TR and Will

Books by William Manners

Father and the Angels

One Is a Lonesome Number

You Call That a House?

Wake Up and Write

TR AND Will

A Friendship That Split the Republican Party

William Manners

HARCOURT BRACE JOVANOVICH, INC.

NEW YORK

ISBN 0-15-191081-2

Library of Congress Catalog Card Number: 69-14838

Printed in the United States of America

D.6.70

The quotations from *The Letters of Theodore Roosevelt*, edited by Elting E.
Morison and John M. Blum, Cambridge, Mass., Harvard University Press, copyright
1954 by the President and Fellows of Harvard College, are reprinted by permission of the publishers. The material from *Letters of Henry Adams*, edited by
Worthington Chauncey Ford, is quoted by permission of the Houghton Mifflin
Company. The quotations taken from *Crowded Hours*, by Alice Roosevelt Longworth, and from *Selections from the Correspondence of Theodore Roosevelt and
Henry Cabot Lodge* are reprinted by permission of Charles Scribner's Sons. The
quotations from Lawrence F. Abbott's *The Letters of Archie Butt* are reprinted with
the permission of Mrs. Laura Abbott Dale.

1-15-79

For Ande,
Julie,
Jane,
and Tracy,
members of the House

Contents

Illustrations

(Between pages 146 and 147)

Cartoons

Acknowledgments

Obviously, thanks should be spontaneous, immediate; spoken thanks are. This is my intention in the following expressions of appreciation, even though they are of necessity belated and suffer from an accepted stylized formality.

First of all, I am deeply grateful to Mrs. Alice Roosevelt Longworth and Mrs. Helen Taft Manning, not only for extending to me the hospitality of their homes, but also for supplying me with singular and invaluable recollections. To Charles P. Taft I am equally grateful for his authorization to use any letters written by his father and by members of the Taft family.

Russel M. Smith and the staff of the Manuscript Division of the Library of Congress—by their courtesy and understanding—made the reading of the Taft letters a more successful undertaking. Other librarians who assisted me unstintingly and with enthusiasm, and whom I therefore wish to thank, are Ruth Adams of the Westport, Connecticut, Library and Stanley Crane of the Pequot Library in Southport, Connecticut. And I want to thank Father Francis Small of the University of Fairfield Library in Fairfield, Connecticut, and the staffs of the Ferguson Library of Stamford, Connecticut, and the New York Public Library.

My very deep thanks go to Roberta Pryor, of the Ashley Famous Agency, for believing in the book with unwavering constancy from idea to final draft.

To Gordon Carroll and Sam Lawrence I owe a special word of thanks, because they granted me a part-time sabbatical from the Famous Writers School—essential in getting the writing of the book under way.

I also wish to indicate my appreciation to Miriam Butensky, Charles Gorham, Ann and Walter Heintze, George Lowther, and Pierre Sichel for the various ways—concrete and subtle—in which they assisted me.

Finally—though she is really first on my indebtedness list—I wish to thank my wife, Ande. She not only offered perceptive advice and well-timed encouragement, but aided me untiringly with the fascinating, though arduous, chore of research. And I'm also indebted to our daughters, Julie, Jane, and Tracy—for restraint, at times; for constant interest; for their standing offer of assistance; and for specific, constructive deeds.

Part I   Heir Apparent

One　　　　　Dinner Party at the White House

The March rain appeared nothing more than the cold, cheerless, unrelenting rain of any winter. But time and place gave it a singular importance: Washington, D.C., the day before the inauguration of a new Republican President, former Governor General of the Philippines and Secretary of War, William Howard Taft. During the past two weeks, skeletal scaffolding for seats had materialized all along Pennsylvania Avenue, over the mile and a quarter between White House and Capitol—the route of the Inauguration Day parade. The weather's severity rendered pathetic and desolate these structures which one Democratic observer dismissed as "crude and unsightly," and the long loops of light strung along the avenue to express gaiety barely made themselves seen through the wintry gloom. Decorations—flags, bunting, floral baskets—were drenched, desecrated by a savage east wind, their festive purpose opposed and scorned.

Theodore Roosevelt started this day, his last as President, with a customary hurried breakfast of hard-boiled eggs, rolls, and a large cup of coffee sweetened by saccharin. He then jogged downstairs and, with his barrel chest characteristically a bit ahead of the rest of him, walked briskly to his office in the West Wing; there was not, as yet, any external evidence that this particular day was essentially different from any of the almost three thousand others TR had spent in the White House.

But today, well-wishers made up most of the crowd that had already gathered in the waiting room. Beyond it, in the thirty-foot-square office, mail to be signed rose in toppling-high piles on the President's desk. During the past week requests for autographed photographs had been overwhelming, and some had reached the desk with no more of an address than a sketch of teeth and specs or one of a Big Stick.

While these appurtenances were inextricably associated with TR, other characteristics also distinguished him: a "close-clipped brachycephalous head," a rather shaggy mustache of indeterminate color, and a square and

3

"terribly rigid jaw." When he bounded into his office, he also managed
the paradox of pausing for a moment in the doorway, "like a hunter on
point," thereby getting everyone's attention before making his entrance
and immediately setting to work.

The three windows that looked south to the Potomac and the Virginia
hills also displayed in their view the White House tennis court, where
much of his work had been conducted. But this morning there was no
meeting of the Tennis Cabinet. Instead, callers came, brought by congressmen, and TR pumped their helpless hands with both of his and
talked "with all his features working." Cabinet members arrived with
chiefs of bureaus who were introduced to TR. To many, he said, with
great enthusiasm, "Indeed, I need no introduction to you. Your work
brought you before me long ago." Sheer ebullience compelled him to use
an excess of energy—a swatted fly received a blow sufficient for the ex-
termination of a dragon. When seated in a straight chair, he crossed and
uncrossed his legs—his slight paunch notwithstanding. When he was
seated in a rocker, his galvanic energy propelled it from one side of the
office to the other. In not fully occupied moments, he polished his glasses
vigorously. Invariably, his voice—high-pitched and Harvard—rose to
falsetto for emphasis. And when he said "I"—and he used that upstanding
pronoun often—it sounded like " 'I-y-e-e-e' with the final 'e's' trailing off
like the end of an echo."

Today, there was much lively raillery—and the laughter was louder
than usual. It was a determined but transparent attempt to keep TR's last
hours as President from being tainted by melancholy. However, one devoted friend and outstanding member of the Tennis Cabinet was unable
to mask the gloom and apprehension he felt; they were reflected in his
eyes, the huge dark Huguenot eyes of the Chief Forester of the United
States, Gifford Pinchot, whose conservation innovations, enacted by TR,
were a landmark in the Roosevelt administration. Still, the pace was not in
the least affected. TR maneuvered someone into an alcove, for a hurried
confidential word. On the way, he shouted good-bye to someone else
across the room. He marched up and down—or sat on the edge of his
desk, swinging his leg—as he dictated to William Loeb, his secretary.

One letter—which was distinctively TR and weighted with largess and
solicitous coercion—went to Will Taft, his successor. "Dear Will," he
wrote. "One closing legacy. Under no circumstance divide the battleship
fleet between the Atlantic and Pacific prior to the finishing of the Panama
Canal."

In his four-hundred-and-twenty-first message to the Sixtieth Congress
—with the ineffable satisfaction of one who is in the right—TR, a doc-

trinaire moralist, took one last, hard whack at a body who he believed required an occasional therapeutic blow on the snout. "What I like about you, Theodore," Speaker Thomas B. Reed had commented wryly some years earlier, "is your original discovery of the Ten Commandments."

But for TR, his long sustained battle with the legislators had been pure enjoyment; finally, proudly, he declared himself the winner. "I've been full President right up to the end," he wrote in a note to Ted, Jr., "which hardly any other President ever has been."

His nature demanded that he be this kind of a President—strong, invincible; and, fortunately, conveniently, reflection assured him that any other approach to the office was inconceivable. Still, TR realized that a President who used "every ounce of power there was in the office" might endanger democracy itself if he served for more than two terms.

So, high-principled, a despiser of cads, and to set an example, he vehemently rejected the office which he still wanted and could have had. With childish guile, however, he did not abdicate completely; he picked his successor, one who would "continue his policies."

Therefore, the activity in the West Wing on that third day of March may have been more than the natural momentum of seven and a half years of uninterrupted frenetic activity, for TR had reached the point of admitting to himself that he was troubled about his close friend whom he had chosen to succeed him. He even gave expression to his doubts— curiously enough, to a newspaperman. During the afternoon, in the process of saying good-bye, he escorted Mark Sullivan to the door. "He's all right," TR said of Will Taft. "He means well and he'll do his best. But he's weak. They'll get around him. They'll—" TR put his shoulder against Sullivan's shoulder and pushed—"they'll lean against him."

But Taft had been and, rumors notwithstanding, still was a very close friend of TR's. "The two men seem to have a personal affection for one another," Archie Butt, TR's White House aide, had observed. "It is beautiful to see them together." TR earnestly insisted that his friend would keep his policies alive, that on all fundamentals they were in agreement. To buttress this conviction with at least a gesture, he had extended an invitation to Will and Nellie Taft to dine at the White House and to spend the night, literally to move in the evening before the inauguration.

In accepting this preinaugural invitation, Taft, clinging tenaciously to an old friendship, had written TR, "People have attempted to represent that you and I were in some way at odds during this last two or three months; whereas you and I know that there has not been the slightest difference between us, and I welcome the opportunity to stay the last night of your administration under the White House roof and to make as emphatic as possible the refutation of any such suggestion. With love and affection, my dear Theodore . . ."

Mrs. Taft felt differently about the evening ahead. It was merely an obligation, requiring a degree of complaisance.

Three months short of her forty-eighth birthday, gray-haired—but trim and energetic—Helen Herron Taft had serious brown eyes, somewhat protuberant, with a steady, clear gaze. Her mouth and chin were stubborn; when it was necessary to defend her wishes or opinions, she did it, as a contemporary of hers observed, "with almost a masculine vigor." Once when asked who first thought of Will Taft for the presidency, she snapped, "I did!" Consequently, she fiercely resented an idea that was often expressed, most vividly by a cartoon that presented her husband as a ponderous egg about to be hatched by a toothy bespectacled hen.

For Theodore Roosevelt was Nellie Taft's nemesis. Suspicion, dark suspicion pervaded her every thought of him. "The subject of my husband's appointment to the Supreme Court," she wrote sardonically, "cropped up with what seemed annoying frequency." What motivated TR's persistence was patently clear to her: the desire to keep Will in the "groove" of a lifetime appointment on the Supreme Court bench, and out of the presidency. Mrs. Taft's constant anxiety that TR's ambition would inevitably make the realization of her own impossible was so strong that she viewed Roosevelt's aggressive energy with distaste and even the advocacy of her husband with distrust.

Early in their marriage, Taft had described his wife as his "dearest and best critic," praised her for "stirring me up to best effort," but now, as the inauguration drew nearer—relentlessly, inevitably nearer—Taft became irritable and unhappy. A month after he had won the election, he had said dispiritedly, "It is a very different office from that of Governor General of the Philippines, and I don't know that I shall arise to the occasion or not." Now, in spite of what he had written to TR, he dreaded the evening ahead, an evening he was later to refer to as "that funeral."

But the stereotype insists that very fat men do not brood; rather, that they be unremittingly jolly. Taft's eyes were blue, his skin fair; the upsweeping mustachios suited a stout and jovial figurine, a child's toy with a key in its side to be wound. His three hundred and thirty-two pounds were distributed over a six-foot-two-inch frame. When aboard ship, he could only shower, for he literally became stuck in a standard-size bathtub and had to be pried out of it. As a result of this contretemps, a tub weighing one ton, whose dimensions—seven feet long and forty-one inches wide—could easily accommodate four average-sized men, had been installed in the battleship *North Carolina* specifically for his use on a trip. Now this tub was to be ensconced in the White House, and that Taft was so immense as to need it made him eligible to be an honorary member of the Fat Men's Club of the Sixth Assembly District, whose thirteen members were to march in the inaugural parade.

Such farcical but true stories eventually encourage apocryphal ones. Washington conversation in 1909 was punctuated divertingly with reports that the man who was to succeed TR had given up his seat in a streetcar to three women, and that no other swimmer could swim in the Atlantic when Taft was using that ocean. Once when he was to attend a football game in the Yale Bowl, two reserved seats were requested so that he would be perfectly comfortable. However, when the usher escorted Taft to his two seats, they turned out to be on opposite sides of an aisle.

The fat man jokes and Taft's smile—because it was like "a huge pan of sweet milk poured over one"—conspired to distort the true nature of the man. For one thing, Taft's amiability did not prevent him from abhorring politics. It was his wife, his brothers, and TR who were determined that he be President. Big Will Taft merely wished for the peace, the calm, the dignity of a judicial career. Nonetheless, he now found himself at 1801 P Street—a very solid three-story brick-and-stone mansion on Dupont Circle—a guest of his friends, the William Boardmans and their daughter Mabel—and only hours from the presidency.

The dreary March weather matched Taft's forebodings. It was understandable that Mrs. Taft sent frantic wires to the atelier of Francis Smith and Company in New York City concerning the whereabouts of her white satin inaugural gown. Despite its intricacy—for it was embroidered from hem to bust in a goldenrod design, with a court train, also embroidered in ropes of the same flower—and the lateness of the date on which she had ordered it, Mrs. Taft expected the gown to be delivered on time. She demanded of others the high standards—and discipline—she demanded of herself.

After all, there had been over twenty years in which, as the wife of a government official whose salary was always unequal to the expenses his position entailed, Mrs. Taft had practiced a rigid frugality. Unessentials were ruthlessly expelled from the Taft family budget; thus her wardrobe had always been circumscribed. But now the magnitude of her triumph in being the wife of a President-elect was evident in that she could bring herself to order three coats and wraps, a half-dozen hats, and four gowns, in addition to the missing inauguration gown. Of these four gowns,

which had already arrived, Mrs. Taft chose one of white satin, with a
filmy tulle effect about the sleeves and bodice, for that inescapable dinner
with the Roosevelts.

Significantly, Mrs. Roosevelt's gown for the evening was very different
from the incoming First Lady's; it was simple and it was black. But at
least the two women agreed on one point. They both felt the invitation
for that evening, tendered the Tafts by TR, was ill-advised.

Like Mrs. Taft, Edith Kermit Carow Roosevelt had an undemonstra-
tive nature and strong opinions firmly held. But unlike her, Mrs. Roosevelt possessed an elegance that was completely alien to ambition. Despite
a calm, well-bred assurance, she had a distaste for politics and for the social set whom, her stepdaughter Alice said, she regarded as virtually
synonymous with sin. Her insistence on a private life, moreover, led her
to refuse to give newspaper interviews or to make public statements. She
suffered from neuralgic headaches that, at times, accounted for the as-
tringency of her comments. Always, however, there was an air about her
of a detached, amused observer, and so her cool brown eyes gazing
enigmatically at the turbulence her husband was forever creating gave
some credence to a comment by a former classmate, "You could live in
the same room with Edith for fifty years and never know what she was
really thinking."

But there was no question that she regarded her husband as one would
a child. At the White House table, she often checked his exuberance with
an emphatic, "Theodore!" And his small-boy plea was invariably, "Why,
Ee-die, I was only . . ." No wonder after the birth of her fourth son
she remarked, "Now, I have *five* boys."

As Mrs. Roosevelt—in her black silk gown—awaited the arrival of the
Tafts, she was troubled about Theodore. Taft, she felt, shouldn't have
been "pushed into the presidency." If that hadn't happened, her husband
wouldn't have felt the compulsion to go to Africa to hunt big game, to be
so far away that no one could possibly say that he in any way controlled
President Taft. Though he was young for an ex-President, TR wasn't
young enough, his wife was certain, for the hardships of big-game hunting. After all, he was fifty, somewhat overweight and a bit soft. He was
blind in one eye, the result of a blow he'd received while boxing, and
without his glasses his vision was so bad that he couldn't recognize his
own sons. Still, Mrs. Roosevelt believed that Theodore could hold his
own with wild animals; that he might be felled by jungle fevers, however,
terrified her.

Her worry magnified irritations. Before her husband was out of office,

Mrs. Taft, in her eagerness, announced changes that she was going to make in the White House staff and that automobiles would displace all carriages. What aggravated the situation was that, in spite of TR's close friendship with Will Taft, Edith Roosevelt and Nellie Taft had never been friends. Their relationship had been one of politely exchanged amenities. Just the day before, as Mrs. Roosevelt was showing Mrs. Taft around the White House, Mrs. Roosevelt heard her say in an undertone to a friend, "I would have put that table over there."

The prospect of giving up this home was in itself emotionally upsetting. Even young Quentin said, "There's a hole in my stomach when I think of leaving the White House." With the exception of Quentin in school in Virginia, and Alice, married to Congressman Nicholas Longworth and living in Washington, the other children—Ted, Jr., Kermit, Ethel, and Archie—had left for Oyster Bay by the evening of March 3. Along with them, lingering only as a tenuous echo in memory, had gone the movement, the exuberance, and the incredible energy that had permeated every inch of the White House. The staccato clatter of stilts, the roar of roller skates on the hardwood floors, the hollow knock of pony hoofs in the elevator, and the complete anarchy of the obstacle races— which Theodore and the children staged in the large entrance hall— were activities that often led Mrs. Roosevelt to escape to her small sitting room on the second floor for quiet contemplation. The magic of nostalgia, however, had already cast a pleasant aura and a feeling of longing over that which was irrevocably in the past.

But always the good hostess, Mrs. Roosevelt directed that all the fireplaces be lighted; when her guests arrived, she wanted the house to radiate welcome.

In a White Steamer, not by carriage, the Tafts traveled south on Connecticut Avenue for the scant mile from the Boardman residence to the White House. Winter had stripped the trees lining the driveway on each side of the north portico. Wet-black, their branches were powdered with snow that had begun to fall shortly after six that evening and that now sparkled with light reflected from the White House.

Soon after being admitted by attendants, a few minutes after eight, the Tafts were greeted by the President and his wife. Then the future occupants of the Executive Mansion were shown to the suite on the southeast side of the second floor, known in the White House as the Blue Bedroom —a large bedroom, and bath, with an adjoining smaller bedroom or dressing room.

Mrs. Taft found the view inspiring. Beyond the windows were the

Washington Monument, the lights of the bridge stretching across the Potomac, meeting the lights of Arlington, and the darkness of the Virginia hills.

Downstairs, meanwhile, illumination from a central rococo chandelier —a vast nest of lights—and from wall sconces gave an air of festivity to the oak-paneled State Dining Room. About the table—set with Wedgwood plate, purchased by Mrs. Roosevelt and bearing the President's seal—high-backed Queen Anne chairs waited to be pulled out and occupied. By virtue of its nature and height above the fireplace, a bull moose head, a trophy of TR's, not only surveyed the room, but also dominated it.

The other guests arrived: Admiral and Mrs. William Sheffield Cowles, Mr. and Mrs. Nicholas Longworth, Senator and Mrs. Elihu Root, Mabel Boardman, and Archie Butt. It was a group compounded of family ties, friendship, and close association; yet, before the divisive elements of 1912 played themselves out, everyone gathered in the State Dining Room that night would take sides in the conflict and hate with "violent hate." Tormented loyalties would lead one of them to a dramatic, tragic death.

Will Cowles, a portly figure in his panoply of well-cut naval uniform and gold braid, was an affable and gregarious gentleman. Nevertheless, it was his wife Anna—TR's eldest sister, usually called Bamie or Bye—who commanded attention. "She has no looks, she is very nearly ugly," a friend remarked of her, "she is almost a cripple, and yet no one for a moment thinks of these things. One is only aware of her charm." It was true. Despite the effects of a spinal injury in her infancy, made evident in a slight deformity, Bamie Roosevelt Cowles had the same incisive intelligence as her younger brother, the same political shrewdness; she also had the ability to invest even the dullest of individuals with an engaging personality, and was also a sharp, stimulating conversationalist. Had she been a man, her admiring niece Alice once contended, "*she* would have been President."

Alice herself was an original. Intellectually honest, with an easy, irresistible manner and a wit that took a mischievous delight in shocking conventional minds, she was predisposed to pleasure. At twenty-five, she had a past that included driving from Newport to Washington without a chaperone, getting drunk on rose wine in Peking, jumping fully clothed into a ship's swimming pool, smoking cigarettes, and being the subject of a suit against a scandal magazine that had reported she had entertained Newport gentlemen by dancing in her chemise. All of which, according to that well-worn anecdote, had driven a friend to implore TR to "look after Alice more." "Listen," TR had answered, "I can be President of the United States—or I can attend to Alice."

In 1905 when Will Taft, then Secretary of War, prepared to head an expedition to the Philippines, it was arranged that Alice should be in the party. Also accompanying the group was a thirty-five-year-old congressman from Ohio, Nicholas Longworth, "who has a bright manner and a quick way of saying bright and new things that attract Alice very much." The Taft family and the Longworths had been friends for many years; so Will Taft remarked to old Mrs. Longworth, Nick's mother, that he was certain if Nick and Alice went on the expedition together, they would return engaged. Mrs. Longworth, however, complacently assured Taft that Nick was a confirmed bachelor. Taft chuckled his chuckle, but he had not altogether approved of Nick Longworth or his un-Ohio-like sophistication. "I know," Taft had written to Mrs. Taft in shocked disapproval during the Philippine trip, "that she and Nick indulge in conversations on subjects that are ordinarily tabooed between men and women much older than they are and indeed are usually confined to husband and wife."

Nevertheless, by the third of March, 1909, the Longworths had been married three years, and Alice was "still the drawing card in Washington society and she will be just as popular after the 4th of March as she has been, if not a little more so."

The last of the five married couples assembled at dinner that evening were also the oldest: Elihu Root, Senator from New York—formerly Secretary of War for McKinley and TR and Secretary of State for TR— and his "funny bustling little wife," Clara. Root, austere in appearance, could on occasion be moved to tears. He wore a thick gray bang cut square across his forehead, and he had an incisive intelligence which TR admired enormously and a sardonic wit which delighted him. One of TR's unrealizable ambitions had been to make Root President, but Root's reputation as a corporation lawyer would have made him anathema to the Western progressive voter.

The remaining two dinner guests—Mabel Boardman and Archie Butt were unmarried. Miss Boardman—tall, formidable, and forty-eight— appeared "a congenital spinster." In later years, she grew to resemble Queen Mary to a marked degree and, viewed as "a splendid executive creature," was the dominant power in the Red Cross, having vanquished Clara Barton and sent her into retirement. She had accompanied the Taft party to the Philippines in 1905, and had proven "most useful in the management of Alice." Her devotion to Will Taft and his devotion to her were so well known that after his election the young people had taken to teasing her, calling her "the Pompadour of the Taft administration." "*Now*, Mabel," they would exclaim, "you're going to be a Power!"

Archie Butt, military aide to TR, was at Taft's request to remain in the same capacity in the new administration. His full name and rank, Captain Archibald Willingham de Graffenreid Butt, led the Roosevelt children to recite it with a downhill lilt and claim it sounded like "a big load of coal falling down the stairs." Captain Butt was a Southern officer and gentleman, a sentimental, conscientious bachelor, who enjoyed his position immensely, and was now showing obvious emotion over the departure of the Roosevelts. Unknown to both his chiefs, he had begun writing letters to his mother and, then after her death, to "Dear Clara," his sister-in-law, Mrs. Lewis F. Butt, in Georgia. They were, in effect, a journal—colored by his romantic, antebellum outlook—of life in the White House.

Intimate friends though they all appeared to be, they nevertheless nurtured grievances—some old, others newly arrived at—that lay festering not far beneath the surface of their relationships. Though Will Taft was very fond of Mabel Boardman, his wife did not have "much feeling one way or another about Mabel." Of Senator Root, Mrs. Taft had declared, "As he is perfectly uninterested in me, I can never talk to him." Rankling inside her, moreover, was the conviction that TR actually preferred Root to her husband as the man to succeed him. In Will Taft, too, there lingered in memory the jealousy he'd felt when he'd succeeded Root as Secretary of War only to hear Root's virtues in that office extolled. Root's mordant humor, his puns, which TR found so outrageously funny, Taft found merely irritating. On this point, Mrs. Roosevelt agreed with Taft. She had never forgiven Root for his reaction to a mishap involving her husband. TR had often dragged a reluctant Root along on his strenuous crippling, precipice-climbing walks. One day when TR went alone on his precarious way, he fell and was lamed for a time. When Mrs. Roosevelt reported this to Root, he laughed and remarked unfeelingly that he was very glad.

Other, more immediate tensions made the smiles stiff, the conversations self-conscious, and the dinner an ordeal to be lived through. Mrs. Roosevelt avoided any reference to the fact that on the next day Mrs. Taft would be First Lady, "and the question of housekeeping or domestic affairs was never mentioned by either." Mrs. Taft, moreover, harbored a long-standing resentment of Mrs. Roosevelt. And disturbingly present was Alice Longworth, whose imitations of Mrs. Taft were by now a well-known and popular feature of Washington parties, and of all the Roosevelts. "This, my darlings," she would say to her family, tucking in her chin and forcing her eyes to bulge in a satirical, uncanny resemblance to Mrs. Taft, "is what is coming after you."

Mrs. Taft had never liked Alice, regarding her as one who was always "showing off a good deal." Alice's mockery was added fuel to her smoldering hostility toward TR and contributed to the eventual bitter breach between TR and Will Taft.

Of all those present, TR alone spoke with ease, with his customary jubilance, giving no indication that a door was being closed with finality on great times. Actually, in lieu of conversation, TR performed as a skilled monologist, spacing words with slow deliberation for emphasis and following such leisurely passages for variety and contrast, so it seemed, with staccato bursts.

The evening somehow passed, and the prediction of one guest that it would be "replete with interesting incident" was wrong. Though tears were seen to drop into Senator Root's soup, the salad course was reached without overt drama. Then custom sent the women upstairs to the library for their coffee, the men to the President's study.

Alice Longworth strode to a library window for a look at the weather. When Will Taft had been elected, the Longworths—who were her in-laws and close friends of the Tafts—had irritated her with their adulation of Taft, which by implication was a disparagement of her father. Though she was very fond of Taft himself, "there was something not quite pleasing in the idea of 'my dear Mr. Taft' as a great man and still less as a great President, rubbed in by my in-laws, too!" The attitude of members of the Taft family that Will could become President without any help from TR was also a source of annoyance. "I looked out the window," she recalled, "and turning to the room said, 'It's snowing,' in a voice that, I fear, did not indicate regret at the prospect of a wretched day for the inauguration."

In the President's study, TR, as always, addressed Taft as "Will" and, as always, gave him advice. Taft continued to address TR as "Mr. President."

Before long, it was time for Taft to leave for the New Willard Hotel, where his fellow Yale men were having a smoker in his honor. "I hope, with nerve," he was to tell them, "to be able to stand just criticism . . . and not care a dern [sic] for unjust criticism." However, one Yale man and future Taft critic, Gifford Pinchot, recalled the President-elect's speech as "curiously full of hesitation and foreboding. I cannot remember a single confident note in the whole of it."

Taft's having gone accelerated the departure of the other White House guests. "Finally," Archie Butt wrote his sister-in-law that night, "there were left only the President, Mrs. Taft and Mrs. Roosevelt and myself. Mrs. Roosevelt finally arose and said she would go to her room and advised Mrs. Taft to do the same. She took her hand kindly and expressed the earnest hope that her first night in the White House would be one of sweet sleep. . . ."

The Blue Bedroom, which had been assigned to the Tafts, had formerly been Lincoln's Cabinet Room, before renovation had converted it into a state bedroom. A bronze plate under the mantel, against a side wall, caught Mrs. Taft's eye.

While struggling with the hooks in taking off her white satin gown, she read the inscription on the plate:

> IN THIS ROOM ABRAHAM LINCOLN
> SIGNED THE EMANCIPATION PROC-
> LAMATION OF JANUARY 1, 1863
> WHEREBY FOUR MILLION SLAVES
> WERE GIVEN THEIR FREEDOM AND
> SLAVERY FOREVER PROHIBITED IN
> THESE UNITED STATES.

That she, too, by being in this room on this night was becoming a part of history touched Mrs. Taft with a sudden swell of pride. However, she lay sleepless, haunted not by the great tragedy of Lincoln and the Civil War, but by a cloud of "petty details." A messenger had arrived at the Boardmans with her gown for the inaugural ball; but since she did not know this, it proved an admirable subject for worry. And then there was the despicable weather about which she could fret. One newspaper's headlines stated flatly, "Inauguration tomorrow will have smiling skies." But there was something ominous in the hedging report of the Weather Bureau: "The weather probabilities for Thursday are still too uncertain to forecast." The weather was Mrs. Taft's special concern, because she had won her war with the Inaugural Committee. This meant that after her husband was sworn in, though it meant breaking all precedent, she would ride triumphantly back to the White House with him. Helen Herron Taft—not Theodore Roosevelt—would be sitting beside the twenty-seventh President of the United States.

Two

"And Now—
That Meant
My Husband!"

The snow that had been light and innocent at six in the evening turned into a meterological nightmare during the night: seventy-mile-an-hour winds yanked telephone and telegraph wires from poles, which were toppled, isolating Washington. The snow became heavy, fell endlessly, as from an inexhaustible feather bed.

Not even Alice Longworth's mischievous filial allegiance, framed in a definite wish, could have conjured up this blizzard, rivaling the one twenty-one years earlier. Some situations, however, can cause individuals to suspend belief in natural law's complete authority and to see, with a touch of the poet and the savage, personality and portents in nature. Certain individuals, therefore, interpreted the storm as a symbolic warning of stormy times for Taft. Others said TR was merely going out strong. To many it was obvious that the storm equaled the heavens' protesting TR's departure and blocking Taft's taking the oath of office.

The storm's severity gave a semblance of credibility to all these disparate views. With telegraph wires down, having been broken by heavy, wet snow—or by a combination of snow and ripping winds—telegrams to New York were routed by Atlanta, Memphis, and St. Louis. The New York *Times* attempted to circumvent the storm in a similar fashion by sending its copy to Philadelphia, hoping it might reach its destination from there.

No comparable expedient could be employed by Washington trolley cars. Trains heading into Washington also became immobilized. The twenty Pullman cars bearing the Seventh Regiment, for example, took up what appeared, to the passengers, to be permanent residence north of Baltimore.

More than communications and transportation were affected; the residents of Washington, upon awakening in the morning, saw "that the storm, instead of abating had increased in violence."

15

Nature might very well be providing a fitting Wagnerian overture—there's no end to signs and omens—an overture for this day and the years of drama that would be an inevitable continuation of it.

Mrs. Taft awakened in the gray light of night merging into day. Then she realized that sounds had awakened her. Motionless, attentive, she identified them as crackling sounds, localized them as coming from the windows. She left her bed, crossed to the windows, and looked out. "The world was ice-bound." Had this taken place during the campaign, it might have struck her, with the irrationality of irritability, that TR was in some way involved. But now, she was excited, "a condition," she wrote later, "quite rare with me."

While her husband, making a vast mound of the covers, continued to sleep, she dressed—though the full light of day had not yet come. Her eagerness made it appear she was the one who was going to be sworn in.

Taft had returned early from the smoker the evening before, at eleven o'clock, but still he slept. His need for sleep was great, though no correlation exists between size and the quantity of sleep required. Psychologically, sleep fit his temperament, reducing strife to an absolute minimum, offering procrastination without guilt. Public functions caused him to doze off. Inured to this, Mrs. Taft would dutifully nudge him awake to the reality of droning speakers.

Now, finally, Taft awoke, rose ponderously, reluctantly. He pulled on his pants, big pants, the gift of a big state, Texas. Dark gray and striped. They had been made with the co-operation of Admiral Tago, a three-year-old Angora goat, who had given ten pounds of its wool to make the inauguration pants a reality.

At that moment, all over stormy Washington, men were pulling on their pants, committing themselves by that symbolic act to the life of that day. In Taft's case, the symbolism covered at least four years.

The storm may have concerned him, but there was work to be done on his inauguration address, work that even he could not put off. He eliminated paragraphs, for the speech was too long, according to a theory of Mrs. Taft's "that no audience can stand more than an hour" of a speech.

He did not eliminate a paragraph on tariff reform—which TR had regarded as too hot to handle and had left for his successor. "I shall call Congress into extra session to meet on the 15th day of March, in order that consideration may be at once given to a bill revising the Dingley Act." And the paragraph on conservation, "saving and restoring our forests and the great improvements of waterways," remained intact. Conservation would become the Pinchot-Ballinger controversy. And in the very second paragraph of his typewritten address, he would speak of the reforms of his "distinguished predecessor" and say that "I should be untrue to myself, to my promises, and to the declarations of the party platform upon which I was elected to office, if I did not make the maintenance and enforcement of those reforms a most important feature of my administration."

As to this intention, Jonathan Dolliver—the huge, shambling Senator from Iowa, with a wit always honed sharp and ready for attack—was to say, "Yes, Taft carried out TR's policies, carried them out on a shutter."

"For you're going, for you're going, and one scarce believes it's true," mourned humorist Wallace Irwin in the New York *Times* on March 4. "Yes, a sort of lonesome feeling, like an arrow shoots us through— / By the Laws that got the scrubbing / And the Trusts that took the clubbing, / 'Twill be many a cold, hard winter 'ere we see the like of you!"

The weather's significance also touched the repartee of the protagonists themselves. "I knew there'd be a blizzard when I went out," TR greeted Taft genially when the President-elect came down to breakfast on the morning of Inauguration Day. "You're wrong," Taft replied with a chuckle, "it is my storm. I always said it would be a cold day when I got to be President of the United States."

The President's laughter and his display of energy could not conceal that in merely a few hours he would no longer be President, and that he was acting as host in a house that was hardly his. The White House had been shut to the public on the second and would remain so until the fifth, in order that the Roosevelt family belongings might be removed and the Executive Mansion readied for its new occupants. The stable had already been converted into a garage to shelter the new White House automoblies, among them a White Steamer—Model M—driven to Washington from the factory in Cleveland. (In an artful display of merchandising, the Washington White Steamer dealer had taken a half-page ad in the *Post*, listing four reasons for buying a White Steamer. The first one stated: "Those in whose judgement the Nation has the most confidence have selected the White Steamer for their personal use, thereby stamping it as 'the correct car.' ")

Inevitably, sadness and regret attend the ending, the death, of a part of one's life. They colored TR's last full hours. Now, to all this feeling, a new emotional quality was added. TR, whose personality required power, was about to "give" the presidency to Will Taft in a minute's ceremony surrounded by hours of festivity. His friendship could not offer more. Could Taft's reciprocate?

Verbal evidence maintained that the affection felt by TR and Taft for each other was as strong as ever. And in a souvenir, a bonus accompanying each ticket for the inaugural ball, TR, reviewing Taft's career, concluded, "No man of better training, no man of more dauntless courage, of sounder common sense and of higher and finer character, has ever come to the Presidency than William Howard Taft." As though not to be outdone, that very week a laudatory article, written by Taft, appeared in *Collier's Weekly.* Entitled "My Predecessor," it stated that "the relation between Mr. Roosevelt and myself has been one of close and sweet intimacy. It has never been ruffled in the slightest degree and I do not think we have ever misunderstood each other. When the friction of the last few months shall have disappeared, the greatness of Theodore Roosevelt as President and leader of men in one of the great moral movements of the

"He's All Right." By H. C. Davenport, New York *Evening Mail,* 1908.

country's history will become clear to everyone and he will take his place in history with Washington and Lincoln."

Now these two men, each eulogized by the other, finished breakfast. Then, posing for a photographer, they stood together on the south portico of the White House, each in a Prince Albert coat, Taft exuding a substantial joviality, TR jaunty with a flower in his lapel.

A dozen carriages, with Cabinet members and congressmen, arrived; they would follow the carriage of the President and the President-elect. (Incident quickly followed incident, as to a preordained denouement.)

At about ten o'clock, TR, dressed for the weather, moved with the rapid jerky short steps of silent movies from the main entrance of the White House. Galoshes and Boston gaiters covered his legs in tight embrace all the way from his feet to his knees. He also held an umbrella and a weekly periodical as he stepped briskly through the swinging glass doors.

Immediately, he started bowing and nodding vigorously. "Good-bye! Good luck!" he said repeatedly to the numerous newsmen, photographers, and White House attachés, as he both made his way to a waiting carriage and shook hands with friends. Taft, in an overcoat with a fur collar, and wearing a silk hat, smiled and nodded, too. He evoked a picture of a child emulating an older one, a child reduced by age and status to a position of tagging along.

Before entering the carriage, in which TR, Philander Knox, and Henry Cabot Lodge waited, Taft bowed. The carriage door slammed; the finality of the slam, a sharply isolated and distinct sound in the cold wet air, proclaimed that TR was definitely on the way out.

A current rumor would have disagreed. The incredibility of TR's departure from the presidency, it maintained, grew out of the inexhaustible energy, freshness, and drama that had characterized his "reign." The "imitation Caesar" could not simply step down of his own free will. At the very least, he would on this day do something characteristically spectacular to steal the show from Taft. The vagueness of what that something might be made it all the more provocative, even menacing.

But the ritual of the day, ritual's special power, could not be discounted. Once its hoopla, traditions, and legality had been completed, Taft would definitely, irrevocably, be the twenty-seventh President of the United States.

Moreover, this whole matter had been placed in capable hands; M. D. Weller, Chairman of the Inaugural Committee, was acting in that capacity for the fifth time. His efficiency made possible an announcement early in January that plans for the reception of the two hundred thousand visitors expected during inauguration week were "practically perfected." Attention had been given to the most minute of details. Marchers would take steps thirty inches in length and at a cadence of one hundred and twenty steps per minute. Drum majors were to use batons as staffs only and not throw them into the air; thus dignity would be preserved, and horses pulling the carriages in the presidential party would not be frightened. The first motion of a salute of an individual passing the President's stand was to be made at six paces in front of the President and the carry resumed at six paces beyond. Parking of carriages at the inaugural ball . . .

By nine thirty, so that the minutiae of all this ritual could go on unimpeded, Pennsylvania Avenue had been cleared of snow. To accomplish this, six thousand street cleaners had worked hard, goaded by the urgency of a deadline, and they had spread eighteen thousand pounds of sand.

Even before the avenue had been cleared, in the ground-floor window of an undertaker's parlor near Tenth Street, four aged women sat immobile. With hands folded macabrely, they waited like mourners, or the mourned, for the sights to begin. Spectators filled windows of upper stories, too; store windows had been emptied for this purpose and were being rented for ten to twenty dollars. The sums paid by the Vanderbilts, the Whitneys, and Senator Boies Penrose for the best view of Pennsylvania Avenue from hotel windows were released by an awe-inspired, reverential press as "mysterious amounts."

Spectators also filled the slushy streets. Thousands wore little cards that ordered gaily, "Smile, Smile, Smile," for smiling had become synonymous with the big man who was about to become President. Although smiles would not reduce the high cost of living, they would do no harm either.

Some of the detectives, moving among the crowd, may have smiled to make themselves as one with the crowd, unobtrusive. They had been brought to Washington from many of the big cities. By this maneuver, any well-known criminal who had come to Washington for the inaugural pickings would be certain to be recognized by a detective from his locality.

The weather had wiped smiles from the faces of men selling seats erected outdoors, for they were begging that three- and five-dollar ones be taken for a dollar. Ten-cent and twenty-five-cent sandwiches were eagerly being sold for two or three cents.

At least one salesman, standing near the Capitol, profited by the blizzard, for he hawked umbrellas for fifty cents, umbrellas which he maintained were large enough for two.

The principals, responsible for all this anticipation and activity, sat in the carriage whose door had been slammed and had just started to be drawn by four sleek bays—their reddish brown color and fine breeding making them indistinguishable. Silk hats lent formality to the two Negroes sitting up high on the driving seat. Eight Secret Service men and four detectives from the metropolitan police force walked beside the carriage, keeping protectively close to it.

As if on cue, no more than a dozen yards down the drive, the horses became skittish. The leaders were shying nervously at the snow—sparse flakes, remnants of what had seemed an inexhaustible abundance. The tension enveloping the carriage added to the menace of snowflakes; the expectancy that "something" would happen charged the air. The horses reared and backed, eyes wide, breath frozen gray. The Secret Service men rushed to the lead horses, in the process of becoming snarled with the wheel horses, held their bridles, quieted them with orders and soothing words.

Soon the procession of carriages once again continued down the West Drive, and passed out the West Gate.

A new problem presented itself to the Secret Service men and the detectives. Because the presidential carriage top was up, crowds ran along beside the carriage, kept pace with it, wanting to catch a glimpse of TR and Taft. They saw TR wiggling his silk hat at the window in acknowledgment.

Applause sounded and was continuously renewed as the carriages approached new sources of applause. For the next four years, all circumstances related to TR and Taft would be heatedly compared. Even the reaction of the crowd to this procession to the Capitol would be the subject of speculation and controversy. TR advocates would say the response four years earlier at his inauguration had been far more enthusiastic. Taft people might counter that the weather hadn't been so severe then. This would give the other side a chance to agree, to point out that the sun had shone brightly and the air had been warm, but they'd also be implying that TR deserved credit for this.

"Oh, you, Teddy!" someone along the curb shouted appreciatively.

"Where's Taft?" another spectator called. Belligerence gave the question a special meaning. "Why don't you give Taft a chance?"

Taft obviously didn't want this chance, for he didn't know what every politician knew: crowds must be flattered by recognition, if it be no more than a wave of a hand, a nod. During the entire trip, not once did Taft look out of the carriage or acknowledge the crowd.

All the way up Capitol Hill, crowds stood in slush; finally they were rewarded for their patience and discomfort. The carriages arrived and

TR and Taft climbed the broad Capitol steps together. But the pleasure of the crowd proved momentary. It turned to disappointment and anger when government employees appeared with megaphones and announced that owing to the inclement weather the inauguration ceremonies would be held indoors, in the Senate Chamber.

The announcement had precisely the opposite effect on congressmen. Though they hadn't stood in the slush, many had slogged through it. Profanities resounded through the Capitol cloakroom, rapped out in accents of the pioneer West, the rural South, and the effete East, all deploring the weather or suggesting that the inauguration should be held at the end of April, a date that had been good enough for George Washington.

Actually, the blasphemies and the more constructive outpourings of the Republican members reflected mere annoyance. Deep down, they rejoiced. After all, there were many newly elected Republican governors, and so numerous were the Republican senators and congressmen that "like a widening Spring freshet they flowed over into the half-empty Democratic side of the chamber."

As for the Democrats, they could give joyful thanks that TR's departure was finally at hand. Now they would no longer have to endure his flayings. So regular, so enduring had they become that printers could set the headline "TR FLAYS" in type and then merely add whatever or whoever was being flayed on a particular day.

But with TR gone, all would not be well with the Republican party. In the last few years of his "reign," TR, in swinging to the left, had helped deepen a growing cleavage. Old Guard Nelson Aldrich still ruled the Senate; Old Guard Joe Cannon remained as czar of the House. In spite of this, and though a strong conservative element existed, the progressives, "assistant democrats," were rapidly gaining strength.

This was a situation that required the attentions of a master politician like TR: bluster, wild self-confidence, the ability to know when to use a hammer lock or a smile to get what you wanted, an ego bursting with energy.

But this very highly qualified individual said, in what was naturally a flat, dogmatic statement, that "the country should not be asked to stand four years more of crusading." He had uprooted and cleared, and now Taft, "a constructive fellow," could build. In the President's room, to which TR and Taft had gone upon their arrival at the Capitol, a Washington *Star* correspondent observed the two men. Because the reporter in him was looking for newsworthy animosity, he noted that "while they were cordial, they did not spend very much time together."

In the Senate Chamber, the regular whirling chairs had been removed, ostensibly to make more room for the cane-seated ones that were placed in semicircles about the chamber. Those in the front row, because they had the distinction of being first and of having brown leather seats, were reserved for justices, the diplomatic corps, and retiring Cabinet members.

In the front row of the executive galleries—also an honored position, at the south end of the chamber—the Tafts sat together, as a unit.

They were all there, too. Even young, cheerful, freckle-faced Charlie had made it, though he had had the problem of being excused from Taft School, his Uncle Horace's school in Watertown, Connecticut, whose rules forbade absence on any account during the school year. However, resourceful Uncle Horace had formulated a new rule: "Any boy whose father becomes President of the United States might be excused to attend the inauguration."

With Charlie and her two other children, Mrs. Taft sat arrayed in elegance. This high point in her life demanded elegance: large pearls in her ears, a string of pearls about her throat, a gown of mauve chiffon velvet— embroidered in gold and mauve velvet with an aigrette. Seated on her right, in order of seniority, were Robert, a junior at Yale; then Helen, a freshman at Bryn Mawr; and then Charlie.

Charles P. Taft, after whom young Charlie had been named, sat at his sister-in-law's left. As she equaled her husband's presidential aspirations, he represented monetary patronage. For eighteen years—from the time Will Taft was Solicitor General—his half brother had subsidized him devotedly. The annual contributions had been from six to ten thousand dollars.

Directly behind him, white-haired, ancient, but with alert eyes and a new hat, sat Aunt Delia. She was Miss Delia Chapin Torrey, oldest sister of Taft's mother, who, along with others in the family, had determined that Will shouldn't accept a Supreme Court appointment, but be President.

Another maker of a President—retiring Senator Thomas C. Platt, the "Easy Boss" who unwittingly helped TR to become President by dumping him in the obliterative hole of the vice-presidency—sat looking about with half-closed eyes as he nervously clutched a cane. Old, ill, he was no longer a power. Just as he had changed, deteriorated, so his political world was changing.

With the appearance at 11:45 A.M. of the justices of the Supreme Court, in voluminous black silk gowns and headed by Chief Justice Fuller, a stir spread through the galleries and chamber. The movement and sound of which it was composed indicated excitement and the realization that the inauguration was getting under way. The justices filed in and were seated. The diplomatic corps followed; their elaborate trappings of gold lace, colored sashes, and jeweled orders contrasted so sharply with the black frock coats and white linen of the American legislators that it appeared something profound—though elusive—should be deduced from this. Governors and officialdom in every branch followed.

This parading to seats consumed a half hour, during which the excitement occasioned by the arrival of the justices continued to mount. Everyone knew, felt, that the moment was drawing near when the power of the presidency would pass from TR to Taft. Theoretically, TR's term of office had ended at twelve noon, and the United States had been without a chief executive for over fifteen minutes; even the old, deluding subterfuge of turning back the hands of the clock to circumvent this predicament had not been used.

Shortly after 12:15 P.M. an announcement heralded the entrance of the President and the President-elect. Then, ceremoniously, a pair of senators and a pair of representatives escorted TR and Taft to chairs reserved for them. After being seated, as though continuing the tribalistic formality of their arrival, they looked straight ahead. Finally, Taft ignored the sacred ritual and glanced up at his family and smiled. But TR, restrained by the inaugural's prescribed rites, hampered in "stealing the show," stared grimly ahead.

A prayer. Assisted to the platform, Edward Everett Hale, Senate chaplain, author, patriot, who—forty-six years earlier—had spoken before Lincoln at Gettysburg, beseeched God with a voice that trembled with infirmity and entreaty.

The prayer ended; Taft arose. For him not to be smiling made him appear especially somber. He left the seat next to TR which he had occupied and walked to the platform. With Taft no longer beside him, TR appeared isolated, alone.

Clerk James H. McKinney approached Taft with a Bible used in the Supreme Court and which was being used now at Taft's request. Even this crumb of symbolism meant much to him. By kissing a Bible on which members of the Supreme Court had been sworn in for generations, he would be expressing his love for the Court. The presidency had merely been an arrangement, and—as in such family arrangements—love was not really considered. Eventually, it was felt, Will would come to love the presidency.

It was part of an ironic set of circumstances that Chief Justice Melville Weston Fuller should administer the oath of office to President-elect

Taft. Fuller—small, brisk, with silky white hair that draped on his shoulders—was a relic of another era. He had been appointed by his fellow Democrat Grover Cleveland, and his qualifications for his position were not highly regarded, particularly by TR and Taft. In 1904, when he had already sat as Chief Justice for sixteen years, TR circulated the rumor that he might retire "and that Governor Taft [then in the Philippines] would be a suitable man for the vacancy." However, at a dinner given by Fuller, Mrs. Fuller directed a guest who was on his way to the Philippines to "tell Willie Taft not to be in too much of a hurry to get into my husband's shoes." Faded hopes for Fuller's resignation were succeeded by references to the inevitability of his death, though Taft wrote dejectedly that Fuller "was as tough as a knot," and it was Elihu Root's conviction that "they will have to shoot him on the day of judgment."

Now, at 12:55 P.M. on March 4, 1909, the infirmities of old age were apparent in the Chief Justice. He spoke the words of the oath, but they could not be heard by those assembled in the chamber. Taft, towering over him, repeated his apparent silences in the shape of words that could be heard by everyone on the floor and in the galleries. It was in these words of the presidential oath, read haltingly by Chief Justice Fuller, that Taft detected indications of Fuller's senility. Instead of asking the President-elect to swear faithfully to "execute the office of President," Fuller said "faithfully execute the Constitution." (Standing next to Taft, Philander Knox, the incoming Secretary of State, whispered, "Don't do it!")

As soon as the last words of the oath, "defend the Constitution of the United States," had died away, a signal flashed from the dome of the Capitol, proclaiming that he had been sworn in. A ten-inch gun responded; it was in the navy yard, a mile and a half away. The boom it created was joined by every noisemaker in the District of Columbia: steam whistles, horns, rattles, cheers. For fifteen minutes, the manufactured echo of that boom continued, an arranged spontaneity, insisting shrilly, raucously, deafeningly that the Taft administration was welcome.

More significantly, the brokers on the floor of the Stock Exchange in New York hurrahed when it was announced that Taft was in and Roosevelt out.

"The office of an inaugural address," President Taft was saying, while the festive noises in his honor continued, "is to give a summary outline of the main policies of the new administration so far as they can be anticipated."

He then went on to deliver those paragraphs that he had not deleted that morning before breakfast. He would carry out his distinguished predecessor's policies: fight the domination of trusts; revise the tariff downward; build a "proper army" and a "proper navy" that would insure peace; conserve the nation's natural resources; protect the workman in industry. He also touched on the misuse of labor injunctions, work on the Panama Canal. . . .

Mrs. Taft sat throughout the ceremony with "perfect poise and self-command"; serenity, it appeared, had completely displaced thought. But there were thoughts, and some dwelt on the eagerly anticipated ride back to the White House with the President of the United States; she left immediately after his address in order to meet him in the Rotunda, from which place they would go to the carriage.

But she didn't leave before TR had leaped to his feet and hurried up to her husband, who later reported to her that TR had said, "God bless you, old man. It is a great state document." (Mrs. Taft thought TR's comment had been, "Bully speech, old man.")

As Taft clasped TR's hand, "for a moment the two were almost locked in an embrace."

"Good-bye and good luck, again," TR said quickly. "I'm off."

Rules forbade applause in the chamber, but it broke out for TR as he made a hurried exit, moving as though pursued. Speed was certainly not alien to him, but now it smacked of escape.

At this point, the mood changed abruptly, becoming one of celebration, for a vast number of cheering New York Republicans closed in on TR, eager to accompany him the three short blocks to the new Union Station. They surrounded the double surrey in which he rode with his secretary, William Loeb, and marched along with it. Spectators also streamed on each side of the street and thus declared that the devotion to TR did, indeed, run over. At the height of the whole emotional outpouring, a big brass band pounded and blew TR's favorite tunes, "There'll Be a Hot Time in the Old Town Tonight" and "Garry Owen." At one with the spirit of the procession, the band began to play "Auld Lang Syne."

During the two-hour wait at the station, there was an impromptu reception in the presidential suite. Shortly after 3:00 P.M. TR and Mrs. Roosevelt made their way to the parlor car "Clytie." To the three thousand people present—two rows lining each side of the station, a dozen deep—TR declared that while he had had a "bully time" as President, he was glad to lay down the duties of office. "Good-bye all," he said, lifting his hat. "Good luck to you."

Inside the train, TR and his wife went to the drawing room and began to unpack flowers sent to him by well-wishers. As the train pulled out, those lining the platform fortified themselves and each other by repeating a comforting phrase, "He'll be back! He'll be back!"

Obviously, the New York *Sun* did not hold that view. One of TR's attempted reforms during his presidency concerned itself with simplified spelling. "Nuthing escapes Mr. Rucevelt," Henry Watterson, a Louisville, Kentucky, journalist had written sardonically. "No subject is tu hi for him to takl, nor tu lo for him tu notis. He makes treatis without the consent of the Senit. He inforces such laws as meet his approval and fales to see those that du not soot him. He now assales the English langgwidg, constitutes himself a sort of French Academy, and will reform the spelling in a way tu soot himself." Thus the *Sun* could express its joy over TR's departure with a one-word editorial that stood distinct, clear, emphatic, surrounded by white space in the middle of the column: "THRU."

Wex Jones in the New York *American* expressed a more kindly derision:

> There's a moaning in the Jungle;
> a wailing on the plain;
> From all across the continent there's an
> awful cry of pain.
> 'He is coming!' shrieks the parrot, and
> the ostrich hangs its head. . . .

All these farewells—no matter what their form or degree of virulence—would substantiate Irvin S. Cobb's observation, "You had to hate the Colonel a great deal to keep from loving him."

As the train took TR to Oyster Bay, the first step of the journey about which the animals were so apprehensive and the *Sun* rejoiced, Taft, in fur-collared coat and silk hat, stood in the reviewing stand watching the parade in his honor. In order not to keep people waiting in the cold for the parade, he had hurried lunch. Mrs. Taft was there beside him, bundled up in a heavy fur coat, not wanting to miss any aspect of the inauguration. Earlier, when she had reached the White House after the trip from the Capitol, she had stood in the entrance hall on the great brass seal, embedded in the floor, which bore the national coat of arms. Around the seal were the words, "The Seal of the President of the United States." After reading them, she thought, "And now—that meant my husband!"

Snow on the roof of the reviewing stand melted and dripped disrespectfully over the front and on her husband. But President Taft kept smiling. TR had told him to keep smiling.

That the Roosevelts were really not present was paradoxically emphasized by a Roosevelt's being there. Quentin had cut classes at the Episcopal High School in Alexandria, in order to see the parade; he watched

it with his good friend Charlie Taft and was "the only Roosevelt anywhere in evidence."

"Theodore has gone off in a wild hurricane of the frozen elements,"
Henry Adams wrote next day to his brother Brooks, "and today dawns
with a Taftas [sic] smile. Most fervently I hope it will be my last
Inauguration. These ruptures of social relations depress me horribly.
They are nearly always final."

Three   Nineteen Years

The events of nineteen years, interlocked in a cause-effect pattern as finely wrought as a snowflake or a dynamite blast, brought Will Taft to the presidency. But such patterns can be seen in all historic events, given the clear, unobstructed view of the present. And it is in such patterns that the fatalist finds confirmation, the determinist sees glands and reflexes, and the reverent are inspired to say that "God works in mysterious ways, his wonders to perform." In this instance, the mysterious ways ranged from idyllic friendship, to war, to assassination, to America's debut as a world power, to an obsessively ambitious wife—the panorama and melodramatic ingredients of a not-too-credible novel. They started when one of its principals—who, ironically, had a strong fatalistic streak in his make-up —came to Washington in the decade before the twentieth century arrived.

Washington's streets in that era knew the peace of dim, yellow gas-light, and—during the day—horses, between buggy shafts, unwittingly added to the tranquillity by waiting hipshot at curbs with somnolent patience. Only in January—the height of the calling season—did traffic noticeably pick up. Afternoons, carriages of every degree of affluence, from the shabby little coupé pulled by an old horse to the grand, highly polished equipage drawn by a spanking team of bays, moved up and down the fashionable streets.

The White House, usually the cynosure for the highest level of Washington society, was in eclipse in 1890 because of the personality of its occupants. The Benjamin Harrisons, though a worthy couple, were unpopular. Mrs. Harrison was a quiet little woman whose two interests were her grandchildren and painting china. President Harrison—little, gray, and cold, "with a handshake like a wilted petunia"—was disliked even by his fellow Republicans. The wife of a Republican senator claimed "he had a trick of turning a Republican into a Democrat that was almost sleight-of-hand."

Therefore, the obligation of establishing stimulating society for sophisticated Republicans was assumed by the Henry Adams-John Hay set, composed of Thomas Reed, Cabot Lodge, Cecil Spring-Rice of the British Embassy, and "Dear Teddy," the new Civil Service Commissioner. The relations of this group with the White House "were sometimes comic, but never intimate."

Despite the presence of this pocket of sophistication, Washington appeared a "very pleasant big village." The White House grounds were even open to the public, and the Roosevelt children—Alice, Ted, and Kermit—played there. Afterward they would saunter, as though they had no destination, but it was to the small frame house at the corner of Jefferson Place and Nineteenth Street.

Sometimes, before going all the way home, they would stop at Farragut Square and watch for the trolley car that would be bringing their father home from the Civil Service Commission office at Eighth and E Streets. There would be the hard grinding sound of metal wheel on metal track, and just as they had been watching for their father, so he had been watching for them, for he would hop off the trolley and walk with them the few blocks that remained.

Restlessness had brought TR from New York to the bucolic atmosphere of Washington, as an inner turmoil would be a factor in his departure. Though he had been prepared to settle on writing as a lifework, he preferred politics even if it meant an annual salary of thirty-five hundred dollars and a minor office, not much sought after.

Benjamin Harrison had grudgingly granted TR the appointment to the Commission, but only after Cabot Lodge and Tom Reed had spoken in their friend's behalf, and only after Harrison had refused him the position of Assistant Secretary of State. TR—a man who "wanted to put an end to all the evil in the world between sunrise and sunset"—irritated Harrison. And his relentless energy also rubbed the President the wrong way; even TR was aware, after bounding up the stairs of the Executive Mansion and into Harrison's presence, that Harrison drummed his fingers nervously on table surfaces.

But TR didn't let the discomfiture of others slow him down or keep him from getting things done. Upon his arrival in Washington, he rushed into the Concordia Building—a misnomer from that time forth—identified himself as the new Commissioner, and roused his colleagues with a barrage of questions, directions, and suggestions. From that time on, said one of his fellow commissioners, "every time I went to the office it was as to an entertainment. I knew something was sure to turn up to make our work worthwhile, with him there." That work, reforming civil service—

previously only the concern of a few cranks—was not easy, for President Harrison's support for such reform was, at best, tepid.

During the heat of the Washington summers, when Mrs. Roosevelt and the children would depart for Sagamore Hill, TR shared a bachelor establishment with Cecil Spring-Rice and continued to lash out for reform. He also acquired new friends, the Bellamy Storers, who were to become all-important elements in the pattern of his future. Storer, of a wealthy old Cincinnati family, had the distinction of being considered "the handsomest man in southern Ohio!" The symmetry of his Roman profile notwithstanding, it was his wife, the former Maria Longworth—of the Cincinnati Longworths—who attracted an admiring circle around her. Mrs. Storer's most absorbing interest was politics—national and Church (she was a Catholic convert). Her character was conspicuous for tenacity, and her "bright bird-like eyes" could both impress and intimidate. TR, who would one day have the full power of Maria Storer's tenacity trained on him, during this summer had his spare meals at the Storer home on Rhode Island Avenue. There, with his voice rising in emphasis to falsetto and his emphatic words spaced out dramatically, TR dominated the conversation and the attention of both guests and hosts. The general view was contained in one emphatic evaluation: "What a human dynamo!"

So great an impression did he make on everybody that few failed to predict greatness for Theodore Roosevelt. TR himself responded to these predictions with a negation that springs naturally from fatalism and is its counterpart. "My future," he said sadly to Brander Matthews. "How can I have a future in public life? Don't you know as Civil Service Commissioner I have made an enemy of every professional politician in the United States? I can't have any political prospects."

Scene two, act one, occurred nine months after TR stormed into Washington. In it, thirty-two-year-old Will Taft—ponderous, lonely, bag in hand—arrived from Cincinnati. It was six o'clock of a bleak February morning in 1890. Weary, rumpled after a sleepless night in a Pullman berth too small for his bulk, Taft faced the city and a position his wife hoped would give him "an opportunity for exactly the kind of work I wished him to do."

For the previous two years he had been a judge of the Superior Court of Ohio, doing the kind of work *he* liked to do and that might very well lead to the achievement of his most compelling dream: appointment to the Supreme Court. But, instead, President Harrison appointed him Solicitor General and, "with a few regretful glances at his beloved Bench," he accepted.

From the grimy old Pennsylvania Station Taft proceeded to the disappointing discovery that his office, a shabby cubicle, was up three flights of stairs and that his stenographer, also functioning as a telegrapher, had to be summoned from the chief clerk's office. To add to the gloom, the desk was piled high with the work of his predecessor, who had died the month before. Taft felt lonely, depressed, uncertain that he could handle the job that faced him.

Two weeks later, Mrs. Taft arrived with their six-month-old son, Robert, rented a small house at 5 Dupont Circle, and tensely anticipated all the rewards of being in the midst of things. At sixteen, as Helen Herron, she had also come to Washington; then it had been to be a guest of President Hayes, a former law partner of her father's. That week of her adolescence spent in the White House had made a deep and lasting impression on her. Following her engagement to Will Taft, she had, therefore, been profoundly struck by the fact that many believed Will would attain "some very important position in Washington." To her way of thinking, there was only one important position in the nation's capital.

Far from being prepared for that high position, Will Taft continued to be uncertain about his new job. His knowledge of federal law, he felt, was inadequate; as a speaker he wasn't fluent. "I have difficulty in holding the attention of the Court," he wrote his father glumly. "They seem to think when I begin to talk that that is a good chance to read all the letters that have been waiting for some time, to eat lunch, and to devote their attention to correcting proof. . . ." The justices were not merely being perverse; an anxiety to include all relevant facts lent a quality of interminability to Taft's briefs and speeches. Mrs. Taft also noticed it. "Don't make your brief too long, dearest," she cautioned him. "The court will appreciate it much more if they don't grow weary over reading it."

Like her husband, Mrs. Taft knew uncertainty and disappointment. Instead of becoming part of the intellectually select Adams-Hay group, whose preoccupation was derisive commentary on the art of politics and the uses of power, her husband was attracted to the more parochial society of the Attorney General and the Supreme Court justices, whose conversation orbited about the law. This circumstance might have prevented any intimacy springing up between Will Taft and Theodore Roosevelt—or their meeting at all—had it not been for the Storers. As members of old Cincinnati families, the Storers, the Longworths, and the Tafts all belonged to the same social circle in Ohio. Moreover, Charles Anderson, whose mother was a Longworth, and thus a cousin of Maria Storer, married Mrs. Taft's sister Jane; so "Bill Taft was considered to be quite within the family circle." During Mrs. Taft's occasional visits to her family, Taft was often at the Storers' Rhode Island Avenue residence. "You go so much to the Storers," she wrote him from Cincinnati, "that I really cannot keep track of your engagements with them."

Since TR also spent a great deal of time at the Storers, it is quite likely that he and Taft met there for the first time. Following this meeting, they saw each other often. Because they lived near each other, they frequently walked to work together, lunched together. It may have been the very physical and personality differences that made them appear so incongruous which served as a bond between them.

One of these differences related to adjustment. TR was forever restless, caught between alternatives, not sure what work he would do next. But the White House—the seat of power, the center of the arena—which the two men passed on the way to their offices, undeniably had the magnetic appeal for him that it also had for his friend's wife. Taft, unlike TR, knew precisely what he wanted—a place on the Supreme Court, preferably the chief justiceship; the achievement of this goal would give him power and dignity without the worry inherent in the presidency. He was in full accord with a tenet once propounded by his father, "To be Chief Justice is more than to be President."

Because he was the grandson of a former President, albeit one who had died a month after his own inaugural, at which he had contracted pneumonia, Benjamin Harrison was in the habit of stating dispassionately that he was "predestined for the presidency." Providence, he claimed, had ordained the matter. (However, to forestall any providential slip up, at his own rain-sodden inauguration Harrison wore a complete armor of chamois under his suit. "No Inauguration pneumonia for him!")

With comparable mysticism, Will Taft felt preternatural forces determining the direction of his life. "I have a kind of presentiment," he wrote his wife, from the deathbed of his father, "that Father had been kind of a guardian angel to me and that his wishes for my success have been so strong and intense as to bring it and that, as his life ebbs away and ends, I shall cease to have the luck which has followed me thus far."

Following his dying father's advice, and his own inclinations, Taft accepted an appointment, "for it would be in the line of promotion to the Supreme Court," as United States Circuit Judge for the Sixth Judicial Circuit.

This was a move of which Mrs. Taft deeply disapproved, a situation which she feared, for with older, settled men as his colleagues, Will, at the age of thirty-four, would be "fixed in a groove for the rest of his life." It would, she wrote him in alarm, "put an end to all the opportunities you now have of being thrown in with the bigwigs." Added to this disadvantage, there was her dislike of Cincinnati. While visiting her parents she wrote her husband that, except for her family, "there is hardly a soul here whom I care to see, I feel almost as if I were in a strange place."

But back to Cincinnati the Tafts went. For the next eight years, they were to be surrounded by stolid, judicial society, live on an income of six thousand dollars a year—one thousand dollars less than the salary a Solicitor General received—an income that was not in the least improved by Will Taft's conscientious return of unused expense account money. Assuming consistency in the supernatural world, if Will Taft's father had been able to control events by simple desire, so conceivably might Mrs. Taft. Her poignant yearnings were for the excitement of Washington and the "bigwigs" who would ease Will past the pitfalls of a Supreme Court appointment and into the White House.

It wasn't Theodore Roosevelt's guardian angel, but, rather, one whom some regarded as his evil angel who prophesied TR's future. "I do not say that you are to be President tomorrow," Cabot Lodge wrote him, "I do not say that it will be—I am sure that it may and can be." Notwithstanding such encouragement, because defeatism was bedfellow with wild enthusiasm in TR's nature, he continued to be glum over his prospects. The battle had gone out of his work as Civil Service Commissioner—even rows with Cabinet members and party regulars had become "fairly chronic," and he maintained the war with himself. "The trouble is," he wrote his sister Bamie, "that my career has been a pleasant, honorable and useful career for a man of means; not the right career for a man without means. If I can I shall hold this position another winter; about that time I shall publish my next two volumes of the Winning of the West; I am all at seas as to what I shall do afterwards."

Opportunities arose and were dismissed: an offer of the New York City mayoralty nomination; the post of New York City Street Cleaning Commissioner (turned down with the somewhat lame excuse that he was unfamiliar with the work "of cleaning the streets, dumping the garbage, etc."). But when he was offered a New York City police commissionership, he accepted with the speed of snapped fingers. Here at last was a job for a man of action and fortitude, because, as TR knew, with anticipatory delight, the core of civic corruption was the Police Department itself.

So remunerative was the income of a dishonest New York City policeman derived from blackmail and bribery, that appointments to the Police Department were sold in a manner reminiscent of the Purchase System in the old British Army. A patrolman's appointment cost from two to three hundred dollars, a captaincy from twelve to fifteen thousand dollars.

On a day in early May, 1895, after receiving a stern injunction from his political mentor, Cabot Lodge, not to lose interest in national politics while acting as Police Commissioner, TR, trailed by his three fellow police commissioners, ran up the crumbling steps of the New York Police Headquarters at 300 Mulberry Street, exclaiming, "Where are our offices? Where is the board room? What do we do now?"

It was observed by the keen eyes of police reporter Lincoln Steffens that one of the other police commissioners "hated the way TR took command of the police from the first day and kept saying 'I' and 'my policy.' "

Despite the formidable problems of his job, and the presence of an unco-operative associate, TR stated irrevocably four weeks after his arrival, "I am getting the Police Department under control." Five months after that, he reported buoyantly to Lodge—with no evidence now of an "all at seas" depression—that though he had rough times with his fellow commissioners, he kept each one in line "by a mixture of tact, good humor, and occasional heavy hitting."

While his family stayed at Sagamore Hill for the summer, TR spent two or three nights a week in town, nights which had a horrendous and sobering effect on the New York police force. Dressed in black cape, a broad-brimmed black slouch hat, pink shirt, with a black silk sash trailing to his knees, his spectacles and teeth flashing with equal menace, TR prowled the streets to investigate the conduct of his policemen. "I make some rather startling discoveries at times," he reported with amused understatement.

In the course of "flaming with indignation," dealing "slashing blows," engaging in "savage tilts," and finishing his four-volume history, *The Winning of the West*, TR recommenced worrying about his future. He wrote to his sister, "The only thing I am afraid of is that by and by I will have nothing to do and I should hate to have the children grow up and see me have nothing to do." Although he reiterated that he was politically dead, his friends police reporters Steffens and Jake Riis were convinced he was working toward the presidency. When they asked him point-blank if this was not so, TR reacted violently.

"Don't you dare ask me that," he shouted at Riis. "Don't you put such things into my head." Calming down a bit, he explained to Riis and Steffens, "Never, never, you must never either of you ever remind a man at work on a political job that he may be President." He paused thoughtfully, then continued, "I must be wanting to be President. Every young man does. But I won't let myself think about it. I must not because if I do, I will begin to work for it, I'll be careful, calculating, cautious in work and act, and so—I'll beat myself."

In the fall of 1896 TR took a respite from his police duties and, with Cabot Lodge, stumped enthusiastically for McKinley, even though "we are not among his favorites." With the election of McKinley, new appointive offices were tantalizingly accessible for loyal Republicans. "There is one thing I *would* like to have," TR wistfully informed Maria Storer, "but there is no chance of my getting it. McKinley will never give it to me. I should like to be Assistant Secretary of the Navy."

TR had expressed his desire to the right person; not only the Storers, but also Cabot Lodge and Will Taft—making contact with his friend again, and most significantly—converged on the President-elect to ask that something be done for Theodore, specifically that he be given the assistant secretaryship of the Navy. Even TR's enemy, Tom Platt, boss of the New York Republican machine, agreed to the appointment, commenting that TR "could do less harm to the organization as Assistant Secretary of the Navy than in any other office that could be named." Still McKinley was reluctant. "For the truth is, Will," he said in answering Taft's appeal, "Roosevelt is always in such a state of mind." But McKinley's objections were dissolved by the force of Mrs. Storer's personality, her air of "conscious priority," plus the fact that, several years earlier, the Storers had donated ten thousand dollars to a fund collected to relieve McKinley of an embarrassing hundred-thousand-dollar debt, and the unassailable fact that if McKinley refused this request "the Storers might come after him for something bigger." As Taft was to say later, "We got Theodore in the Navy Department." (And, more significantly, they set off a cause-and-effect chain reaction that got Theodore—and Will—into the presidency.)

TR was now not only back in Washington, the center of political power, but in a position—considering his propensities—to wield that power. Most assistant secretaries, it is true, wouldn't "have continually meddled" with what wasn't their business; and most secretaries wouldn't have countenanced their assistants' doing so. However, Secretary of the Navy John D. Long, former Governor of Massachusetts, a stout, kindly, tolerant, conservative, white-bearded gentleman, was, as TR described him, "a perfect dear." His poor health conveniently and often kept him away from the Navy Department; thus unusual authority was delegated to his assistant.

On February 25, 1898—ten days after the sinking of the *Maine*, during which period TR frantically feared McKinley was bent on peace—

Secretary Long stayed home from the office, but carefully cautioned TR not to take "any step affecting the policy of the Administration without," he said, "consulting the President or me," and to handle matters routinely. The next day, Long returned, only to discover that TR had meanwhile begun "to launch peremptory orders, distributing ships, ordering ammunition, and had cabled Admiral Dewey to be ready in case of war with Spain."

A week later TR requested his brother-in-law Douglas Robinson, who managed his finances, to "find out from the Life Insurance Company if my policy would be vitiated if I should go to Cuba in the event of war." Immediately upon declaration of war, in late April, with the can't-wait eagerness of an adolescent, TR resigned from the Navy Department. Secretary Long strongly advised against his going off to war. And, indeed, unarguable reasons confronted TR. His wife had had their fifth child, Quentin, the previous fall and was now recovering from a serious operation. Ted, Jr., was sick. Moreover, such a precipitous act might very well put an end to his public career. "I really think [TR] is going mad," his friend Winthrop Chanler wrote worriedly to his wife. "The President has asked him twice as a personal favor to stay in the Navy Department, but Theodore is wild to fight and hack and hew. It is really sad. Of course this ends his political career for good. Even Cabot says this." But as Secretary Long was eventually to admit in his diary, with a postscript wisdom, "His going into the army led straight to the Presidency."

The first solid step toward the White House occurred in mid-August, when TR and his Rough Riders steamed up to Montauk Point in the transport *Miami*, back from their "splendid little war" of twenty-three days, and the Republican party in New York was in need of a hero. The incumbent governor, Frank S. Black, was favored for renomination by Senator Tom Platt, but it was brought to Platt's attention that Black's scandalous administration of funds for the repair of the Erie Canal would bring them down to defeat. Consequently, with reluctant pragmatism, Platt sent his lieutenant, Lem Quigg, down to Montauk. According to Platt, the exchange was brief and direct.

" 'Would you accept the Republican nomination for Governor?' " Quigg asked TR.

"Like cracks from a rifle, the gallant Colonel came back with: 'Would I? I would be delighted!' "

" 'Then count upon Senator Platt's support. Come to the Fifth Avenue Hotel to see him.' "

Aware of TR's weakness for "various altruistic ideas all very well in their way," Platt demanded and received assurance from TR that Platt would be consulted on all policy and political appointments. TR was duly nominated and elected, after a picturesque campaign, in which he—wearing full Rough Rider uniform—was sourly described by Platt as having "fairly pranced about the State."

As he had promised Platt, Governor Roosevelt consulted him on party policy, legislative matters, and appointments. But after scrupulously consulting him, Platt complained, TR frequently did precisely as he pleased. For one thing, TR levied a tax on the franchise of public service corporations; this bitterly offended the business community, which, Platt grimly informed TR, supported the Republican party. And the Governor's refusal to appoint Platt's men infuriated the New York boss.

In his anger, Platt thought Washington to be a safe distance from Albany and the office of the vice-presidency a suitably malicious dead end for TR's ambitions. Though TR fiercely resisted, Platt was aided in his effort by Cabot Lodge, who, unlike Platt, was convinced, he told TR, that the vice-presidency would be a "true steppingstone for you either toward the Presidency or the Governor Generalship of the Philippines." The latter office was one for which TR yearned with almost as much fervor as the former, but, as he wrote Cecil Spring-Rice at the end of 1899, "it would not occur to the President to appoint me."

This was reckoning without the persistence of Cabot Lodge. For, about six weeks later, at the end of January, 1900, Lodge brought the matter to McKinley's attention by asking him directly, Lodge told TR, "whether he was thinking of sending you as Governor General of the Philippines."

McKinley's reply held hope, for he said, Lodge wrote TR, "that you were the ideal man to be the first pioneer Governor in those islands. . . ." But the President led Lodge to believe that this wouldn't take place until the military rule of the islands ended and all authority would be in the hands of a civil governor.

After McKinley's assassination, one of his political appointees tearfully blurted out, "He was the *purest* man that ever lived. Often, often I've heard him say, 'Boys, if there's dirty work to be done, don't tell me of it. *Do* it—but don't tell me of it!'" Apart from this purity, among William McKinley's other attributes was a notable reluctance to disappoint or say no. Therefore, with his customary solicitude, the President neglected to mention to Lodge that, only the day before, he had wired Judge Will Taft in Cincinnati to come to Washington—at which time he was to offer him the appointment of President of the Philippine Commission, with the assurance that he would be named Governor General when that post was created. (Astonished by this offer, Taft said, "But Mr. President, I am sorry we have got the Philippines. I don't want them and I think you ought to have some man who is more in sympathy with the situation." To this, McKinley replied, "You don't want them any less than I do, but we have got them and in dealing with them I think I can trust the man who didn't want them better than I can the man who did.")

Meanwhile, Lodge deluged TR with letters, urging that he seriously consider the vice-presidency. TR advanced a practical objection. Since he had a growing family whose education would require a great deal of money, he couldn't afford the level of entertaining that such former Vice-Presidents as Levi Morton and Garret Hobart, both millionaires, had maintained. Lodge replied that the matter of entertaining need not deter him, that Adlai Stevenson, Cleveland's Vice-President, had lived in three rooms in a Washington hotel. (As it turned out, the Roosevelts would not have had to resort to hotel living. The Storers would once again come to TR's aid, offering their Rhode Island Avenue residence at a nominal rental, while they were in Spain, where Bellamy Storer was Minister.)

Alarmed at the growing possibility of TR's being shunted off in the vice-presidency, his friend, reporter Joseph Bishop, wrote John Hay, McKinley's Secretary of State, imploring him to oppose TR's nomination. "There is no instance on record," Hay replied sardonically, "of an election of a Vice-President by violence. . . ." Indeed, Hay and Elihu Root viewed TR's strenuous efforts to avoid the vice-presidency with cynical amusement. In early June, several weeks before the Republican convention was to be convened in Philadelphia, TR hurried down to Washington in order to protest vehemently to members of the administration that he didn't want the vice-presidency. Root favored him with what John Hay called "a murderous smile" and then said, "Of course not, Theodore, you're not fit for it."

By the time the convention met, Boss Platt had assured TR's nomination by ingenuous, characteristic political maneuvering; despite the outraged opposition of Ohio Boss Mark Hanna—"Don't you realize that there's only one life between that madman and the presidency?"—TR was nominated by acclamation. "Platt and Hanna took opposite positions," TR wrote, "but each at the time cordially sympathized with the other's feelings about me."

In Cincinnati at this time, Will Taft stifled whatever qualms he had about going to the Philippines, because of his wife's enthusiasm for the trip. To her, the advantages were significant: they could leave Cincinnati and the narrowing confines of the judiciary; in such a high executive office, moreover, Will's White House potential would be infinitely improved. His brothers, whom he consulted, also felt that he should go. "So

he resigned from the Bench; the hardest thing he ever did," and before
the fall elections in 1900, the Tafts were settled in a large high-ceilinged
house on Manila Bay.

In that election, the McKinley-Roosevelt ticket triumphed. When
Thomas Platt was asked if he planned to go to the inauguration, he
replied with lip-smacking pleasure, "Yes, I am going down to see Theodore Roosevelt take the veil."

Young Alice Roosevelt's opinions paralleled those of Mark Hanna,
rather than of Platt; she maintained an "ever-present resentment at Father's being shoved into the Vice-Presidency." Therefore, as she stared
down at the inaugural parade from her vantage point in rooms over
Madame Payne's Manicure Shop on the corner of Fifteenth Street and
Pennsylvania Avenue, she eyed the portly—the impressively stable—figure of President William McKinley in a speculative manner and "wondered, in the terminology of the insurance companies, what sort of 'risk'
he was."

The Constitutional Convention may have felt that the Vice-President
should be an important official, but the details concerning the nature of
his office were drafted hurriedly, over a weekend, and accepted perfunctorily—without debate. John Adams, the first Vice-President, with his
customary irascibility, in a sense evaluated the shabby genesis of the vice-
presidency when he branded it "the most insignificant office that ever the
invention of man contrived or his imagination conceived."

TR, experiencing Adams' frustrations, upon becoming Vice-President
stated flatly that the office "ought to be abolished." After all, he and it
were irreconcilable; for while he was—as John Adams' great-grandson
Henry described him—"pure act," this office offered only one meager
task: presiding over the Senate. Eager to make the most of this duty, TR
went over the old files of the *Congressional Record*, but his heart was not
in it, for, as he had remarked before assuming office, he would inevitably
be bored by debates he couldn't be in. Although he presided for only five
days, from March fifth to the ninth, that sufficed to convince him he
"was the poorest presiding officer the Senate had ever had." This deepened his gloom, and led him to conclude that the vice-presidency was
not a "steppingstone" as Lodge had led him to believe, but the shelf—
oblivion—that Platt had intended.

TR also had a burden which Adams did not have, for George Washington had stated with lofty magnanimity that the person "elected Vice-
President cannot be disagreeable to me in that office." But the plain fact
was that TR's impulsive nature and his aggressiveness *were* disagreeable

to McKinley. Consequently, the President kept him at a distance; TR's communication with McKinley was by letter, letters that received "courteous acknowledgments," but which TR felt were not "even looked at by the President."

And, worst of all, most frustrating of all, TR had no power, an elementary requirement for him. So bereft was he of power that in response to a request for a political favor, he had to say, "I will try to get it for you, but you must not build up high hopes upon my succeeding." He even had to express uncertainty when a general had asked for an appointment to Annapolis for his grandson.

"An hurrah cannot last for five years," TR had once said, and therefore, in his desperation, he looked to the future. Seizing upon the fact that in 1881 he had spent a year in the New York Law School, he considered studying law during the empty years of the vice-presidency. He wrote James Lowndes, a Washington attorney, asking simple, practical, affecting questions as to how he should proceed. Though he said he didn't think it "quite proper" while Vice-President "to do any real practice of the profession," obviously contemplation had lingered on this pleasing prospect.

At the start of the summer of 1901, when he wrote to Taft that he wasn't doing enough to justify his existence, he attended the opening of the Pan-American Exposition in Buffalo. McKinley, however, merely sent a message of good wishes and the information that he would be coming to the Exposition in September.

While writing Taft that he wasn't going to get "the presidential bee" in his bonnet, TR was planning a nationwide tour for the following year to ignite presidential bonfires. In August he went West to do some political scouting—and hunting. At the beginning of September, when President McKinley headed for Buffalo, TR was in Vermont and gratified by the evidence there of support for him.

On September 6, 1901, Leon Czolgosz, a schizophrenic anarchist, inspired by the recent assassination of King Humbert of Italy, decided he would kill a President. For a week, it appeared his attempt had been unsuccessful, and that the President would recover. So certain did this appear that TR, who had rushed from Vermont to Buffalo, took men aside to talk about 1904. His energy and drive required that he take care of "the unknown quantity of the next three years." But the next few days negated that necessity, for McKinley's condition deteriorated and, in the early morning hours of September 14, he died.

As soon as he was sworn in as President, TR assured the country, and thereby calmed the agitated nerves of Republican business leaders, that he would continue the policies of President McKinley, for "the peace, the prosperity, and the honor of our beloved country."

At last, after six arduous, inactive months, the vice-presidency—by means of its one virtue—had given TR the power his personality required. Immediately upon entering the White House, he told reporters, "I was voted for as Vice-President, it is true, but the Constitution provides that in the case of the death or inability of the President, the Vice-President shall serve as President, and, therefore, due to the act of a madman, I am President and shall act in every word and deed precisely as if I and not McKinley had been the candidate for whom the electors cast the vote for President."

Shortly after the funeral train bearing the body of William McKinley left Buffalo, cursing—vehement and desperate—desecrated it. The man who many believed had controlled McKinley was damning the new President, who was riding in a nearby coach with his Cabinet.

In his despair and grief, Mark Hanna broke into his swearing as though the slain man were alive and should be censured. "I told William McKinley it was a mistake to nominate that wild man at Philadelphia."

The following month, still with an air of desperation, Hanna wrote to that "damned cowboy" pleading with him to "go slow."

As December and the time for TR's first message to Congress drew ominously nearer, conservative United States held its breath. But after hearing the wordy, over twenty-thousand-word document, it breathed again—with relief and amazement. The feared message could have been delivered, the New York *Evening Post* reported, by "a man of sixty, trained in conservative habits." Actually, TR was forty-three, the youngest President the country had ever had. Concealed in all the verbosity of his message to Congress were references to the country's evils and the need to correct them, the groundwork of policies that would require a progressive point of view for their continuation. Although TR objected to misconduct and not to wealth, each had chemical affinity for the other.

TR was, indeed, going slowly, cautiously, but for his own, rather than Hanna's, reasons. To a man who had been a weak, asthmatic child, strength was the goal, not popularity—which he dismissed with "I am not a college freshman." His presidency, he was therefore determined, would be like Lincoln's, "subject only to the people," and not hamstrung by the Constitution or by Congress—with whom, he said, he'd get along, if he possibly could.

When congressmen trooped amiably into TR's office, with prepared requests for their little illegal favors, they were astounded that the President would not oblige. Finley Peter Dunne's Mr. Dooley suggested the need for an "emergency hospital f'r office holders an' politicians acrost th' sthreet fr'm th' White House."

But TR found that though he did not have to be a menial servant to Congress, he had to contend with the Supreme Court; the Founding Fathers, who had created the vice-presidency that had given him so much trouble, were also responsible for the lofty specifications that made it difficult for him to "jump over the Supreme Court."

Since a powerful President, TR felt, was a President who got things done, he went at the job of negating the Supreme Court as a hurdle by getting his supporters—"men of my type"—on it. In 1902, he appointed Oliver Wendell Holmes and wrote to Taft, with the urgency of one about to light a fuse, that it was "of the utmost importance to get our strongest men on the Court at the very earliest opportunity."

His urgency made sense; in that year, he stopped going slowly. The Sherman Anti-Trust Act, since its enactment in 1890, had not inhibited corporations in any degree. All its ferocity was in its name. But in mid-February, 1902, without a word to anyone except his Attorney General, TR reactivated the Sherman Anti-Trust Act by instituting a suit against the Northern Securities Company, a colossal railroad monopoly established by J. P. Morgan and James J. Hill. When Morgan heard of this ungentlemanly action, he rushed to Washington to ask if his other interests would also be attacked. "Certainly not," TR told him, "unless we find out that . . . they have done something we regard as wrong." Misconduct—not wealth—was the evil. Regulation—not destruction—of big business was TR's panacea. And in that same year, in settling the anthracite coal strike, TR was the first President to involve himself in a dispute between capital and labor, going so far as to make the socialistic threat of taking the mines and turning over the mining of coal to the army.

Having made these powerful, novel thrusts, TR decided he needed Taft's backing on the Supreme Court. In late October, 1902, he cabled Taft in the Philippines, "On January first there will be a vacancy on the Supreme Court to which I earnestly desire to appoint you. . . ."

This unexpected offer disturbed Will and Nellie Taft, for making a choice was extremely difficult. More than ever, more than anything, Taft wanted a place on the Supreme Court bench, but important work remained in the Philippines that he felt it was his duty to complete. And though Mrs. Taft "yearned to be safe in Washington," she continued to be most reluctant to have Will's future confined, limited, by a lifetime appointment. "Great honour deeply appreciated," Taft cabled back, "but must decline. . . ."

With regrets, TR accepted Taft's decision, but then changed his mind, informing Taft that he would have to put him on the Supreme Court. "After all, old fellow," he reminded him, "if you will permit me to say so, I am President and see the whole field."

"Recognize soldier's duty to obey orders . . ." Taft cabled in answer, and then he went on to "presume on our personal friendship" to make one more appeal. This appeal, and numerous protests by the Philippine people, pleading that Taft remain, caused TR to answer, "All right, stay where you are. I shall appoint someone else to the Court."

But TR was still intent on getting Taft back in Washington, a first step in appointing him to the Supreme Court. Therefore, six months later, he urged Taft to return and be Secretary of War. "This," wrote Mrs. Taft, "was much more pleasing to me than the offer of the Supreme Court appointment, because it was in line with the kind of work I wanted for him and expected him to have. . . ." In accepting, Taft complained of the small salary a Cabinet officer received, the high cost of entertaining, and the burden this would place on his wife.

TR responded with advice, similar to that which he received from Cabot Lodge in the matter of vice-presidential economies. "I hope you will live just exactly as you and I did when you were solicitor general and I, civil service commissioner." Mrs. Roosevelt, he pointed out, didn't mind not having champagne for dinner. And they'd discovered that they could do most of their entertaining at "Sunday evening high tea." He concluded, "Thank Heaven, you are to be with me!"

("You should see Nellie's lip curl," Taft wrote an old friend, "at the suggestion of Sunday high teas and dinner parties without champagne.")

During the first year after they returned, Mrs. Taft felt alone and friendless—a sharp contrast to the social prominence she had enjoyed in Manila. In the hope of relieving all this emotional despair, she had expected some attention from Mrs. Roosevelt; and being eager for this attention, she bitterly resented not receiving it.

Will Taft busied himself with campaigning for TR's election in 1904. Even a maligned, castigated big business—after some misgivings—supported TR, instead of the Democrats' Judge Alton B. Parker, though he was strongly against TR's "usurpation of authority." The representatives of obese trusts, with dollar signs on their checked waistcoats, remained in the Republican party, because, as the conservative New York *Sun* explained, it preferred "the impulsive candidate of the party of conservatism to the conservative candidate of the party which the business interests regard as permanently and dangerously impulsive."

TR's victory was overwhelming. Immensely pleased, he said jubilantly that he could now be addressed as "Your Excellency" instead of "Your Accidency." On the night of his victory, he made an impulsive statement that, later on, he admitted, he would cut off his right hand not to have made. It was a statement that in 1912 became a perfect weapon for his enemies. He proclaimed that under no circumstances would he "be a candidate for or accept another nomination."

"I can see him," his daughter Alice recalled, "standing in the hall near the door of the red room as he gave it to a secretary." Mrs. Roosevelt, with her usual calm sagacity, felt that her husband had tied a knot with his tongue that he "could not undo with his teeth." It was to prove a knot that would also hold Taft captive.

On the eve of his inauguration, TR was reported to have said, "Tomorrow I shall come into my office in my own right. Then watch out for me."

This vow he kept, wielding the Big Stick frenetically against all wrongdoings, so that he appeared a cross between "St. Paul and St. Vitus." He fought against "embalmed beef." He got after railroad evils. The Monroe Doctrine, he decided, need not apply to the United States; we, but we alone, could intervene when necessary to preserve order and stability in the Americas. With the aid of James R. Garfield and Gifford Pinchot, he served future generations with a fighting, far-reaching conservation policy. He shoved through the Pure Food and Drug Act, the Employer's Liability Act, the Hepburn rate law for railroads. Confusing his identity with the nation's, its power with his own, he took Panama, started the dirt flying in constructing a canal. To show the nation's power —his power—to the world, he sent battleships around the globe in a feel-my-muscle gesture.

Not all of TR's presidential battles were of either the St. George or conquistador variety. His sensational encounter with Maria Storer had far more of the ludicrous than of the heroic. Its genesis lay in those years of close friendship between the Roosevelts and Storers, and in Maria Storer's absolute—and artless—faith in political influence in the pursuit of her two goals: that her husband be given a suitably high position in government and that Archbishop Ireland of St. Paul be elevated to the cardinalate. Eight days after TR became President, Mrs. Storer requested a Cabinet post for Bellamy. "Please," she wrote ingeniously, "give him either Navy or War." A month later, after TR apologetically explained that this would be impossible, Mrs. Storer asked for an ambassadorial post for

Bellamy, "suggesting London or Paris." When this, too, was denied, her importunate demands were unrelieved until the fall of 1902, when TR appointed Bellamy Storer Ambassador to Austria-Hungary.

Having placed Bellamy satisfactorily, Maria now turned her attention to the advancement of the Archbishop. While TR admired Archbishop Ireland, for an American President to request the Pope to name him cardinal was most improper. Nevertheless, the Storers showed TR's letters to Vatican officials, and Bellamy in an audience with Pope Pius X quoted the President as saying he "desires emphatically for Mgr. Ireland all the honors of the church. . . ." Upon hearing of this, TR wrote a stern letter to Bellamy Storer with the injunction, "I must request you not to quote me in any way or shape hereafter."

After an exchange of letters that taxed TR's dwindling patience, he sent off a letter with an ultimatum; either the Storers were to drop their ecclesiastical politicking or Bellamy must resign from the diplomatic service. To these alternatives the President received no reply. He sent another letter, which also remained unanswered. Finally, upon TR's demand, Bellamy Storer wired his resignation, and a sixteen-year friendship was dissolved.

An obvious irony lay in the fact that, just at the time of Bellamy Storer's resignation, Maria Storer's nephew, Nick Longworth, married Alice Roosevelt, a wedding the Storers refused to attend. A more acute irony was also discernible. With a cousin married to Mrs. Taft's sister and her nephew now married to TR's daughter, Maria Storer, under normal circumstances would have represented a family link between the Roosevelts and Tafts. As it was, disappointed and embittered, she could only signify disunity.

As TR bounded from one field of combat to another, the election year of 1908 approached, and TR the politician was confronted by TR the moralist, the expounder of the simple basic virtues of fair play, clean living, courage, self-respect, decency. He believed that no "harm comes from the concentration of power in one man's hands provided the holder does not keep it for more than a certain definite time. . . ." He had therefore given his word that he would not run again, and so he must not run again.

Three prominent men were seriously considered as potential nominees by TR: Elihu Root, Charles Evans Hughes, and William Howard Taft. While TR admired Root immensely, Root, as a former corporation counsel, was too closely associated with big business to be tolerated by the Western progressives. On the other hand, Hughes, an admirable Governor of New York, was "a strong-willed, forceful character," and very popular with Western progressives, but TR cordially disliked him. As for Taft, another Supreme Court appointment had become available in the spring of 1906, which the President offered Taft, with the additional proviso that if the chief-justiceship became vacant while TR was still in the White House, Taft would become Chief Justice.

But upon asking young Charlie Taft if his father was going to become a Supreme Court justice, a family friend was told, "Nope."

"Why not?" he asked Charlie.

"Ma wants him to wait and be President," Charlie answered.

One day shortly after this encounter, following a Cabinet meeting, Taft explained to TR, "Nellie is bitterly opposed to my accepting the position and . . . she telephoned me this morning to say that if I did, I would make the great mistake of my life."

In the fall of that year, while Taft was out of Washington, Mrs. Taft was invited to lunch at the White House. After lunch, TR drew her aside, saying he wished to speak to her. "He seems to think," Mrs. Taft wrote her husband indignantly, "that I am consumed with an inordinate ambition [for you] to be President and that he must constantly warn me that you may never get there—and now he says that while you are his first choice that in case you are not persona grata to the powers that be, it may become necessary for him to support someone else like Hughes, for instance, should he win in New York. I felt like saying, 'D— you, support whom you want for all I care.' But, suffice it to say, I did not. . . ."

By January, 1908, a final decision was forced upon TR by his energetic secretary, William Loeb. If he didn't choose a candidate and throw the strength of the administration back of him, Loeb told TR, people would believe he meant to disregard his pledge and force his own nomination.

After briefly considering Root again, TR arrived at a conclusion. Although the incidents leading to it may have had all the farfetched melodrama of a not-too-credible novel, the narrative was certainly not pat, because it took nineteen years—and their complexity—for TR to say, "We had better turn to Taft."

Four

"Smile, Smile, Smile"

The convention city of the Republican party was to be Chicago, the date June 16, but long before then the preparations and anticipation charged Chicago's atmosphere with politics. Even the AMA convention, which preceded the Republican party's, had political overtones. Its keynote speech demanded more doctors in the Cabinet, urged that more doctors enter politics. Women doctors arose in defense of Theodore Roosevelt's policy that women have as many children as possible.

The political battle would take place in Chicago's somber stone Coliseum, the Midwest's heavy-handed version of a castle. Mrs. Taft wanted to be there, for she feared TR plotted to use Will as a stalking horse to whose candidacy delegates would be committed; then at the last moment, according to his Machiavellian scheming, he would snatch them away to support his own nomination. Gravely alarmed though she was by this possibility, friends were able to persuade her to remain in Washington.

The Tafts' side, however, didn't lack for representation. Charles P. had arrived on June 5, eleven days prior to hostilities, to do preparatory work. Young Bob Taft, a wide-eyed eighteen, was on hand for his first convention, sleeping on a folding bed in his Uncle Charlie's office in the Coliseum, and meeting more Tafts than he knew existed. Mabel Boardman had come, too, and had taken rooms in the Auditorium Annex. There were only two Roosevelts present; Alice and Alice's Aunt Corinne (Mrs. Douglas Robinson). The idea of a TR coup, which loomed as such an overriding fear in Mrs. Taft's mind, was to Alice Longworth a wild yearning. She had wished "in the black depths of my heart," she recalled, " 'that something would happen' and that Father would be renominated."

Knox and Hughes—and other hopefuls—could not be completely discounted as threats to the Tafts. Philander C. Knox, former Attorney General and now Senator from Pennsylvania, might prove invincible if

Taft did not win on the first ballot, for not only was Knox capable, but also big business would support him. As for "the bearded lady," TR's pejorative for Hughes, his chances had been seriously damaged at the beginning of the year when, at the same time Hughes was to make a definitive speech in his own behalf before the Republican Club, TR had released his highly sensational "Wall Street message," in which he referred to his enemies among the "malefactors of great wealth" as "men with hard faces and soft bodies." Accused of having sent the message to Congress for only one purpose, to blanket Hughes's speech in the press, TR grinned and said, "If Hughes is going to play the game, he must learn the tricks."

But nothing TR might do to promote Will Taft's nomination could convince Nellie Taft of his sincerity. The contest, she felt, remained one between him and her husband. A similar view was held by conservative Republicans and was articulated by Mrs. George M. Pullman, a well-known Chicago society matron, who declared, "We must have Taft, for if we don't we'll have Roosevelt."

The possibility of a last-minute stampede to TR also charged the Coliseum's atmosphere, bringing "a flavor of excitement" to the convention. In addition, blue and white bunting, with red rosettes, managed in a small way to make something special of the hall's vast hangarlike interior with its grim steel-girder ceiling. And there was, of course, the noise of persuasion, the strident carpentry of party platform making, with delegates punctuating personal pronouncements with spits aimed perfunctorily at cuspidors.

On the first day of the convention, the temporary chairman, Senator Julius C. Burrows of Michigan, dutifully, platitudinously, interminably extolled the Republican party, including obligatory, reverential mention of Abraham Lincoln and his contemporary counterparts, Theodore Roosevelt and William Howard Taft. The names alone, in each instance, touched off applause. It was considered noteworthy that the applause evoked for Lincoln was second in clamorous enthusiasm; that for Taft, third.

Obviously, Theodore Roosevelt's influence was dominating the convention. That a great deal of it would be necessary to "put Taft over" was a view generally held, a view the Tafts were aware of—at one conscious level or another—and resented. A minor display of this influence at work occurred in a little convention vignette, and its efficacy should have pleased the Tafts, however much it also might have irritated them. This influence dealt with a major problem of the convention audience—the extreme difficulty of seeing the speakers on the dais. The problem was aggravated by the huge, broad-brimmed straw hats worn by the ladies and kept securely pinned on, despite the complaints and entreaties of the men seated in back of them.

In Section 63, on one of the Coliseum's twelve thousand seats, sat Alice Roosevelt Longworth, equated with TR by the Tafts, for both father and daughter possessed ego, energy, quick intellect, personal magnetism, and in proportions making them disquietingly similar. She wore a large black lace straw hat, trimmed with a black aigrette and with drapings of tulle and a band of blue circling the crown, which effectively obscured the view of those behind her. After she was asked to remove her hat to set an example for the other women, Alice carefully unpinned her hat and removed it. Shortly, all over the Coliseum a curious phenomenon occurred—one by one, two by two, in groups, as the ripple of Alice's influence spread, women carefully unpinned and removed their hats.

The convention's first day had been overture—traditional ceremony and ritual, to be endured for what was to come. The second day, however, started with the dullness of the first; there was still really no indication of what lay ahead. Taft's delegates were seated—precisely as expected. Then the spare figure of the permanent chairman, Senator Henry Cabot Lodge, rose and surveyed the assemblage through ice-blue, heavy-lidded eyes. Although his mustache and beard hid his mouth, his manner revealed that its lines were cast down in its usual fixed expression of disapproval. "In discussions," a friend once remarked of Lodge, "he was one of those who care more for downing his adversary than for discovering common ground for possible agreement." His customary aloofness and arrogance stemmed simply from an unaffected reliance on being a Boston aristocrat, a regular Republican, and an acute politician. Nevertheless, it always created resentment in those whose faith in one or another of these verities was not as firm as his. Cabot Lodge did have a very real charm and an engaging wit, but they were reserved for his family and friends. His close friendship with TR was on a different basis from that of TR with Will Taft, one that gave it added durability; Edith Roosevelt and Nannie Lodge shared their husbands' attachment for each other and, indeed, were close friends themselves.

As permanent chairman, Lodge was now confronted by an oppressive task which TR depended upon him to perform: to make it clear to the convention delegates that Theodore Roosevelt would not accept the nomination. Beginning the long, formularized speech of a chairman, Lodge's rasping voice sounded, as usual, like "the tearing of a bed sheet."

Though conservative Republicans reiterated their belief that the delegates were anti-TR, "the spirit of the convention," journalist Henry Stoddard recalled, "was wholly Rooseveltian." The mere unemphasized mention of "the President" caused deafening cheers. But Lodge's metallic voice doggedly made itself heard. "The President has enforced the laws as he found them in the statute book," he declared. "For this performance of his sworn duty he has been bitterly attacked." More cheers, a louder outbreak than before, cut him off.

Finally he was able to begin again, pointing out that "the President is the best-abused and most popular man in the United States today," a statement that set off an explosive demonstration. Soon a chant, "FOUR, FOUR, FOUR YEARS MORE!," started in the galleries and was taken up by those on the floor.

Smiling, pleased, Lodge indulged the demonstration, made no attempt to stop it.

The Alice-watchers turned to Section 63 to see Alice's reaction to the ovation. She sat quietly, smiling occasionally; her husband, beside her, had an unlighted cigar in his mouth.

Seated in the front row with the Ohio delegation, Charles P. Taft appeared "ominously aloof." "It is nothing," he told a Chicago *Tribune* reporter. "They are working off a little steam."

As the demonstration went on and on, despite the band's loud but futile rendition of "The Star-Spangled Banner," Lodge declared to friends on the platform, "They said there was no Roosevelt feeling in this convention, but I will show them that there is."

During the forty-nine-minute ovation—the continual chanting of "FOUR, FOUR, FOUR YEARS MORE!"—pink-haired, pink-faced Frank Hitchcock came down from the Alaska delegation to whisper to Charles P. Hitchcock, who was Taft's campaign manager and looked, it was maintained, like a conventional play character named Reggie. "They whispered and shook their heads a great deal." It was observed by vigilant reporters that all the Tafts, especially the women, looked worried.

Cabot Lodge finally brought the demonstration for TR to an end by making himself heard above the roar. He then did what was, he declared, "the hardest thing I ever did in public life"; he said that TR's decision was "final and irrevocable" and that "anyone who attempts to use his name as a candidate for the presidency impugns both his sincerity and his good faith." Anyone who would do that, Lodge concluded in eloquent pronouncement, "was no friend to Theodore Roosevelt."

Directly in front of the platform and ten feet above the heads of the delegates were four black disks through which wires were looped and joined to a small central cable leading from the hall. By this combination of telephonic and phonographic mechanisms all the proceedings of the convention were picked up and transmitted through a wire cut into a White House telephone. TR, receiver to ear, heard the forty-nine-minute ovation. Afterward he came into his office, "in as gay a humor," noted Archie Butt, "as I have ever seen him."

TR was undoubtedly pleased by the intensity and duration of the demonstration in his honor, but it is more likely that his pleasure expressed an ambivalence to power. His daughter Alice may have expressed his true feelings when she said, "It was against human nature, against mine anyway, not to feel that the prospect of all those great times coming to an end was something to be regretted, though most secretly."

Earlier, at lunch, TR's ambivalence and the arrival of an occasional telegram marred the tranquillity of the meal. Friends were wiring insistently that if he didn't make a fresh refusal of the nomination, the convention would name him, but TR decided he could not be more emphatic than he had been and that there was a danger of appearing to protest too much.

In any event, his gaiety after the long ovation did not extend across the street and into the office of the Secretary of War, where Will and Nellie Taft, with young Charlie and Helen, waited in a state of ferment. Although they had not heard the Roosevelt demonstration directly, telephone and telegraph bulletins were constantly handed to Mrs. Taft, which she read aloud. When the demonstration had gone on for about thirty minutes, Taft rose from his chair abruptly, snatched up his hat, and strode hurriedly over to the executive offices. He spoke to TR briefly, and then, evading the reporters gathered in front of the President's office, not wanting to reveal the nature of their conversation, he returned to the War Department. There, in a crisis-ridden atmosphere Mrs. Taft still sat, receiving and reading aloud the bulletins from the Coliseum describing the continuing ovation for TR.

The heavy red hangings draping the windows of the office of the Secretary of War and the gilt-framed solemn portraits of former War Secretaries on the walls did nothing to lighten the mood of the Tafts, who, on the third day of the convention, once again gathered to receive bulletins from Chicago. Secretary Taft's huge flat-topped desk was in the middle of the room. Behind it, in her husband's swivel chair, Mrs. Taft sat as though enacting a cartoon charging her with overt political power. Taft was off to one side with friends. Young Charlie, serving as courier, rushed about bearing bulletins.

The nominating speeches started, and glib oratory dispensed with favorite sons in a cursory fashion. Charles Evans Hughes was nominated by a man who failed to mention Hughes's name. Taft's name, however, was mentioned when he was nominated, and it started a demonstration, with the delegates participating. Those from Texas had an immense pair of pants on the end of a flagpole, with a sign that read, "As pants the hart for cooling streams, so Texas pants for Taft."

During this demonstration, while a series of bulletins was received—characterizing the cheering, reporting its volume, appraising its degree of enthusiasm, and estimating its possible duration—Taft sat calm, composed. But Mrs. Taft was wild with excitement. "I only want it to last more than forty-nine minutes," she exclaimed. "I want to get even for that scare that Roosevelt cheer of forty-nine minutes gave me yesterday."

"Oh, my dear, my dear!" Taft said, smiling.

The Taft demonstration ran down, and stopped, finally, after twenty-five minutes. Word came that balloting was about to begin; "breathless eagerness followed." Into this excitement Charlie came rushing with a bulletin that he immediately handed across the big desk.

His mother "went deathly white." With obvious difficulty she read aloud, "A large portrait of Roosevelt has been displayed on the platform and the convention has exploded."

"A silence as of death fell upon the room. Mrs. Taft sat white as marble and motionless." Her husband's fingers tapped the arm of his chair, and he whistled quietly. No one spoke or glanced around.

Into this strained scene Charlie rushed with yet another bulletin, which he also handed across the desk to his mother. Impassively she read, "A huge American flag with a Roosevelt portrait upon it is being carried about the hall, and the uproar continues with increased fury."

(During "the awful silence that followed" in Washington, Senator Lodge, in Chicago, had started calling the roll for balloting. So loud was the uproar that he reached Massachusetts, alphabetically, before the reporters were able to put down how the vote was going.)

Then Charlie raced into his father's office, clutching still another bulletin, and Mrs. Taft, "almost leaping from her chair in excitement, read 'Massachusetts gives 25 votes for Taft. . . .' "

In just a matter of minutes, the nomination was announced. The vote stood at Taft, 702, Knox, 68, and Hughes, 67. A motion to make the nomination unanimous was made and so ordered.

Mrs. Taft's color had returned.

Loeb relayed the news of Taft's nomination to TR through the open bay window of his office, overlooking the tennis court. TR paused in his game with Assistant Secretary of State Robert Bacon just long enough to express delight; he then ordered Bacon to serve. Loeb, meanwhile, sent out press releases of TR's comments on the outcome of the convention, which TR had dictated before leaving the office, thus assuring an uninterrupted tennis game.

In spite of his devotion to tennis, TR "had never learned a real stroke"; he also played poorly because he talked while playing, a practice that also marred the technique of his opponent. Now, "charging the ball fiercely with teeth gritted," bounding back and forth on the court, he "expressed his delight with characteristic emphasis" on the subject of the convention.

The gratification, the sheer exaltation of the entire Taft family at Will's winning the nomination at the very least equaled TR's delight, but the vexation of being under obligation to TR for this triumph had already begun to intrude on their pleasure. They, therefore, reviewed and minimized the degree of obligation and TR's influence at the convention. "The cheering for the President on Wednesday worried the family, especially the ladies," Bob Taft wrote his mother from Chicago, "but it really wasn't as bad as it seemed because a great deal was carried on by a kind of rough class around the back of the hall, and the delegates with a few exceptions weren't particularly excited." ("Not only did the people want him," Corinne Roosevelt Robinson said in speaking of the ovation for her brother, Theodore, "but the *delegates* wanted him as well.")

Nevertheless, relations between the two men continued to be felicitous and without apparent strain. "In fact," TR wrote his friend Sir George Trevelyan the day after Taft was nominated, "I think it has been very rare that two public men have ever been so much at one in all the essentials of their beliefs and practice." It was therefore more than a mere expression of the amenities when Taft thanked TR after the nomination; TR was later to say, acidly, that "he exhausted the English language for words with which to express his obligation to me."

At the end of June, Taft resigned as Secretary of War in order to begin the work of the campaign, and TR discussed with him possible successors to that office. Since it would be difficult to get a first-class man for only the remaining months of the Roosevelt administration, TR told him, "I would prefer to name a man whom you will continue, but if you do not care to commit yourself I will go ahead and do the best I can without involving you at all."

TR's choice to fill the War Department secretaryship was Luke Wright, a Southern Democrat, who had been in the Philippines with Taft. How did Taft feel about Luke Wright?

He would, Taft assured TR, "be more than pleased to continue

Wright." "Then," TR pressed him, "I can tell Wright when I offer him the place that I am speaking for you as well as myself?"

"You can."

About the same time, according to TR, Taft advanced the subject of his Cabinet. "I wish," he said, "you would tell the boys I have been working with that I want to continue all of them. They are all fine fellows and they have been mighty good to me. I want them all to stay just as they are."

"Why don't you tell them so yourself?" TR asked.

"No, I don't want to do that. I don't want to make any promises," Taft replied. "I want to be in a position to say that I have no promises out. I wish, though, that you would tell them just how I feel and let them know that I want the Cabinet to stand just as it is."

Only four members of the Cabinet wished to stay on, TR told him: Oscar Straus, George Meyer, James Wilson, and James R. Garfield. "If you really want me to talk with them about it," TR said, "I will gladly tell them of your intentions."

"Yes," Taft assured him, "I wish you would."

In addition to these arrangements, it had also been settled that Taft would deliver his speech accepting the nomination on July 29, in Cincinnati. To prepare that speech—and to rest—Will Taft went to Hot Springs, Virginia, with his wife. TR's summer was to be spent in Oyster Bay.

During this period, letters came to Hot Springs frequently and regularly from Oyster Bay, embodying advice on everything from how to handle extreme prohibitionists to the writing of "your little speech of acceptance." On July 17, TR concluded a long letter with, "I suppose (for your sins) you will have copies of my speech and letter of acceptance before you. You will notice that I made my speech comparatively short, but made it as aggressive as possible. . . ." In a handwritten postscript he cautioned him to be "very careful to say nothing, not one sentence that can be misconstrued, and that can give a handle for effective attacks. I have always had to exercise lynxeyed care over my utterances!"

In addition to giving him advice, TR invited Taft to stop off at Oyster Bay for a day or two so that he could go over the speech with him. Without checking with his family first, Taft accepted TR's invitation and announced publicly that he wanted to "get the President's judgment and his criticism" on the speech. Consequently, when he arrived in Cincinnati, a wrathful brother Charlie confronted him, wanting to know why he had to come to Cincinnati by way of Oyster Bay.

There have been many efforts to fix the specific event that instigated

the dissolution of the friendship of Theodore Roosevelt and William
Howard Taft—and the precise moment of its occurrence. What is more
significant is the primary originating force behind the breakup—the Taft
family: Nellie Taft, Charles P. Taft, Henry W. Taft, and Horace Taft.
Purely personal antipathy was a factor; Horace, gentle and usually
trenchantly witty, expressed the basis for it, seriously, succinctly, when
he told Will that he did not like TR "because he was so conceited and self-
centered." Will—always a conscientious but somewhat ineffectual
counterforce—replied, "That is because you don't know him."

At no time oblivious to the Taft family's feeling toward him, TR
ignored it so that he could plunge ahead as though it did not exist. He
wired Will his reactions to the acceptance speech: "Both of the first two
paragraphs should certainly be omitted. The rest of the speech is I think
admirable, with two or three corrections." He then went on to point out
five—not two or three—corrections. Another suggestion was curiously
similar to one made by both Nellie and Horace—that the name Roosevelt
be invoked fewer times in the speech. "You are now the leader," TR
reminded Taft, "and there must be nothing that looks like self-depreciation or undue subordination of yourself. My name should be used only
enough thoroly to convince people of the identity and continuity of our
policies. . . ."

So, on one of the hottest days of the summer of 1908, during city-wide
festivities, Will Taft stood on a platform in front of his brother Charlie's
home on Pike Street and said in his acceptance speech, "Mr. Roosevelt led
the way to practical reform. The chief functions of my administration
shall be to complete and perfect the machinery by which the President's
policies may be maintained."

The next four months, which Taft accurately predicted would be "a
kind of nightmare for me," began a tug of war between the Taft family
and TR with—if the figure is to be maintained—Will Taft serving as the
rope.

Will and his brother Horace agreed that the campaign should be dignified; even assuming the efficacy of such an approach, it was not TR's idea
of a campaign. Because the Tafts had their way in the early stages, the
campaign was "loaded down with calm."

Neither did drama appear to be forthcoming from Taft's opponent.
William Jennings Bryan, after an ovation that lasted for an hour and
twenty-seven minutes—a frenetic attempt to create optimism—was nominated for the third time. The main items for which he stood, however—
income tax, inheritance tax, and corporation control—had been taken
over by TR. Bryan, who claimed he was the candidate who would really

carry out TR's policies, had adopted one of his own that was certain to kill him at the polls—government control of railroads. Understandably, a depressed conservative Democrat pointed out bitterly, "The Democrats will now resume their accustomed occupation of electing a Republican President."

TR, nevertheless, drew back from overconfidence, for it bred inaction. Certain though he was that voters could not help but be drawn to Taft's admirable qualities, he had selected only half the ticket; the other half was "Sunny Jim" Sherman, one of the "high priests" of the Old Guard who, during a long twenty years in the House, had not backed a single thing of value and was "a bone allowed the reactionaries."

A major anxiety of TR's—one shared by the Republican party generally—was that Taft, not accepted wholeheartedly by the progressives, and now burdened with Sherman, might not carry the West. A neat stratagem was needed to make Taft appear a conservative to Eastern voters and a progressive to the Western electorate.

TR, like an overconcerned father writing to a son who had just left the family nest, told Will Taft precisely what to do: Don't talk on delicate

"Alone I Didn't Do It." Mr. Taft (breathless but triumphant): "Thank you, Teddy!" By Bernard Partridge, London *Punch*, November 11, 1908.

subjects; stop citing court decisions; treat the political audience as one coming to see a poster, not an etching—no soft colors or fine lines, just streaks of red and blue and yellow to catch the eye; don't define your religious beliefs. There was advice to cover all occasions. Golf, Taft's game (though, owing to what his wife called his "unusual proportions," he was unable to place the ball on the tee), should not be played until after the election, for the public viewed the game with suspicion. If he went fishing, voters sobered by the Panic of 1907 might think him indolent. He should stay in hotels, not in private homes, so more people would have a chance to see him. And, above all, Taft, that "big generous high-minded fellow," must *smile, smile, smile!* In the absence of a dynamic personality, a vigorous speaking style, and a combative nature, only a Hobson's choice remained—an unflagging affability.

Before long, reporters became aware of "a certain kind of indiscreet talk that began about that time, to be heard occasionally in the corridors of the hotel where the Taft family were stopping. It was talk gratuitously critical of Mr. Roosevelt, and it seemed to proceed from, if not originate with, those very close to Mr. Taft."

The Tafts, jealous, quick to take offense, saw condescension in TR's incessant flow of advice, and the implication that Will "was not capable of standing on his own feet." Upon urgent request from those whom he euphemistically called "some of Taft's friends," John Hays Hammond, an old college friend of Will Taft's, undertook "the delicate mission" of telling TR that "in his effort to help Taft he was keeping himself too much in the limelight" and perpetuating an impression that Taft was "forced to rely on the President for everything he did." This sort of thing, Hammond told him, "had made a bad impression in political circles."

For a moment TR eyed Hammond quizzically, then said, "I guess you're right. In the future I'll put on the soft pedal."

But certain facts could not be side-stepped by TR: "dear old trump" though Will Taft was, he did, indeed, need someone to take him by the hand. This judgment had been arrived at early in what Alice Longworth referred to as the "game of putting Taft over," and had been quickly hardened in the fire of Taft's ineptness as a campaigner.

Earlier in the year, Taft spoke at the tomb of Ulysses S. Grant, and in the course of his speech, with complete innocence, had woven in comments on Grant's drinking, thus outraging GAR veterans, whose support he was after. And his idea of the most fascinating subject on which to speak before a Boston audience was the Philippines—a choice that sent a convalescing Alice Longworth into such whoops of laughter that they broke a stitch of her appendectomy incision.

The ten thousand dollars that Charlie Taft added to his brother's income each year was to allow Will to be "able to do as he pleased politically," but no amount could make adhering to the basic principles of politics a matter of choice. Nor could this money substitute for even a moderate aptitude for politics and a taste for its challenge.

"The most obvious political moves," despaired New York *Times* reporter O. K. Davis, "pass right under his nose unnoticed." Once Frank Hitchcock sent Taft a wire from the top of Pike's Peak, saying, "We are on top and intend to stay there." Astonished by what he regarded as a silly communication, Taft snorted and said, "What does he send me a message like that for?" and threw it in the wastebasket. A reporter who was in his office at the time explained that the wire was a publicity stunt: "Hitchcock expects you to answer with a message he will give out and every newspaper in the country will print it."

"Oh," said Taft, "I see."

In mid-campaign, because of some fresh political absurdity, TR had exclaimed, "Who with a sense of humor and a real zest for life would not be glad to be prominent in American politics at the outset of the 20th Century?"

Will Taft, for one, would not; he disliked the limelight. He also abhorred playing politics, "buttering people up, as he went around the country." He was to regard his campaign for the presidency as "one of the most uncomfortable four months of my life," during which he and his family were "exposed to all sorts of criticism and curious inquisitiveness," during which reporters dogged his footsteps, whose queries, if not awkward to answer, he found impertinent. While he was Secretary of War, his office had been a haven for newsmen. Every afternoon at about four o'clock reporters would "go Tafting" and congregate for a half hour's genial exchange with Secretary Taft. Now, as a presidential candidate, he was ill at ease with the same men, and they, aware that he might soon be replacing the most colorful and newsworthy President in living memory, found him disappointing. Their stories reflected their attitude toward him. Taft wrote plaintively to Mabel Boardman, "I never get up now and look at the headlines in the newspapers that I do not do so with a fear that there is to be found something in their columns calling for denial or explanation. Those things that can be denied I do not fear. It is those things that have to be partly denied and partly explained that are troublesome."

As the summer progressed into fall, Charles P. Taft continued to pour hundreds of thousands of dollars into his brother Will's campaign, and Theodore Roosevelt continued to rally the candidate with cries of "Hit them hard, old man!" The candidate himself stumped for the job he did

not want with long, dull speeches—418 of them in forty-one days—
which he read with the droning intonation due dusty legal documents.
Thus, despite TR's strenuous efforts "to put a little vim into the campaign," he was worried. "I am not very much pleased with the way Taft's
campaign is being handled," he wrote his son-in-law, Nick Longworth, at
the end of September. "Whether it is Vorys, or Corbin or Keifer or
Charlie Taft who is responsible for it, I cannot say. But I do wish that
Taft would put more energy and fight into the matter."

The following day, he wrote fretfully to Lyman Abbott, owner of *The
Outlook*, "Oh Lord, I do get angry now and then over the campaign. Of
course, I suppose everyone always feels that he would manage things a
little differently if he had the doing of them; but certainly I would like to
put more snap into the business."

TR went so far as to communicate his displeasure to Nellie Taft, who
wrote her husband, "I was so depressed yesterday morning by the President's cross letter, plain cross it was, nothing else. . . ." She was equally
disturbed, while staying in New York with the Harry Tafts, by a call
from the White House, asking her to come down as soon as possible to
see the President. "I can't imagine what Teddy wants," she wrote to
Will—mindful, no doubt, that TR disliked being called Teddy—"but
probably only to complain of something."

If TR wished to complain of something, he restrained himself. Instead,
he encouraged Mrs. Taft, assured her he was most optimistic about the
outcome of the election. His pacification objective succeeded, and TR
wrote Taft, "It was the greatest pleasure to see Mrs. Taft."

Finally, inevitably, all the maneuverings by the Tafts and TR ended,
for the election was at hand.

On the night of Tuesday, November 3, 1908, the great searchlight on
top of the New York *Times* Building would indicate the election results
by flashing to the south if William Jennings Bryan won and to the north
if William Howard Taft won.

Theodore and Edith Roosevelt had arrived in Oyster Bay at nine that
morning, having left Washington at midnight on Monday. Twenty-one-
year-old Ted, Jr., came from Thomasville, Connecticut, where he was
learning the carpet business, to cast his first vote. Father and son went to
Sleet's Hall, the village polling place; their votes were registered on ballots 141 and 142. By six that evening the Roosevelts had returned to the
White House; later, there would be a dinner party for two dozen officials
and their wives, and all would await the returns.

At eight that morning, Will Taft, exhausted, his voice hoarse from speechmaking, arrived in Cincinnati, where Mrs. Taft and the rest of his family had gathered at his brother Charlie's house.

In 1908, Pike Street, in the east end of Cincinnati, was the fashionable residential section of the city. It contained many tall, three-story, solid gray-brick houses, with miens at once ugly and highly respectable. One of them, 69 Pike Street, was the Herron house, in which Mrs. Taft had grown up. Diagonally across the street from it was a low, colonial residence, set back on a green expanse of lawns and shrubbery—the finest house on Pike Street, if not in all Cincinnati. It had once been the home of the Longworths; the first Nicholas Longworth had bought it from the original owner; then it had been purchased by David Sinton, the millionaire iron dealer, whose daughter Annie married Charles P. Taft. Thus, the house had been known, in its span of life, as the old Longworth house and as the Sinton house, and was now called the Taft house. Its style of architecture suggested that of another, even more prestigious residence, for it had been designed by James Hoban, who had also designed the White House. As Nellie Taft had observed from her home across the street, it had "the same classic lines." Under the present circumstances, this architectural affinity was eminently apt.

Among those gathered at the Taft house to hear the election returns were Will and Nellie Taft and their sons; Charlie and Annie Taft; three of Mrs. Taft's sisters; Nannie Wallingford, Nick Longworth's sister; and Nick and Alice Longworth. Three telegraph wires and one telephone wire had been installed to bring them the election returns. This installation was in a side room, from which the returns were brought and read to the assemblage by Gus Karger, who worked for Charles P. on the *Times-Star* and was a publicity agent for Will Taft.

The first returns were from New York, and they were good; those that followed continued to be good, "without a setback anywhere": Massachusetts, New Jersey, Connecticut, Michigan, Tennessee, Wisconsin, California. Karger reread reports that were especially favorable, and Taft himself read one that said he had carried Maryland.

By midnight, it was evident he had won. In front of the Taft house on Pike Street victory bonfires leaped high, streaking the clear, cold autumn sky; a band boomed the triumphal strains of "Hail to the Chief" and played the tender, sweet "Beautiful Ohio," and members of the Citizens' Taft Club hurrahed and cheered until Will Taft emerged, acknowledged victory, and declared his administration would be a "worthy successor to that of Theodore Roosevelt."

TR had predicted that they would beat Bryan to a frazzle; consequently, the victorious returns did not surprise or absorb him. He "sneaked off from his party" early; this annoyed Mrs. Roosevelt, for she was left with the guests. She sent Archie Butt for TR, and he found him in the library reading.

Before the evening ended, TR and Will exchanged wires—each sending the other, according to Alice, "as pretty telegrams as possible." TR congratulated Taft, "and the country even more." And Taft responded with a figurative, verbal bow. "It is your administration that the victory approves."

Despite such substantial affirmations of amity, Alice Longworth had found the adulation by the ladies of the Longworth family of Will Taft, "their particular pet great man," to be galling. "I rather think," she recalled, "that then and there I began to indulge a proclivity toward malice that occasionally comes over me." She felt even greater irritation—completely surrounded, as she was, by the enemy camp—with "an unmistakable attitude, on the part of members of his [the Taft] family of 'here he is where he ought to be' and 'We don't owe so very much to Roosevelt anyway; he could have got along quite as well without him.' And as the returns came in there was much comparing them with the returns of 1904. Wherever Taft ran ahead of Father's figures, they fairly gloated; so, as far as I was concerned, the stage was set for the first steps that led to the 'breakup of a beautiful friendship.' "

Five

"He Is Not
the Same Man"

A horizon of mountain and sky and the milk-blue smoke of many forest fires, which hung lazily in the Allegheny Valley, should have contributed to the tranquillity the President-elect was eager to achieve.

He sat before the view's immensity—on the porch of The Chestnuts, a little brown cottage nested in the trees—waiting for its balm, its therapeutic powers, to take effect. The residue of eighteen thousand miles of stumping had to be dissipated.

By way of co-operation, Taft was positive, optimistic. "I really did some great work at sleeping last night," he said. "For good measure," he declared, "a few days of this will take campaign kinks out of me."

His resolve had been unequivocal when he and his wife had left Washington on November 6 for Hot Springs, Virginia, on the Cowpasture River, and "a complete rest of at least two weeks." He had even specified that he would consider neither "cabinet construction nor political appointments."

As soon as he arrived in Hot Springs, however, he wrote a letter of thanks to TR. With his seemingly unerring gift for choosing an innocent phrase into which others might read explosive significance, he told TR, "you and my brother Charley made that possible which in all probability would not have occurred otherwise." Or had Taft's letter read, as some accounts insisted, "my brother Charley and you," or, "I owe my election more to you than to anybody else except my brother Charley"?

President-elect Taft had also been naïve in assuming he could go a mere one hundred and sixty miles southwest of Washington, as a crow or a politician would travel, and find "absolute rest and quiet." He actually believed that the "important work of the Hot Springs sojourn" would consist of deciding where to go next for more rest when the weather grew cold. (The report that he would visit his brother Charlie's one-

hundred-and-sixty-acre ranch in Taft, Texas, for a ten-day hunting expedition, Taft immediately denied.)

The very day after Taft's vacation began, his illusion burst. Representative Joseph H. Gaines of West Virginia arrived, seeking out a troublesome issue: Taft's views on tariff revision. In quick order more men
swooped into the idyllic retreat: Frank Hitchcock, whose pink face had
"a good many more seams about the eyes and mouth" than before the
campaign; Theodore Burton, candidate for Joseph Foraker's Ohio Senate
seat; and Vice-President-elect James Sherman.

Still, there was some escape from these men and the uncertainties they
aggravated. Taft played golf, for he had gained "considerable flesh during
the campaign" and needed the exercise, as he did the diet to which he
could now return. One evening he and his wife attended an illustrated
charity lecture at the nearby Homestead Hotel; the subject was "Rou-
mania," the lecturer, a Mrs. Walker Fearn. The following night they
were at the Homestead Hotel again, at a dinner given in their honor by
Mr. and Mrs. D. Holmes of Kentucky.

A promise made while he was Secretary of War meant interrupting his
rest, going to Brooklyn to attend the unveiling of a monument to soldier
and sailor heroes who had died on British prison ships during the Revolutionary War. To leave the porch with the tranquil view, to travel again,
to speak again did not appeal to Will Taft. But he made the trip, for,
lacking the agility of a politician in evasion, he could only keep or break a
promise.

On the return trip to Hot Springs, Taft planned to stop off at the
White House to see the President, who, by this time, of course, had read
Taft's letter of gratitude. Already in circulation was a rumored reaction
by TR on sharing honors with Charles P. Taft for Will Taft's election.
"He puts money above brains," TR reportedly snapped.

As Taft approached Washington this letter did not concern him, for,
having written it in innocence, he remained unaware of the trouble it
might cause. His annoyance focused on the train in which he rode with
Secret Service officers, his secretary, and a few newspapermen, and on the
interruption of his rest. Even a private car, he realized during the campaign, can become cramped quarters after several weeks. He also felt a
below-the-surface discomfort, endemic to the procrastinator, for the
tariff problem and the puzzle of his Cabinet he knew would eventually
have to be faced and solved.

In Philadelphia, when the train stopped and he was interviewed, he
joked about not being in politics. And he was serious, slightly plaintive,
when he said, "I want more rest."

But snow and rain delayed the train's arrival in Washington by twenty-two minutes. The President's carriage, which awaited him was, moreover, to hurry him to the White House and a few additional unanticipated problems.

Though the next day, a Sunday, started with worship at the All Souls' Unitarian Church for Taft and at the Dutch Reformed Church for TR, it proved not to be a day of rest.

In the afternoon, while TR went off on a walk with Ambassador Jusserand of France, Postmaster General George von L. Meyer, and George B. Cortelyou, Secretary of the Treasury, reporters faced Will Taft in the East Room. They wanted to know the substance of his talk with TR. He gave them a sample of his famous chuckle and said, "No, we did not confine our conversation entirely to a discussion of the weather." The reporters brought up the matter of his Cabinet. "Seriously, boys," he said, "I haven't given the subject of my Cabinet any consideration at all." He followed this extraordinary statement with one whose substance was made of dreams and wishes. "I shall not take up that matter until sometime in February. I suppose I must do it then."

As Taft turned to leave the reporters, Representative John Dalzell of Pennsylvania appeared to pay his respects. Taft could not have been delighted to see Congressman Dalzell, known as the "great high priest of high protection," for the Republican convention had pledged a downward revision. White-bearded, sturdy, with a tendency when standing to lean slightly back, Dalzell told Taft that the revision of the tariff was in excellent hands.

Will Taft's visit continued to provoke speculation. There was the matter of the President's annual message to Congress, a draft of which was completed. TR, the speculation ran, wanted Taft's approval, for it would be up to Taft to follow through on the suggestions made. Did Taft see the message specifying Roosevelt policies that were more radical than any TR had ever before enunciated? TR had gone so far to the left as to declare that the man who worked should receive "a larger share of the wealth." He asked for a revision of the Sherman Anti-Trust Act to make it more effective, and blasted the judiciary for its abuse of the injunction that trampled labor's rights. Did Taft utter any protest? He had, of course, pledged himself to carry out TR's policies—those policies extant at the time of his pledge, not altered alien policies. But TR, always politically alert, saw the steady growth of a progressive element in the party and a labor union opinion; neither, he felt, could be ignored. Now that he wasn't up for re-election, restraint wasn't necessary; he could reveal his deepest convictions, thoroughly enjoying one last good fight with

Congress. Thus, the Roosevelt policies showed themselves to be not as fixed as the North Star, as immutable as dogma, and to a basically conservative Will Taft, this fact held cause for alarm.

According to his original plan, Taft was to leave Washington for Hot Springs on Monday, November 16. Instead, he took the 7:05 P.M. train, the first train possible, due to arrive in Cincinnati the following day. Before leaving, he explained the change of plans to the press. "I have received a summons for home that I must obey, and I trust you will believe me when I assure you it has to do solely with family affairs."

That Taft's sudden trip to Cincinnati did involve family affairs was precisely what the reporters suspected. For the same Senate seat being sought by Congressman Burton and Senator Foraker now had a new candidate, Charles P. Taft. Quiet, slim, white-haired, Charles P. had multiplied his wife's vast inheritance—the largest individual fortune in Ohio. His investments, as beautifully varied as the Ohio terrain, were in the Cincinnati baseball club and in the city's gas works, streetcar lines, opera house, leading hotel, real estate, and newspaper, the *Times-Star*. His generosity to the Republican party was well known; in lordly domination of the list of campaign contributors, Charles P. Taft's name stood beside one hundred and ten thousand dollars. Equally well known was Charles P.'s generosity to his brother Will. (Commenting on the cost to the bride's family of a marriage to a European nobleman, Charles P. remarked, "If they think it costs a lot to get a lord in the family, getting a president cost $800,000.") But widespread feeling opposed the President's settling the obligation with a United States senatorship. This would set a precedent. Friends in other states would point to it and try to get Taft to come to their aid in local controversies. Then, too, Taft was certain to be embarrassed on another score: many members-elect of the Ohio legislature—who in those days chose members for the Senate— reluctant to pledge themselves to Charles P., for whatever reasons, would have to be whipped into line by the party. And should Charles P. succeed in reaching the Senate, it might well be asked how this would affect his brother Will's pledge to carry out TR's policies. A parallel of another senator and President—both from Ohio, too—had a startling similarity. Mark Hanna, to be close to his protégé, William McKinley, had arranged a place for himself in the Senate.

Long before Will Taft's train reached Pennsylvania Station in Cincinnati and a waiting automobile took him to his brother's house, speculation and suspicion had solidified to an intriguing conclusion: TR had sent Taft back to Cincinnati to convince Charles P. that he must withdraw from the Senate race. By the time Will Taft was ready to leave, a more specific reason for his sudden visit than the weak "family affairs" was given. Charles P.'s daughter was ill—as, indeed, she was—and a concerned uncle had come to see her.

Whereas TR found special delight in a day so filled with engagements that he could not make them all, such pressures wearied Taft. He therefore looked forward to his return to Hot Springs; there, at least, he intended to rest. Mrs. Taft met the morning train and her husband. Taft saw the snow on the Virginia mountains, saw it as interference with his golf. The sun was bright and would melt the snow, but William L. Ward, a New York Old Guard Republican leader, and Vice-President-elect Sherman had solidity, permanence, as they converged on him. The frivolity of brilliant red vest and Scotch tweed suit and cap made Sherman, who had been ill during the summer, appear particularly fit—and durable. A different meeting that was imminent, moreover, seemed almost as troublesome. Theodore E. Burton—his brother's opponent for the Ohio Senate seat—waited in the hotel, eager and anxious to see Taft.

Most ominous of all were two men not even present in Hot Springs, the twin specters of tariff revision—slouch-hatted, tobacco-chewing, steel-eyed House Speaker Joe Cannon and icy, aristocratic, arrogant Senate Majority Leader Nelson W. Aldrich. For even before the tariff struggle in the hot summer ahead, Taft felt caught between the party's pledge to revise the tariff down and the opposition to such revision by the powerful congressional Republican leaders Cannon and Aldrich. In order to emerge victorious from an encounter with such political masters, one had to be a superlative politician. Will Taft felt, as he admitted, "like a fish out of water." Moreover, he was quite aware who had thrown him out of his element: Nellie, TR, and his brother Charlie. "However," he maintained, "as my wife is the politician and will be able to meet all these issues, perhaps we can keep a stiff upper lip and overcome the obstacles that just at present seem formidable." If Taft really hoped his wife would "be able to meet all these issues," he was to learn with a terrible sadness that a grinning sadistic fate had other plans.

An orgy of conjecture now gripped Washington. What innovations would Mrs. Taft bring to the White House? Would Taft make any changes in the Roosevelt Cabinet? Would Taft, for example, keep Secretary of War Luke Wright on? The majority of the Metropolitan Club thought he would. So did Mrs. Roosevelt. Would Mrs. Taft allow Isabel Hagner, Mrs. Roosevelt's secretary, to remain as her secretary? Archie

Butt thought not, since, he remarked, "she has made enemies in her position, and these will do all in their power to undermine her to Mrs. Taft; in fact, they have already done so."

As Captain Butt observed, Mrs. Taft was "a woman of wonderful executive ability," and he wrote, "I have no doubt she will make some startling changes." Before the end of November, Mrs. Taft sent word from Hot Springs that she and her husband wished Captain Butt to continue as White House aide, that she would not retain Miss Hagner, and that liveried servants would replace the frock-coated ushers. ("Oh," Mrs. Roosevelt exclaimed tearfully, when she heard of this change, "it will hurt them so.")

Rumors of arbitrary changes in the diplomatic service also went the rounds of Washington parties. In particular, the position of Henry White, Ambassador to France, was believed by some to be in jeopardy. (Years before when White had been attached to the American Embassy in London, the Tafts, on their honeymoon trip, had asked him to get them tickets to the House of Commons. Unable to obtain these, White sent tickets to the Royal Mews instead. The Tafts were indignant, "especially Mrs. Taft.")

Disturbed by this report, TR, obviously feeling it was an awkward kind of question for him to ask Taft, had his daughter Alice inquire of the President-elect if the rumor had any foundation. Alice's report was reassuring. "Mr. Taft was his most good-humored self, though he neither denied nor affirmed the truth of the alleged 'slight' but said with his friendly chuckle, in a most sincere and rather reproachful voice, 'Alice, knowing me as well as you do, you could not think me capable of doing such a thing for such a reason. You must believe that I am big enough to forget that sort of thing.' "

No doubt inspired by the changes Mrs. Taft planned for the White House, "rather grander than ours," Alice Longworth began giving her wickedly mischievous imitations of Mrs. Taft. "It was really," she admitted, "rather a good piece of mimicry," and one soon enjoyed by most of Washington.

Perhaps in recognition of the changes his successor would inevitably make, and the gossip and rumor they would stir up, TR in a lighthearted spirit sent off a Bible to Taft, with the following verses in Ecclesiastes marked for his attention:

Therefore I hated life; because the work that is wrought under the sun is grievous unto me: for all is vanity and vexation of spirit.

Yea, I hated all my labour which I had taken under the sun: because I should leave it unto the man that shall be after me.

And who knoweth whether he shall be a wise man or a fool? yet shall he have rule over all my labour wherein I have laboured, and wherein I have shewed myself wise under the sun. This is also vanity.

On the morning of December 4, Taft played his last game of golf in Hot Springs, finishing it just as it started to snow. Two to three inches accumulated on the ground within an hour, making it most pleasant to anticipate the place he had chosen to continue his rest—Augusta, Georgia. This choice had been made much against Mrs. Taft's wishes. For one thing, she felt Augusta was too far from Washington, too remote a spot, where a President-elect—or his wife—"could not be in it or know what's doing."

This aspect did not trouble Will Taft; he had written a letter pleading for complete rest, and he had not sent it to an individual, but simply to Augusta. Perhaps a city would listen; one could more credibly ascribe compassion to the inanimate where President-elects were concerned. In Hot Springs, senators had continuously dropped off on their way to Washington, just to shake his hand—nothing political—or merely for rest, to take the waters—nothing political. But somehow "extended conferences" did develop, and they were fatiguing.

The idea of Augusta—quiet and far from Washington—was fortunately in itself a balm and a healing, for before Taft could reach its peaceful boundaries he had to go to Washington and New York. His first stop was Washington, where he was to speak at the Joint Conservation Conference, in company with TR and Gifford Pinchot, and where he and Mrs. Taft could consult with Archie Butt about personnel changes in the White House. The Tafts had also been invited by the Roosevelts to an informal luncheon in their honor at the White House.

So on a Thursday morning in the second week of December Archie Butt arrived at the Boardman house, where the Tafts had two bedrooms and an office on the third floor for their use while they were in the city. As Captain Butt approached their rooms, he heard Mr. Taft's hearty laugh; and when he entered, he observed Mrs. Taft's annoyed expression.

"Well, I don't see anything to laugh at," she said to her husband. Then, on seeing Archie, she added, "Now we must get to business while Captain Butt is here."

"Nothing to laugh at!" Taft exclaimed. "I think it is the funniest thing I ever heard." Turning to Archie, Taft said, "I was Cabinet-making early this morning, and I had thought that I had settled one place at least, and just as you were announced I had told my wife. She simply wiped him off the face of the earth and I have got to begin again. The personal side of politics has always been funny to me, but nothing has been quite as funny as to have a man's career wrecked by a jealous wife."

"Not jealous at all," Mrs. Taft replied defiantly, "but I could not believe you to be serious when you mentioned that man's name. He is perfectly awful and his family are even worse. I won't even talk about it."

As Taft turned from Cabinet-making to personnel changes, Archie "by the utmost use of diplomacy," he later recorded, "saved the heads of those men of whom Mrs. Roosevelt is the fondest." Later, Mrs. Roosevelt asked Archie to let Mrs. Taft know she would be glad to discuss these matters with her and give her any assistance. But she also wished him to assure Mrs. Taft that if she did not care to do so, Mrs. Roosevelt would not be at all offended. Upon being given this message, Mrs. Taft informed Archie that she didn't wish to discuss these matters with Mrs. Roosevelt. Aware that he was adrift in "the twilight zone" of the two administrations, Archie then suggested to Mrs. Taft that she at least thank Mrs. Roosevelt for her kind offer, "which she agreed to do next Saturday when she lunches there."

At the lunch TR and Taft did most of the talking, "most of the conversation being a kind of good-natured banter." Before the Tafts left TR had taken Taft aside and urged him to go to Panama to see the progress of the work on the canal. Then he remarked, linking their administrations, making them as one, "You ought to see that work for yourself, for it is going to be the biggest thing in your administration, as it has been the biggest thing in mine." Taft agreed to go at the end of January.

The next day the Tafts were in New York City, at the home of Henry Taft on Forty-eighth Street, and the President-elect talked with Senator Philander C. Knox, former Attorney General under TR, "a splendid-looking man, small but cultured and keen," and offered him the key post in the Cabinet—that of Secretary of State.

Taft did this bit of business, but he put off preparing a speech which he, as guest of honor, was to deliver at the Twenty-third Annual Dinner of the Ohio Society on December 16 at the Waldorf-Astoria Hotel. Henry Taft, President of the Society, was toastmaster; Charles and Horace also attended. Because he had not yet written his speech, Will Taft asked to be put last on the program. Then, quietly, but observed, he made notes with a stubby pencil. The subject he chose for his speech was the tariff. (In the following year, because an unfailing attribute of character is consistency, Taft would deliver another unprepared speech on the tariff, but because conditions do change that speech would have catastrophic repercussions.)

Another speaker, immediately preceding the President-elect, was ex-Senator John Coit Spooner of Wisconsin, who, as a corporation lawyer, defended railroads. Spooner, an excellent speaker, made pointed criticism of Roosevelt policies. He spoke highly of the Constitution and "in a veiled way indicated a deviation from it on the part of Roosevelt."

Those among the guests who expected Taft to take sharp exception to Spooner's references to TR were disappointed. He said nothing about them, explaining his inaction the next day to Oscar Straus. He "had thought first that he might say something in reply, but on second consideration he decided to let it pass."

A few years earlier, when Taft was Secretary of War, a similar situation had taken place at a dinner in Boston. A speaker on that occasion had made derisive comments about TR, and Will Taft's response at that time had been forceful. "When I love a chief," he had said, "and when I admire him from top to toe, I cannot be silent and permit such insinuations, although they may be hidden in a jest." But the situation and pressures on Will Taft at that time had been different.

Finally, after the middle of December, the Tafts reached Augusta, Georgia—a refuge for women and children during the Civil War, for it is situated one hundred and thirty-five miles from the coast and had been safe from damage by gunboats. But the President-elect, approximately only five hundred miles from Washington, was not out of danger of political annoyance. Still, Taft went down Augusta's Greene Street, a street lined with live oaks, draped solemnly and yet festively with Spanish moss; he headed for the Terrett Cottage—adjacent to the Bon Air Hotel —in Summerville, with its warm East Georgia sunshine, for which the natives felt rich Northerners were willing to pay. (Fifty years, after all, had sharpened rather than dimmed the animosities between Northerners and Southerners.) Though Summerville and its grand Bon Air Hotel offered golf, the male population of Augusta whose profession was cotton found their entertainment in more virile sports, in scrub horse racing and cock fighting.

But Taft, oblivious to the inimical emotional climate surrounding Summerville, liked whatever opportunities Augusta offered for rest. Thoughts of his Cabinet—or the thought that he should be thinking about it— disturbed Taft's serenity. He played golf on Augusta's sandy links daily for exercise, but then resisting the frequent barbecues raised an inner conflict. Dieting aggravated all his problems. When he was under the care of a Harley Street physician, Dr. N. E. Yorke-Davis, Taft's weight had gone down from three hundred and twenty-two pounds to two hundred and fifty pounds, but that had been over two years ago. He had now ballooned up once more to well over three hundred pounds, which meant six-ounce beefsteaks for breakfast instead of twelve-ounce ones and ruled out popping salted almonds into his mouth to quell hunger and alleviate frustrations, among which was choosing the rest of his Cabinet.

At Christmas the Taft children came down to join their parents: Bob from Yale, Helen from Bryn Mawr, and Charlie from Taft School. Basking in the warmth of the Georgia sun, his children around him, with the mantle of the presidency about to descend on him, its eventual burdens yet only lightly felt, Will Taft felt his spirits lifting—except when he thought about his brother Charles P.

TR, bitterly opposed to Foraker, had applied pressure on Charles P. to withdraw from the Ohio Senate battle so that Burton would be victorious. At the end of December, Charles P. *did* withdraw, but the implication in the press was that Will, embarrassed by his brother's candidacy, had forced him to withdraw. "It seems too hard," his sister-in-law Annie Sinton Taft wrote him, "that such a thrust should appear to come from you."

It was not surprising that in his New Year's letter to TR, Taft wrote somewhat despondently, "I look forward to the future with much hesitation and doubt as to what is to happen."

Now 1909 had arrived, and only two months lay between Will Taft and the presidency of the United States. The curious diffidence that had sprung up between him and TR after the election had grown. They still wrote pleasant, friendly letters to each other; when they met, they exchanged good-humored, pleasant conversation; when they spoke of each other, it was in terms of the highest praise, but underneath these superficialities the old camaraderie was gone, and in its place there was a wary reserve. A protective coterie—rival teams—surrounded each of them. It is axiomatic in politics that between two such groups there should be suspicion and mistrust.

"People," recalled Alice Longworth, "were always coming with reports of 'he is going to—' or 'he is not going to—' "

TR hoped to learn something definite about Taft's plans for his Cabinet when Cabot Lodge came back from his visit to Augusta. Immediately upon Lodge's return, "he hurled discord into the Roosevelt and cabinet camps by announcing that he had been in Augusta two whole days before he was allowed to see Mr. Taft alone for a minute, that he was kept constantly under the watchful eye of either Mrs. Taft or of his brother, who is with him from New York." Lodge's explicit report did make TR uneasy. "It was evidently the intention," he told him, "to get rid of every person who might keep President Taft in touch with the Roosevelt influence." Of the Roosevelt Cabinet only George Meyer, the Postmaster General—who was to become Secretary of the Navy—and James Wilson, Secretary of Agriculture, would remain. Oscar Straus would not be retained, nor would the two men about whom TR had been most anxious: Luke Wright, who had accepted the War secretaryship as Taft's successor for a few months, with the understanding that he would be retained by Taft; and James R. Garfield, whose administration of the Department of the Interior pursued the Roosevelt-Pinchot conservation policies with militant purpose.

The morning following Lodge's disclosures TR asked Archie Butt if he had definite assurance that the Tafts meant to keep him at the White House. Archie replied that he was "reasonably sure."

"Because, if you are not," TR told him, "and know of anything I can do for you, I want you to let me know. I cannot leave my favorite aide hanging by his heels."

In his letter to Taft, TR wrote of the Cabinet changes with commendable detachment. "I think it would be well," he suggested, "for you to write them all at once that you do not intend to reappoint them; they will be making their plans, and less than two months remain and I do not think they ought to be left in doubt."

In his letters to those Cabinet members whom he did not wish to retain, Taft gave the same explanation: that since the problems facing him would be different, these problems would require other men to solve them. But he had remarked cryptically, "The reason I kept Garfield out of the Cabinet was because I knew him."

Beyond this somewhat inadequate reason, there was much speculation of a more substantial cause for dismissing one of TR's closest associates. Garfield was, of course, a fellow Ohioan, but from Cleveland—northern Ohio—while Taft was from southern Ohio, and the two sections had their own regional, recondite political differences. Then, too, Garfield's vigorous administration of conservation policies had antagonized many Republican heavy campaign contributors in the West, and he was regarded by regular Republicans as a radical.

But Taft's decision to drop Garfield from his Cabinet might very well have sprung from a more basic consideration. Though James Garfield was a lawyer, he was not Taft's kind of lawyer, who would characteristically feel less concern with any particular policy than with the legal processes employed to execute it. Garfield was, instead, TR's kind of lawyer. The Rooseveltian legal philosophy was made graphically clear by a story—possibly apocryphal. After the construction of the Union Station in Washington, the old dilapidated Pennsylvania Station still stood blighting the Mall. TR, eager to remove this eyesore, was informed by his Attorney General that he had no authority to remove it. TR then ordered him to find some law that would permit the removal, but the Attorney General was unable to find such a law. Was there any law, asked TR in exasperation, that specifically said he could *not* tear down Penn Station? The Attorney General said no, there wasn't; so TR had the station torn down.

Taft accounted for Luke Wright's dismissal by ascribing a trait to him that Will Taft apparently considered a serious flaw. Taft said he'd known Wright in the Philippines and felt he wasn't certain enough of himself.

But TR was not impressed by Taft's reasons for his actions in regard to Jim Garfield and Luke Wright. While publicly he said, "Taft is going about this thing just as I would do," privately he told Garfield, "Jim, something has come over Will, he is changed, he is not the same man." A little over two weeks before Taft's inauguration, TR said to Luke Wright, "I am distressed, General, that you will not continue to be Secretary of War, but unfortunately you have been too close to me, I fear."

Though Henry Adams could never be charged with having any intimate kinship with the general public, he spoke for many less patrician Americans when he asked rhetorically, "If the new President is bent on making a clean sweep of Roosevelt men, why did we elect him expressly to carry out the Roosevelt regime?"

"Receptions, dances, balls and luncheons," Archie Butt reported with tender awe, "have filled every minute for the President, his wife, and Ethel." In addition, while the carpenters hammered and sawed in preparing the physical structure of the inauguration, the personal effects of TR and his family had to be packed, readied for removal from the White House.

Other details arose—emotionally charged, many of them. Though Captain Butt was going to remain at Taft's side, his loyalty could not be switched automatically and with ease. For one thing, he wondered if the Tafts would continue to use "The White House" on their invitations and stationery or go back to using "Executive Mansion." The change, if they made it, would be evidence of bad taste—and more than he could bear.

A similar problem—similar, at least, in subject matter—confronted the

Roosevelts. TR, as a private citizen once again, would need calling cards. After March 4 he could not, of course, use his card that read, "The President"; he therefore had cards printed that bore his name—simply that, nothing more. His wife objected. "Mr.," a form all gentlemen used, she felt, should be added to the "Theodore Roosevelt." When TR resisted this suggestion, Mrs. Roosevelt said, with obvious irony, "Then why not simply have Roosevelt or Theodore, or even The ex-President?" "I want him to be the simplest American alive after he leaves the White House," she explained to Archie Butt, "and the funniest thing to me is that he wants to be also and says he is going to be, but the trouble is he has really forgotten how to be."

The transition for the Tafts was equally difficult. On their return from Panama, the President-elect appeared tanned and in good humor, but his worries and uncertainties would on occasion bob to the surface. For one thing, TR's public assurance that Taft had gone about selecting his Cabinet just as he would have done failed to dispel a stubborn residue of uneasiness. Taft therefore took exception to the customary arrangement on Inauguration Day for the "wife of the President-elect to take with her to the Senate Chamber the wives of the incoming Cabinet." He declared to Archie Butt, "I will have no other Cabinet on the 4th of March but the one now in. Neither the members of the prospective Cabinet and certainly not their wives will have the slightest standing on the 4th of March. I will continue to meet with the present Cabinet until my own will have been confirmed by the Senate."

This was a well-intentioned gesture; though symbolic, it was open to a single interpretation. TR matched it with a forthright statement: "Give Taft a chance." This was an apostrophe to all the criticism of Taft in the air. "He has a legal mind—he can round out and shape up the policies of the last four years better than if I were to remain here."

But despite the gestures of both men, many people saw changes in Will Taft. Reporters noticed that he did not act with "the old cordiality and friendliness." Instead, they noted "a reserve that almost amounted to coldness."

Closer and closer, Taft drew near to the irrevocable step, the few minutes, the thirty-five words that were the inauguration—all the rest was fanfare, ceremony.

The day that would contain these words, that would make Taft President of the United States, arrived, and Ike Hoover, the chief usher of the White House, observed that Taft appeared "cross and uncomfortable."

As prescribed by the Constitution, Will Taft said, "I do solemnly swear that I will faithfully execute the office of President of the United

States and will, to the best of my ability, preserve, protect, and defend the Constitution of the United States."

Then he rode back to the White House with his wife for the luncheon with one hundred and seventy-five guests which TR would not attend, but which custom required that he pay for, and later Taft rushed off to review the parade. Finally, when the parade was over, when the hordes of people left for their homes and hotels, the Tafts returned to the White House. There, the first thing Will Taft did was to drop down in a large comfortable chair, stretch out his legs, and declare, "I am President now, and tired of being kicked around."

Part II   The White House

Six   Ordeals

"Down at the bottom," TR had written William Allen White the previous August, "my main reason for wishing to go to Africa for a year is so that I can get where no one can accuse me of running, nor do Taft the injustice of accusing him of permitting me to run, the job."

Now that the trip was at hand, and all plans intended the departure to be a quiet one, TR—now simply Theodore Roosevelt, according to his calling card—did not want the press to publicize his embarkation. But in the nineteen days since the inauguration there had been more in the papers about the ex-President than about the President. And on this clear, cool, beginning-of-spring morning, a vast, wildly excited crowd appeared at the pier in Hoboken, fought its screaming way to the side of the German steamship *Hamburg*, whose masts, fore and aft, were gaily bedecked with bunting.

The Hoboken police tried, with shouting and shoving, to control the pushing mass. It surged around TR, knocking off his gray slouch hat, ripping the gilt buttons from his olive-green military overcoat—the black braid on its sleeves indicating his rank in the Rough Riders. Some women had even climbed on the rails of the companionway to catch a glimpse of the great man.

A reporter caught in the crush took advantage of his nearness to TR to ask him if he was going to run for President again. By leaping ahead to 1912, the question, in a sense, negated his departure. TR merely "looked sorrowfully at him and said good-bye."

Catching sight of Archie Butt, TR managed to grasp his arm and greet him warmly.

Taft had given Butt the opportunity to wish TR *bon voyage*, for he needed someone to deliver a gift and a message, which Taft had not thought of sending "had I not suggested to him," Butt wrote, "that his predecessor would appreciate some word at parting . . . that it would be highly gratifying to the friends of Mr. Roosevelt."

Butt had also selected the gift, purchased at Galt's, a gold ruler that extended to a foot and had a pencil in it. Because TR used the expression "Good-bye, good luck" when he parted from someone, Butt suggested that this be the inscription. To it, using some initiative in the whole matter, Taft had added, "And a safe return."

TR told Butt that he appreciated the gift and said that he'd read Taft's message at sea. Then he asked about individuals at the White House— Jimmy Sloan, a Secret Service man; Major Loeffler, the elderly door-keeper; Charlie Lee, who worked in the stable. His main concern was whether they still had their jobs; mere departure, obviously, could not sever emotional ties.

A brass band played as loudly as possible to express depth of feeling. Friends—Jusserand, Root, Lodge, Garfield, Pinchot, Loeb—came on the tug *Timmons* from Pier A, North River. TR's sister Mrs. Douglas Robinson and her son Theodore came on board. Roosevelt shook over five hundred hands between nine and eleven.

Eleven was sailing time, but General Leonard Wood arrived late to see his friend depart, and the *Hamburg* therefore tarried seven minutes past the hour. Finally, all who were going ashore went down the gangway. As the ropes were cast off the pier, TR, accompanied by nineteen-year-old Kermit, who was to be the official photographer of the expedition, went to the port side of the bridge.

When the *Hamburg* moved off slowly, effortlessly, regally down the river, the March sun glinting incongruously on the somber gray water, tugboats, like ladies in waiting, accompanied her.

Left behind were the band music and cheers. They continued, however, to express a reluctance to let TR go, and this same feeling could be sensed in the *Timmons*' escorting the *Hamburg*, after the other tugs had fallen behind, until the ship was abreast of Forts Wadsworth and Hamilton, where a twenty-one-gun salute was fired.

Before the ship was out at sea, TR went to his suite, on Promenade Deck Number One. Telegrams from friends who had been unable to come made high piles on the table. Pacing, he read Taft's long emotional letter, which expressed his individual need for TR and a disquietude over his departure. Taft had written:

If I followed my impulse I should still say "My dear Mr. President," I cannot overcome the habit. When I am addressed as "Mr. President" I turn to see whether you are not at my elbow. When I read in the newspaper of a conference between the Speaker and the President, or between Senator Aldrich and the President, I wonder what the subject of the conference was, and can hardly identify the report with the fact that I had a talk with the two gentlemen. . . .

Many questions have arisen since the Inauguration with respect to which I should like to have consulted you, but I have forborne to interrupt your well-earned quiet and to take up your time when it must have been so much occupied with preparation for your long trip. . . .

I have no doubt that when you return you will find me very much under suspicion by our friends in the West. . . . I knew . . . I should make a capital error in the beginning of my administration in alienating the good will of those without whom I can do nothing to carry through the legislation to which the party and I are pledged. Cannon and Aldrich have promised to stand by the party platform and to follow my lead. They did so, I believe, for you in the first Congress of your administration and this is the first Congress of mine. Of course I have not the prestige which you had or the popular support in any such measure as you had to enable you to put through the legislation which was so remarkable in your first Congress; but I am not attempting quite as much as you did then, and I am hopeful that what I do offer will be accepted and put through. . . .

I want you to know that I do nothing in the Executive Office without considering what you would do under the same circumstances and without having in a sense a mental talk with you over the pros and cons of the situation. I have not the facility for educating the public as you had through talks with correspondents, and so I fear that a large part of the public will feel as if I had fallen away from your ideals; but you know me better and will understand that I am still working away on the same old plan and hope to realize in some measure the results that we both hold valuable and worth striving for. I can never forget that power that I now exercise was a voluntary transfer from you to me, and that I am under obligation to you to see to it that your judgment in selecting me as your successor and bringing about the succession shall be vindicated according to the standards which you and I in conversation have always formulated.

I send you this letter . . . that it may express to you what I would say to you if I were on the deck of the *Hamburg*, where I should be delighted to be and once again to clasp your hand and say the fond farewell, or rather to say "*Auf wiedersehen*. . . ." With love and best wishes, in which Mrs. Taft joins me, believe me as ever, Affectionately yours. . . .

Immediately upon finishing the letter, TR sent Taft a telegram: "Am deeply touched by your gift and even more by your letter. Greatly appreciate it. Everything will surely turn out all right, old man. Give my love to Mrs. Taft."

A half hour later, reflexively, as an overflow of energy, TR sent a second telegram. "Greatly appreciate your greetings and the autographed picture, which hangs in my stateroom. With love and every good wish for your success and welfare."

The picture had arrived by the morning mail; in it, Will Taft was situated between large portraits of Washington and Lincoln—in whose company TR had several times said Taft belonged. It was signed, "With best wishes for a pleasant voyage and a bully good time. William H. Taft."

TR had enjoyed the crowd swarming on and about the *Hamburg* because he enjoyed crowds, their movement, their expenditure of energy, what they meant politically. To Taft, however, crowds were the antithesis of rest, which was what *he* prized. No degree of rest, of course, surpassed sleep.

In it, he found sanctuary from public speeches; usually, on such occasions, his alert wife would dutifully nudge him awake. Once sleep befell him when Speaker Joe Cannon "was leaning over his chair and talking most earnestly."

And it even overtook him during an "interminable reading of the scriptures" at funeral services for Mrs. Dalzell, wife of the Pennsylvania Congressman. Laid out in white satin on a white divan in the parlor, the late Mrs. Dalzell had roses in her hand and lilies draped across her feet. By attention to color and floral detail, death had been rendered both ornamental and sacred; and human frailty could easily sully and profane it. Thus, when Archie Butt heard an "incipient snore" and realized its place of origin, he felt sudden alarm. Never again, he resolved, would he leave President Taft's side, for he felt it was just as much his duty to guard him "from such situations as his person from anarchists."

Less ludicrous intimations of trouble arose as early as the day after Taft's inauguration. "Taft's First Day," a New York *Times* headline read, "A Severe Ordeal." Taft had made a proclamation that a special session of Congress would meet on the fifteenth of March to revise the tariff, and tariff framers had called on him.

Then at the very first big dinner of the new administration—a "Harmony Dinner," for an explosive mixture of insurgents, standpatters, and Democrats were present—portents occurred that pointed an ominous finger at both Taft and his wife.

Custom decreed that the President enter first, but Mrs. Taft "bolted in ahead of him," and she was halfway down the line of guests before the President had finished with the first couple. She was virtually done before he reached the halfway point.

The next day, Mrs. Taft ascribed her charging in ahead of the President and her frenetic pace to nervousness; she had never been so "nervous and upset" in her whole life. As though Will would not be surpassed by his wife in this regard, he said, "I was not nearly so nervous the day I took the oath of office." After the dinner, he had bad dreams concerning it, and talked while he slept—tortured, strangled sleep talk.

It is not surprising that after this harrowing experience, when Taft spoke of TR, he spoke of him—with obvious wishful thinking—as "the President."

Mrs. Taft corrected him once with a stern "You mean the ex-President, Will."

"I suppose I do, dear," Taft answered plaintively, "but he will always be the President to me, and I can never think of him as anything else."

To Mrs. Taft, the President meant President William Howard Taft, and her ambition and drive, which had helped make him President, now impelled her in all the social and political life of the White House. Absorbed by a session of the Senate, she went without lunch. Cannon's talks with the President were also talks with her. At social gatherings, when she spotted her husband taken aside for a private conversation, she would immediately join in.

Archie Butt also observed that "Mrs. Taft loves the worry of housekeeping." Really, economy rather than love was the catalyst. Duty entered into it, too, for she often expressed the wish that Will were as adept with money matters as he was with legal ones, but since he would never be, the family finances had to remain her province.

State dinners, she thought, were dinners paid for by the state; the news that the President had to foot the bill shocked her. Keeping up with the Roosevelts entered into this matter, too. Their state dinners had been prepared by a caterer—Rauscher—at seven dollars and fifty cents per plate; this did not include the champagne and cigars. And TR, a nonsmoker, made sure that the cigars were of the best, for he stated axiomatically that a poor cigar could wreck the best of dinners. (It can only be hoped that Mrs. Taft did not know of the rumor that it had cost TR thirty thousand dollars of his own money for his stay in the White House.)

Independent—and, above all, frugal—the new First Lady had an answer to all this. Dinners would be prepared in the White House, a step which Archie Butt felt would prove an ordeal for Mrs. Taft—and her assistants. She also hired a housekeeper. Though Mrs. Roosevelt had never had one, Mrs. Taft felt one was needed for efficiency. (Ironically, Elizabeth Jaffray, the housekeeper, remained in the White House until the Coolidge administration, when she was dismissed for being too extravagant.)

Mrs. Taft made changes for aesthetic as well as monetary reasons. That big bed of Lincoln's in which she had slept the night before the inauguration she replaced by two smaller mahogany beds that were without canopies—the first twin beds to be installed in the White House. Chintz took the place of the heavy brocade of drapes and upholstery.

And now, at last, she had the opportunity to discontinue a custom instituted by Mrs. Roosevelt—the weekly morning meeting of the Cabinet ladies. She had found those meetings distasteful; they had made her feel like a school child going to a class to be lectured by the teacher—and the teacher, of course, was Mrs. Roosevelt.

These concerns of the slashing, driving executive, coupled with an overly ambitious social schedule, made for constant strain. At one afternoon reception she received visitors with her husband and shook two thousand hands. There were also dinner parties, official receptions, musicales. A special tension was involved in the establishment of Riverside Drive in Potomac Park, where she went twice weekly to attend a Marine Band concert, and where, it was reported, "the automobiles hiss and snort and smell dreadful."

Strain also bore down heavily on the President. His consumption of food, therefore, increased. He railed against time for not being reasonably commensurate with the things that had to be done. Still, he was not an early riser; he didn't finish breakfast before nine or ten. Making conflicting appointments, a casual habit of his, did not help matters. On one occasion, the Cabinet expected to meet with the President at eleven, but by precise mismanagement that hour had also been reserved for the Supreme Court. Understandably, Archie Butt complained worriedly, "If the President continues to transact business as he is transacting it now, he will be about three years behind when the fourth of March, 1913, rolls around."

Though Will Taft had assured Alice Longworth that he was not the sort to hold a grudge against Ambassador Henry White, White was recalled from Paris in April. "And there was another to add to a mounting list of black marks, or betrayals, as they began to seem." Taft was aware of the talk such dismissals caused, and it gnawed at his composure. (Deep in British East Africa, TR heard of the dismissal and wrote White, "This letter must be personal, for the last thing I must do is in any way to criticize my successor. But if as I hear to be the case you are to be displaced I wish you to know that everything I could do was done in your behalf, not because of my affection for you, great though that is, but because as I told Taft I regard you as without exception the very best man in our diplomatic service.")

Will Taft's general discomfort in the presidency was a factor in determining his negative relationship, bordering on belligerency, with the press, which made for additional discomfort. Not only did he and Fred Carpenter, his secretary, refuse to release news, but they were also exceedingly reluctant to see reporters. To get news, reporters frequently had no choice but to go to those who were opposed to the administration, or indulge in rumors, or resort to what was intriguingly labeled "bedroom politics."

Taft's acidulous, standoffish, un-Rooseveltian approach to the newsmen soured editorials. To avoid "anger and contemptuous feeling," Taft simply didn't read them, but he could not escape the ever present, though under the surface, awareness of their existence.

He became sensitive about eyes staring at him when he was riding horseback.

"Did you notice people laughing at him?" Mrs. Taft asked Butt. "For he seemed to think he caused amusement."

While standing, posing for a portrait, Taft fell asleep. Weariness lined his face.

Cold and fever forced him to stop working and stay in bed. He improved in a few days, but did not feel up to keeping a dinner engagement. Mrs. Taft went without him.

At one dinner, there was evidence that though her combativeness toward TR had not diminished, her nerves were wearing thin.

One of those editorials from which Taft hid made mention of an interview of TR by a correspondent, which had reportedly taken place in Naples. It quoted TR as saying that Taft had been elected to carry out his policies and that "if he faltered he would return and put him aside or something to that effect."

In coming to TR's defense, Butt declared the whole thing a fabrication.

"Oh, I don't know," Mrs. Taft shot back. "It sounded just like him. It is just as well to recognize what has got to come sooner or later, and let people and papers like the *Sun* take sides."

At another dinner, near the end of April, the wife of a Democratic congressman from Texas noticed that Mrs. Taft's white satin dress "with bands of cut-steel beads around the low neck showed wear." Then, with compassion, she observed that Mrs. Taft was "direct and sincere" as usual, "but she looked dreadful and spoke of not being well." She also mentioned that throughout the campaign—because her husband traveled in crowds, where bombs and guns might lurk—she had suffered from nerves.

Insidiously, erosively, the White House rained unseen blows upon Mrs.

Taft; it could not have been living up to the aura that had surrounded it in her fantasies, fantasies in which she ruled with complete authority and *élan*.

Later, after the tragic event that lay just ahead, Mrs. Roosevelt made the observation that very few women had found happiness in the White House. She mentioned that she had been one of the few, and that possibly Mrs. Grant may have been happy, but "it is hard to tell." She also included Mrs. Grover Cleveland. (When Mrs. Cleveland was asked if she would like to live in the White House again, she referred sarcastically to the absurd stories circulated about her, her husband, and her children while they were in the White House. "What! There where my husband was accustomed to drag me about the house by the hair and where my children were blind, deaf and deformed? Never!") Then Mrs. Roosevelt concluded, "I doubt if even I was entirely happy, for there was always that anxiety about the President when he was away from me. I never knew what a strain I was under continuously until it was over."

On May 17, at one o'clock in the afternoon, young Charlie Taft was to have an adenoid operation at the Episcopal Eye, Ear and Throat Hospital, a simple operation, the removal of tissue obstructing nasal and ear passages and inducing mouth breathing, but to parents *an operation*. And being the youngest child made Charlie appear all the more defenseless; his enthusiasms and energy and freckles—all the characteristics of a regular boy—gave him an especially endearing quality, and to anxious parents would render him, somehow, all the more vulnerable.

The President wanted to get to the hospital as soon as possible after the operation—by two fifteen at the latest. Mrs. Taft would be there during the operation.

The First Lady's decided pallor caused Archie Butt to question the advisability of her being there, to suggest that she have someone go in her place. "She merely smiled at the suggestion."

She was dressed in a white dress, with Japanese embroidery, and her large purple straw hat had pink roses on its crown; after the operation, at four, she and her husband were due to sail to Mount Vernon on the presidential yacht, the *Sylph*.

Making it to the hospital and to the *Sylph* on time would be difficult for the President. Characteristically, he immediately ran behind schedule. At two o'clock he was still closeted with a South American commission. Finally, finished with that duty, he went to the Green Room for a meeting with J. P. Morgan, Jr., and two Englishmen. Consequently, it was almost three by the time he arrived at the hospital.

His wife was at the phone—a familiar husband-wife scene—at the point of calling to find out what was keeping him. But this scene dissolved immediately to one involving parents delighted over a successful operation on their son. Nonetheless, and in spite of her white dress, Nellie Taft's pallor was still noticeable; Charlie, after all, had lost a considerable amount of blood and—on coming out of the ether—had been in a somewhat hysterical condition.

What followed had the quality of retribution, of one struck down by a curse, rather than being the inevitable natural result of stress, strain, and flaw.

The *Sylph* had not yet reached Alexandria when Attorney General Wickersham—the Wickersham family had been invited for the sail—turned to Archie Butt and said, in what seemed casual statement of fact, "Mrs. Taft has fainted. See if there is any brandy aboard."

The boat's captain hurriedly produced rye whisky. Cracked ice was applied to Mrs. Taft's temples and pulse. This revived her, but she was "deathly pale." Butt arranged for the captain to head back to Washington immediately, and this was done before the President even knew of his wife's collapse. Taft went "deathly pale" when Butt called him and told him. On entering the room where his wife lay, he closed the door after him.

On this day, TR, innocent of what was happening to the Tafts, concluded a note to Elihu Root in which he made mention of the six lions he had killed. "Fixing up a Tariff," he went on, "is, of course, much more important than my present occupation; but it's not nearly so alluring! Give my warm regards to the President when you see him. From all I can gather, he seems to have been doing excellently. Of course, he will have his little worries and bothers, but that simply is what has to be expected. It is all right!"

After they reached the White House and Mrs. Taft was put under Dr. Delaney's care, Butt observed that "the President looked like a great stricken animal. I have never seen greater suffering or pain shown on a man's face."

The last of six dinners that Mrs. Taft had arranged were scheduled for that very evening. In order to keep Mrs. Taft's condition secret—its seriousness had not as yet been determined—Mrs. Taft's sister Eleanor (Mrs. Louis) More took her place, and it was agreed that all questioners would be told that the day in the hospital had exhausted Mrs. Taft.

Taft, of course, had the leading, most difficult role in this deceit. With the music blaring behind him, he entered the room smiling the Taft smile and then proceeded to pass "in a most nonchalant way" among his guests. The dinner proved even more difficult, for "every mouthful seemed to choke him."

Later, when the men were smoking, Taft slipped away to have a talk with the doctor. Because the newspapers had gotten wind of Mrs. Taft's illness, Taft prepared a statement that might be given to them in case it became necessary. It explained that the excitement, heat, and exertion had been too much for Mrs. Taft's nerves, but that after a few days of complete rest, according to the doctor, she might be able to resume her social duties.

The next morning, to console by praise, the New York *Times* stated: "In the ten weeks of her husband's administration, Mrs. Taft has done more for society than any former mistress of the White House has undertaken in as many months."

No paper reported that Mrs. Taft had suffered a stroke which was to affect her speech and face.

"She expects to receive guests on next Friday's at-home as usual, and on Saturday to accompany her husband on a week-end trip to Hampton, Virginia." The New York *Times* reported this cheerfully, having no way of knowing the complete error of her expectation.

Seven

Cannon, Aldrich, and Sereno Elisha Payne

Nellie Taft's dream, the White House, had become a prison—the second floor, the area in which she was confined. There, Eleanor More, as well as Mrs. Taft's other sisters, a nurse, the housekeeper, Mrs. Jaffray, and Dr. Delaney became the inhabitants of her daily routine. Only when she was sure she would not be seen would she dare venture from them and into a corridor.

A face-to-face encounter with someone other than those she saw regularly was unthinkable, for it would reveal a First Lady who had difficulty walking and who was incapable of clear, unimpeded speech. (In teaching her to speak again, Will had struggled pitifully, patiently, seated beside her on a sofa. With his hands over hers, he would plead, "Now please, darling, try and say 'the'—that's it, 'the,'" as though he felt that if she could only say that little word, she would soon say all the others to which the definite article is introduction.) She had to avoid being seen. If she did not, pity—even if unspoken—would surely follow, and she had reserved pity of herself as her own prerogative. There was also anger, frustration. And if she, who had been driven by ambition, turned to the passage in Ecclesiastes that TR in high good humor had marked for her husband and read that "vanity of vanities; all is vanity," this would only have been an irritant—at best, bitter solace.

The President found himself imprisoned, too, but by the confines of his personality. He and the Republican party had promised in the 1908 platform that the tariff would be revised, and Taft—hopelessly honest—felt obliged to keep that promise.

However, most Republicans—and most were conservative—went along with Cabot Lodge's brazen declaration, "Nobody ever pledged me to revision downward, any more than to revision upward." They were also as one with Speaker of the House "Uncle Joe" Cannon. In expressing his perplexity over tariff revision talk, he asked, with cocky cynicism, "Aren't all our fellows happy?"

Indeed, for over three decades following the Civil War, "our fellows" had quantitative reason for being happy. Their dollar-sign vests became more and more bloated, owing, in part, to the government's magnanimous protective tariff, which its opponents, with justification, branded as a "mother of trusts." Small businessmen, because of it, couldn't possibly compete. And the harried consumer, innocent of economic complexities, embraced a satisfying, simple equation: high tariffs equal a high cost of living. Many votes had been cast for Taft simply to lower both sides of that equation. When this was done, the voter felt, Taft would be carrying out TR's policies.

But the tariff posed a difficult, complicated question, because Taft, although he believed the tariff should be reduced, was innately conservative and really spiritually akin to those who didn't want the tariff reduced. (His progressivism was merely reflected light: the conjunction of TR, inherently a believer in change, and Taft.) By temperament, Taft couldn't feel kinship with "Western progressives," but he couldn't deny *they* wanted to do what he felt honesty demanded.

Though his Nellie was the politician in the family, he couldn't go to her now for the answer he desperately needed. Instead, he had to maintain a façade of cheerfulness in her presence, to help her and to conceal his constant fear, a fear she also felt, that other, more terrible strokes might come. As for TR, though Taft might have "mental talks" with him "over the pros and cons of a situation," this could not prove sufficiently effective in resolving the tariff tangle.

This, moreover, was the summer of the tariff, and both the weather of that summer and the battles over the tariff made the front pages and tortured Taft. The thermometer in the kiosk on Pennsylvania Avenue was watched with a blend of scientific curiosity and masochism; it disappointed no one, for it registered a record-breaking 104 degrees at three in the afternoon of June 26. On such days, the streets were "like hot rubber; at night they gave off heat and odor like a pitch kettle." City officials, in an attempt to do something about this, went so far as to speak of flushing the asphalt streets after the sun set to dissipate their heat. But there was the heat of the daylight hours, during which the senators toiled long and hard, "steamin' away," Dooley observed, "undher th' majestic tin dome ov the capitol thryin' to rejooce th' tariff to a weight where it can stand on the same platform with me frind big Bill Taft without endangerin' his life."

Taft escaped from his problems by playing golf, and he played even on the very hot days, for he believed that this would do more to lessen the "measurement of his girth" than anything else. He also went "automobiling" and for canters down Potomac Drive on his big bay. (Not till a month after her collapse was Mrs. Taft able to take her first automobile ride.) Though he skipped lunch—so as to say he was dieting—he made up for it at dinner; one evening Butt noticed him eat all the candied fruit in a large bonbon dish, bit by bit, absently.

The heat, his overeating, and whether he should align himself with the insurgent minority or the standpatter majority remained constants. Equally unchanging were the individuals—strong, complex personalities —who loomed on both sides; they would have to be handled by Will Taft with a Theodore Roosevelt dexterity.

A confrontation had already occurred. One morning, five days after the inauguration, three formidable politicians—Nelson Aldrich, Joe Cannon, and Sereno Elisha Payne—confronted Taft. This trio believed devoutly and with fervor in a high tariff. Aldrich bore witness to the extent of his convictions by declaring that he had been a protectionist before the Republican party came into existence, and that he would be one until he died.

Taft, therefore, had reason to feel apprehensive when he learned that the purpose of the visit directly concerned "Uncle Joe" Cannon, whom he intensely disliked. Cannon's vulgarity grated on Taft's sensibilities. (At one time it had also grated on the sensibilities of his constituents; Cannon lost one term in office several years earlier for using foul language on the floor of the House. He had thereby earned another, less avuncular name, "Foulmouth Joe.")

The President was unable to accept this sinewy, slight—he was considerably less than half Taft's weight—chin-bearded, swearing, spitting caricature of a politician. TR's warning to his daughter Alice when she was to play poker with Cannon, *never* to get between him and a cuspidor, was sound advice. Cannon swore as easily as he spit. His thin voice had the capacity to go on endlessly, and habit had synchronized a gesticulating left fist to it. But control of committee appointments, rather than oratory, gave him his power—as did his determination of the course and outcome of debates, for he alone decided who would speak in the House and who wouldn't. The enactment of legislation, as a consequence, depended on him; those whom he appointed to committees voted in accordance with his wishes, for the sake of their political lives.

However, a coalition of thirty insurgent Republicans and Democrats in the House had arisen and, with the indignation of the wronged, challenged Cannon's authoritarian rule. They saw no humor in the rube role he had assumed for the sake of his rural, uneducated constituents, in the cracker-barrel wit and the affected, untidy clothes—which were really expressly tailored for him, and expensive. (Contrary to insinuations by some of his enemies, Cannon had come by his impressive wealth honestly; it had been amassed for him, through investments in Illinois, by his albino brother, Bill, a financial genius.) What really impressed the insurgents was Cannon's power to block progressive legislation.

The threat of these men—to unseat Cannon, destroy "Cannonism"— had brought Cannon, flanked by Aldrich and Payne, to Taft. Though Cannon looked at Taft with his usual heavy-lidded, speculative gaze, his proposition appeared clear-cut and a matter of simple choice. All Taft had to do, Cannon, Aldrich, and Payne informed him, was use his influence to squelch the coalition opposing Cannon. In return, Cannon would get behind the tariff of the party's platform.

Taft's big body squirmed. He knew if he accepted these terms, the word would be out that he was allying himself with the reactionary forces in Congress, acting counter to Roosevelt's policies—although TR had always advised caution and suggested co-operation whenever a matter involved Cannon.

Still, simple arithmetic told Taft that he must accept. Obviously, logically, if he were to get legislation through he must be on the side of one hundred and eighty representatives rather than on that of a numerically ineffective though vociferous thirty.

And so by the time old Joe Cannon, preparatory to departure, put on his black slouch hat, turning green at the edges, Taft had agreed to support him. The result, moreover, turned out precisely as planned: the House's tariff bill—the Payne Bill, with enough reduction in it at least to suit Taft—moved on to the Senate; Cannon was picked once again as Speaker, his power remaining intact; and the rebels in the House viewed Taft with suspicion.

The Payne Bill, however, didn't suit the insurgents. One of them, Robert La Follette of Wisconsin, a short, rugged, intense individual with a high forehead which he accentuated by brushing his stately mop of hair straight up, decided that the "House bill was in violation of the pledges of the party and against the public interest."

La Follette's intensity must have been infectious, for Taft advised La Follette and his colleagues in the Senate to "criticize the bill, amend it, cut down the duties." He assured La Follette, "when they lay that bill down before me, unless it complies with the platform"—his fist struck the desk emphatically, as TR's might have done—"I will veto it."

So Taft didn't touch the House bill, because he didn't "much believe in a President interfering with the legislative department while it is doing its work." They had their responsibility; he had his.

Three days after the House bill went to the Senate, Nelson Wilmarth Aldrich, acknowledged boss of the Senate, whose six-foot frame was imperiously erect at sixty-eight, who was appropriately adorned with a grand and arrogant white mustache, and who had snapping dark eyes that could intimidate or charm, introduced a revised bill in the Senate. The nature of that revision should really not have shocked and surprised anyone—as it did—considering Aldrich's attributes and personal history.

Born in a poor Rhode Island mill town, Aldrich left school early to set about the business of becoming a self-made man. Starting as a clerk in a wholesale grocery, he rose with incredible, Alger-like speed; but while Alger's Dick Darewells courageously stopped the runaway horse of the wealthy employer's daughter, Aldrich simply saw the great value in combining business and politics. (It must be said, he also married well.) As a consequence, by the time he was in his thirties, he had become president of both the First National Bank and the Providence Board of Trade, and before he reached forty, he was a member of the Senate. At sixty, he had accumulated great wealth in rubber and tractions, lived at 110 Benevolent Street in Providence, and when his daughter married John D. Rockefeller, Jr., he was able to think only of her happiness. (Consequently, according to one acute observer, among Aldrich's other distinctions, he was responsible for bringing "charm to the Rockefeller family.")

Nelson Aldrich's wealth and philosophy made him admirably suited for membership in the Senate. State legislatures—not the consumer, whom Aldrich damned—selected the ninety-two members of that body; the dominant interest in the state, in turn, controlled the state legislature. Literally and figuratively, therefore, there was a senator from Sugar, a senator from Steel, a senator from Wool. . . . Naturally, Aldrich believed in them with all his heart, for he was "the interests' " strong right arm and, naturally, he had very much in common with the twenty other millionaires who were his colleagues in the Senate.

Understandably, this man could introduce his revised bill in the serene manner of one telling the truth. His bill, he said, had lowered the rates of the House or Payne Bill. He was also able, with the air of a just man crying out against a wrong, to state that action should be prompt, for delay would be injurious to business.

Close scrutiny was not needed to see that many amendments—847 of them—had been made, and that the changes, in approximately six hundred cases, had been increases rather than reductions.

Dooley had nothing but praise for the bill. In his opinion, the good senator from Rhode Island had put many "familyar commodyties within th' reach iv all." On the free list now were such "familyar commodyties" as curling stones, false teeth, canary-bird seed, hog bristle, and silkworm eggs.

The senators and press of the Midwest were too incensed to employ sarcasm; only the direct thrust of anger fit their mood. The Senate, the House, and the President should unite to depose Aldrich, "the New England Tyrant." Because they were speaking in the spirit of TR, they assumed Taft was with them. At this point, when all the maneuverings still lay ahead, Taft may have been, for he said, "I fear Aldrich is ready to sacrifice the party, and I will not permit it."

Vice-President "Sunny Jim" Sherman strongly advised Taft to use patronage as a club to get what he wanted. Like Dooley, he believed "Politics ain't bean bag. 'Tis a man's game."

But it went against Taft's placid nature to use political weapons. Roosevelt, he knew, had used patronage with consummate skill. (Once TR, in order to get the vote of a senator who always opposed him, made what he considered his "most outrageous appointment"; he put into the office of city attorney the brother of the senator's mistress.) TR had also manipulated public opinion so that the sweep of its fury made members of Congress knuckle under. But Taft knew his limitations, brooded on them.

In dealing with the situation confronting him, he tried a Roosevelt strategy that was least alien to him: he would be friends to both the progressives and the standpatters and, he hoped, would evolve a solution in the process.

Before Nellie Taft became ill, the numerous unexpected guests—and the impossibility of planning for them—disturbed her. Senators and representatives, both insurgents and standpatters, came for lunch and dinner, frequently even for breakfast. Automobile rides—at night—also had political objectives, as did sitting on the porch.

Senator Dolliver reported sardonically to La Follette, "Bob, I was invited up to the White House to a tariff breakfast. The muskmelon he served was not very good."

The word that he had for Senator Albert Beveridge of Indiana was not couched in oblique terms. One day on the Senate floor, Dolliver, white with emotion, whispered to Beveridge that they had been deserted by Taft.

The very next day, Beveridge was led to believe that this was true, for he received a very cold reception at the White House.

In a few weeks, however, he was able to write his wife, "One o'clock. Just home. Saw Taft—he is with us."

It took only four days for the swing of the pendulum. Taft had angered the insurgents; once again Beveridge viewed the administration as hopeless, doomed.

Taft's fraternizing with Payne and Aldrich didn't help matters; he dined with them, sat on the porch with them, took night automobile rides into the country with them.

Aldrich—his piercing brown eyes still on the welfare of business—tried to force his bill through the Senate. He used a simple, painful measure; he saw to it that the senators worked a thirteen-hour day—from ten in the morning to eleven at night.

The heat wave, as though co-operating with Aldrich's little plan, continued unabated. To get some relief, "Senators sneaked out into the cloakroom to sit under the electric fans." Free lemonade, another cooling device, had only the virtue of being free. Up in the galleries, the few visitors "kept their hats busy" in a vain effort to create some circulation.

To get away from the heat—and for the sake of her health—Mrs. Taft was to spend the summer at Beverly, Massachusetts. Though her health had improved, she feared she might at any moment become paralyzed, for paralysis had struck her father and other members of her family, and she dwelt morbidly on this knowledge. Hypochondria and logic assured her that since fate had been capable of striking her down as it had, it could be even more sadistic.

On July 1, three days before the Tafts left, an excavator obliterated TR's tennis court, the first step in the construction of an addition to the cramped executive offices of the White House. So closely had this tennis court been identified with TR that its destruction could lead, via symbolism, to only one conclusion.

On the day that Taft left to accompany his wife, daughter, younger son, and Dr. Delaney to Beverly, he gave strict instructions, as though to counteract what the excavator had done, that no employee of the White House should give out anything that would have so much as a flavor of hostility to the Roosevelt administration.

Beverly had already been honored by two Presidents—Washington and Harrison—and eagerly anticipated the arrival of a third. The City Hall's windows, those that could be seen from the street, had even been washed for the occasion—and this had not been done for Washington or Harrison. The *Sylph* also rode at anchor in Salem Bay, convenient and ready for the President's use. ("Fool name for a craft," a native remarked irritably, "for a craft that has to carry him.") And the vine-clad Mont-serrat railroad station had been bedecked for the Tafts' party's arrival.

Taft—who was always essentially Taft, rather than TR—immediately upon arrival drove off to the summer "White House," not giving the Mayor of Beverly a chance to deliver his speech of welcome and not saying a complimentary word for the painstaking way in which the station had been decorated.

Taft wanted to see to it that his wife and Helen and Charlie were settled in this temporary summer environment. The cottage's setting could not have been more reassuring. All its details were on a grand, majestic scale—towering elms, wide verandas—and it provided a salubri-ous vista of Salem Bay, dotted decoratively with rocky islands and the pretty white sails of small craft. The view could not help but trigger the thought that Nellie would surely feel "the good effects of the sea air."

In the afternoon, Taft motored to Windcliffe, the Boardman summer home. His wife would have the opportunity for what social life her strength would permit, because although the Boardmans were six or seven miles away—a considerable distance in 1909—both families had automo-biles, and the two houses were linked by an excellent road. (Equally con-venient, as the insurgents pointed out with some venomous pleasure, were the palatial summer homes of J. P. Morgan and Nelson W. Aldrich.)

Before the afternoon was over Taft made one reconnaissance that re-lated to his personal need; he went to the Essex Country Club. He wanted to have a look at their golf course, for he would be playing that course and the Myopia Club course before the summer was over. Moreover, he would be playing when he should have been working on speeches, and those particular games of golf, as a consequence, would, oddly enough, be responsible for a critical situation in the Republican party.

Burdensome speeches lengthened the trip from Beverly back to Wash-ington. Honesty, once again, made one of them obligatory. He had to speak in Norwich, Connecticut, for when he was there during the cam-paign, he had promised, if elected, to return for the town's two hundred and fiftieth anniversary. He also had to go to Blue Ridge, New York, to speak at the three-hundredth-anniversary celebration of the discovery of Lake Champlain.

There were other obligatory speeches, and he approached them with the tremulous state of mind of young Will Taft, coming to Washington for the first time to be Solicitor General. "I have to make two more speeches this day," he wrote his wife, "and how I shall do it I do not know. It is awful." And he wailed over their content: "My speeches get thinner and thinner and I shall just drivel in a little while."

Taft needed a speech writer, and he still needed—as events would prove—the big-brother direction that TR had supplied before going off to another continent.

What the President found waiting for him in Washington was not really preferable to speechmaking. After three months of debate, on July 8 the Senate passed the tariff bill, one whose rates soared above those in the House bill. Ten progressive Republicans had voted vehemently against it. Blind Senator Thomas P. Gore of Oklahoma was able to visualize TR, upon his return from Africa, being elected by going before the people on a platform that promised a real revision downward. He was certain, moreover, that had TR been in the White House he would have vetoed this bill. Across the country the press screamed its outrage. Only the Democrats rejoiced; no sight could be more delightful than this Republican Civil War; the Aldrich Bill had been the firing on Fort Sumter.

To quiet the uproar, Taft announced he would work with the Conference Committee to affect a revision of the rates downward. Hadn't Cannon and Aldrich said that they would make it possible for him to "exert a great influence" on the committee? The function of this committee, composed of members of the House and Senate, was to iron out the differences between the bills of the two houses and create a compromise bill.

Hopeful though Taft said he was, the Midwest and the progressives generally believed, with despair and bitterness, that it was too late; the Senate bill could not possibly be transformed into the bill they had in mind. This conflict and Washington heat kept Taft awake at night. "I slept in three beds," he wrote his wife, "and changed because each time I waked up I found myself so bathed in perspiration that the bed was uncomfortable." He also moved about in his size fifty-four pajamas, positioning whatever bed he was sleeping in out in the middle of the floor, in order to get the most of whatever breeze there might be.

Then Taft experienced an act of politics; it shocked him. Old Joe Cannon, the czar, the vulgarian, the tyrant, had loaded the Conference Committee with members of the House who espoused a high tariff. One of them revealed the emotional depth of his credo, saying, "I sweat blood every time they reduce a schedule."

Will Taft wrote to his brother Horace, in the plaintive tone of a small boy suddenly faced by injustice in the world. "I don't think Cannon played square." In what might have been an answer, Dooley said, "Thrust iveryone, but cut the cards."

On July 18 Taft's awakening progressed. In a letter to his wife he pointed out, "I am dealing with very acute and expert politicians, and I am trusting a great many of them and I may be deceived; but on the whole I have the whip hand." (In his innocence and honesty, he could not conceive the illegality and ingenuity of a plan that was actually attempted—one that would lower the duty on a particular schedule and yet increase it. For example, a set of dishes valued at ten dollars at a sixty per cent duty would pay six dollars. The nefarious plan would lower the duty to forty per cent, a substantial reduction, one sure to please those baying for reduction, but would see to it that those dishes were valued from fifteen to twenty dollars instead of ten. The duty paid would then be at least as much as the old one—and possibly a few dollars more.)

The debates started in the Senate on the tariff schedule; they were bitter and dramatic. "Jokers" in the bill were uncovered, exposed. The insurgents stayed up far into the night, studying tariff schedules, ruining their eyes and health, but hopefully gathering information that would confound Aldrich and his henchmen.

Instead of drawing closer to the insurgents—and their objective—Taft became more and more friendly with Aldrich, whose levelheadedness had always appealed to him. Before long, Taft reached a point where he regarded an attack on Aldrich as one against himself.

Daily he wrote Nellie—who, at least, still had to know about the bigwigs. In his letters to her, he damned the progressives as being "rather forward," which appeared to assess their dedication with the criteria of etiquette. In particular, Beveridge's ego, "so self-centered and so self-absorbed," bothered Taft. He "has been home to Indiana," Taft wrote his wife, "and has become convinced that his attitude is the perfect attitude." As for Bob La Follette, his feelings concerning him were also unmixed. Against his will, Taft had agreed to be part of a church cornerstone-laying ceremony in which La Follette would also participate. "I shall have the pleasure of listening to Mr. La Follette," Taft wrote acidly, "and somebody else equally objectionable, before I come to my part of the ceremony. . . ."

Nellie Taft had become a general out of action, receiving the communiqués far behind the lines, reading them on the large piazza swept by cool breezes. Her circumscribed life included automobile rides along the North Shore, a band concert at Salem Willows, and Will's letters, which were full of references to "free hides," "duty on shoes and harness and leather," "iron ore at 12½ cents a ton," "a fight on gloves." Though she had to have all this information, there was such a tedious amount of it that she had to complain, at least by subtle indirection, "I got your letter full of tariff discussions." Golf news might make the tariff reports more palatable, so he wrote her, "This afternoon I went around in 96." Then there was his weight. By "curtailing some of my food," he told her, he had dropped from three hundred and fourteen pounds to an ounce or two under three hundred and ten, and he planned on losing half a pound a day. But he was reticent, fearful, about making inquiries concerning her health. He approached the subject on tiptoe, with stealth. "You do not write me anything about yourself, I wish you would." When she informed him that she had made considerable improvement in talking, Will was "delighted" by this news. He told her he was sure improvement "will come by jerks so to speak," urged "continual practice to bring about changes."

Another side to his solicitude appeared in his letters—written in bold copperplate—in the declarations of love with which they were concluded. Sometimes it would be "with loads and loads of love, Lovingly, Will." Always the comparative was too meager and the superlative did not suffice—"and believe me, as much in love with you as ever and more, lovingly yours, Will." Mrs. Taft signed her letters, "Devotedly, Helen." That his outpourings stemmed from fear and served as a shield was indicated by the extreme, obsessive diligence with which he wrote; not a single day must be missed, and if missed, an apology followed posthaste. "He was afraid she'd be mean to him," a perceptive spectator maintained, "make him stand in the corner like a little boy."

To assert himself took conscious, arduous effort and was, therefore, unpleasant. But deep down, a vital part of his ego demanded it, and the lingering image of TR still influenced him, and so he took a stand, of sorts, on the tariff. Cannon wanted a high tariff on gloves, "in the interest of a friend named Littauer," and he went so far as to threaten the President with defeating the bill in order to have his way. Appalled by this blackmail, Taft stood firm, and Aldrich, always ready to make a small concession for a large advantage, backed Taft. Cannon, as a consequence, capitulated. When Aldrich, Senator Jonathan Bourne, and a Mr. Heinz of the lumber interests lay in wait for him and made demands, Taft stood erect and said, "I refuse to be bossed."

He was firm, too, with Sereno Elisha Payne, who favored a particular duty on gloves and stockings. "Then, old man," said Taft, "I will have to fight you. We won't quarrel, but I shall use all the influence I have to defeat this schedule." He also stood up to Francis E. Warren, senator from Wyoming (and father-in-law of General Pershing), a wealthy sheepman, senator of Hides and Wools, whom Dolliver had called "the greatest shepherd since Abraham."

"I have tried persuasion with Warren," Taft told Archie Butt, "and if that does not do he can go to hell with his wool schedule and I will defeat him without compromise."

This, Butt wrote, "smacked so much of President Roosevelt that it made my blood tingle."

The resemblance, however, had only the depth of an outburst. TR enjoyed a fight; Taft did not. There was a question, therefore, as to how long Taft would hold out on tariff issues, which the insurgents had linked inextricably with the Roosevelt policies and their own.

That summer Taft did not labor constantly in the tariff vineyards. He appeared to be especially busy, for he insisted on devoting the entire afternoon to golf. Worry about the tariff didn't help his game.

There were other diversions, too. One afternoon, he and a party went to a five-cent picture show on Ninth Street, and for about twenty minutes they saw a flickering likeness of the President delivering a speech at Petersburg, Virginia, at the unveiling of a monument honoring Pennsylvania soldiers who had died in Petersburg during the Civil War; solemn though this occasion was, the jerky mechanized representation of Taft's gestures caused laughter.

The following week, on a Monday evening, after an afternoon of golf, Taft went to Fort Myer to "see the Wright aeroplane in flight," an aeroplane being tested for the government. Fort Myer and the Wright brothers' flights became a focal point of social activity that summer. Alice Longworth often drove out in her electric, bringing food and several thermoses of Tom Collinses with her and running "a popular lunch wagon." On the day of Taft's visit to Fort Myer, Joe Cannon appeared out of nowhere and sat at Taft's left. Then, in a minute or two, Nelson Aldrich materialized and took a chair at his right.

In spite of a fifteen-mile-an-hour wind, Orville Wright, in order not to disappoint the President, took the plane up. It rose to a height of about one hundred feet, circled the field, and came down—all in two and a half minutes. Taft arose and applauded heartily. As soon as he settled back in his seat, he engaged in earnest conversation for several minutes with Aldrich, so earnestly that the topic may well have been tariff rather than aeroplane.

The next day, Taft saw Orville Wright set a new world mark by remaining aloft with a passenger for one hour, twelve minutes, and forty seconds, breaking his brother's record by two minutes and fifty-nine seconds. Taft could not have paid the feat a higher compliment than when he said, "I've missed my dinner, but the show was worth it." TR, he told the Wrights, would probably ask for a plane ride, but he himself wouldn't. "I don't believe," he said, "I am built along aviation lines any-way."

Meanwhile, Beverly, Massachusetts, grew restive; it was summer, and President Taft, therefore, belonged in the summer "White House." The board of aldermen, who had been responsible for getting the City Hall windows washed prior to Taft's brief visit, met to pass resolutions that would put the blame for Taft's absence where it belonged.

Their action proved unnecessary, for on August 6 Taft signed the Payne-Aldrich Tariff Bill and was, finally, able to depart for Beverly. During the signing, a thunderstorm broke out, with melodramatic meteorological effects. Just as meaning had been read into the blizzard at the time of his inauguration, newspapermen now saw this storm "as a note of warning from the country." They predicted that this storm would be followed by a "storm of protest."

Taft, however, said that he was pleased by the bill; at the same time, he pointed out to Nellie, "Your husband will be damned heartily in the Capitol and elsewhere." Just as he expected, and the newsmen predicted, the "storm of protest" descended. The bill helped the East and manufac-tured goods, but not the West and South and raw materials. It helped the malefactors of great wealth, TR's enemies. It split the party: a minority West against a majority East. Instead of an income tax it substituted a minuscule corporation tax, which Aldrich accepted in order to destroy the income tax. Summing it all up, the outraged progressives stamped the Payne-Aldrich Bill as "just plain dishonest."

Taft, of course, would not agree with that evaluation. He conceded that it was "not a perfect bill," but he felt it represented "a sincere effort." Before the summer would end, he would alter this estimate—and this alteration would prove catastrophic.

This time no crowd greeted Taft on his arrival in Beverly; decorations no longer brightened the Montserrat station. Mrs. Taft had come in a "motor," and she sat in it until Will came to her. The only apparent change from the norm in his wife was a decided pallor. (A few days later, Taft wrote his brother Horace, "She is quite disposed to sit as a Pope and direct me as of yore, which is an indication of the restoration of normal conditions.")

Golf immediately became part of Taft's daily routine. It was as much therapeutic as recreational; the clubs were long and heavy. His partners at the Myopia Club were William Boardman and John Hays Hammond. Before he went off to the golf course, and before breakfast, Taft spent a salutary hour exercising with Dr. Charles Barker: boxing, wrestling, throwing the medicine ball. Afternoons Taft reserved for Nellie, for conversation and motoring and trying to distract her from her illness.

Not much of the day remained for the President to spend in executive offices, but his position required them, and so they were available, over a department store in the Mason Building, just off the main street, staffed with a secretary, an assistant secretary, three stenographers, and three clerks.

One important visitor, an investigator for the Interior Department, heralded a controversy that would be equally as damaging as the tariff "reduction." It would have been better for the Republican party if Aldrich had not suggested that Taft go on a speaking tour, to be as oil upon the troubled political waters of the Midwest and West.

One important aspect of the imminent Western trip bothered Taft. "If it were not for the speeches," he pointed out, "I should look forward with the greatest pleasure to this trip." Reason then jerked him rudely from the euphoria of fantasy and made him conclude, "But without the speeches there would be no trip, and so there you are."

A man in his predicament had to resort to a brilliant idea: he would outline about four speeches—"about" made it possible to do three instead of four. Parts of these master speeches could then be used in each speech he made and garnished with local color so as to appear completely fresh. But this plan had a serious flaw; it required that "about four speeches" be outlined. To his routine of golf and keeping Nellie company he added putting off doing the speeches.

Taft finally had to leave the golf course and mount the speaking platform. The first speech was in Boston; the garnish on it was Aldrich, whom Taft declared the "real leader of the Senate." He then proceeded to Winona, Minnesota, to help in the re-election of Jim Tawney, arch standpatter and an apostle of high tariff.

That September night in the Winona Opera House, Taft made history —with one sentence. Ironically, he read the speech, because "care of expression was required." He also read that one epic sentence: "On the whole, however, I am bound to say that I think the Payne bill is the best bill that the Republican party ever passed."

The following day he wired Nellie, "Speech hastily prepared, but I hope it may do some good." Afterward, he admitted he had dictated the speech—and that sentence—as he traveled between stations, "and glanced through only enough to straighten out the grammar." He sent a wire to Nellie, one of his daily wires to her during the trip, telling her, "I said what I thought and there is that satisfaction."

There certainly was no other consolation, because the newspapers pounced on that one sentence and made headlines out of it. For one thing, the gist of that sentence was news; for another, the newspapers of the country were incensed by the Payne-Aldrich Tariff Bill, because it had not put Canadian wood pulp and newsprint on the free list.

The newspapers in a state that Dolliver believed would be stoutly Republican to the day hell went Methodist made an especially violent frontal attack. The Des Moines *News* wished the ghosts of animals that TR had killed in Africa should "ever haunt him for having foisted on the country this man Taft." The Des Moines *Register and Leader* stated flatly that "TR need merely ask and he can have the nomination in 1912."

Even brother Horace had an adverse comment to make about the Winona speech. "I did not write to you about it," he wrote, "because my secretary is a lady and no language that suited the speech could be dictated. I will swear at you about it when I see you."

Eight

"What Will Roosevelt Think?"

When Cyril Pinchot, leading a company of soldiers from Breteuil, France, arrived at Waterloo in 1815 to reinforce Napoleon, he was too late. The battle was over. Such a fate never befell Cyril's grandson, Gifford, who always appeared on the battlefield well ahead of time. Subsequently, Cyril was obliged to leave France for his part in a plan to rescue his leader from St. Helena. Thus, it was perhaps appropriate, in view of his heritage, that Gifford Pinchot be the driving force in the effort to rescue *his* leader, Theodore Roosevelt, from political retirement and restore him to the presidency by means of that incubus of Taft supporters, the "Back from Elba" movement.

In 1909 Gifford Pinchot was forty-three; he had a lean, handsome face with a commanding dark mustache and uncompromising, fiery, evangelical eyes, and his considerable inherited wealth did not diminish the spirituality of his appearance. His habits were eclectic: Spartan and sybaritic, for he slept on the floor and in the morning had cold water thrown on him by his valet. His six-foot-one frame was attenuated, as if some inner fire had consumed excess flesh. Physically, as well as in many other ways, he was the antithesis of William Howard Taft. A bachelor—the most eligible in Washington—he still mourned the death, in 1894, of his fiancée ("For years he wore a black band on his sleeve, understood to be for a loss so long past that none of his friends could recall it"), and would not take the marriage vows until 1914. He lived in Washington with his devoted mother, Mary Jane Pinchot—or "Mamee," as her three children called her—who blended a "very grande dame" manner with a militant spirit and had almost as keen an admiration for Theodore Roosevelt as her son.

Nominally, Gifford Pinchot was head of the Forest Service, a minor agency of the Department of Agriculture. As such, he would normally have communicated with the White House through his superiors; in Pinchot's case, this was not so. He always went directly to the President, a practice that Taft, seven months after he took office, found pernicious. "The truth is," he wrote Mrs. Taft, "the whole administration under Roosevelt was demoralized by his system of dealing directly with subordinates."

However, Pinchot and the Secretary of the Interior, James R. Garfield, son of the twentieth President, occupied a unique position in TR's administration. "No two men have been as closely identified with so many of the policies for which this administration has stood," TR wrote at the end of his term. This statement, part of a foreword for a proposed book by Pinchot and Garfield on the Roosevelt policies, was not mere hyperbole. Both men were frequent guests at Sagamore Hill, and they could be found at the White House at almost any time, as the leading members of TR's Tennis Cabinet. In addition to the slashing, driving games played on the White House courts—in boiling heat, pouring rain, and snowstorms— other Roosevelt-inspired activities occupied Pinchot and Garfield: boxing, wrestling, tossing medicine balls, achieving a precarious balance in walking "the Crack," a sloping fissure in a vertical wall of a quarry in Rock Creek Park (those who fell, fell also in the estimation of TR), chopping wood on Cathedral Hill, and drinking mint juleps on the White House lawn. Less ephemeral was their influence on policy matters, as ghost writers of TR's speeches, his messages to Congress, and many of his public statements. The readiness with which TR accepted and delivered their speeches—often without any change at all—indicated his reliance on, and respect for, their point of view. "There has been a peculiar intimacy between you and Jim and me," TR wrote to Pinchot, "because all three of us have worked for the same causes, have dreamed the same dreams, have felt a substantial identity of purpose as regards many of what we three deemed the most vital problems of today."

Garfield wholeheartedly admired TR, and Pinchot's idolatry was manifest to all, including the idol himself, who analyzed it cheerfully as "almost fetish worship." It was TR's conviction that Pinchot worshiped his capacity for sheer ruthlessness. "He thinks," TR explained to Archie Butt, "that if we were cast away somewhere together and we were both hungry, I would kill him and eat him, AND," he said, turning to Archie and showing his teeth in a ferocious grin, "I WOULD, TOO."

Actually, Gifford Pinchot's most passionate devotion was given not to an individual, but to a crusade. His eyes looked, wrote Owen Wister, "as if they gazed upon a Cause." That "Cause" was conservation; the crusade, its acceptance as national policy.

Since its inception, the Government Land Office (part of the Department of the Interior, which had jurisdiction over minerals and water

power) had permitted—really encouraged—extensive settlement of public lands on the theory that this would advance the country's economic
development. Corruption and sheer incompetence also prevailed in the
Land Office, springing from the presence of so many political appointees,
superfluous brothers-in-law and unemployable cousins; consequently,
large tracts of land were dealt out to individual and private interests with
alarming speed. The United States was vast, its natural resources seemingly limitless.

However, by the beginning of the twentieth century, through Pinchot's
and Garfield's extraordinary efforts, with the help of dedicated colleagues
in the Reclamation and Forest Services—who were all given complete
support by TR—forest conservation and federal irrigation programs began to be accepted practice. Public land had begun being withdrawn for
forest reserves before TR's administration, but he increased the acreage
to such an extent—sixty-three million acres in two years—that powerful
interests in the West were outraged. This led Congress in 1906 to pass a
bill prohibiting any more withdrawals in six Western states. TR put off
signing the bill to the very last possible moment. By the time he finally
lifted the pen from his desk to sign, Garfield and Pinchot had already, as a
result of frenetic speed and the time TR had made possible, withdrawn
sixteen million acres in those six states, enough acreage to create twenty-
one new national forests. "The opponents of Forest Service," TR wrote
with enormous satisfaction, "turned handsprings in their wrath."

Still, the rapidity with which large corporations—General Electric,
Westinghouse, the Aluminum Company of America—were taking control of water sites, mineral deposits, and timberlands bothered only a
comparative few. "The relation of the conservation of natural resources,"
wrote TR, "to the problem of National welfare and National efficiency
had not dawned on the public mind."

Indeed, before that bleak day in February, 1907, on which the idea of a
federal government policy covering conservation of *all* natural resources
first dawned on Gifford Pinchot, it had never, to common knowledge,
occurred to anyone else. To Pinchot, riding along on his horse, Jim, on
Ridge Road in Rock Creek Park, lost in solitary thought, the concept
seemed "like coming out of a dark tunnel . . . like lifting the curtain on
a great new stage."

The Pinchots—rich, enlightened, and humanitarian—entertained almost
nightly at their mansion, at 1615 Rhode Island Avenue at Scott Circle.
The motif running through virtually all their social life was the conservation movement. Governors, Cabinet members, senators, congressmen,
federal administrators, and Western lumbermen and cattlemen flocked to

the Pinchots, dined in patrician abundance, and listened to Gifford Pinchot preach the gospel of conservation.

Consequently, it was only natural that during the winter of 1907–1908 TR, Pinchot, and Garfield would engage in many discussions concerning the future of conservation. Over and over again TR repeated, "How lucky we should be if it were possible to get Will Taft into the Presidency." The election of Taft having been accomplished, a curious apprehension then overtook the trio. On the positive side, Pinchot noted the strong conservation speech Taft had given during the campaign. ("Not a bad speech, either," commented Pinchot. "I wrote it myself.") However, Pinchot recorded later, "Our reluctant dread that something was wrong with Taft gradually crystallized into the fear that, under pressure, he might go back on his salt."

To erase niggling doubts about Taft's commitment to conservation, TR called both Pinchot and Taft to the White House one evening shortly after the election. Upstairs, in the President's study, formerly the Cabinet Room, Will Taft, a bland three-hundred-and-twenty-two-pound man with a penchant for inactive pursuits and a distaste for fanning public opinion, was confronted by Theodore Roosevelt and Gifford Pinchot, who shared somewhat different characteristics: combativeness, a propensity for strenuous sports, an insatiable appetite for basking in the public eye, and an undeviating conviction of being right. (Indeed, Mr. Dooley's definition of a fanatic could conceivably have been applied to the Chief Forester: "A man that does what he thinks th' Lord wud do if He knew th' facts iv th' case.")

"Taft pledged himself to TR," Pinchot reported, "and incidentally to me, to stand by and carry on the Conservation fight."

On Monday evening, December 7, 1908, *Aïda*—an opera whose tortuous plot involves the king of Egypt, high priests, and slave girls, and which concludes with the hero and heroine entombed in a dungeon—was performed on the stage of the Belasco Theatre in Washington. The next afternoon, the audience that had packed the theater viewed an entirely different kind of melodrama. The Joint Conservation Conference was meeting, and sitting on the stage, among governors of twenty states, were Theodore Roosevelt, Gifford Pinchot, and William Howard Taft.

This was the first time since the election that TR and Taft had appeared together on a public platform. The main address was to be given by TR, but Taft, serving as chairman, was also to speak. Upon Pinchot's introduction of Taft as "the President-elect," Taft rose and, with every appearance of good humor, including his notorious chuckle, said, "Mr.

President, ladies and gentlemen, there is one difficulty about the conservation of natural resources. It is that the imagination of those who are
pressing it may outrun the practical facts. I have been introduced as the
President-elect. I am not the President-elect, except in the imagination of
Mr. Pinchot. . . ."

This seemed to be merely a bit of heavy-handed humor, based on the
technicality that the electoral college would not meet until the following
Monday and, therefore, not until then would Taft's status as President-
elect be official. But it was more than that; it provided an irresistible
opportunity for Taft to aim a dart at what he considered the conservation
movement's—and Pinchot's—chief characteristic: hysterical overstate-
ment. To an irritated Pinchot, it displayed a prime example of what TR
was to call Taft's "hair-splitting legalisms."

As Taft set aside the speech that Pinchot had written for him, he
smiled, veiling in his eyes what William Allen White had observed as "the
hint of a serpentine glitter." "I had some notes that I was going to read,"
he said, "but the truth is they contained so many expert statements that I
am afraid you might suspect their authorship. . . ." Though Taft's brief
statements harmlessly reiterated his plan "to carry on the work so admirably begun and so wonderfully shown forth by President Roosevelt,"
the remarks introducing them bitterly antagonized Pinchot and served
"notice of the coming of a new and darker day."

From then on, everyone wondered: "Would Taft stand by his promise? Or would he turn our great Conservation victory into defeat?"
Since thought—in the case of TR and Pinchot—never went unaccompa-
nied by action, in the ten weeks that remained of the Roosevelt administration, nearly four million acres along the courses of sixteen rivers in the
West were withdrawn. This was done by Secretary Garfield, under the
direction of Chief Forester Pinchot, and approved by President Roosevelt. The last of these withdrawals was made only forty-eight hours
before TR left office. The reason for such frantic action was patently
clear to Pinchot, Garfield, and TR: to save "the water power sites on
public lands for the people, and from the grabbers." But fear arose that
"the same power that had saved them—the power of the President—
could also undo them."

During this time, an entirely unexpected blow fell. Immediately following the election, James Garfield had been assured by TR, who in turn had
been assured by Will Taft, that he was to be kept on as Secretary of the
Interior. He had therefore renewed the three-year lease on his Washington house. But at the end of January, 1909, Garfield was informed that he
wouldn't be retained in the Cabinet.

"In a sense," TR wrote Pinchot, "I did Jim a personal injury by getting him to take office seven years ago. . . . His law practice has, of course, gone to the winds, and his work for the Government has not been such as to make it easy for him to resume this practice with profit to himself. He has sacrificed much for the privilege of giving as good work for the public as any man of our acquaintance has done."

However, Taft regarded Garfield's predicament with a sanguine philosophy, both glib and difficult to deny. When his brother Horace ventured the opinion that "poor Jim will have a hard time," Taft replied that "it will probably be the best thing that could happen to Jim, if he only knew it."

Immediately upon Garfield's dismissal came the disturbing news that his successor would be Richard Achilles Ballinger. On the surface, Ballinger's appointment seemed unobjectionable. An erstwhile reform mayor of Seattle, Washington, Ballinger had not only gotten rid of the slot machines in that city, but had also been, as even Gifford Pinchot grudgingly admitted, "a fairly good Mayor as Mayors go." His father had read law in Lincoln's office and had commanded a Negro company during the Civil War. A Williams College schoolmate of Garfield's, Ballinger had been appointed commissioner of the General Land Office by TR on the recommendation of Garfield himself.

Despite all these noteworthy facts, Ballinger's one-year stay in the Land Office was regarded by Pinchot and Garfield as a disaster. They discovered to their horror that he was in favor—highly in favor—of selling coal and grazing land outright to private individuals and companies, and very much against TR's policy of merely leasing them for fair royalties for limited periods. Equally shocking was his opposition to one of Pinchot's major projects, the creation of Chugach National Forest in south-central Alaska, and his questioning of the legality of many of the Conservationists' procedures. Perhaps Ballinger's conservation philosophy agitated Pinchot and Garfield most of all, for it appeared to be precisely that of Western businessmen who wished to open land for private development and private profit.

Described by Pinchot with evident hostility as "a stocky square-headed little man of no inconsiderable energy and no little executive punch," Ballinger was also small, nervous, with iron-gray hair and a quick temper.

Finally—after exactly a year of acrimonious exchange with Pinchot, Garfield, and their colleagues—Ballinger resigned and returned to Seattle to practice law. Among his closest associates in Seattle were those whose political philosophy and financial interests collided with a strong federal government conservation policy and, particularly, with the virulent form, "the accursed Pinchotism," that it assumed under TR's administration.

Pinchot expressed his reaction to Ballinger's replacing Garfield. "I couldn't work with him as I have with Jim," he told a magazine editor. "Jim and I think alike concerning the matters in which the Forest Service and the Department of the Interior are closely related. Ballinger and I might clash." This comment was promptly passed on to Taft, who not only remained unmoved by Pinchot's anxieties, but also added to them. The implementation of the Roosevelt conservation program was based on an idea wholly obnoxious to Ballinger, "that the Executive is the steward of public welfare." This stewardship concept had been formulated by Pinchot's close friend, George Woodruff, Assistant Attorney General for the Interior Department, who shortly after Ballinger's appointment was made a federal judge by Taft and sent off to Hawaii.

If any doubts about Ballinger's views on conservation lingered in Pinchot's mind, they were immediately dissolved after Taft's inauguration. After seven years of the "whoop 'er up boys business," Ballinger declared, with an emphasis that fell ominously on the ears of the Chief Forester, "the soft pedal is on and on to stay." The new Secretary spoke with assurance, for only the day before he had restored to private entry many of the water sites withdrawn so hurriedly at the end of the Roosevelt administration.

In the two weeks that followed, the withdrawals of fourteen more large tracts were canceled. Hardly had the ink dried on Ballinger's signature than Pinchot, who had been on a fishing trip, returned to Washington. In a spirit of raw indignation, he descended on the White House to protest "as vigorously as I knew how," he declared, "against Ballinger's action." The next day he saw the President again; two days later, Taft conferred with Secretary Ballinger, who subsequently informed the Reclamation officials that President Taft wished to have the restored water sites rewithdrawn. It was a jubilant Pinchot who now balanced his fear "that Taft had gone wrong against my fervent hope that he would prove he hadn't."

Poor Will Taft! Having been President for six weeks, he was beginning to see the precise nature of "that splendid misery." On the same day that he first heard Pinchot's agitated protests, insurgent Senator Beveridge preached at him for three hours about tariff rates. Then upon Taft's emerging, wilted, from his office, he was trundled off in the White House touring car to the ball park, for the opening of the baseball season. His presence, Archie Butt said, "rattled the home team, for it played worse than it is wont to do and it never plays exceptionally well."

By the time the season was over, the standing of the Washington Nationals had not improved, and President Taft's troubles had been intensified by a conscientious and dedicated young man from the West.

Louis Russell Glavis was twenty-six years old in 1909—part of an era in which young men of that age did not make trouble. In this respect, Glavis was ahead of his time.

He seemed to appear out of nowhere; and when it was all over—when the effects of the congressional investigation, the sensational magazine articles, the exchange of harsh epithets had somewhat subsided (they never entirely subsided for the participants and their supporters)—he faded away, presumably into obscurity. He might have been conjured up by Gifford Pinchot's mystical powers—Taft men thought it quite likely —to produce precisely the result he achieved: forcing into the public arena, in sharp and graphic contrast, the conservation policies of Theodore Roosevelt and William Howard Taft, and, inevitably, the fundamental points of conflict between the two friends.

In actuality, Glavis was a solid young man, pleasant-looking in a subdued Gibson-man fashion, with a memory for detail and a remarkable ability to assess facts and place them in relevant sequence. Coming up in the Land Office Field Service in the Far West, he had been a special agent; then, in the fall of 1907, Chief of the Portland Field Division. Almost immediately his suspicions were aroused by some Alaskan coal land claims, known as the Cunningham claims, with whose history he was already familiar.

Alaskan coal lands had, for several years, provoked a profound longing among land speculators. They were hampered by a law whose provisions stated that a claim was only for the claimant's use, and which limited the size of an individual's claim to one hundred and sixty acres and the number of claims which could be consolidated to four. Moreover, it was required that a claimant—or an association of four claimants—swear that no intention existed to consolidate further with other claims.

Despite the ease with which this sworn declaration was made, it was the transparent object of many of the claimants to gain possession of land at ten dollars an acre from the government and then transfer an interest, at an enormous profit, to the financial titans waiting off stage, J. P. Morgan and the Guggenheims. They had formed the Alaska Syndicate, which already controlled the copper mines, railroads, and steamships in Alaska. For this reason, in November, 1906, TR had withdrawn one hundred thousand acres of Alaskan coal lands from public entry. Among the nine hundred claims pending at that time, there was a group of thirty-three, staked out by Clarence Cunningham, an Idaho miner, for himself and thirty-two others. Eight of his fellow claimants resided in Seattle and were friends of Richard Ballinger.

It was the belief of Glavis and several other agents in the field service that, as one reported to the then General Land Office Commissioner

Ballinger, "from the talk of different attorneys and individuals interested in the Alaskan coal lands, I feel that the disposal of the lands all tends toward one direction, and that is the Guggenheim companies. . . ." Consequently, the claims were illegal.

Commissioner Ballinger told Glavis to go ahead and investigate. However, two weeks later Ballinger ordered Glavis to clear-list—that is, record as valid—the Cunningham claims. When Glavis wired a strong protest, Ballinger "suspended the clear-listing order." He also wired one of the claimants, "Temporary delay caused by report of field agent." Very shortly after that, Ballinger's resignation took effect, and he left the General Land Office to return to Seattle and his law practice.

The advantage of being legally represented before the General Land Office by a former commissioner of that agency was lost neither on the Cunningham claimants nor on the government, whose Revised Statute, Section 190, explicitly forbade such a situation.

Nevertheless, within a month after he returned to private law practice, Ballinger was not only being consulted by the Cunningham claimants (as well as by other coal, water, and land claimants), but was also writing letters to the new commissioner, his close friend, Fred Dennett, urging immediate clear-listing of the Cunningham claims. But though Dennett was agreeable, Secretary Garfield was not. The claims, therefore, lay dormant.

Following Taft's victory, Glavis was informed that the Cunningham forces were demanding of their senators and congressmen that they induce Taft to drop the troublesome Garfield from his Cabinet.

After Garfield was dropped—whether it was, as Taft said, "because I knew him," or because of the influence of the Cunningham claimants— Ballinger succeeded him and began to press Glavis to finish up the investigation. Implicit in the pressure was the request that the conclusion be favorable to the Cunningham claimants. But, as Dennett later observed, "Glavis has these coal cases on the brain," and though Glavis maintained he had uncovered important evidence of fraud, Secretary Ballinger insisted on ending the inquiry. Finally, an order came taking Glavis off the case. (The report of the man replacing him agreed with his belief that the Cunningham claims were fraudulent.) This led Glavis to the understandable conclusion that the sympathies of Ballinger—and Dennett, too —lay with private interests rather than with the public welfare.

Casting about for a compassionate ear, Glavis went to the Forest Service, since many of the claims in question were located in the Chugach National Forest. Glavis appealed to Pinchot for advice. Should he, he asked the Chief Forester, resign and make public the whole case with its charges of malfeasance against Ballinger and other officials in the Department of the Interior? Pinchot, exercising uncommon caution, advised Glavis to make a full report of his findings directly to President Taft.

Nine days later, armed with a fifty-page report (prepared with the aid of Assistant Forester Overton Price and Law Officer Alexander Shaw of the Forest Service) and a letter of introduction from Gifford Pinchot, Louis Glavis journeyed to Beverly, Massachusetts, where President Taft was enjoying golf and relaxation before embarking on his speaking tour of the West. Taft read Glavis' report. But after having waited in vain to be called into the executive presence, Glavis returned to Portland. Taft, meanwhile, consulted with his Attorney General, George Wickersham, and then informed Ballinger of the charges against him and directed him to prepare a statement of rebuttal, making it "as full as possible."

By this time, Taft's mildly negative estimate of Gifford Pinchot as a "transcendentalist" had progressed even beyond his being "a good deal of a radical and a good deal of a crank." Taft now felt a deep, burning resentment. To a caller at the Beverly cottage rash enough to defend the Chief Forester, Taft's voice rose in fury, denouncing Pinchot as a fanatic who had no knowledge of discipline or interdepartmental etiquette. He would, he said, not stand for such insubordination. On hearing the tone of her husband's voice, Mrs. Taft explained, rather needlessly, to Archie Butt, "Yes, he is angry. When he raises his voice like that he is always mad."

Taft was not the only one incensed by the actions of Glavis and Pinchot. In early September, while giving reporters an account of his activities, Ballinger lost his temper. "Incidentally," he told them, "I propose to kill some snakes." Ballinger's snake-killing weapon took the form of hundreds and hundreds of pages of documents, reports, records, exhibits, and other substantiating material, "all bearing on the case of Pinchot," that he and Oscar Lawler, an assistant attorney general in Interior, carried to Beverly with them on September 6.

When they arrived, Taft was on the golf links. But that night the three of them sat up "thrashing out the matter." After their departure Taft stayed up until three in the morning, digesting the records.

On September 13 Taft sent a letter to Ballinger exonerating him and authorizing him to fire Louis Glavis. The letter was also released to the press. Though this letter was of shattering importance as a catalytic agent, two other letters—*not* released to the press—were perhaps more revealing. A copy of the public letter of exoneration to Ballinger accompanied each. One Taft had addressed to "My Dear Gifford"—just then emerging from the seclusion of a Southern California island fishing trip—

pleading with him not to take up "Glavis's cause" and above all, not to resign. The other was written to Ballinger; in it, the President cautioned him to see to it that his subordinates in Interior would not "involve Mr. Pinchot in this matter and to rest silent in view of the complete acquittal they receive from my letter. Should it be necessary, as is not unlikely, to submit all this record and evidence to Congress, I shall be glad to have your authority and that of your subordinates to leave out of your answers any reference to Pinchot or the part he took in bringing Glavis's report to my attention."

Anticipating the dire consequences if Gifford Pinchot left his administration was a source of anguish to Taft. Such an event would signify just one thing to Republican politicians—conservative and progressive—and to the country as well: the old TR-Will Taft friendship was over, irrevocably over. Although Taft certainly did not want this to happen and publicly was still clinging to the old shibboleth—"meeting at the armory of six or seven thousand people, where I talked for an hour about the Roosevelt policies"—he had already begun to remark privately on the affinity between TR and Pinchot. They, he wrote Nellie, "sympathize much more than he and I can, for they both have more of a Socialist tendency."

After a brief conference with Pinchot in Salt Lake City, at the end of September, Taft lamented glumly in his daily wire to Nellie, "I don't know how long I shall be able to get on with him." To his brother Horace he betrayed even more despair. "I am convinced," he wrote, "that Pinchot with his fanaticism and his disappointment at my decision in the Ballinger case plans a coup by which I shall be compelled to dismiss him and he will be able to make out a martyrdom and try to raise opposition to me on Ballinger's account."

Despite his grave doubts, Taft continued to placate Pinchot in minor matters, hoping this would avoid a ruinous public controversy. At the same time, Louis Glavis, no longer an agent for the Department of the Interior but still a most determined man, wrote the story of his investigations and speculated as to what publication would be the best showcase.

By October, Taft was writing Nellie that "Pinchot has spread a virus against Ballinger widely, and has used the publicity department of his bureau for the purpose." And from Milford, Pennsylvania, from Grey Towers—a huge stone country house resembling a French château, the home of the Pinchots for thirty years—the virus was being directed to East Africa, six thousand miles away. In his dark-paneled study Gifford Pinchot and his house guest, James Garfield, composed a seventeen-page letter to TR, which assessed Taft's administration up to that time and gave their account of the Pinchot-Ballinger controversy. Though they never sent it—perhaps second thoughts prevailed—its opening gave some indication of their explosive feelings. "Not until now," they wrote, "have we felt like interfering with your hunting of African beasts by telling you anything about the beasts in this country who have been coming again into the open since you left."

By 1909, *Collier's Weekly* had a circulation of a half million and had eclipsed *McClure's* in its publication of the hard-hitting exposé article styled by TR as "muckraking."

The magazine, published by an Irish immigrant and former book sales-man, Peter F. Collier, but run by his son Robert and Norman Hapgood, had already unmasked the fraud and deception in patent medicines, in food and drugs, and in Congress, and had uncovered the social blackmail practiced by *Town Topics,* a scandal magazine.

In late September, Louis Glavis informed President Taft in an open letter that he planned to publish "the facts in my possession concerning which I firmly believe you have been misled." Because of their liberal crusading spirit, he chose *Collier's* as the perfect outlet for his charges against Ballinger and the Interior Department. Though he had already been offered three thousand dollars by another magazine, he was so eager to have *Collier's* publish his disclosures that he offered it to Hapgood "with the preliminary condition that nothing shall be paid for it." Such a proposition would have appealed to even a far less liberal editor than Hapgood. He read the article and accepted it.

In early November, as the President returned from his two months' tour of the West, advance copies of the November 13 issue of *Collier's* were released to the press. Its flamboyant cover displayed a large greedy corporate hand engulfing a mountain and its natural resources and the huge query: "ARE THE GUGGENHEIMS IN CHARGE OF THE DEPARTMENT OF THE INTERIOR?" Framed in a large red question mark was a picture of Richard Achilles Ballinger. Glavis' article, titled by Hapgood "The Whitewashing of Ballinger," was not quite as sensational as the manner in which it was presented. His account of his investigations was direct.

I assert that the Land Office ordered the Cunningham claims to patent, without due investigation, when Commissioner Ballinger knew they were under suspicion; that while in office Commissioner Ballinger urged Congress to pass a law which would validate fraudulent Alaskan claims; that shortly after resigning from office he became attorney for the Cunningham group and other Alaska claims. . . .

Ballinger, who had been reacting with increased irascibility to reporters and their persistent queries, now, understandably, became even more resentful. "The Glavis story is a tissue of falsehoods and insinuations," he declared heatedly.

The *Collier's* article stepped up the speculation in the daily papers as to whether Ballinger or Pinchot would be the first to leave the Taft administration and how the whole matter would affect the relationship between TR and Will Taft. Glavis himself, dwarfed by the personalities who assumed his cause, became such a nebulous figure that even his initials, "L. R.," were transformed by the newspapers; they referred to him variously as "L. T. Glavis," "R. L. Glavis," and, provocatively, "T. R. Glavis."

The December 18 issue of *Collier's Weekly* contained another article on the Ballinger case, "Can This Be Whitewashed Too?" Written by a lawyer-journalist, C. P. Connally, it traced political and financial machinations deeply involving Ballinger with the Cunningham claimants.

Both sides now demanded a congressional investigation of the charges. Ballinger was particularly anxious for such an action, specifying that an inquiry should include a complete probe, not only of the Department of the Interior, but also of Pinchot's Forest Service. What was more, "Secretary Ballinger," reported one paper with journalistic delight, "is preparing to carry the war into Africa."

But shortly before Congress authorized the formation of a Joint Congressional Committee, *Collier's* received some disquieting information. Payne Whitney, a former classmate and a friend of Rob Collier, disclosed to Collier that the Taft administration planned formidable revenge against what it considered a radical publication. The investigation would, by its preponderance of regular—*i.e.*, conservative—Republicans, chosen in the House by Speaker Cannon and in the Senate by Vice-President Sherman, exonerate Ballinger completely. Fortified by this exoneration, Ballinger would then institute a million-dollar libel suit against *Collier's*.

The success of this plan was all too possible, and an alarmed Rob Collier, together with Norman Hapgood, held a crucial strategy conference during the week of Christmas at the New York home of Gifford Pinchot's hunting companion, Henry L. Stimson, then a New York lawyer. Also present for consultation were Pinchot, his brother Amos, Jim Garfield, and George Wharton Pepper, another lawyer, who had been recommended to Pinchot by Stimson. Pepper, to Pinchot's "immediate satisfaction and ultimate regret," agreed to act as counsel for the Chief Forester.

Glavis and, through him, *Collier's* were in the most vulnerable position. As Hapgood pointed out, though *Collier's* had no standing before the

Joint Congressional Committee, Glavis did; and it would be proper for the publication to protect the interests of its contributor. It was also to *Collier's* interest that the committee should not exonerate Ballinger, for then he could not bring a libel suit. Thus, this vital question confronted the meeting: Who should be attorney for Glavis?

Though other individuals were proposed, Hapgood persistently favored one man—eventually retained at a fee of twenty-five thousand dollars plus expenses—a brilliant and controversial Boston attorney who had, in the past, investigated the practices of insurance companies, Boston utilities, and the New Haven Railroad: Louis D. Brandeis.

Following that Christmas-week meeting, Pinchot purposefully set about declaring his position in a speech, in the unlikely event that anyone might find his stand unclear. Because of a blizzard, his audience in the University Club in New York consisted of only a half-dozen friends. But the speech was, as he pointed out later, "more widely printed than any speech I had ever made."

Its extensive dissemination was understandable, for this speech vividly portrayed the sides of the conservation fight in the only colors Pinchot could distinguish: black and white. "There is," he said, "no other question before us that begins to be so important, or that will be so difficult to straddle, as the great question between special interest and equal opportunity, between the privileges of the few and the rights of the many, between government by men for human welfare and government by money for profit, between the men who stand for the Roosevelt policies and the men who stand against them."

It was not surprising, therefore, that the press, which had been a muted chorus of foreboding throughout the summer and fall, now trumpeted a blast of omniscience. "Practically the whole attention in political circles," wrote the New York *Journal of Commerce*, "is now centered upon the proposed Congressional Investigation of the doings of Secretary Ballinger. With but few exceptions members of Congress still in the city regard this investigation as of unusual significance because they think it is practically an investigation of the President himself." "Scent a TR cabal" read a front-page Washington *Post* story. Another paper made the same interpretation with pithy alliteration, viewing the conflict as "a tilt between Taft and Ted."

It was the opinion of hardened Washington reporters that the conservation controversy might have ended had Taft, in the style of the former White House occupant, simply "cracked the heads of both Ballinger and Pinchot together on the spot, and thrown them both out of the Government service."

But as Taft plaintively confided to Archie Butt, "I cannot do things that way. I will let them go on, and by and by the people will see who is right and who is wrong. There is no use trying to be William Howard Taft with Roosevelt's ways."

Before long, Taft began to share the conviction held not only by the press, but also by his closest associates and relatives, that there was, unquestionably, a "Back from Elba plot" to undermine his administration and restore TR to the presidency in 1912. However, as Archie Butt reported to his sister-in-law, Clara, "He does not believe that President Roosevelt will endorse such a thing, but the fact that Pinchot seems to be behind most of it gives the President great concern, for there is no doubt of the devotion of President Roosevelt to Pinchot and his belief in him."

And it gave Charles P. Taft great annoyance. "Personally, I am tired of Pinchot," he wrote succinctly to his brother Will.

The Chief Forester actually aroused the suspicions of Charles P. to an almost paranoid degree. The elder Taft had been approached for a donation of five thousand dollars to form a new association for the conservation of natural resources to be headed by ex-President Eliot of Harvard. Replying balefully that there were already too many conservation associations, Charles P. refused any donation. "It struck me," he wrote his brother in the White House, "that possibly the new association would be controlled by him [Pinchot] and aid in boosting him in his fight with Ballinger. . . . Another queer circumstance is, that Collier and Son who are running *Collier's Weekly*, are publishing and boosting President Eliot's book shelf idea. I do not mean to say that there is any combination between Collier and President Eliot and the attack on Ballinger, but after all, the combination looks a little peculiar."

A few days after Christmas, when both brothers were attending the marriage of their niece in New York, Charles P. again alluded to the situation. "Will," he said, "I am getting tired of this Forestry Bureau business, and I don't know but it would be a good thing to let Pinchot out!"

"I am beginning to think that is just what he wants to force me to do, and I will not do it," Will Taft replied. "If the whole contention is the result of some sort of conspiracy, Pinchot's dismissal would only bring about what they are trying to do, an open rupture between Roosevelt and myself, and I am determined if such a rupture is ever brought about that it shall not be through any action of mine. Theodore may not approve of all I have done and I don't expect him to do so, but I shall try not to do anything which he might regard as a challenge to him. No, Charlie, I am going to give Pinchot as much rope as he wants, and I think you will find that he will hang himself."

On the last day of 1909, Gifford Pinchot wrote his long-delayed letter to "Dear Theodore." "In my judgment," he wrote, "the tendency of the Administration thus far, taken as a whole, has been directly away from the Roosevelt policies." He didn't ascribe "deliberate bad faith" to Taft, but "a most surprising weakness and indecision." In analytic elaboration, Pinchot gave sixteen indications of Taft's abandonment of the Roosevelt policies. But a brief sentence at the beginning of the letter sounded Pinchot's real lament, anguished and heartfelt: "We have fallen back down the hill you led us up."

An oppressive holiday lull hovered between 1615 Rhode Island Avenue and 1600 Pennsylvania Avenue. The Tafts held a reception at the White House on New Year's Day, attended by fifty-five hundred people, among them Gifford Pinchot and his mother. "Taft spoke to me pleasantly," Pinchot recorded in his diary. "Wished me a Happy New Year, and I him."

The amenities of the season having been observed, the state of hostilities could resume. Taft, beset by his brothers, by members of his Cabinet, and by hardheaded Republican politicians to fire Pinchot, clung to the hope that he need not fire Pinchot and that the congressional investigation would reveal "just how lenient he has been toward Pinchot."

One criterion pointed to the right path: there must be nothing for which TR could reproach him. Although Taft was most apprehensive over TR's reaction to the conservation quarrel, the appraisal of each of his acts in terms of what TR would have done had become a source of mounting irritation. "I get rather tired," the President said testily, "hearing from his friends that I am not carrying out his policies."

Taft could not face quarrels—controversy—with equanimity. "He wants every man's approval and a row of any kind is repugnant to him." Consequently, in pursuing peace of mind, he grew pale and worried, snapped at his associates, and consumed salted almonds. By contrast, the Chief Forester was in the highest of high spirits, bounding from one lecture platform to another in propounding the conservation policies of Theodore Roosevelt. Conservation was receiving more publicity than it ever had, and so was Pinchot. The probability of being dismissed fazed him not at all; in many ways, it seemed a provocative prospect. "Maybe my head is coming off," he wrote a friend, "but if it does I shall try to be like a gentleman in the Arabian Nights whose most important remarks were made after decapitation."

While Pinchot had been on the West Coast, occupied with his speaking engagements, his assistants in the Forest Service, A. C. Shaw and Overton Price had aided Glavis with his *Collier's* articles. They had also given considerable information on the Cunningham claims and Ballinger's activities to *Collier's* and other magazines, and this resulted in a barrage of anti-Ballinger articles. "Technically," Pinchot admitted, "Price and Shaw were wrong. Without question they had instigated attacks on the Secretary of another Department and furnished the ammunition. But also without question they had taken their official lives in their hands in defense of the public interest."

Since the congressional investigation would most certainly reveal these facts, Pinchot determined, he said, to "lay all our cards on that table, of our own motion tell the whole truth, admit that Price and Shaw had been wrong, and so give no one a chance to uncover anything that could be held against us." So, immediately after the first of the year, he, with the help of his counsel, George Pepper, and his friend Harry Stimson, drafted a letter of justification to his chief, Secretary of Agriculture Wilson.

However, when Senator Jonathan Dolliver, Chairman of the Committee on Agriculture and Forestry, asked Pinchot to write him a letter on the Ballinger case, Pinchot, to the "dismay" of Stimson and Pepper, modified the letter to Wilson "in substance and form," as Pepper later wrote reproachfully, and sent it to Senator Dolliver. This action disregarded an executive order issued by President Taft to all department officials to maintain silence on the Ballinger case. The purpose of this "chloroform system" was to stop the flow of information from the Forest Service to publications hostile to Ballinger and the Taft administration.

On January 6, 1910, Pinchot's letter was handed to the clerk and read in the Senate. The senators—astounded at Pinchot's boldness in going over the head of his chief, over the head of the President himself, in order to appeal to the public—listened incredulously to the Chief Forester's defense of Price and Shaw, who, Pinchot wrote, "deliberately chose to risk their official position rather than permit what they believed to be the wrongful loss of public property," his sweeping vindication of Louis Glavis as the "most vigorous defender of the people's interest," and his assertion that Glavis was dismissed from government service because of President Taft's mistaken impression of the facts.

In conclusion, Pinchot generalized fleetingly on law and public interest, which, according to frequent accusations, he and TR viewed as incompatible.

While "the little bomb in the shape of a letter" was being read, a mass of documents accompanied by a message from President Taft lay on the desk of the Vice-President. They were all the papers on which Taft had based his exoneration of Ballinger; they also included the Glavis charges and the report of Attorney General Wickersham, in which the Attorney General had alluded to Glavis as suffering from "a species of megalomania."

"What is a Megalomaniac?" asked the Washington *Post* the next day. It answered its own query with the Funk and Wagnalls dictionary definition of a megalomaniac set inside a thick black-edged box at the head of a front-page column, captioned, "Pinchot Doomed, Rumor Asserts."

And, of course, Rumor was right. A furious Taft had called a Cabinet meeting after the reading of the Pinchot letter, which the President regarded "as a piece of insubordination almost unparalleled in the history of the government." Upon emerging, the Cabinet members were "mum as clams and painfully serious when Mr. Pinchot was mentioned."

For a day, Taft, haggard and careworn, looking "like a man almost ill," wrestled with the problem of Gifford Pinchot. "He is weighing Pinchot in the balance," Archie Butt wrote Clara, "but he is weighing also the consequences of his own act with Roosevelt. All else is nothing to him. I know it. I believe he loves Theodore Roosevelt, and a possible break with him or the possible charge of ingratitude on his part is what is writhing within him now. He can't say to his advisers, 'What will Roosevelt think?'"

By late afternoon of January 7, Taft had made his fateful decision and, several hours later, a White House messenger rang the bell at 1615 Rhode Island Avenue. Pinchot, on his way to a dinner party, casually holding a shining silk hat, his tall figure magnificent in evening dress, answered and was handed the letter he "half expected."

Bounding upstairs to the dining room, Pinchot waved the letter at his mother and exclaimed, "I'm fired."

Mrs. Pinchot's eyes flashed, her son recalled, "she threw back her head, flung one hand high above it, and answered with one word: 'Hurrah!'"

Mrs. Pinchot herself chronicled the event briefly in her diary. "Great rejoicing," she noted. "Lots of reporters."

On that same January day in 1910, TR and his party, with thirty porters and two hundred pounds of supplies, sailed down the White Nile to the Lado Enclave, on the Congo side of the Bahr el Jebel, about two degrees north of the equator. They were searching for a rare species of African heavy game; the square-mouthed rhinoceros, known more dramatically, but less accurately, as the white rhino. After ten days of inordinate heat and nights of malicious mosquitoes, TR shot two of the nine white rhinos that he and Kermit would eventually down, and discovered the rhinos were "not as white as they are painted."

On the seventeenth, a native runner arrived at the enclave with a cable from the Press Agency, informing TR that Pinchot had been dismissed and asking the former President for a statement. "Of course," TR wrote Cabot Lodge later that day, "I said nothing."

In addition to this letter to Cabot Lodge, the African postman—"a wild savage who runs stark naked with the mail"—also picked up another letter TR had written that day. It was to Gifford Pinchot, whose own long letter containing his charges that Taft had almost completely abandoned the Roosevelt policies TR wouldn't receive for yet another month. TR had written:

Dear Gifford:
We have just heard by special runner that you have been removed. I cannot believe it. I do not know any man in public life who has rendered quite the service you have rendered; and it seems to me absolutely impossible that there can be any truth in this statement. But of course it makes me very uneasy. Do write me, care of the American Embassy at Paris, just what the real situation is. I have only been able to follow things very imperfectly while out here. . . .

"Expecting a Roar from the Jungle." By De Mar, Philadelphia *Record*, January 10, 1910.

Nine

"A Perfectly
Frivolous Waste
of Time"

To observe that small events shape lives and that fate hangs on trifles may not be fresh reflections, but they do apply admirably to certain situations. One such situation was the manner in which the House membership on the congressional committee to conduct the Pinchot-Ballinger investigation would be determined by Representative John Dalzell's fixed habit of leaving the House chamber at precisely one o'clock each afternoon for a sandwich, coffee, and a piece of pie in the House restaurant.

Since the administration's primary aim in the investigation was to justify President Taft's support of Secretary Ballinger and his dismissal of Pinchot—or, in the language of the antiadministration men, "to whitewash Ballinger"—it was vital that those Republican members selected to sit on the Joint Committee be loyal, regular—that is, conservative—Republicans.

In the Senate, the Vice-President was authorized to name the committee members. It was confidently expected that "Sunny Jim" Sherman's choices would be staunch Taft men, and so they were.

In the House, the authorization was to go to Speaker Cannon. But on the same January day that Gifford Pinchot was dismissed as Chief Forester, a tough little fifty-year-old insurgent congressman from Nebraska, George W. Norris, determined to take that right of appointment from "Uncle Joe" and have the committee members named from the floor.

In order to do this it was necessary for him to be recognized by Representative Dalzell, who often occupied the chair for the Speaker. However, Norris knew he could not hope for recognition from the archconservative Dalzell; so, with his eye on the huge House clock, he waited for 1:00 P.M. and Dalzell's customary departure for lunch. As Dalzell moved down the aisle to the door, Norris quietly approached Representative Walter Smith of Iowa, substituting for Dalzell, and asked for two

123

minutes' floor time. Smith, a close friend of Norris', agreed. Norris took the floor and, from hastily prepared notes, declared that if the committee was to make a real investigation, one in which the American people would have confidence, the committee members would have to be selected by someone other than Speaker Cannon. He then proposed an amendment to the resolution calling for the appointment of a joint committee, which would delete the words "appointed by the Speaker" and substitute "elected by the House."

"Immediately," Norris recalled, "there was excitement in the House; everybody saw that if my motion prevailed there would be a real investigation, instead of a whitewash. There was a scurry at once to get everybody into the House to answer the roll call. . . ."

Despite the efforts of the regular Republicans, Norris' resolution carried, but by a slim margin: 149 to 146. (This was the beginning of the end for "Uncle Joe." In early March, 1910, Norris, with the aid of other Republican insurgents and Democrats, would complete the defanging of the Speaker by removing from Cannon the source of his power—the chairmanship of the House Rules Committee. In a bitter and remorseless three-day battle, Cannon, likened by Alice Longworth to an "old gray wolf at bay," was defeated.) The caucuses held by the three forces— regular Republicans, Democrats, and Republican insurgents—decided that the insurgents would name one committee member, the Democrats two, and the regular Republicans three.

The trio chosen by the regular Republicans was Samuel McCall of Massachusetts, Marlin E. Olmsted of Pennsylvania, and Edwin Denby of Michigan, who as Warren G. Harding's Secretary of the Navy would achieve notoriety in another conservation scandal, Teapot Dome. The House Democrats selected two uncommonly able men, James M. Graham of Illinois and Ollie M. James of Kentucky, whose obesity rivaled that of Will Taft, and for whom a special chair had to be installed in the committee room. That Judge E. H. Madison of Kansas represented the insurgents proved most significant. He wrote a masterly minority report of his own at the end of the investigation which greatly affected public opinion.

The Republican Senate members chosen to sit on the committee were Knute Nelson of Minnesota, who became chairman, Elihu Root of New York, Frank P. Flint of California, and George Sutherland of Utah. The Senate Democrats were Duncan Fletcher of Florida and Thomas Paynter of Kentucky, soon to be replaced by William E. Purcell of North Carolina.

Charles P. Taft's Cincinnati *Times-Star,* a newspaper the *Literary Digest* accurately described as "probably closer than any other to the Administration," declared "the personnel of the investigating Committee has pretty effectively downed all talk about Congressional 'whitewash' of the Secretary of the Interior." Nevertheless, it was no coincidence that the voting of the committee—composed of seven Republicans, four Democrats, and one insurgent—on all questions during the hearings had an immutable consistency: seven to five.

Though the legal and parliamentary technicalities involved in the preparation of the Pinchot-Ballinger investigation briefly obscured the political overtones for some of the participants, they didn't for all. "The situation," Pinchot's attorney, George Pepper, wrote his wife, "is not in the least degree a legal situation but wholly political. Nobody in this crowd understands it—but I seem to be the only one who is willing to admit this obvious fact."

To the rest of America, too, the significance was clear. Two weeks before the hearings began, the Cleveland *Press* published a cartoon graphically emphasizing the view held throughout the country. It showed President Taft and Secretary Ballinger cowering in bed and staring at each other in alarmed fright, both asking, "Did you see the same thing I did?" Outside the window, a huge familiar face hung in the dark sky, grinning balefully at them. It was composed of a large set of teeth, a pair of pince-nez, and a hat that could conceivably be either a Napoleonic tricorn or a Spanish-American War campaign hat. The caption read: "The Return from Elba."

Room 210, the largest in the Senate Office Building, was the scene of the Pinchot-Ballinger investigation. "The stage set is not elaborate," a reporter from *The Outlook* was to sum up at the hearing's conclusion. "The actors are not in good view of the spectators . . . the action often drags . . . nevertheless, a number of people have been attending the performance continuously, and at times there has not even been standing room."

Viewed in its entirety, it had the static, monotonous quality of a tableau. At the head of a long table at the far end of the room sat the committee chairman, Senator Knute Nelson, with his short pepper-and-salt beard, looking "like a prosperous Yankee farmer" instead of a Norwegian immigrant turned Minnesota politician. On Senator Nelson's left sat the six Senate committee members; on his right, the six House members. At the other end of the table was a raised oak chair, on which thirty-three witnesses sat in turn, few finding either comfort or satisfaction in their tenure there. On each side of the witness chair sat the counsel. Chief among them were George W. Pepper, tall and urbane, with a distaste for the direct appeals to the press and public engaged in by his client, Gifford Pinchot, and Louis Brandeis, the attorney for Glavis. Early in the hearings Secretary Ballinger and the Interior Department had not been represented by counsel, but on February 5, after a few days of dispassionate testimony by Louis Glavis, the committee suggested that such counsel be engaged.

The choice, however, proved to be unfortunate. Colonel John J. Vertrees, though a personal friend of President Taft's, was a heavy-handed lawyer from Nashville, "rather prone to epithet" and in the habit of addressing the committee "as he would a rural jury in Tennessee." Ill-equipped for the task, Vertrees was further handicapped by having Louis Dembitz Brandeis, one of the cleverest lawyers in the United States, as his opposing counsel.

Lean, with shoulders that displayed the stoop of a very tall man, Brandeis was incisive of speech and imperturbable in manner, with dark eyes that shone brilliantly behind his pince-nez, and his clean-shaven features had not yet achieved that Lincolnesque grandeur of his later years. He was a twentieth-century urban man whose mind worked with ease, speed, and implacability, providing a vivid contrast to Colonel Vertrees, older in years, narrower in outlook, and considerably slower in understanding. A rangy lawyer of another era, Vertrees had a drooping mustache startlingly similar to Gifford Pinchot's and he possessed the manner of "a fire-eating Southerner," a characteristic which became increasingly conspicuous in the course of the forty-six days of hearings.

For each of those days a large and vocally partisan audience— overwhelmingly feminine—packed Room 210. They awaited some electrifying piece of evidence that would reveal, according to individual allegiance, either that a Machiavellian Pinchot and Garfield were conspiring through Glavis to bring about the ruin of the Taft administration so that TR could return in 1912, or that Ballinger with President Taft's support had attempted to destroy the Roosevelt-Pinchot conservation policy. Flaunting their loyalties with hissing and applause, they reacted toward the proceedings, George Pepper recalled, like "rooters at a football game."

Profound and unequivocal partisanship characterized the Pinchot-Ballinger investigation. It was a rare individual who attended the hearings in any capacity who did not owe allegiance to one of the contesting sides. Spirited encounters resulted from the presence on most days of Mrs. Richard Ballinger and her loyal friends, who sat in the front row near the press table, and of Mrs. James Pinchot, the seventy-two-year-old mother of the former Chief Forester, accompanied by equally loyal friends, who

sat directly in back of the Ballinger party. Loud disparaging comments
—meant to be overheard and resented by those in the opposing group—
were made by the ladies of both parties. On one day, within fifteen
minutes of each other, Chairman Nelson received a complaint from a
friend of Mrs. Ballinger's that the Secretary's wife found remarks made
by those in Mrs. Pinchot's entourage "perfectly disgusting and dreadfully
annoying" and a charge from a Pinchot adherent that comments made by
the Ballinger ladies were "abhorrent and annoying" to Mrs. Pinchot.

Nor was the press table removed from the prevailing partisan spirit:
the Associated Press, according to Gifford Pinchot, was proadministra-
tion, while the United Press "was with us."

The magazines were more one-sided. "Most of the magazine writers
will never see anything but Roosevelt," Will Taft told Archie Butt, "and
will never approve of any methods except those of Roosevelt." Whether
the national magazines were driven simply by their enthusiasm for TR or
by their outrage at Taft's desire to raise second-class mailing rates, the
majority *were* antiadministration.

The committee itself radiated bias; its chairman, Knute Nelson, exhibited his pro-Taft partiality with undeviating consistency. His intractable
silence when it was obvious that Colonel Vertrees or a pro-Ballinger
witness should be called to account for some transgression was only
equaled by the ferocity of his attacks on Brandeis and all the pro-Pinchot
witnesses. The other Republican committee members shared, in varying degrees, Senator Nelson's partisanship. Similarly, the committee
Democrats—Senators Fletcher and Purcell and Congressmen Graham and
James—vigorously supported the Pinchot side, James in an acute and
witty manner, and Graham through artfully judicial questions. Judge
Madison, the insurgent House Republican, alone exemplified determined
objectivity. He was antiadministration, too, but only, in each instance,
after judicial consideration.

A cold that Will Taft contracted at the Requiem Mass for the late
Leopold II of Belgium hung on; his enormous bulk was unable to resist
"any microbe, however small." Tired and pessimistic, he viewed the political landscape with many misgivings. Next time it would be impossible to
elect a conservative man to the presidency, he told Senator Bourne on the
day Louis Glavis began to testify before the committee. The drift of the
country, he said, was toward radicalism. But he was determined not to
play politics. He would ignore radicals—to whom he referred as "this
element." "I am going ahead as if there were no second term," he declared.

Louis Glavis' testimony was presented over a period of three weeks, and it was pronounced by old Mrs. Pinchot to be "admirably given." Undeniably, Glavis made an excellent impression. "Cool, self-possessed," wrote a reporter, "modest in demeanor, ready with his answers and brief in stating them, he did not present in person the figure of a suspicious egotist, ambitious megalomaniac as he has been pictured." Throughout cross-examination by a blatantly sarcastic Vertrees, Glavis, his voice low and clear in spite of his Western drawl, held firmly to the charges against Ballinger he had made to President Taft. Even Glavis' own counsel was impressed. "I have never seen his equal," Brandeis wrote his brother, "*Der junge Mensch* is only 26."

But the relationship between Gifford Pinchot and *his* counsel, George Pepper, held irreconcilable differences. "The newspapers at the press table were never part of the audience to which George spoke," Pinchot complained. "After he had made an important point and got it in the record, it never occurred to him that a minute or two would be well spent in getting that point to the general public through the press. Again and again I had to supplement George's failure to connect with the larger audience by making a public statement of my own, and again and again George, horror-stricken, threatened to resign." Perhaps because of what his counsel called "grandstanding," the testimony of Gifford Pinchot, who followed Glavis in the witness chair, was, as he himself admitted, "less impressively accurate than Glavis's." Indeed, when Vertrees asked him his age, Pinchot replied, "Forty-four or forty-five."

Stripped of its emotional and political aspects, the Pinchot-Ballinger controversy consisted of a difference in philosophy as to conservation procedures and stemmed from the star-crossed ineptitude of the Taft administration. But few disputes of such national prominence can be laid to rest with so simple a verdict. A situation that might erupt into a battle between two old friends could not be easily resisted. "Pinchot was regarded as in some sense representing Theodore Roosevelt's administration," George Pepper wrote, "and both newspapermen and spectators were eager to have the proceeding develop into a sensational controversy between President Taft and his predecessor." It was left to Colonel Vertrees to express this attitude in the hearings. In his opening defense of Ballinger—after a derisive summary of the TR-Pinchot conservation policies and a pejorative description of Gifford Pinchot ("vain and flattered," "self-exaggerated," harboring a "spirit of resentment and revenge")— Vertrees declaimed, "Here was the reign of men, March 4, 1909, there came the reign of law." Though this disparagement was ostensibly directed at Pinchot and Garfield, some members of the committee and many reporters and other spectators interpreted it as a fling at TR.

So the promise of melodramatic conflict and of sensational disclosures held the audience captive through weeks of tedious technical testimony on reclamation by former Secretary of the Interior James R. Garfield and officers of the Forest Service. Even wearisome readings of complicated documents, heavy with figures and diagrams, failed to discourage attendance. Occasionally, there would be some reward: the excitement of a bitter clash between Brandeis and Chairman Nelson, the numerous instances of Elihu Root's Olympian scorn with the whole proceeding. "Let us get on with the testimony," he would implore. "What we want, Mr. Brandeis, is to go on with extraordinary swiftness." "I think you are wasting our time." So many areas into which Mr. Brandeis probed were, according to Senator Root, "a perfectly frivolous waste of time." As the investigation wore on, the power of his anguish reached new heights of expression. "We've been here forty days, and it is time the children of Israel should get out of the wilderness." At no time, however, did he reveal any indication of his real concern. The Pinchot-Ballinger controversy was, he had written Harry Stimson a few months earlier, "pregnant with immense evil for the Administration and the Republican Party. It is difficult for me to see how it can be averted, but I hope it may, and I shall do all I can to help in doing so."

But despite this resolve, Root could not keep the annoying Brandeis from harping on one request, day after day after day. "Mr. Chairman, I would like to renew my daily complaint in reference to the papers not produced which have been called for. I suggest that the committee address a special communication calling for the production of the papers not yet delivered."

What were these mysterious papers that Brandeis called for with such persistence? President Taft had been requested by Congress to send to the committee "any reports, statements, or documents upon which he acted in reaching his conclusions" on the charges against Ballinger by Glavis. Voluminous records and documents, as well as the elaborate summary and opinion on the case drawn up by Attorney General George W. Wickersham and dated September 11, had been sent.

But one document which Brandeis had reason to believe existed was not among them. That document—the Lawler memorandum—together with the date on the Wickersham report was to attach a stigma to the Taft administration from which it would never recover.

When Taft's letter of exoneration of Ballinger was made public, Frederick Kerby, a twenty-four-year-old stenographer in the Interior Department, told a friend of his, Hugh Brown, also in the Interior Department, "Just between you, me and the gatepost, we wrote that letter in

Ballinger's office." Shortly after, Brown confided this information to his former chief, James R. Garfield. Consequently, one evening in mid-February, 1910, Kerby went to the Rhode Island Avenue home of Gifford Pinchot and there, in the presence of Pinchot, Garfield, and Louis Brandeis, revealed in an astonishing story the circumstances surrounding the Lawler memorandum.

When Secretary Ballinger had journeyed to Beverly in early September of the previous year to defend himself and his associates from the Glavis charges, he had been accompanied by a friend and subordinate, Oscar Lawler, Assistant Attorney General attached to the Interior Department. Upon their return to Washington four days later, Lawler moved into Ballinger's private office and began dictating to Kerby and another stenographer a number of drafts of a letter exonerating Ballinger. "It was obvious from the way Lawler dictated the letter," Kerby later wrote in his statement to the press, "what it was intended to be. Moreover there was no attempt at concealment. The letter began: 'Sir,' it referred to Ballinger as 'you' in each case and the personal pronoun 'I' was used throughout. From the context the 'I' could be no other than Taft himself." Unquestionably, Kerby felt, "Lawler was *drafting* a letter for Taft's *signature reviewing the Glavis charges and exonerating the Sec'y.*"

After completing a few drafts, Lawler held a long conference with his colleagues in the Interior Department, prominent among whom was the subject of the exoneration, Richard A. Ballinger. "The conference cut the draft to pieces with criticisms and suggestions," Kerby wrote, "and the whole thing was revamped. By night we were ready to make the final draft that was to be submitted to the president at Beverly." One original and three copies of the letter were prepared, addressed to Ballinger and written in the first person, a person who was quite clearly the President of the United States. It had been typed triple-space, presumably so Taft might make additions or deletions. Lawler placed the original and one copy in his briefcase; then, before he left that night, he supervised a crucial chore, disposing of the rough drafts. Since "it wouldn't be safe," he told the stenographers, "to trust them to the wastebasket," the drafts were placed in a closed grate in one of the offices and set afire. "The papers blazed up and burned furiously," Kerby wrote. "We stood around the fireplace and watched the smoke curl around the pages and the fire lick up line after line of typewriting. We didn't leave until every bit of paper had been consumed and the drafts were reduced to an unrecognizable mass of black ashes."

Then Lawler, briefcase in hand, caught the Owl Express to New York, changing there for a train to Beverly.

It was Brandeis' hope that he could force the administration to produce a copy of the Lawler draft without having to call Kerby as a witness. Having a wife, baby, and mother to support, and ambivalent loyalties to rationalize, Kerby didn't want to testify. Although he was promised a job by the Scripps-McRae News Association if he would make a statement for the press, he still resisted. So when the fiercely defensive Secretary Ballinger came to the stand on April 29, Brandeis set out to expose Lawler's role in the preparation of the Taft letter of exoneration.

"I hope," wrote Horace Taft to his brother in the White House, "that Ballinger will keep his head level when he testifies." But this was a vain hope, for Richard Ballinger was high-strung, and the effects of his battle with Gifford Pinchot were evident even when he was being questioned by Colonel Vertrees. "Frequently," wrote a reporter, "when some phrase in the question of his own very friendly counsel brought to his mind some grievance, then, with voice raised and with face flushed and with shaking arm, he burst out with angry speech." His attitude toward Brandeis blended fright and belligerence, and he regarded every question by the opposing counsel as an attack. Often he would ask the stenographer to repeat a question, "so that it might be rid of Mr. Brandeis's intonations."

The intensity of Ballinger's feelings was evident, and the possibility of his breaking down completely led some spectators to breathe a sigh of relief when one crisis or another had passed. Although none of this emotionalism reflected on his official integrity, it nevertheless left a bad impression on the public. Of all Ballinger's erratic conduct in the witness chair, the most damaging was his obvious evasiveness.

"Now, why," Brandeis asked him, "did Mr. Lawler go to Beverly?"

"At the request of the President," Ballinger answered.

"Why did he go?" Brandeis persisted.

"I decline to state any conversation with the President in connection with the matter."

"I did not ask you to state any conversation because it has been agreed that no conversation with the President should be stated here," Brandeis responded. "What did Mr. Lawler take with him when he went to Beverly the latter part of the week?"

"A grip," Ballinger said, "with some clothes in it. I do not know what else he took."

"You know that he did have something else?"

"And some records," the Secretary replied reluctantly. "I know that he had other things; yes."

"What were they particularly, bearing on the Glavis-Pinchot controversy?"

"He had some records of the case or memoranda."

"What?" asked Brandeis.

"I cannot definitely define just what he had in his portfolio or what he took with him," Ballinger answered stubbornly.

Aggressively, implacably, Brandeis pursued his line of questioning and Ballinger—red-faced and with vehemently angry voice—in turn, denounced, denied, and indulged in patent circumlocutions. Finally, driven into a corner by Brandeis' probing, Ballinger admitted, painfully, unwillingly, to Lawler's having transported to Beverly "a sort of résumé of the facts as set forth in the records," and that he himself "went over his memorandum." Nevertheless, the Secretary insisted, "I know nothing about the copy or copies of that memorandum."

Ballinger's heated denials of "any specific knowledge" of the Lawler memorandum were supported by Lawler and Attorney General Wickersham, who maintained that they had no copies of the paper. In addition, a committee ruling was passed, by the customary seven-to-five division, that directed the members not to call on President Taft for information on the Lawler draft. It was made increasingly clear that the document could not possibly be produced without an effective catalyst.

Frederick Kerby therefore came to a decisive conclusion. After a long consultation with his wife, he dictated to two executives of the news association a lengthy detailed statement concerning the preparation of the Lawler letter. It was published on Saturday, May 14, 1910. Its specific detail had the inescapable ring of truth. It included an explicit physical description of the Lawler final draft (typed on a Number Three model Monarch typewriter on Crane twenty-four-pound Bond paper and held together at the upper left corner with a McGill fastener), disclosures of Ballinger's covert activity in his own exoneration, and an account of the furtive midnight burning of the rough drafts.

Immediately upon seeing the story, a highly agitated Ballinger rushed to the White House, only to learn that the President was playing golf at Chevy Chase. Prodded by Ballinger, Fred Carpenter, the President's secretary, called the clubhouse and told General Clarence Edwards, one of his golf partners, what had occurred. When Edwards returned to the President on the links and repeated Kerby's story, "Mr. Taft declared at once and with emphasis that he didn't know anything about it," and went right on with his game. (His game for Saturday, however, had been ruined, he complained the next day, "for I could not put my mind on it. I was thinking about that damned scoundrelly stenographer who sold himself to betray the private correspondence of the man he was working for. It would have been bad enough had his affidavit contained the truth, but when it consisted of a lie, or to say the least a perversion of the facts, it seems to me that there was no excuse for his offense. However, I got him off my mind by ordering Ballinger to dismiss him today, and so with a clean conscience I can buckle down to this game. The beauty of golf to me is that you cannot play if you permit yourself to think of anything else.")

Armed with the President's denial, Ballinger released the following statement:

With reference to the published affidavit of F. W. Kerby, the stenographer in the office of the Secretary of the Interior, to the effect that the President's letter of September 13, 1909, exonerating Secretary Ballinger was substantially prepared for the President's signature by Assistant Attorney General Lawler, it was said at the White House today that there is absolutely no foundation for any such statement. The President dictated his letter personally as the result of his own investigation of the record and in consideration of documents and papers in his possession at the time and upon the general report to him.

On that same afternoon, unknown to Ballinger and President Taft, Attorney General Wickersham, after reading the Kerby revelations, dispatched a newly discovered copy of the Lawler memorandum to the committee. A letter accompanying it offered the somewhat weak explanation that "it seems to have been overlooked in collecting papers in answer to your previous communications."

It was all awkward, undeniable, embarrassing. Sometime later, Taft "volunteered" an explanation of the incident to reporter O. K. Davis which illustrated, Davis thought, "the rather easy way in which he sometimes took matters that were liable to be of great importance." Taft explained that, when reached at the golf course, "he had just plain forgotten all about the memorandum," and that same night when Colonel Vertrees came to the White House to find out what to do, "he [Taft] had to go back over the events of the time when it was written, step by step, before he got it, it had passed so thoroughly out of his mind."

For the unfortunate Taft administration, the episode of the Lawler memorandum was only one of what TR's Attorney General, Charles J. Bonaparte, was to call "the most notable unbroken succession of colossal blunders known in American politics." For at the same time that Brandeis fished for conclusive evidence on the Lawler memorandum, he was also on the trail of another related administration skeleton.

When Congress had asked the President for all the papers on which he had based his dismissal of Glavis and his exoneration of Ballinger, Taft had sent the Wickersham "Summary and Report." This bulky mass of papers consisted of the Glavis charges, the Ballinger defense, maps, technical data, and memoranda—documents of all sorts—plus Attorney General Wickersham's thorough, carefully prepared summary and opinion of it. It comprised 717 pages in all, more than five hundred thousand words.

What struck Louis Brandeis as peculiar was that the "Summary and Report" was dated September 11, 1909. In order for that date to have been valid, Wickersham, who had been given all the material in the case on September 6, would have had to study and absorb all its complex technical matter, summarize it, and write a detailed opinion of the whole, in addition to performing his many other duties as Attorney General, in a period of five days. A most remarkable feat!

Moreover, it also seemed highly improbable that Taft could have "dictated his letter [of exoneration] personally as the result of his own investigations of the record and in consideration of documents and papers in his possession at the time and upon the general report to him" in the two days between the eleventh and the thirteenth. This was particularly hard to believe, since Brandeis discovered that, on the two days in question President Taft had also played golf, attended the Sonderclasse yacht races and presented the Taft cup, received foreign visitors (among them, the grandson of the Mikado), reviewed the Beverly firemen, prepared a speech he was to deliver before the Boston Chamber of Commerce, and readied himself for his Western trip.

Brandeis' deduction that Wickersham's report was actually written several months *after* September 11 and predated was verified when he came upon an incredibly wonderful error in the report itself. Wickersham, in summing up his opinion, "undertook to answer a charge which had not been made in any way by Mr. Glavis in his letter to the President, which had not been answered by Secretary Ballinger or by Mssrs Schwartz or Dennett or Pierce in their answers, but which had appeared in a statement by Mr. Glavis two months later, namely, the statement which was published in *Collier's* of November 13th."

Two such severe blows to the integrity of his administration as the Kerby revelations and the predating of the Wickersham report could not be disregarded by Will Taft; he hurriedly sent off a letter of explanation to Committee Chairman Nelson.

In it, he wrote that, after studying the records, he had decided there was no basis for the charges against Ballinger and he had said to Oscar Lawler, "I was very anxious to write a full statement of the case and set out the reasons for my decision, but . . . the time for my departure on a long western trip, occupying two months, was just one week from that day; . . . I had some six or seven set speeches to deliver at the beginning of that journey, and I could not give the time to the preparation of such a detailed statement and opinion as I would like to render in the matter." Will Taft's sheer ingenuousness in this situation was demonstrated in this artless admission to Chairman Nelson: "I therefore requested Mr. Lawler to prepare an opinion as if he were President."

Lawler's draft, the President went on, "contained references to the evidence which were useful, but its criticism of Mr. Pinchot and Mr. Glavis I did not think it proper or wise to adopt. I only used a few paragraphs from it containing merely general statements."

As for the date on the Wickersham report: The Attorney General had given him an oral analysis of the record and the conclusions at which he had arrived in studying the record. "I was very sorry not to be able to embody this analysis in my opinion," the letter continued, "but time did not permit. I therefore directed him to embody in a written statement such analysis and conclusions as he had given me, file it with the record, and date it prior to the date of my opinion, so as to show that my decision was fortified by his summary of the evidence and his conclusion therefrom."

Senator Root, frenetically impatient throughout the investigation, now stormed in outrage. "We are not here to investigate the President of the United States! We are here to investigate the Department of the Interior. Counsel has been endeavoring assiduously and not altogether ingenuously to lead the investigation into a trial of the President."

But Elihu Root, with his air of irrefutable hardheaded wisdom, erred. Though not on trial in *fact*, William Howard Taft was, in effect, to be tried in the minds of the American electorate; and the verdict would not be kind, nor even accurate. Neither ghostwriting nor predating of documents were in themselves unusual procedures in government. "It was the kind of thing done continually by presidents," editorialized one magazine, "whether of a railway company or of the United States." And the President had quite accurately pointed out that he had used only a small portion of Lawler's draft. Nevertheless, with a curious ethical insensitivity, he had employed Oscar Lawler to ghostwrite the exoneration of Lawler's own official superior. "Why," editorial opinion asked, "in the name of common sense, was the production of the Lawler document—even the acknowledgement that there was such a thing—resisted inch by inch . . . ?" Similarly, it was not the predating, simply as a matter of form, that troubled anyone; it was the use made of the predating—to give the impression that Taft's decision to exonerate Ballinger was based on a study of an elaborate summary and opinion rather than on rough notes and conversation.

The furtiveness, the attempt to cover up, made a commonplace appear a conspiracy. Moreover, for the legalistically proper Will Taft to have been involved in such a transaction was a shattering disillusionment. But in spite of a nationwide criticism of President Taft, many in Washington agreed with Iowa Republican Henry C. Wallace, who said, "If you put Taft and a trap on a section of land in the night, and wanted to find him, you would simply need to go to that part of the square mile where the trap was located and you would find him in it."

Louis Brandeis himself had been shocked by what he had uncovered. "It was the lying that did it," he told Pinchot years later. "If they had brazenly admitted everything and justified it on the ground that Ballinger was at least doing what he thought best, we should not have had a chance."

It all added an emotional burden on a bitter, depressed Will Taft. For he had his personal anguish, too. "No one knows how he suffers over his wife's illness," Archie Butt recorded. "He bears up beautifully under it, but as the weeks go by and there does not seem to be any permanent improvement, his hope sinks pretty low at times." One evening in late April, Archie came upon what he felt was "as lonely a picture as I have ever seen. . . . They were sitting together on the long sofa in the Blue Room, he asleep and she very wan and pale in appearance."

A trip to Cincinnati in early May, 1910, had shocked Archie. It was sad "to see the little enthusiasm shown on his [Taft's] arrival at his old city the first time since his inauguration." This tepid welcome, however, was, Archie felt, "compensated for by the warmth of reception he received from people of his own social class."

Returning after a visit to St. Louis, the President made a fifteen-minute stop at Cincinnati, where his brother Charlie waited at the depot to advise him to fire Ballinger, a recommendation Will Taft firmly resisted. He was, he said, determined "to take no action in the matter as long as nothing is proved against him."

With a mood "black and pathetic," he reacted to the humiliations brought on by the investigation. "For a long time," he said on the same day he wrote his letter of explanation to the committee, "I did not believe the reports that the whole trouble is the outcome of a well-organized conspiracy on the part of Garfield and Pinchot to discredit my administration but I am beginning to believe it to be true. I have tried to have this investigation impartial and conducted on legal lines, but I am to be forced to enter the fight, and if I do, I shall make public such facts as will utterly annihilate Garfield and those who are behind this matter."

But utter annihilation was not Will Taft's kind of strategy; rather, it was considered a predilection of Theodore Roosevelt's. Taft observed of him one day, wistfully, "You know, you hear now that he is not unlike Napoleon and it is becoming popular to speak of him in comparison to Napoleon." Will Taft was also the subject of comparison. A similarity had been seen between him and the hapless Washington baseball team. "He, too," *Harper's Weekly* observed sadly, "has not had all the luck."

Producing a report of the committee's findings should have been a simple task. It was, after all, a foregone conclusion that the Republicans would find Ballinger innocent of everything and the Democrats would find him guilty of everything. However, a strong suspicion based on durable political precedent indicated the Republican majority did not wish to issue their report until after the fall congressional election, for their defense of Ballinger would hardly enhance their already dwindling prospects.

So a committee meeting, held in Minneapolis in September, 1910, was attended by only three of its Republican members: Nelson, Sutherland, and McCall. Senator Nelson undertook to handle the awkward situation of delaying the committee's action with a round of congenial entertainment. One day he escorted the visiting committee members to a fair in St. Paul; the next, he offered a trip to an old soldier's home. Nevertheless, the four Democrats and one insurgent rebelled, insisting that a meeting be held.

Only Nelson appeared at the hotel meeting room, where the Democrats and Judge Madison proceeded to enter resolutions to have Secretary Ballinger removed as an unfaithful public servant and the Glavis charges sustained. At this point Senator Nelson departed for the men's room. Shortly afterward, and presumably from there, he sent a message adjourning the meeting.

Consequently, the Democratic minority issued their report, gleefully anticipating that it would embarrass the Republicans. Highly critical of President Taft and the Interior Department, the report concluded "that Mr. Ballinger has not been true to the trust reposed in him as Secretary of the Interior, and that he should be requested by the proper authority to resign his office as Secretary of the Interior." As for Gifford Pinchot, the report declared him "a man of high character, of fine honor, of stainless integrity and of patriotic purpose," and pointed out that "he dared to be insubordinate, if such he was, in the interest of his country."

In December, a month after the Republican election disaster, the Republican majority of the committee finally issued their report. "Neither any fact proved," it read, "nor all the facts put together exhibit Mr. Ballinger as being anything but a competent and honorable gentleman, honestly and faithfully performing the duties of his high office with an eye single to the public interest." On the other hand, Gifford Pinchot, it declared, "had not always been considerate in his dealing with other public officials" and he "could at times assume a threatening attitude."

Judge Madison, the Republican insurgent, did not sign either the Republican or the Democratic report; instead, he issued his own, which Gifford Pinchot, in a commendable attempt at objectivity, regarded as "the least partisan as well as the ablest of the three."

After a painstaking summary of the charges, the testimony of the witnesses of both sides, and the evidence, Judge Madison stated that in his opinion the charges of Glavis and Pinchot should be sustained, and that Ballinger "has not shown himself to be that character of friend to the policy of conservation of our natural resources that the man should be who occupies the important post of Secretary of the Interior in our Government, and he should not be retained in that office."

Madison did not dwell (nor did, of course, the Republican report) on the embarrassing subjects of the Lawler memorandum and the predating of the Wickersham report. But these were major elements, in the view of the general public. The Providence *Journal* listed the two real contentions of Brandeis: that "(1) Mr. Ballinger is unfitted [*sic*] to exercise to public advantage the peculiar trusteeship for which Mr. Taft selected him, and (2) that, in order to sustain him, the administration has pursued methods which are palpably disingenuous, not to say unworthy." It was the general opinion of the American people that both these contentions had been proved.

But months before these final reports, another report—a verbal one, in March, 1910—caused Will Taft to suffer the greatest uneasiness. "He was rather thoughtful," Archie Butt noticed, "all the afternoon after he learned that Mr. Roosevelt had sent for Pinchot to join him in Europe." Though Archie comforted the President with the conjecture that Pinchot was going to see TR uninvited, Taft wasn't convinced.

His apprehensions were justified. After learning of Pinchot's dismissal, TR had written the former Chief Forester that since he felt it was ungracious for an ex-President to criticize his successor, he would remain silent for the time being. "But," he had added, "I do wish I could see you. Is there any chance of your meeting me in Europe?"

It was not too much to ask of Gifford Pinchot. As the investigation continued in Washington, a very tall, unusually lean gentleman, with a distinctive dark, drooping mustache and deep, zealous eyes, journeyed to New York and boarded the liner *President Grant*. According to the passenger list, he was "Gaylord Smith." He was bound for Porto Maurizio on the Italian Riviera to have a reunion with an old friend.

Part III Renominated by Europe

Ten   "Viva Roosevelts!"

At the point in the Sudan where the Blue Nile and the White Nile intersect lies Khartoum, a city of turbulent political activities. The Mahdi, a Moslem messiah, and his followers, in their mission to free the Sudanese people from those they considered their oppressors—the Anglo-Egyptian government—had besieged the city for ten months and, upon capturing it, had killed its defender, General Charles Gordon, and massacred his men.

A quarter century had passed since that event, but the city—although rebuilt—still presented a scene of political unrest in 1910. And in early March of that year, this was unusually so. Egyptian nationalists in their red tarbooshes raged against British rule, while British civil administrators and army officers sat over whiskey and sodas in the seclusion of their white Anglo-European clubs, displaying what an eminent visitor was to call "an uncomfortable flabbiness in Egyptian matters." Added to these normal conditions were great crowds of foreigners, Americans and Europeans, who had suddenly descended on the city, filling its hotels, lining its streets. Many waved banners reading "Welcome Teddy!" American flags flew from numerous buildings, and bunting appeared up and down Khartoum's streets.

Besides the throngs of tourists, newspaper correspondents were also swarming into Khartoum at a startling rate, all determined to be the first to interview Theodore Roosevelt on his arrival. TR had ended his eleven-month African expedition at the end of February by shooting a giant bull eland in the Belgian Congo. He was now steaming down the Nile, "passing through stratum after stratum of savagery and semi-civilization," toward Khartoum and his re-entry into a particularly savage stratum of civilization: politics.

Cabot Lodge had admonished TR that some of the newspapermen "will be very hostile to Taft and will try to rouse your indignation against him

141

by what they say. They will try to get you to say things. I think it is of
the first importance that you should say absolutely nothing about American politics before you get home."

The reporters, not content to wait in Khartoum for TR to appear,
chartered launches and steamboats at "fabulous charges" and lay in wait
all along the river. "Ex-President Roosevelt," exclaimed the headline of
the London *Daily Mail,* "is now becoming the hunted instead of the
hunter!" The *Pasha,* a battered old steamer with broken paddles, chartered by Cal O'Laughlin of the Chicago *Tribune,* strove heroically to
compete with the *Cairo,* the "fastest ship on the Upper Nile," chartered
by rival reporters who, according to O'Laughlin, were impeded by "overconfidence and lying up nights." One hundred miles above Khartoum,
while the *Cairo* stopped to take on wood for fuel, the *Pasha* lumbered
past it. Consequently, its passengers were the first to sight the huge stern
wheel of the Sudanese government steamer *Dal,* carrying the Roosevelt
party and towing a barge loaded with giant elands and Mrs. Gray's water-
bucks.

Looking tanned and fit, TR greeted them cheerfully. He was helmeted,
dressed in a khaki suit, knee-high pigskin boots, and a gray flannel shirt,
and, apparently to dignify the occasion of his entering the great world
once again, he sported a green tie. To the questions with which he was
bombarded—What about Pinchot? What did he think of the Payne-
Aldrich Tariff Act? What had he to say about Taft's first year in office?
What about 1912?—TR had a remarkably un-TR-like, all-inclusive answer, a model of circumspection. "I have nothing to say and will have
nothing to say on American or foreign political questions or any phase or
incident thereof. I will give no interviews, and anything purporting to be
in the nature of an interview with me can be accepted as false as soon as it
appears. This applies to our entire stay in Europe."

Upon arriving in Khartoum, TR was received enthusiastically by Rudolf von Slatin, the right-hand man of absent Governor General Reginald
Wingate and a legendary figure in his own right. During Slatin Pasha's
ceremonious welcome, it was observed, TR kept looking about Khartoum in every direction and, at a break in the amenities, he was heard to
inquire of an official, "Where's the railroad station?"

As soon as he could escape his admirers, TR—with Kermit—went
directly to the railway station to meet Edith Roosevelt and eighteen-year-
old Ethel, who had arrived by train from Alexandria at about five thirty
that afternoon for "the happiest of meetings." TR had been "dreadfully
homesick for Mrs. Roosevelt," he wrote Cecil Spring-Rice months before. "Catch me ever leaving her for a year again if I can help it!"

Mrs. Roosevelt brought news of Ted, Jr.'s engagement to Eleanor Alexander, and her husband's evening clothes, so that he need not attend the dinner to be given in his honor the next evening at the Sirdar's palace in khaki suit and green tie. She also had been given a special mission by Cabot Lodge. Fearing the inadequacy of his written entreaties—"not to express an opinion on anything before you reach the United States"—and hoping that the rumor that TR would meet Gifford Pinchot was not true—"because the mere fact of his meeting you would at once produce misapprehension"—Cabot trusted in Edith's "commentary and explanation" to restrain Theodore from impulsive speech.

This was not a task easily accomplished by one woman, even one as perceptive as Mrs. Roosevelt. After all, as TR wrote disarmingly to Cabot, "everybody turned to me precisely as if I were in my own country. They were hoping and praying for leadership. . . ." In the two days before he and Mrs. Roosevelt and their two children left by train for Wadi Halfa, where they boarded the *Ibis* and steamed down the Nile one thousand and seven hundred and fifty miles to Cairo, TR responded to their need with a speech of characteristic candor before the Egyptian Officers' Club. Though a picture of the anti-English Egyptian nationalist leader hung in a prominent place in the club, TR spoke to the Egyptian and Sudanese officers "with unmistakable plainness as to their duty of absolute loyalty and as to the ruin which would come to both Egypt and the Sudan unless the power and the prestige of the English rule were kept undiminished." The English, he explained it to his sister Bamie, "hail me as half ally, half teacher and are wild to have me instruct the Egyptians here and their own people at home what the facts are."

By March 24, when the Roosevelts arrived in Cairo, his speech had thoroughly incensed the Egyptian nationalists. The kindest of them observed sourly, "Mr. Roosevelt does not know what he is talking about, but he means well." Even a much-publicized nighttime visit to the Sphinx failed to mollify the proponents of "Egypt for the Egyptians." (The vision of a momentarily silenced TR standing in the moonlight before the mighty inscrutable colossus of the desert provided endless material for American political cartoonists.)

But the reporters trailing TR, while intrigued with his forays into foreign politics, continued to plague him with questions about Taft, about 1912, about the whereabouts of Gifford Pinchot. "With the mystery of the Sphinx," wrote an inspired reporter for the New York *Times,* "he made his reply, 'I am observing my usual reticence on all questions relating to American affairs, political and otherwise.' "

TR underscored his determination to maintain this vow of silence, despite the persistence of obviously provocative newspapermen. On a visit to the Necropolis, as he was examining a hieroglyphic on one of the tombs which portrayed a native in a court of law being beaten by officials to force him to testify, a newsman mischievously suggested that the Pinchot-Ballinger investigating committee might want to adopt this method to produce testimony favorable to Secretary Ballinger. TR merely smiled and changed the subject. A further test of his resolution came the following afternoon—a Saturday—when he held a reception for the seven hundred Americans visiting in Cairo who were clamoring to see him. As he stood in the garden of Shepheard's Hotel, each tourist approached, shook his hand, and made warm outspoken comments: "Won't you straighten up old man Taft when you get home?" "We want to see you in the White House again." "We want you in 1912." Finally, after a pair of eighty-year-old twin ladies from New Britain, Connecticut, confronted him with "We want you back again," he said to them, "I am not going to make a speech, but I am pleased to meet you Americans so far from home. I am glad to furnish you evidence that the lion did not do his duty."

But the day before, in a private talk with Oscar Straus, his former Cabinet member, who had come to Cairo to see him, TR had relaxed his guard. "He spoke," Straus recalled, "of Taft's having told him he would retain Garfield and myself, and said Taft was aware that he was specially attached to us both. I showed him an article in a current *North American Review*, entitled 'The First Year of Taft's Administration,' which plainly showed much ground had been lost."

With relief, he was able to turn from the awkward, ubiquitous appeals for some comment on the success or failure of William Howard Taft's administration by speaking at Cairo University on "Law and Order in Egypt." ("I must say," he wrote Whitelaw Reid, "I should like to handle Egypt and India for a few months.") As might be expected, his speech caused an outcry among nationalists, whose demands for a constitution TR declared to be premature. Self-government, he told them, was a goal toward which one worked slowly and righteously. "God is with the patient," he further informed them, quoting an old Arab proverb, "if they know how to wait."

A nationalist newspaper retaliated with another old Arab proverb, containing a curious and no doubt accidental allusion to American political parties: "They are able to make a donkey's tail look like an elephant's trunk when so inclined."

The next day, a band of students from the university marched on Shepheard's Hotel to protest TR's speech. "*Vive le Constitution*," they shouted. "*A bas les hypocrites.*" It was shocking, one of the students declared, that Theodore Roosevelt, a prominent citizen of a free nation, should oppose granting a constitution to Egypt. This seeming paradox, however, they explained by TR's Dutch ancestry, for, they said, the Dutch were notorious imperialistic oppressors. Proving that there is an old Arab proverb for every occasion, one was produced to account for TR's support of English rule: "*El erk masse*"—"Blood will tell."

On the last day of March, TR, his wife, and their two children boarded the steamer *Prinz Heinrich*, bound for Naples. Awaiting TR on a different continent were new and extraordinary triumphs, fresh international incidents in which to become embroiled, and a newsworthy conference with an old comrade. "I don't agree with you about not seeing Pinchot," TR wrote Cabot from Rome. "I am delighted to see him. . . . I shall listen to all he has to say, I shall not commit myself." Although Cabot's letters preached discretion, to which TR vigorously subscribed, TR nevertheless wrote him, "I am very uncomfortable about all I hear from home."

Despite the dedicated myopia of *Avanti*, an Italian Socialist newspaper, which warned its readers that Theodore Roosevelt might merely be "an overestimated bourgeois," by March 31 no more hotel accommodations were available in Naples. During the twenty-four hours the Roosevelts remained in that city TR was received, he wrote his friend Sir George Trevelyan, "in a way that really embarrassed me." His appearance at the opera set off such ringing expressions of enthusiasm that a remarkable phenomenon took place: in a country containing the most devout opera lovers in the world, the performance actually stopped for ten minutes while the audience cheered Theodore Roosevelt. After it had once again resumed, processions of Italian admirers "persisted in coming up to be introduced."

The next three days were spent in Rome, where even more unreserved demonstrations of esteem occurred. "We look again to see him at the head of the great Republic," proclaimed the Mayor of Rome at a dinner given in TR's honor.

In Rome, too, the climax of his "elegant row" with the Vatican took place, filling the front pages of papers in Europe and the United States. An audience with Pope Pius X had been arranged for TR. However, an American Methodist missionary in Rome, B. M. Tipple, had, with singular inappropriateness, alluded to the Pope as "the whore of Babylon," and the Vatican was understandably offended. The Papal Secretary, Cardinal Merry del Val, communicated to TR, then still in Egypt, that his audi-

ence with the Pope depended upon TR's agreeing not to see the Methodists. Though TR regarded Tipple as "a crude, vulgar, tactless creature,"
he responded that, while he hoped to have an audience with the Pope, "it
must be distinctly understood that I would not make any stipulation in
any way impairing my liberty of conduct to see anyone else that I
chose."

Through an intermediary who went to Rome to attempt to settle the
matter, Merry del Val suggested that if TR would secretly agree not to
visit the Methodists he would have no objection to a public announcement that TR had made no such agreement. "Why," TR wrote indignantly to Trevelyan, "a Tammany boodle alderman would have been
ashamed to make such a proposal." After his adamant refusal, TR wrote
Cabot, the Methodists "issued an address of exultation which can only be
called scurrilous . . . and with equal promptness I cancelled the arrangement I had made for seeing them. . . . The only satisfaction I had out of
the whole affair, and it was a great satisfaction, was that on the one hand I
administered a needed lesson to the Vatican, and on the other hand, I
made it understood that I feared the most powerful Protestant Church
just as little as I feared the Roman Catholics." TR had good reason for
gratification with his part in the whole affair, for detached observers
readily admitted that he had come off the victor in the dispute with the
Cardinal, regarded in Europe as "an astute and able politician."

In a special cable which Merry del Val arranged to have sent to an
American newspaper, the Papal Secretary gave his version of the incident,
summing up the altercation with TR not as one involving principle, but
as "simply a question of common courtesy, and surely common courtesy
is not incompatible with the rights and freedom of an American citizen."
That Cardinal Merry del Val's reputation for political shrewdness had a
firm basis in reality was substantiated by his choice of an American
newspaper to which to send his special cable: the Cincinnati *Times-Star*,
owned by Charles P. Taft.

With the sound and fury of his controversy with the Vatican still
reverberating throughout Rome, and indeed, around the world—the New
York *Times* even called up memories of the TR-Maria Storer-Archbishop
Ireland imbroglio—Theodore and Edith Roosevelt set off northward in
"an old-style three-horse carriage" to repeat the drive they had taken
twenty-three years earlier on their honeymoon. They drove through the
lovely Italian hill country of Tuscany, to the delight of the Italians, who
were astonished to discover that romance was a characteristic of American politicians.

But by the end of two days, TR wrote Cabot, "when everybody had

Mrs. Theodore Roosevelt (Edith Kermit Carow), 1902

Mrs. William Howard Taft (Helen "Nellie" Herron)

Theodore Roosevelt with his family, 1907. *L. to r., seated*: Quentin, the President, Archibald, Mrs. Roosevelt, Ethel; *standing*: Kermit and Theodore, Jr.

William Howard Taft and his family, 1909. *L. to r.:* Charlie, Taft, Helen, Mrs. Taft *(seated)*, and Robert

Archibald Butt, White House aide to Theodore Roosevelt and William
Howard Taft

Alice Lee Roosevelt, 1904

Elihu Root

Nelson W. Aldrich

Richard A. Ballinger

Henry Cabot Lodge

Theodore Roosevelt speaking in Asheville, North Carolina, 1904

William Howard Taft making a campaign speech at Cedar Rapids, Iowa,
October, 1908

Theodore Roosevelt and Gifford Pinchot on a trip of the Inland
Waterways Commission down the Mississippi River, October, 1907

become advised by telephone and telegraph of where we were going, it became out of the question to continue. We were simply swamped with people, Italians in all the little Italian towns, Americans wherever we came near a winter hotel, and others, all of them with great good nature and friendliness joining to make it impossible for us to go out of our rooms unless we cared to be accompanied by increasing crowds; and wherever we wanted to admire anything, from a view to a picture, having local officials start amiably in to help us in our admiration!"

On April 9 the Roosevelts stopped briefly at Genoa and then made their way westward, along the thin coastal strip of the Italian Riviera—flanked on one side by the Alps and on the other by the Ligurian Sea—to the ancient town of Porto Maurizio. Here, Edith Roosevelt's spinster sister, Emily Carow, lived in a villa that she rented from a friend; and here, it was reliably rumored, the long-awaited meeting between Theodore Roosevelt and Gifford Pinchot would take place.

Surrounded by groves of orange and olive trees, backed by the gracefully terraced hills of the Ligurian Alps, the whole town of Porto Maurizio basked under a sky of deep azure blue on the afternoon of April 10, 1910. Its Moorish buildings were lavishly decorated and, from many windows, Italian and American flags flew side by side. A regiment of infantry in striking uniforms stood at attention, and almost all of the town's population of six thousand—the women carrying brightly colored parasols and the children dressed in holiday white—lined the still uncompleted boulevard fronting the Riviera Palace Hotel.

The arrival of TR, accompanied by his wife and sister-in-law Emily, set off a burst of ecstatic cries of "Viva Roosevelts!" Then, following a ceremony in which Mayor Carretti made him an honorary citizen and named Porto Maurizio's new boulevard Roosevelt Boulevard, TR delivered a speech in English which Emily Carow, in a heroic attempt, translated for the crowd. TR concluded with "Viva Porto Maurizio," "Viva Mayor Carretti," and—with a mischievous look at his sister-in-law—"Viva Miss Carow!" The Roosevelts then repaired to Emily Carow's home, Villa Magna Quies—Villa of Great Quiet.

Late that night another well-known American, Gifford Pinchot, arrived and checked in at the Riviera Palace Hotel. The next morning Pinchot rose early, breakfasted, and by 9:00 A.M. was at the Carow villa. Under the avidly curious eyes of reporters, TR came out of the villa, shouted, "Hello, Gifford," and ran to shake Pinchot's hand. There then followed what the former Chief Forester recorded in his diary as "one of the best & most satisfactory talks with T.R. I ever had. Lasted nearly all day, and till about 10:30 P.M." The next day brought a resumption of the conference between the two old friends, both of whom declined to make any statement to reporters.

"It was a good talk," Pinchot recalled many years later. "I brought him up to date—took him the facts. We discussed them, and he understood them. They left him in a very embarrassing position, but that could not be helped." Gifford Pinchot had come not only armed with verbal "facts," which he articulated with intense conviction, but also fortified by letters from Senators Dolliver and Beveridge and William Allen White, filled with criticism of the Taft administration.

In those two days, when TR and Pinchot were not walking and climbing along picturesque trails and talking, or riding in the Caramagna Valley and talking, they sat at a wooden picnic table, talking, in Emily Carow's garden, overlooking the Ligurian Sea. Some one hundred and forty miles south of the Italian Riviera, the blue waters of that part of the Mediterranean washed the shores of Elba. The two men could not, of course, see that historic island from the villa garden, but the significance that the catch phrase, "Back from Elba," had acquired in American politics, added to the import of Pinchot's revelations, caused Elba to seem portentously at hand.

Whether or not the comparative proximity of Elba weighed on TR, Pinchot's disclosures certainly did, for on the very day he first talked to the former Chief Forester, TR wrote Cabot Lodge a long letter.

I don't want you to think that I have the slightest feeling of personal chagrin about Taft. The Presidency of the United States, the success of the Republican Party, and above all the welfare of the country—matters like these cannot possibly be considered from any standpoint but that of the broadest public interest. I am sincere when I say that I am not yet sure whether Taft would with wisdom have followed any course save the one he did. The qualities shown by a thoroughly able and trustworthy lieutenant are totally different, or at least may be totally different, from those needed by the leader, the commander. Very possibly if Taft had tried to work in my spirit, and along my lines, he would have failed; that he has conscientiously tried to work for the objects I had in view, so far as he could approve them, I have no doubt. . . . Probably the only course open was not to do as he originally told me before the nomination he intended to do, and as he even sometimes said he intended to do between nomination and election but to do as he actually has done. . . .

He amplified for Lodge what Pinchot had called his "very embarrassing position."

You do not need to be told that Taft was nominated solely on my assurance to the Western people especially, but almost as much to the people of the East, that he would carry out my work unbroken; not (as he has done) merely working for somewhat the same objects in a totally different spirit, and with a totally different result, but exactly along my lines with all his heart and strength. Of course you know that among my heartiest supporters especially in the West, and, curiously enough, also in Eastern states like New York and New Jersey, there has been any amount of criticism of me because I got them to take a man on my word who they now find understood his own promise in a totally different sense from that in which both I and the men who acted on my word understood it. There is only a little harsh criticism either of my sincerity or of his, but there is a very widespread feeling that, quite unintentionally, I have deceived them, and that however much they may still believe in my professions when I say what I myself will do, they do not intend again to accept any statement of mine as to what anyone else will do. . . .

Then TR summed up his position and attitude.

I myself cannot help feeling that even though there has been a certain adherence to the objects of the policies which I deemed essential to the National welfare, these objects have been pursued by the present Administration in a spirit and with methods which have rendered the effort almost nugatory. . . . I do think we had the Republican Party in a shape that warranted the practical continuance of just what we were doing. To announce allegiance to what had been done, and to abandon the only methods by which it was possible to continue to get it done, was not satisfactory from my standpoint. I have played my part, and I have the strongest objection to having to play any further part; I very earnestly hope that Taft will retrieve himself yet, and if, from whatever causes the present condition of the party is hopeless, I most emphatically desire that I shall not be put in the position of having to run for the Presidency, staggering under a load which I cannot carry, and which has been put on my shoulders through no fault of my own. Therefore my present feeling is that Taft should be the next nominee, because if the people approve of what he has done, they will elect him, and if they don't approve of what he has done, it is unfair to me to have me suffer for the distrust which others have earned, and for which I am in no way responsible. This represents not a settled conviction on my part, but my guess as to the situation from this distance. Of course things may entirely change, and my attitude change with them. . . .

The night before TR wrote his letter to Cabot Lodge—just about the same time in the evening that Gifford Pinchot arrived at the Riviera Palace Hotel—Will Taft sat in the Blue Room of the Executive Mansion with a former Yale classmate, his sister-in-law Mrs. Louis More, and Archie Butt. They listened to Caruso on the Victrola, and Taft, his thoughts evidently on what was transpiring in Porto Maurizio, dwelt hopefully on Theodore Roosevelt's readiness to change his mind.

"I suppose Pinchot will fill his ears with prejudicial tales," the President said, "but that I cannot help and I cannot checkmate. If he comes to Washington I shall discuss with him most frankly every act of the Administration, and even should he have committed himself to Pinchot, I have no doubt but that he will change his mind after he learns the facts from me or Root in conversation. It is a strange contradiction in Roosevelt's nature, but he has no pride of opinion at all. He does not mind how often he changes his mind if he thinks there is some reason for doing so. I have known him to commit himself to some proposition in the morning and reverse himself five times before evening. But each change was the result of some new information rather than the result of indecision. . . . Pinchot is a socialist and a spiritualist, a strange combination and one that is capable of any extreme act. I think Roosevelt knows him thoroughly and will possibly reach the truth of the matter out of his own mouth."

If Will Taft needed any further reminder of that meeting in Porto Maurizio, he received it from Mayor Carretti, who, possibly in a moment of excessive affability, sent off a cable stating that Colonel Roosevelt had arrived and been received enthusiastically by the whole population. "Porto Maurizio," he concluded expansively, "is proud to welcome this great American citizen and send the President of the United States its heartiest greetings."

Taft responded with a cable to Mayor Carretti, acknowledging his "courteous telegram announcing that President Roosevelt arrived. . . . In reply I assure you and your countrymen that the American people are very grateful for and greatly appreciative of the receptions which Italians from the sovereign to the humblest subject have accorded to our most distinguished citizen."

The New York *Times*, in reporting the exchange of cablegrams, was quick to point out certain unusual features: that President Taft had referred to TR as "President Roosevelt" rather than former President Roosevelt; and that the encomium "our most distinguished citizen" was a phrase normally reserved for the President of the United States. The *Times* speculated that in wording his cablegram as he had President Taft wished to show America and Europe that he had nothing but admiration and affection for Theodore Roosevelt.

| Eleven | "Confound These Kings, Will They Never Leave Me Alone?" |

Virtually every sovereign or consort of the countries in Europe was linked not only by a network of German princes and princesses who had married into every royal house, but also, almost invariably, by relationship to King Edward VII of England. The Emperor of Germany was a nephew of King Edward; the Czarina of Russia, a niece of King Edward; the Queen of Spain, Edward's niece; the King of Norway, Edward's son-in-law; the Crown Prince of Sweden, Edward's nephew-in-law; the King of Denmark, Edward's brother-in-law. Queen Sophie of Greece was Edward's niece and so was Queen Marie of Rumania. The late Crown Prince Rudolf, son of the Emperor of Austria, had married Princess Stephanie of Belgium, whose father, the King of Belgium, was Edward's cousin. Even Ferdinand, the lowly Czar of Bulgaria, had a grandfather who was a brother of Edward's grandmother.

In consequence of all these interwoven relationships, the members of European royalty lived in an exclusive inbred world of pompous display and affronted feelings, of family alliances and intrafamily intrigue, of maneuverings for power and manifestations of superiority—conditions that would seem to make a world war inevitable. The European tour of Theodore Roosevelt provided all these individuals with an exciting new gambit and was, according to TR, "a relief to the tedium, the dull narrow routine of their lives."

In great part, the competition of the royal houses dictated his itinerary. Having accepted invitations to speak at Oxford and the Sorbonne, TR said, "I was certain that the Kaiser would not stand my speaking in England and France and not in Germany; and sure enough, I soon received from the German Ambassador, by his direction, a request to speak at the University of Berlin." He found this sensitivity to be prevalent among the smaller countries, too, and pointed out, "while the different rulers did not care a rap about seeing me, they did not like me to see *other* rulers and pass them by."

To be obliging, he went to Vienna, called on Archduke Franz Ferdinand, whom he characterized as "a furious reactionary," and had dinner at the Schönbrunn with the Archduke's great-uncle, the old Emperor, Franz Josef, not "a very able man," TR thought, but a gentleman with good instincts. (However good these instincts, one Austrian dinner habit of his horrified TR: "The finger bowls were brought on, each with a small tumbler of water in the middle; and the Emperor and all the others proceeded to rinse their mouths and then empty them into the finger bowls.")

Extravagant enthusiasm characterized his popular reception in Vienna. "The streets and squares around the hotel were blocked with crowds and when I drove to the Schönbrunn to dine with the Emperor, the whole route was lined on both sides with onlookers." TR probed the extraordinary fascination he held for Europeans and decided that they thought of him "as still the great American leader, the man who was to continue to play in the future of American politics something like the part he had played in the past." He wrote a friend: "Moreover this was the view that almost all the statesmen took. No explanations of mine were treated as anything but rather insincere and affected self-depreciation, and my statement of the bald fact that under our system and traditions an ex-president became of little or no importance was always greeted with polite but exasperating incredulity." (At the White House Will Taft was also giving some thought to the subject of TR's popularity. "I don't suppose there was ever such a reception as that being given Theodore in Europe now," he mused. "It does not surprise me that rulers, potentates and public men should pay him this honor, but what does surprise me is that small villages which one would hardly think had ever heard of the United States should seem to know all about the man. The receptions which are accorded him in small obscure towns and hamlets are significant. It illustrates how his personality has swept over the world. . . . It is the force of his personality that has passed beyond his country and the capitals of the world and seeped into the small crevices of the universe." The title of an article in the *Literary Digest* explained TR's European reception differently, and more succinctly: "Mr. Roosevelt Renominated by Europe.")

In Vienna, too, TR had a reunion with an old friend, Henry White, "the best man in our diplomatic service," who, he later wrote, "for reasons of unspeakable triviality," had been dismissed from the service by Taft. "When he saw me," White informed his wife, "he bounded with joy, and I have been constantly with him ever since. He made me break-fast with him alone, and talked most freely on matters political."

TR's tumultuous welcome in republican Paris, where he and Kermit went next to join Mrs. Roosevelt and Ethel, exceeded those extended to any reigning monarch. On the evening of the day he arrived, the Roosevelts attended a Comédie Française performance of *Oedipus Rex*, occupying the presidential box. At first TR didn't respond to the volleys of applause from surrounding boxes and from the gallery, but since they continued, he bowed his acknowledgment. At the end of each act, the actors came forward on the stage, as they did when royalty was present, and bowed to TR with profound humility and respect.

On the twenty-third of April, TR delivered an address at the Sorbonne on "The Duties of the Citizen"; one of these duties, he pointed out, was not to let the race die out. The French appeared impressed by this advice.

The Parisian literary world, also avid to meet TR, had its opportunity to do so at a salon held by Mrs. Roosevelt's cousin, Edith Wharton, at her home in the rue de Varenne. However, few of that world could speak English, and TR spoke French badly, "with a rather bewildering pronounciation," according to Mrs. Wharton.

A visit to Napoleon's tomb, during which TR stood bareheaded for a few minutes, "seemingly deep in solemn thought," was noted as significant news by an idolatrous French press. Viewing TR and Napoleon dispassionately, Frederick Masson, a distinguished member of the French Academy, in his article in *Echo de Paris*, stated, however, that there was "no point of resemblance between the two men. . . ." He could more readily see a resemblance—physical, at least—between "the unfortunate Taft" and the obese Louis XVIII, whose royal career was sharply curtailed when Napoleon returned from Elba, and who, according to Masson, "although a clever dancer, could not walk a tightrope without a balancing pole."

Twenty-four hours in Belgium was sufficient time for TR to lunch at the American Embassy and dine at Laekon Palace with King Albert, "a huge fair young man, evidently a thoroughly good fellow," and Queen Elizabeth, "really cultivated and intellectual."

A proprietary interest in his Dutch descent led Holland to await eagerly the visit of Theodore Roosevelt and his family. They arrived on the day before the first birthday of Princess Juliana and lunched at Het Loo Palace with her parents, Queen Wilhelmina and Prince Henry. Although TR had a sentimental regard for the home of his ancestors, "Alas," he wrote, "Queen Wilhelmina was the only royalty we did not like at all." Evidently, domestic life in a matriarchal royal family entailed singular pressures. Wilhelmina "ruled her fat heavy, dull husband with a rod of iron," TR related. "He was leading a dreadful life. . . . When we got up from the lunch table, the queen said to him: 'Take Mr. Roosevelt into your room.' He did not catch what she said, turned round with his mouth open, and asked what it was; whereupon she promptly lost her temper, grew red in the face, almost stamped her foot, and snapped out at him: *'I said, take Mr. Roosevelt into your own room,'* whereupon he gave a little start and took me into the room, in gloomy silence. Hoping to distract him, I said: 'I am glad that your daughter the little princess seems so well.' However, he declined to be diverted, and responded more gloomily than ever, and with appalling frankness: 'Yes; I hope she has a brother; otherwise I pity the man that marries her!' "

But the Roosevelts were delighted with the Danish Crown Prince Christian and his wife, and with the monarchs of Norway and Sweden, all of whom they visited in the following week. The Norwegian royal family—King Haakon, Queen Maud, and little Crown Prince Olaf, with whom TR romped ("as I used to romp with my own children when they were small")—proved particular favorites. "They were dears . . . if ever Norway decides to turn Republic we should love to have them come to live near Sagamore Hill," TR reported.

By early May, Roosevelt cartoons began to fill Berlin papers, and a popular weekly issued a special Roosevelt edition preparatory to TR's visit. Germany's leading Roosevelt admirer, Kaiser Wilhelm, prepared to inundate him with honors, personal attention, and military maneuvers. The Roosevelts were even to stay at Potsdam Palace, an unparalleled honor for an unofficial American. But King Edward VII of England died on May 6, and all European courts plunged into mourning. Consequently, the Kaiser—though he had detested his Uncle Bertie and had been equally detested in return—had to relinquish his plans for having the Roosevelts as his palace guests.

A headline on the first page of the New York *Times* on the day following the royal death proclaimed a unique type of *lèse-majesté:* "KING'S DEATH UPSETS ROOSEVELT'S PLANS."

It was often remarked that Theodore Roosevelt and Kaiser Wilhelm II had similar characteristics. (General Alfred von Tirpitz, the German Secretary of State, made such a remark to Edith Roosevelt at dinner one night, without defining these similarities.) TR and the Kaiser were both compulsive talkers and shared a mutual weakness for military uniforms. Before leaving the United States, TR had wanted to buy a dress uniform of a cavalry colonel—brilliant with yellow plumes and gold lace—an idea squelched by his wife. "Theodore, I would never wear a uniform that I had not worn in the service," she had said firmly, "and if you insist upon doing this I will have a *vivandière*'s costume made and follow you throughout Europe."

The Kaiserin Augusta Victoria, intimidated by her imperial husband, had no such influence. On the afternoon of May 10, when the Kaiser and TR clasped hands in greeting on the marble steps of Frederick the Great's New Palace at Potsdam, the Kaiser was resplendent in the white uniform of a general of the *garde du corps,* wearing a helmet surmounted by a shimmering silver eagle. TR, on the other hand, wore a black business suit and slouch hat.

The next day, the Kaiser presented a thrilling panorama of military might in honor of "*Mein Freund* Roosevelt." For five hours, the two—the Kaiser again arrayed in gorgeous uniform, TR now in a khaki jacket, riding breeches, tan leggings, and the familiar black slouch hat—sat astride magnificent chargers and watched twelve thousand cavalry, artillery, and infantry engage in a sham battle on the Field of Döberitz. During the entire five hours the Kaiser—according to TR, at least—"talked steadily."

The following day, the University of Berlin, honored TR with a Ph.D., and he spoke on "The World Movement." The day after, American politics intruded again, for he learned a Washington paper had reported during the previous week that he had written President Taft that he endorsed his administration and would support him for renomination. When reporters queried him about this, TR threw up his hands and told them, "This reminds me of the story of the hunting of the snark. I've got to say a thing apparently ninety times over before I can command belief. I've never discussed the subjects mentioned in this article either verbally or by letter with a living soul."

In Pittsburgh, President Taft, on being asked whether he had received such a letter from TR, replied with a simple "No." But Taft had contacted TR on another matter. "The President," Archie Butt noted, "has named Mr. Roosevelt to represent us at the King's funeral. With him and the Kaiser present, it will be a wonder if the poor corpse gets a passing thought."

In mid-May of 1910, the front page of the London *Daily Mail* dwelt on only two subjects: the funeral plans for the late king and the imminent arrival of Theodore Roosevelt. After crossing the North Sea on the Flushing–Queensborough steamer, the Roosevelts reached Victoria Station early on Monday morning, the sixteenth. TR—dressed in deep mourning, with a heavy black band around his silk hat and a black crepe band on his left arm—and his wife and two children were taken by royal carriage to Dorchester House, where they were to stay as guests of American Ambassador Whitelaw Reid.

London had already begun to teem with royalty, assembling for the funeral. Emperors, kings, princes, archdukes, minor czars—all arrived with great entourages. TR had already met many of them in the past two months, but others who had never met him wished to remedy this without delay. As a consequence, a few hours after the Roosevelts arrived at Dorchester House, a liveried, silk-hosed footman announced to TR, busily catching up on his correspondence, that a king had come to call on him and was waiting downstairs. "Confound these kings," TR exclaimed with testy amusement, "will they never leave me alone?"

On the evening before King Edward VII was to be laid to rest in the royal crypt at Westminster Abbey, what TR always referred to as a wake took place. "I hardly know what else to call it," he wrote a friend. "King George gave a dinner to the special ambassadors in Buckingham Palace, the palace in which the dead king his father was lying in state. There were some seventy of us all told. Each man as he arrived said some word of perfunctory condolence to the king our host, and then on with the revel! It was not possible to keep up the pretence of grief any longer, and nobody tried, and it was precisely like any other entertainment."

And highly entertained TR was. Indeed, the events of that evening and of the funeral the next day provided him with a series of hilarious anecdotes with which he regaled his friends for years afterward. They would even serve to divert, briefly, and elicit a few kind words from a long-time critic. "He told us many stories of his adventures with the world's elect," Nellie Taft would recall, "and with his keen appreciation of the ridiculous and his gift of description, gave us as merry an afternoon as we ever spent with him."

One episode, disclosed to TR in all seriousness by the Kaiser, was a Graustarkian farce over precedence; it had taken place on the Orient Express carrying Archduke Franz Ferdinand of Austria-Hungary and Czar Ferdinand I of Bulgaria to London. Each demanded that his private car be ahead of the other. "The archduke triumphed," TR said, "and had his placed nearest the engine, the czar's carriage coming next, and then the dining carriage. The archduke was much pleased at his success, and rode next to the engine in purple splendor; and all went well until dinner time, when he sent word to the czar saying that he should like to walk through his carriage to the dining saloon, and the czar sent back word that he could not! Accordingly, breathing stertorously, he had to wait until a station came, get out and get into the dining saloon, and after eating his dinner wait until another station was reached, get out again and pop back into his own carriage."

Kaiser Wilhelm had evidently appointed himself *arbiter elegantiae* as to which members of royalty were worthy of TR's attention. "Roosevelt, my friend," he declared loudly, planting himself squarely between TR and the Bulgarian Czar, "I want to introduce you to the King of Spain; *he* is worth while talking to!" And the "unfortunate Prince Consort of Holland" had only to approach TR; the Kaiser appeared immediately, ignored the Prince completely, and the poor Prince "drifted off with fat meekness." When the Kaiser's vigilance relaxed the kings thronged around TR, "fairly scrambling," Henry White wrote his wife, "for a share in his conversation." "Oh, I would never have taken that step at all if I had been in your place, your Majesty," White heard TR tell one king. "That is *just* what I would have done," he heard him tell another.

TR and Stephen Pichon, Minister of Foreign Affairs of France, were the only nonroyal persons present, in behalf of the only two republics represented. Pichon held himself tense, alert to affronts to his country's status. "Before dinner he got me aside," TR reported, "and asked me in French, as he did not speak English, what colored coat my coachman had worn that evening. I told him I did not know; whereupon he answered that his coachman had a black coat. I nodded and said yes, I thought mine had a black coat also. He responded with much violence that this was an outrage, a slight upon the two great republics, as all the Royalties' coachmen wore red coats, and that he would at once make a protest on behalf of us both. I told him to hold on, that he must not make any protest on my behalf, that I did not care what kind of coat my coachman wore, and would be perfectly willing to see him wear a green coat with yellow splashes." Unfortunately, TR's command of French was inadequate. "My incautious incursion into levity in a foreign tongue met appropriate punishment, for I spent the next fifteen minutes in eradicating from Pichon's mind the belief that I was demanding these colors as my livery."

Returning to Dorchester House that night, TR found his family— including Alice, who had arrived in London several days before—sitting up to hear what had happened that evening. His account proved diverting.

The next day, as the funeral procession stood ready to start from Windsor, Pichon fretted and fumed that while all the royalty were to ride in glass coaches, he and TR were not. "As I had never heard of a glass coach excepting in connection with Cinderella," TR declared, "I was less impressed with the omission than he was." Throughout the whole funeral TR, between bouts of helpless laughter, endeavored in his imperfect French to keep Pichon from creating a row. Despite TR's levity, Sir Arthur Conan Doyle, writing his impressions of the King's funeral in the *Daily Mail*, was inexplicably struck by "the strong profile of the great American, set like granite, as he leans back in his carriage."

In the week following the funeral, the Roosevelts visited the country home of the Whitelaw Reids, went sight-seeing, met innumerable eminent men—though refusing to meet Winston Churchill, whom TR unaccountably disliked—and paid a condolence call on Queen Mother Alexandra, who expressed immense satisfaction over her husband's posthumous state of preservation. ("It must have been the oxygen they gave him before he died," she told them. "It was most remarkable. He was so well preserved.")

On Thursday, May 26, TR spoke at Cambridge Union, and as he received an honorary degree, the students, by means of a pulley, lowered a very large Teddy bear on him. (Darwin, they told TR, had a monkey lowered when *he* received a degree.)

Although he was preoccupied with kings, queens, and academicians, the subject of American politics continued to crop up. On his elder daughter's reunion with him, she had presented a firsthand account of "what had been going on at home." She later recalled, "Father was greatly disappointed in most of the course taken by the administration and felt at that time that he could not possibly speak for it in the coming congressional elections."

On the Monday morning following his having been honored at Cambridge, TR had a meeting—the first of its kind—with a defender of Will Taft. He had written Elihu Root, "I really think you ought to try and see me for a moment while abroad . . ." so no one could charge him with not seeing "men representing the other side." Root, therefore, stopped at Dorchester House on his way to The Hague for an international conference and gave *his* version of the Taft administration's actions. In February, as though by way of preparation, Root had written TR, giving him what he felt was desperately needed—a balanced account.

Of course we have missed you immensely & not only your personal friends but the people of the country generally seem to find your return the most interesting thing on the horizon. The change has been a good deal like that from an automobile to a cab. Taft is big & good natured & easy going & lets things drift considerably. That is sometimes a good thing but not always. He is making a good president & will I think win his way into the public confidence but he has not yet altogether arrived . . .

Altogether, the Administration has anything but a smooth path. A good many of the so-called insurgents are talking Roosevelt against Taft & you will have to be pretty careful when you get here & before you become familiar with the various controversies, not to say things that may have meanings ascribed to them that you have never thought of. . . .

In person, at Dorchester House, Root urged his old friend to remain silent on politics when he got home. TR agreed. "And if he had done as he promised me—kept out of things," Root said many years later, "we would have been spared much of our past trouble."

English newspapers and magazines, no different from those of other nations, virtually smacked their lips over TR's newsworthy personality. In a gesture of lavish hospitality *The Spectator* asserted, "We sincerely hope that, owing to the condition of national mourning under which Mr. Roosevelt has visited us, we shall not be deprived of one of those plain-spoken addresses such as he has often given his own countrymen."

TR did not disappoint *The Spectator*. At the Guildhall, where he was elected freeman of the City of London, he delivered "A Plain Talk on Egypt." "In Egypt you are not only the guardians of your own interests," he informed the English, "you are also the guardians of the interests of civilization. Now, either you have the right to be in Egypt or you have not; either it is or it is not your duty to establish and to keep order. If you feel that you have not the right to be in Egypt, then, by all means get out of Egypt." But if they stayed, he told them, "show that you are ready to meet in very deed the responsibility which is yours."

Before delivering this speech, TR had disclosed to British Foreign Minister Sir Edward Grey what he proposed to say. Grey, while agreeing with TR's views, warned him to be prepared for protests in the United States and English press. "He replied characteristically," Grey wrote James Bryce, the British Ambassador in Washington, "by a most vigorous improvised sketch of a leading article which would appear in the United States press, denouncing him."

Grey's prediction proved to be accurate. Not only did the English press storm at TR, but he was also attacked in the House of Commons. In the United States, the Chicago *Daily News* summed up the opinion of the anti-Roosevelt papers. "Colonel Roosevelt," it commented acidly, "must think he is mother-in-law to the human race."

On the tenth of June, the Roosevelts were to board the S.S. *Kaiserin Augusta Victoria* at Southampton and sail home. On the morning of June 9, TR disappeared. It was known he had gone somewhere with Sir Edward Grey, but the newspapers were unable to discover where. Grey and TR had never met before TR's visit, but, as TR said, "I do not remember ever meeting anyone else except Leonard Wood to whom I took so strong a fancy on such short acquaintance." Grey wrote a friend that he liked Roosevelt "immensely," and was particularly struck with his faculty "of imparting healthy courage and vigour. I have loved him."

During that day on which they dropped from London's view, TR and Grey were engaged on a remarkable project for two politicians: a walk through the valley of Itchen to hear English songbirds. The day was gray and moist—good singing weather. They saw forty different species of birds and heard the songs of twenty of these. Moreover, during their tramp through the valley and their subsequent evening together at an inn in the New Forest, they talked on many subjects: birds, books, poetry, and politics. "He spoke of Taft," Grey recalled, "and of their work together with very live affection; he had wished Taft to succeed him, had supported him, made way for him. How could he now break with Taft and attack him? Roosevelt spoke of this prospect in a way that left no doubt of sincerity and poignancy of feeling. On the other hand, how could he sit still and see all his own work being undone and the policies in which he believed being ruined? Roosevelt had come to no decision then, but there was evidence of strong internal combustion of spirit. Such spirits as his, however, are not consumed in this process; the result is energy, decision, and action."

Part IV   The Breach

Twelve   "Another Corner Turned"

In the misty haze of a hot Saturday morning in June, 1910, a twenty-one-gun salute blasted the silence at Fort Wadsworth. As the Hamburg-American liner *Kaiserin Augusta Victoria*—designated by zealous newsmen "the back-from-Elba bandwagon"—steamed past Staten Island into the Upper Bay, six battleships, a torpedo boat, destroyers, and a flotilla of yachts escorted her; the harbor itself "was alive with every kind of craft that could float." To acknowledge the waves, shouts, boat whistles, foghorns, and other welcoming sounds, Theodore Roosevelt and Alice Longworth stood on the starboard side of the upper bridge.

At 7:56 A.M. the huge liner dropped anchor at the quarantine station and was boarded by the health officer. A few minutes later, a launch carrying Secretary of the Navy and Mrs. George Meyer, Secretary of Agriculture James Wilson, Archie Butt, Cabot Lodge, and Nick Longworth circled the liner; they were told they would be permitted to come aboard if they scaled the ladder. Though Mrs. Meyer scoffed at this suggestion, the others clambered up one by one: first, Meyer; then Lodge; then Wilson, nearly eighty, whose wavering ascent was watched with much trepidation; then Nick Longworth; and, finally, Archie Butt, who had two letters from President Taft to TR and one to Mrs. Roosevelt from Mrs. Taft stuck tightly in his boot leg.

TR awaited them in his sitting room and, after a delighted exchange of greetings, Butt presented the letters from Will and Nellie Taft to Theodore and Edith Roosevelt. Almost immediately, many of TR's friends appeared on board, all eager to exchange a word or two with him. In substance, those words equaled those whispered by Lloyd Griscom, New York Republican, and Nick Longworth: "Don't for heaven's sakes, say anything about politics." "You needn't worry," TR replied, laughing heartily. "I'll be good."

Cabot Lodge drew him aside for a confidential talk. Soon Mrs. Roosevelt interrupted it, calling from the deck, "Come here, Theodore, and see your children. They are of far greater importance than politics or anything else." Archie and Quentin Roosevelt had boarded the *Kaiserin Augusta Victoria* from a revenue cutter, accompanied by their older brother, Ted, and his bride-to-be. Also on hand were TR's sisters, Corinne and Bamie, and their husbands, Douglas Robinson and Will Cowles; TR's former secretary, William Loeb; his niece Eleanor and her husband, Franklin D. Roosevelt; another niece, Corinne, and her husband, Joseph Alsop; and other relatives.

After a formal welcoming ceremony at the Battery by Mayor William Gaynor of New York City, a parade moved up Broadway and Fifth Avenue; it was composed of a line of fourteen carriages, preceded by a regiment of Rough Riders on sorrel horses, and followed by a hundred-piece Seventh Regiment band, Spanish American War veterans, and Bud and Temple Abernathy, six and ten years old respectively, who had traveled on horseback all the way from Oklahoma to New York to meet TR on his return. (However, they went back to Oklahoma in a car they had bought in New York, a Brush runabout.) Passing five miles of a closely packed crowd, TR received "one continuous ovation," Archie Butt related proudly. "I have never witnessed anything like it," he said, "and when it was to see just one man in a frock suit, it was simply marvelous."

The return of TR had been the subject of endless conjecture. (It had even been the subject of entreaties to a Higher Power. "Help us to bear the man," prayed *Life*, "help us to listen with patience and forgiveness; help us to thank our lucky stars for this last year's vacation; for rested nerves; for freedom from sudden shocks . . . for cumulated strength to bear the future.") Physical preparations for the welcome had been long in the planning. Commemorative medals were struck. Months before, Cornelius Vanderbilt had been named chairman of the reception committee. Because so very many organizations and individuals demanded to take some part in the ceremony—to march, to play, to orate—Vanderbilt had for a time been "up in the air as to what to allow and what to keep out of sight."

The committee had asked President Taft to come to New York to greet TR, and Taft had at first considered the invitation seriously. "The only question in his mind," Archie Butt wrote, "is that of the dignity of his office. He is not so sure that he, as President, ought to go to New York to welcome a private citizen, even if that citizen is an ex-President, a great personal friend, and the man to whom he acknowledges he owes the fact that he is now President. . . . He fears, too, that going to New York he may appear in the attitude of trying to placate Mr. Roosevelt if the latter has become disgruntled for any cause."

As all attention focused on the impending arrival of TR, Taft's normally placid temper became edgy, irritable. Perhaps he was, as he had written a friend a few months earlier, "schooling myself to bear the shafts of criticism whether proceeding from a hostile feeling, contemptuous indifference or patronizing friendship."

A letter from Taft that TR had received in London before sailing—the first such communication since he left the United States in March of 1909—was heavy with pathos and self-justification in the account Taft gave of his fifteen months in the White House. He had not written before because, he told TR, "I did not wish to invite your judgment on matters at long range or to commit you in respect to issues that you ought perhaps only to reach a decision upon after your return to the United States." To his credit he had impending conservation and postal savings

But Going the Wrong Way

By Herbert Johnson, *La Follette's Weekly Magazine*, March 19, 1910.

bank bills, but the Payne-Aldrich Tariff Act, though "a good bill and a real downward revision," would very likely result in the loss of the next House to the Democrats. Moreover, the Republican insurgents, he wrote his predecessor, had "done all in their power to defeat us." As for the Pinchot-Ballinger controversy, it "has given me a great deal of pain and suffering," he declared, "but I am not going to say a word to you on that subject. You will have to look into that wholly by yourself without influence by the parties if you would find the truth." Summing up, he wrote plaintively, "I do not know that I have had harder luck than other presidents but I do know that thus far I have succeeded far less than have the others. I have been conscientiously trying to carry out your policies, but my method of doing so has not worked smoothly." Personal anguish had affected him, too. He wrote: "My year and two months [*sic*] have been heavier for me to bear because of Mrs. Taft's condition. A nervous collapse, with apparent symptoms of paralysis that soon disappeared, but with an aphasia that for a long time was nearly complete, made it necessary for me to be as careful as possible to prevent another attack. Mrs. Taft is not an easy patient and an attempt to control her only increased the nervous strain. Gradually she has gained in strength and she has taken part in receptions where she could speak a formula of greeting, but dinners and social reunions where she had had to talk she has avoided." Taft ended his letter with an invitation to TR to come and stay at the White House.

Replying immediately, TR thanked not "My Dear Will" but "My Dear Mr. President" for his letter. "I do not know the situation at home," he went on. "I am of course much concerned about some of the things I see and am told; but what I have felt it best to do was to say absolutely nothing—and indeed to keep my mind as open as I kept my mouth shut. . . . Indeed, you have had a hard time, as you say, and of course the sickness of the one whom you love most has added immeasurably to your burden. We have followed with the greatest concern the news of her trouble, and feel very genuine pleasure at learning how much better she is. Will you give her our warmest regards?"

What remained unwritten was an even more personal subject than Mrs. Taft's illness—the highly charged animus that lay between Mrs. Taft and the Roosevelts, male and female. Alice Longworth, although warmly attached to President Taft, did not hide her dislike of Mrs. Taft, and that she often expressed it in her sharp, stinging wit caused even more resentment. While in Africa, TR had written to Cabot Lodge concerning certain slights to his family. Lodge had replied that he and Nick Longworth were "hurt and galled by the attitude of the White House toward Edith and Ethel of which you speak." On the same subject Nick Longworth wrote his father-in-law with a degree of euphemistic delicacy that "the colored gentleman in the wood-pile was not a gentleman at all, but is Mrs. T."

No one was more aware of this fragile emotive balance than Archie Butt. Just before he left for New York to welcome TR in the name of President Taft, he asked the President whether "Mrs. Taft had written to Mrs. Roosevelt." She had not, Taft answered. Did Archie think "she ought to do so"?

"I think so, Mr. President," Archie told him. "If she does that, then you and Mrs. Taft have left nothing undone and it can never be charged in the future that there was the slightest discourtesy toward Mr. or Mrs. Roosevelt from the White House. If either now feels aggrieved that more attention has not been shown to the children, not understanding Mrs. Taft's condition of health, I think a note of invitation from Mrs. Taft will set this right."

Taft told Archie to come back later in the evening and he would have a letter from Mrs. Taft for Mrs. Roosevelt. Upon Archie's return after dinner, nothing was said for a few minutes; then Taft said to his wife, "Nellie, will you go up and do that for me, dear?"

Mrs. Taft went upstairs, Archie reported, "wrote the note and brought it down to me. I don't know that it will be altogether welcomed, for when women get at cross purposes it is hard to get them straightened out again."

Other emotions clouded TR's return. In one of his periodic melancholy surveys of his public career, he told Lawrence Abbott, an editor of *The Outlook*, that, despite the world-wide idolatry he had received, he was "going down like Dewey." His reference was to the quick descent of Admiral George Dewey from the height of national idolatry to public ignominy, because the Admiral had sold a house given to him by the public. Throughout the voyage back to New York "Remember Dewey" became, Abbott wrote, "almost a slogan or shibboleth in our political conversations, although Roosevelt used it not jocosely but very seriously."

Despite all this foreboding, TR's reception and parade took place under a bright hot sun. But in the late afternoon the temperature fell from 82 to 62 degrees and a sixty-mile-an-hour gale and a torrential rain followed the drop. If any further significance were to be read into this event, it might be noted that TR had made his long-heralded, long-speculated-upon return from Elba on the ninety-fifth anniversary of the Battle of Water-loo.

§§

President McKinley's secretary, George Cortelyou, changed the nature and the salary of his position; considerably more power was invested in the office of secretary to the President, and he received six thousand dollars a year. His successor, William Loeb, TR's secretary, though he "had a faculty for making enemies," was highly regarded by TR, who frequently asked his advice, by Mrs. Roosevelt, who "had great confidence in him and often sought his assistance in bringing the President round," and by reporters, who appreciated his accessibility and political knowledge. Under the resourceful Loeb the position approximated that of an assistant to the President.

But as filled by the diffident Fred Carpenter—inept at handling reporters and with little or no political acumen—the position of presidential secretary "shrank several sizes." Neither he nor President Taft, Archie Butt complained despairingly, gave out "anything of any real interest"; "nor do they understand the art of giving out news," he declared. Thus reporters concentrated on the frequency of presidential golf games and looked to Taft's opponents—insurgent Republicans and Democrats—for weightier news. Moreover, Carpenter did not have the same assured relationship with the Tafts as Loeb had had with the Roosevelts. "When the President scowled at him," the New York *Times* asserted, "he trembled, and when the President scolded he wilted with terror. When Mrs. Taft expressed disapproval of things in general or in particular, Carpenter's teeth chattered." Though this account presented caricatures, Carpenter was obviously by temperament unsuited to his job. Accordingly, in June of 1910—shortly before TR returned—he was appointed Minister to Morocco. (The *Times* maintained: "Had Secretary Carpenter possessed as strong a champion in Mrs. Taft as Mr. Loeb in Mrs. Roosevelt, it is quite likely that he would have found his pathway smoother and would not have fled to Morocco.")

His successor, Charles Dyer Norton—suave, engaging, with ambitions for political power—who was a former Chicago life insurance man and had been Assistant Secretary of the Treasury, "promptly began to attend to his duties in a masterful and able way." Taft's relationship with newspapermen began to improve generally. "It was no longer such a rare thing to get an appointment with him," O. K. Davis of the New York *Times* pointed out. But despite the efforts and proximity of a competent secretary, Will Taft himself did not acquire any political sensitivity and remained perversely blind to the urgencies of a good press.

An interview with Cal O'Laughlin of the Chicago *Tribune* illustrated this blindness. Taft laughingly related to Archie Butt how O'Laughlin, who had been in Europe with TR, waited expectantly for the President to ask about his predecessor. Taft was, said Captain Butt, "rather funny as he told of the interview in which he never asked O'Laughlin any questions about the ex-President and [of] the blank expression which came over the newspaperman's face." O'Laughlin subsequently wrote TR about the interview "and expressed regret that President Taft had never even asked concerning him."

A fear of appearing to fawn or seek favors from TR lent a quality of strained jocularity to the letter of welcome Taft had first composed for Captain Butt to deliver. Both Norton and Butt, however, recommended a letter beginning "Dear Theodore" and written so as "to offer no suggestion that there has come the slightest rift in their friendship."

Taft agreed to this change, but would make no further effort. After Archie left for New York, the New York *World* asked for a comment from the President concerning TR's return. Norton "advised him to make some statement complimentary to the hunter," but Taft "showed irritation and said he would not do it."

Though TR had declared to Secretary Wilson that he would make "no comment or criticism for at least two months" in the days following his return, the papers dwelt exhaustively on the steady march of insurgents to Oyster Bay. Cabot Lodge and Secretary Meyer also joined this parade, but such visitors as Senator La Follette, James Garfield, and Gifford Pinchot stimulated much more interest. The visit of the latter two to Sagamore Hill especially incensed President Taft. He felt that while they might have gone there without an invitation, "they could not have stayed overnight and remained the next day playing tennis without one."

His own invitation to TR to visit the White House had been declined for what seemed a specious reason. "Now, my dear Mr. President," TR had replied, "your invitation to the White House touches me greatly, and also what Mrs. Taft wrote to Mrs. Roosevelt. But I don't think it well for an ex-President to go to the White House, or indeed to go to Washington, except when he cannot help it." The tone of his refusal had been disappointing to Taft; so when it was reported that TR meant to come over to Beverly to see him when he attended the thirtieth reunion of his Harvard class on June 29 Taft reacted petulantly: "The fact of the matter is I hope he will not come. He can scarcely do so without my inviting him, and I don't propose to do that. I invited him to the White House and he declined to come, giving some good reasons from his point of view possibly, but not from mine, so I am not in a position to ask him again. In fact, I do not want to see him until he has plenty of opportunity to think the situation over and has made up his mind definitely what course he wishes to pursue, because I cannot argue my case with him or before him.

He says he will keep silent for at least two months. I don't care if he keeps silent forever. Certainly the longer he remains silent, the better it will please me."

It was Norton's opinion that Taft "was preparing himself for a break of some kind" with TR. Indeed, "a break of some kind" between the two friends was incessantly remarked upon in the press—either in solid confirmation or fierce denial. And the editor of the newspaper from which Taft had the least to fear wished to prepare himself, too. "My dear Uncle," wrote Hulbert Taft, an editor of the Cincinnati *Times-Star*, "Would it be presuming on good nature for me to ask you what you know about Roosevelt's future attitude toward the administration? I have been very confident all along that he would support you, and it seems incredible to me that he will do anything else. At the same time I would like to have more accurate knowledge of the situation in my work out here. . . ."

Ten days following his return to the United States, TR went up to Cambridge to attend the Harvard reunion. While there, he dispatched a letter to Gifford Pinchot—similar in its aim to those he had received in Africa from Cabot Lodge—advising the former Chief Forester to "speak with the utmost caution."

Your enemies are hoping and praying for anything in the nature of an indiscretion on your part, and, I want you to disappoint them. Moreover, Gifford, while I very keenly share your disappointment in Taft, and in a way, perhaps feel it even more deeply than you do, because it was I who made him President, yet it behooves us to realize that it is not only possible, but probable, that two years hence, circumstances will be such as make it necessary to renominate Taft, and eminently desirable to re-elect him over anyone whom there is the least likelihood of the Democrats naming. . . . I do hope you won't take any position which would render it impossible, or even merely exceedingly difficult, for you to support him if necessary. He has not proved a good leader, in spite of having been a good first lieutenant; but neither you nor I can allow any personal disappointment or any chagrin at the failure of our hopes to lead us to take any position save that which we regard as demanded by the interests of the country. . . . As you know my judgment is that in all probability Taft has passed his nadir. He is evidently a man who takes color from his surroundings. He was an excellent man under me, and close to me. For eighteen months after his election he was a rather pitiful failure, because he had no real strong man on whom to lean and yielded to the advice of his wife, his brother Charley, the different corporation lawyers who had his ear and various similar men.

It was his belief, he also told Pinchot, that Taft's advisers realized that "they have almost ruined him," and that "he may and probably will turn out a perfectly respectable President, whose achievements will be disheartening compared with what we had expected, but who nevertheless will have done well enough to justify us in renominating him."

Two days following the writing of this letter, in a spirit of conciliation, TR and Cabot Lodge set off in the Senator's large closed touring car from the Lodge summer home in Nahant, for Beverly and a visit with the Tafts. The reaction to the visit amazed Archie Butt. "I never saw as much interest manifested over any one event in the administration of either man." A great crowd of reporters, with a seemingly insatiable thirst for detailed information, many of them armed with cameras, waited outside the gates of what was still referred to locally as the Evens Cottage— although it now housed the President of the United States and his family.

The next morning's New York *Times* featured a front-page story, headlined "ROOSEVELT AND TAFT IN A WARM EMBRACE." "For a full minute, this afternoon," the *Times* reported, "President Taft and Colonel Roosevelt stood on the broad veranda of the Evens cottage with hands upon each other's shoulders while evident delight shone in every line of their smile-enwreathed countenances. . . . They patted each other affectionately on the shoulder, they laughed in a way that left not a single lingering doubt as to the exuberance of their feelings." In actuality, many doubts lingered. This impression of an affectionate reunion between two devoted friends was not shared by some who observed the somewhat awkward meeting. The most dubious was Jimmie Sloan, the Secret Service agent attached to the White House. He had a deep regard for both men, whose safety had been his responsibility. However, he could be attached to TR and still view him with stern objectivity. The meeting between the two men, he told Archie Butt, didn't mean a thing. "I know this man better than you do," he asserted with a suggestion of belligerence. "He will come to see the President to-day and bite his leg off tomorrow."

Perhaps evincing the strain both felt, TR, when asked by Taft whether he would like a drink, answered that he "needed rather than wanted a Scotch and soda."

Still, there they sat on the wide veranda, sociability personified: President Taft, Colonel Roosevelt, Senator Lodge, Charles Norton, and Archie Butt. When Lodge walked over to a sheltered spot to light his cigar, Captain Butt followed him. "Do you think they want to be left alone?" he asked in a low voice. "If so, I will arrange to have the others leave and to delay the coming of Mrs. Taft and Miss Helen."

Lodge told Butt that he had asked TR the same question on the way over and that TR had said that "he wanted it to be like any other social call and not to be left alone with the President." Consequently, Butt sent word to Helen Taft that the President "wanted her and her mother to come down to meet Mr. Roosevelt."

TR had "evidently been primed not to ask Mrs. Taft any questions," because of her speech difficulty, and he did most of the talking. Although Mrs. Taft was later to recall this visit as "being remarkably pleasant and entertaining," she remained silent until TR suggested Taft appoint Andrew Carnegie to head the American mission to an International Peace Conference. Then she said, "I don't think that Mr. Carnegie would do at all."

Over tea, served on the veranda, with everyone seated around a wicker table, TR regaled them with his adventures among the crowned heads of Europe, amusing even Mrs. Taft. She did not share, she later admitted in somewhat of an understatement, her husband's faith in the sincerity of TR's friendship, "but," she said, "I was glad on this occasion to find the old spirit of sympathetic comradeship still paramount and myself evidently proved to be unwarrantably suspicious."

The memory of TR's visit to Beverly convinced her, she maintained years later, that he still held her husband "in the highest esteem and reposed in him the utmost confidence, and that the rumours of his antagonism were wholly unfounded. I was not destined to enjoy this faith and assurance for very long."

It was extraordinary that Mrs. Taft's distrust of TR—long held and deeply felt—lifted even briefly during that two-hour afternoon visit, for her husband had taken no comfort at all from this reunion. As TR and Lodge rose to leave, Taft said, "This has taken me back to some of those dear old afternoons when I was Will and you were Mr. President." However, despite this nostalgic sentiment, after they had gone Taft turned to Captain Butt, smiled, and said, "Well, Archie, that is another corner turned."

When Butt mentioned that Lodge had said that TR didn't wish to see him alone, Taft observed, "I think he felt just as I did, that it was best to have simply a social personal visit and not give any opportunity for confidences which might be embarrassing."

Thirteen　　　　All for Republican Unity

"I spent a day at Oyster Bay," Nick Longworth wrote to Charles Norton two months after TR's visit to Beverly, "and had many hours' talk with my father-in-law." He warned: "Do not let the President be misled by statements that are made to him by people who are working really in their own interest. . . . There are a great many people who would be overjoyed to see an open break between the two biggest men in the country, but such a break, if even only apparent, would be disastrous, not only to the party, but to the country."

There was an irony in Longworth's having expressed his well-founded fears to Charles Dyer Norton, for Norton, with "his fine appearance and ingratiating manners," was an effective member of those divisive forces that wished to destroy the friendship of Theodore Roosevelt and William Howard Taft. By late August Norton had settled into his new job, which enabled him to be so constantly at the President's side that Taft began referring to him as "under president" and his "alter ego." There was only one flaw that prevented Norton from being a perfect presidential secretary, Taft maintained; he had not "a scintilla" of humor. Archie Butt, who had been disposed at first to like Norton, soon found Norton's predilection for harping "on the President's fears regarding Mr. Roosevelt" both infuriating and frightening. "Nothing upsets the President as much," Butt said, "as these constant reports that Colonel Roosevelt has a dagger out for him."

When Norton announced that TR was out to make Jim Garfield the gubernatorial nominee in Ohio, "in order to humiliate the President," Captain Butt protested angrily.

"True to your old chief," taunted Norton, "—that's right, Archie."

Incensed, Butt advised Norton "to stop dragging in Mr. Roosevelt's name all the time, for some day Roosevelt might hear it and then there would be trouble." Butt thought this warning would be effective, because much as Norton seemed to dislike TR he had "a holy fear of his long arm."

Taft didn't require Norton's hostile deductions, for each new report from Oyster Bay disclosed the visit of yet another insurgent congressman and an accompanying pledge of support from TR. Though he warned Richard Ballinger to refrain from comments to the press on "purported interviews respecting insurgents emanating from Oyster Bay," Taft was greatly distressed. "I do not see," he said to Captain Butt, "how I am going to get out of having a fight with President Roosevelt."

To have the validity of her predictions finally recognized by her husband did not surprise Mrs. Taft. Although now, with the limitations her illness had imposed, the White House, the presidency, and the position of First Lady held little magic for her, she still had an ultimate goal: victory over Theodore Roosevelt. "Well," she asserted, after her husband told her of yet another ardent anti-Taft politician being entertained at Oyster Bay, "I suppose you will have to fight Mr. Roosevelt for the nomination, and if you get it he will defeat you. But it can't be helped. If possible you must not allow him to defeat you for the renomination. It does not make much difference about the reelection."

Plagued by the rebellious progressive Republicans—who were infuriated by offenses in the Payne-Aldrich Tariff Act, the Pinchot-Ballinger investigation, and the general abandonment of Roosevelt's policies—Taft indulged in furtive golf games with Henry Clay Frick of Pride's Crossing as the summer of 1910 wore on. (The furtiveness was understandable. It stemmed not from Frick's repute as an art collector, but from his role as the reactionary lord of the steel industry.) Though Archie Butt, Norton, and Mrs. Taft—who had, she told Archie, prevented Will from playing golf with John D. Rockefeller a year before—all felt that "Frick is a bad name to have coupled with that of the President," Taft stubbornly insisted that "he likes Frick and there is an end to what one can say or do in matters of this kind."

In this emotional setting Charles Norton had lofty ambitions as a political manipulator. He would, he told Jimmy Sloan and Archie Butt, "eliminate Colonel Roosevelt as a factor in national politics." In his efforts he was encouraged and supported by an old pro in political manipulation. Senator W. Murray Crane of Massachusetts was also a dedicated stand-patter, a great power among the Old Guard—and, incidentally, Mabel Boardman's brother-in-law. Tall, slender, with an elongated face, a faint mustache, and a general aura of the ethereal, Crane had an unobtrusive *modus operandi*—working through others, whom he prompted from the wings. Taft called him "Old Pussyfoot."

In order to rid the country of the baleful influence of TR, Crane and Norton felt it was important not to irritate the progressives unnecessarily. This included not playing golf with Henry Clay Frick or permitting an albatross like Richard Ballinger to remain in the Cabinet. To a pair engaged in such a pacification project, it was heartening to have a subject so seemingly open to manipulation as William Howard Taft.

"Will," Mrs. Taft said irritably one August morning at the breakfast table in Beverly, "you approve everything—everything Mr. Norton brings you, everything Captain Butt brings to you, and everything everybody brings to you."

"Well, my dear," her husband replied with a laugh, "if I approve everything, you disapprove everything, so we even up on the world at any rate."

"It is no laughing matter," Mrs. Taft said. "You don't want to fire Ballinger, and yet you approve of Senator Crane and Mr. Norton trying to get him out. I don't approve of letting people run your business for you."

"I don't either, my dear, but if you will notice, I usually have my way in the long run."

"No, you don't," Mrs. Taft retorted. "You think you do, but you don't."

Mrs. Taft had substantial grounds for her doubts. When a senator came to Taft and said that Norton had told him "that the President feared some sinister action from Mr. Roosevelt," Taft replied with remarkable innocence, "You must have misunderstood Norton, for it was he who thought Roosevelt was inimical to me, and he has harped on it so much that I feared he knew something which he did not like to divulge to me."

Possessing such a mind-set, Taft could easily see the sinister in TR's next action. The New York State Republican Committee was to meet on August 16 to name a temporary chairman for the state convention to be held in Saratoga at the end of September. The office was not one of mere form; a temporary chairman made the keynote speech outlining party policy and also named the Committee on Credentials, which had the power over the seating of the delegates.

Lloyd Griscom, speaking for the liberal faction of the New York Republicans, persuaded TR to allow his name to be placed in nomination. But despite a wire from President Taft asking "the boys" to co-operate with Griscom, the Old Guard was determined to nominate "Sunny Jim" Sherman, the Vice-President. That body knew that for TR to have the office would signify "the resumption of the leadership of that part of the Republican Party in New York State, with all sorts of possibilities so far as the national situation was concerned." When the committee met on the sixteenth, one of the conservative Republican leaders surreptitiously circulated the news to each member that he'd "just talked on the telephone to the President and the President says he wants Sherman chosen."

And Sherman *was* chosen, by a vote of 20 to 15. Taft publicly denied having made the statement indicating his preference for Sherman; however, in conversations with "Sunny Jim," he had listened to the plans to defeat TR, making no objection, apart from the injunction that the members were not to drag him into the fight and use it to bring about an open rupture with TR.

Archie Butt, anguished by the widening breach between the two men, began the painful consideration of whether he should stay on with Taft, or whether his loyalty and affection for TR dictated that he leave his White House duties. This dilemma was made no easier for him by Norton's elation over Sherman's victory. "Did you see what they did to Mr. Roosevelt today?" Norton, gloating, asked Captain Butt.

Of course, such satanic glee was to be expected of Norton, who, Butt observed, "hates the Colonel as much as I love him." Actually, Taft's private reaction to the situation struck Captain Butt more grievously. "Have you seen the newspapers this afternoon?" Taft said casually to Butt and Norton. "They have defeated Theodore."

Norton chuckled, and Taft began to laugh. "We have got him—we've got him—we've got him," Norton declared, "as sure as peas we've got him." Then he and Taft laughed again.

Boiling with rage, Butt thought, "Like hell you've got him. He is laughing in his sleeve at the whole kit and caboodle of you, and he'll eat you up when the time comes."

Several days later, a calmer Butt advised Taft to remain silent and to keep Norton silent. In answer, Taft said, "If I only knew what the President"—Taft appeared unable to shake the habit of calling TR "the President"—"wanted, Archie, I would do it, but you know he has held himself so aloof that I am absolutely in the dark. I am deeply wounded and he gives me no chance to explain my attitude or learn his."

The wound deepened as the silence emanating from Oyster Bay gnawed at Taft's nerves. Even golf could not dispel his anxieties; he therefore began refusing to go to Myopia for a game. "Everything seems to be in a state of uncertainty," Archie Butt said. "No one knows just what Mr. Roosevelt is going to do, and everyone about Beverly seems to be sitting over a volcano. . . ."

Reports—inaccurate, as it turned out—that TR would charge Taft with conspiring with Sherman and other New York Old Guardsmen to defeat him profoundly grieved Taft. He took to rising at the unaccustomed hour of five o'clock to read the newspapers, most of which contained editorials implying that Taft was "a weakling and devoid of character."

Although Taft had encouraged Sherman to fight TR—by his assumed neutrality, if by nothing else—he refused to acknowledge that this had been the case. He believed it was unfair that "the press has conspired to harass him with charges of this character."

Still, as Captain Butt maintained, Taft was not responsible for initiating the plans to defeat TR. "Before they were even suggested to him," Butt asserted bitterly, "Norton tried them out on me, just as he might try poison on a dog."

Weak in health and spirits, Nellie Taft was nevertheless very much aware of her husband's despondency. "I have not asked him anything, and he has not talked to me," she confided to Captain Butt. "But this Roosevelt business is perfectly dreadful. I lay awake all last night thinking about it, and I don't see what is going to be the outcome."

"The President has not got himself into this fix," Archie told her. "But Norton has, and the President must not rely on his judgment, for he has none, and you ought to urge him, Mrs. Taft, from now on not to be dragged into the petty squabbles in this fall's election."

"I think so, too," she replied, "and I think Will sees it also. He said the other evening that Mr. Norton was very fresh, so I think he sees through him now, but it may be too late."

When Captain Butt left her, he observed tears in Mrs. Taft's eyes. "When she allows herself to be loved," he wrote his sister-in-law, "she is very lovable, but as a rule she keeps herself buried down deep within herself."

The pressure on Taft lessened when he had the telegram published in which he advised Vice-President Sherman to confer with TR on the temporary chairmanship. Butt observed that the wire made no mention of those phone conversations with Sherman, and that it did give an impression of harmony. Nevertheless, Captain Butt's hopes for a reconciliation had faded completely. "They are now apart, and how they will keep from wrecking the country between them I scarcely see."

If Will Taft found TR's silence unnerving, he was to find TR's speaking tour through sixteen Western states downright infuriating. "His tour through the West has been one continual ovation," Taft wrote bitterly to his brother Charlie in Europe. "I am bound to say that his speeches are fuller of the ego now than they ever were, and he allows himself to fall into a style that makes one think he considers himself still the President of the United States. In most of these speeches he has utterly ignored me. . . ."

To be ignored by his old friend was one thing, but the nation's newspapers, too, had relegated him to the second and third pages. "The papers carry columns on what Mr. Roosevelt is saying and doing," Archie Butt noted, "and it is getting under the President's skin, I fear. He listens to everything which can be said against Mr. Roosevelt, and from the most irritatingly insignificant quarters." Captain Butt observed that Taft was not only listening to abuse of TR, "but says a great deal himself which it would be better for him not to say."

Several days before TR's departure for the West, Lloyd Griscom went to Sagamore Hill on a mission. In the interests of Republican unity, he asked TR, "Would you object to my arranging a meeting between you and Mr. Taft on your return? He's more than willing."

TR answered in the affirmative, but added cynically, "If I do this I'm pretty sure he'll use it somehow to convince the public I'm going out of my way to try to make friends with him."

In any event, the trip West would come first. Since his return to the United States, TR had been inundated with speaking invitations—two thousand, accumulating at the rate of twenty-five a day. Refusing an offer by the Republican National Committee to sponsor his swing through the West, he declared, "My speeches on the trip will represent myself entirely, nobody else," and set off in a special railroad car provided by *The Outlook* on a three-week trip which, he said, "I perfectly dread." Though the Western speeches truly represented Theodore Roosevelt, they represented a less orthodox Republican Roosevelt than the one who had sailed off to Africa. For during his year's sojourn he had read Herbert Croly's *The Promise of American Life*, which consolidated his own political philosophy. Croly's New Nationalism thus became TR's New Nationalism—and, several decades later, FDR's New Deal. It championed individual effort combined with a strong centralized government organization that would regulate big business, unions, and agriculture. TR simplified his philosophy at the Suffolk County Fair by stating: "All that New Nationalism means is the application of certain old-time moralities to the changed conditions of the day."

It is most unlikely that the Republican National Committee would have even suggested sponsorship of his trip had it been aware how incendiary some of his speeches would be—in particular, the one he made at Osawatomie, Kansas, in dedicating a monument to "the Kansas saint," John Brown. Actually, his dedication was a plea in behalf of social legislation—laws concerning compensation, limitation of working hours, a graduated income tax. (William Allen White noted that "in nearly an hour's speech, he devoted less than seven lines to our hero.") TR also enunciated a concept which, although not new—Lincoln had proclaimed it—still had the power to strike terror in conservative hearts: "Labor is the superior of capital and deserves much the higher consideration." And he hurled another stupefying thought: "I wish to see labor organizations powerful."

As Gifford Pinchot wrote his mother, TR's progressiveness "has grown steadily stronger." His progressiveness had grown so strong that he had not only allowed Pinchot to write the Osawatomie speech, but he also delivered it with only "one or two additions and two or three changes."

TR's radicalism outraged the regular Republican organization, members of the Taft administration, and President Taft himself, whose customary philosophical response to a bad stroke in his golf game collapsed completely in the wake of that speech. "The other day," Archie Butt reported, at the beginning of September, "he swore a terrific oath and threw his club twenty-five yards from him in anger. This was so unlike him that even the caddies looked astonished. It makes me think he is losing just a little bit of command of himself."

The paths of the two men crossed briefly in St. Paul, where they attended the National Conservation Congress, but they did not meet. Taft delivered "a most masterly address" on the sixth of September to an unresponsive audience and then left town. On the following day, TR spoke—this speech also drafted by Pinchot—advocating national control of the conservation of natural resources. A thunderous ovation expressed wholehearted agreement and affection.

Upon his return from St. Paul, Taft grew increasingly bitter toward TR; whatever expectations he had nurtured for TR's endorsing his administration in the progressive West had disappeared. Far from considering such an endorsement, TR had barely referred to his successor. "It would not surprise me," Archie Butt predicted ominously about Taft, "if he did not soon come out openly and attack his predecessor, as many are urging him to do."

To his brother Charlie, Will Taft poured out his unhappiness. "When he went away," he wrote, "I wrote him a letter in which I expressed the depth of gratitude that I felt toward him, and classed him with you as the two people to whom I felt most highly indebted for being elected President. I learn directly, and I have heard it in so many different ways in addition to the direct statement from Griscom that he regarded this letter as an occasion for feeling bitterly toward me, because I dared to include

you in the same class with him as assisting me in my canvas[s] for the
Presidency. I venture to say that swelledheadedness could go no further
than this. . . ." And to Archie Butt he said, "No one knows how deeply
he has wounded me. I shall always be gratified for what he did for me,
but since he has come back he has seared me to the very soul." To his
brother Horace he wrote less poignantly: "I think he occupies his leisure
time in finding reasons why he is justified in not supporting me."

Horace had already offered comfort by commenting on TR's ability at
one moment to refuse righteously to meet one corrupt politician and at
another to be excessively friendly toward another. "There was a man in
the witness stand in Wilkes Barre last winter," he wrote Will, "who was
asked what the reputation of a certain woman was in regard to chastity.
He replied, 'About medium.' I think Roosevelt's political chastity might
be rated about medium!"

In contrast with the Tafts' openly acrimonious attitude toward TR,
TR's judgment struck the sneak punches of condescension. "Taft is a
kindly well-meaning man," he wrote a friend in England, "who was a fine
judge and an excellent lieutenant in executive office, but he has no instinct
of leadership and he takes his color so completely from his immediate
surroundings that he is continually finding himself in situations where he
really has broken his word, or betrayed some former associate, and where
in consequence, and very naturally, he himself feels irritated against the
man to whom he has not behaved very nicely."

Ignoring the reality of all this animosity, Lloyd Griscom had blithely
arranged a meeting between the two men in the interests of Republican
unity.

Far from producing a more unified Republican party, the meeting
between TR and President Taft resulted in sharper misunderstandings
between the two men and more vocal recriminations. Even the logistics
of the meeting failed. TR was to cross Long Island Sound from Oyster
Bay and head for Black Rock Harbor near Bridgeport. There, Griscom,
whose summer home was in Fairfield, Connecticut, would meet him; then
they would proceed by car to New Haven, where Taft would be awaiting them at a friend's house. But right at the start trouble occurred.
Though the *Tarpon* was a twenty-seven-knot motorboat and "one of the
fastest speed boats on the Sound," by the time it rounded Lloyd Neck it
had run into the first equinoctial gale of the season. Through binoculars, a
member of the New York Yacht Club, Colonel James B. Ford, saw the
Tarpon in difficulties. He also recognized TR, "swaying from side to side
as it bucked the waves and talking most energetically with the engineer."

It looked to Colonel Ford as though TR "was telling the engineer how to run the boat through the storm."

In consequence of the storm, the party put in at Stamford, and a sodden, bedraggled TR hired a car to drive to Bridgeport. Upon arriving at the Bridgeport Yacht Club, TR found that Griscom's car had just blown a tire; so they all piled into the rented car and, accompanied by shrieking police sirens, they sped up the Boston Post Road until they reached the outskirts of New Haven, where "part of the gearing under the tonneau dropped onto the road." The repair took a half hour, and it was after two o'clock by the time they finally arrived at the private home on Edwards Street in which President Taft was waiting.

Just as the journey had been "dramatic and thoroughly Rooseveltian," the excessive civility attempted at the meeting was an expression of Roosevelt's and Taft's sense of the proprieties. "Roosevelt was very pleasant," Taft wrote Nellie, "and I hope I was." In turn, TR wrote Cabot Lodge, "Taft and Norton were more than cordial and made a point of being as pleasant as possible." Nevertheless, Taft's face was wreathed "with a purely physical smile," and TR's hostility was displayed, at one point, when Norton began a sentence and TR, ignoring him, continued speaking. "I have seen him do this," Archie Butt said, "when he wished to show contempt." It was Butt's opinion that TR knew of Norton's ambition to "exterminate him from politics." In this connection, Norton had received phone instructions from Senator Crane to try to hear all that was said, but Norton heard little. Eventually, Butt thought, Crane would learn what had been said from his sister-in-law, Mabel Boardman, in whom Taft confided.

This encounter was unlike their meeting in Beverly three months earlier, for this time TR and Taft spoke to each other privately. At one point before lunch, they "went into a huddle alone in the corner of the room," while Griscom and several others "sat with our fingers crossed." After lunch another private discussion took place. TR's fight against the New York State Old Guard in the coming fall election was the sole subject, but the need for self-justification clouded what was said or left unsaid. "Of course I did not ask Taft's aid or support in any shape or way," TR wrote Lodge, "and it would never have entered my head to do so." "What he wanted," Taft wrote his wife, "was the prestige of my support."

At cross-purposes with the objective of the New Haven meeting—to convince the American people that the TR-Taft friendship was still as close as ever—a controversy immediately arose as to which side had initiated the meeting. "Norton, who is evidently too slick for genuine wisdom," TR wrote Lodge, "with or without Taft's connivance, got all the newspapermen on his train to publish the statement that I had asked to come because I was in difficulties and needed Taft's support." And Taft wrote to his wife, "It was perfectly characteristic that after having sought the interview, as he undoubtedly did, our friend should at once advertise that it was not at his instance but at Griscom's or wearing around to the point of showing that it was at my instance."

Antipathies, of course, obscured the true nature of the situation. But Taft revealed something of his attitude when he told reporters, following TR's departure, "not to take the meeting too seriously." Moreover, he had a new policy of laughing "at the Colonel and thereby trying to make him ridiculous." The reports given out to newspapermen by Taft and Norton were, Archie Butt felt, "calculated to humiliate the ex-President."

In writing of all these machinations to his sister-in-law, Archie made an incisive, telling statement: "Such is politics as seen from the inside, dear Clara. Aren't you glad that Lewis is in the wholesale cotton business?"

More personal, more deeply felt than the "scenic effect" created on order in New Haven was an encounter several days later between Will Taft and another Roosevelt. At a dinner party at the Longworth family home on Grandin Road in Cincinnati, Taft observed with sorrow that the attitude of Alice Longworth toward him had changed. "I am afraid," he wrote his wife in Beverly, "she is gradually drawing away from me on account of the present situation between her father and me, though she professes to be very affectionate still."

Unhappy in Cincinnati (which she called Cincin-nasty), Alice Longworth found clear evidence in her husband's family of hostility to her father. Maria Storer, Nick Longworth's aunt, had just published in the Springfield, Masachusetts, *Republican* another of the Storer-Roosevelt letters—*circa* 1906—concerning the elevation of Archbishop Ireland, and had accompanied it with a fresh pejorative description of Theodore Roosevelt as "a dangerous influence." Nick Longworth's sisters, Nannie Wallingford and Clara de Chambrun, neglected few opportunities to extol the Taft administration to the detriment of the Roosevelt administration. Moreover, Taft reported to his wife, there was "little sympathy between Alice and her mother-in-law. She dislikes her mother-in-law extremely and her mother-in-law dislikes her extremely." Indeed, old Mrs. Longworth took occasion one evening to assure Taft that she approved everything he had done and was with him all the time, "and not," she added meaningfully, "with some other people."

Additional hostility was present that evening in the person of Mrs.

Taft's sister, Maria Herron, who was not on speaking terms with Alice "because Alice did not return her call when she first came to Cincinnati."

While Alice tried hard to strike a note of cordiality toward the President, "both he & I," Archie Butt noted, "saw the old spark was missing, and when he came home later and we were munching apples together before going to bed, he told me the evening had been one of inexpressible sadness to him, that he felt the difference in Alice and felt their old relations would never be the same again."

At a huge barnlike hotel in Saratoga, the New York State Republican Convention met in the last days of September, 1910. The arrival of the Nassau County delegation—led by Colonel Roosevelt, wearing a sombrero—signaled an impromptu parade down Saratoga streets, a stamping, cheering ovation in Convention Hall, and the onset of immoderate anguish in the hearts of the Old Guard. Its victory at the State Committee meeting six weeks earlier had seemingly presaged the easy election of Vice-President Sherman as temporary chairman, but now no sooner had the presiding officer paused in his enumeration of Sherman's noble qualities than a Nassau County delegate rose and nominated TR. The furor was overwhelming; the final vote: 567 to 443, in favor of TR. The Colonel had, most assuredly, "beaten them to a frazzle."

However, TR, in his keynote address, made gestures of harmony, extolling Taft's accomplishments as President. "I hope you saw the proceedings of the Saratoga Convention," Taft wrote acidly to Mrs. Taft. "Roosevelt made a speech praising me also, which must have gone a little hard with him, but which indicated he found it necessary. . . ." No one appeared to be pleased, for from insurgents came cries of outrage over TR's "endorsing the Administration." Pinchot objected to TR's use of the word "upright" in describing Taft. "But, personally," TR wrote a California insurgent, "I think it is absurd to say that Taft is not upright— just as I think it absurd for Taft's friends to complain to me as they do because although I acknowledge him to be upright, I nevertheless think that he lacks the gift of leadership, is too easily influenced by the men around him and does not really grasp progressive principles."

A steady stream of bulletins from Saratoga came to Taft at the lunch table and at his office, keeping him informed of what was going on at the convention. Neither he nor Norton were able to conceal that they were "greatly cast down" by TR's victory.

As the fall campaign began, Norton's obsession with a demonic TR kept Taft on edge and bitter about his old friend. "The President no sooner gets quieted down," Archie Butt observed, "than Norton repeats more gossip and gets him all upset again." Hiding an attack of gout for fear it would inspire levity among political cartoonists and among his own family, poor Taft even tried to tell his doctor that his ailment was tight shoes, but the doctor laughed heartlessly. Irritated by the strict diet that relief from the gout and his excessive weight demanded, Taft found no comfort in TR's supporting the regular New York State Republican ticket and saying nice things about him, with even a brief but fairly kind word about the Payne-Aldrich Tariff Act.

Though the New York gubernatorial candidate was Henry L. Stimson, a protégé of Elihu Root, that TR was stumping the state for Stimson and vigorously supporting him led Taft to regard Stimson as a stalking horse for TR's presidential candidacy in 1912. In an effort to keep the New York campaign from being purely TR's, Taft came to New York "ostensibly to help get things together for Stimson, but," Archie Butt pointed out, "I don't think he is doing much for he listens too eagerly to everyone who has a word to say against Roosevelt and rather gives the impression that Stimson more or less means Roosevelt." The big money men in Wall Street, usually the pillar of Republican support in New York, actually formed committees in support of the Democratic candidate, so violently anti-Roosevelt were they.

The candidate himself, Harry Stimson, reserved and conscientious, had difficulty emerging from under the shadow of the Colonel. The New York *World* ran a daily box score on the front page of the number of times TR used "I" in his speeches for Stimson. By the end of October, the score had risen to an alarming number; when the Colonel asked young Felix Frankfurter, Stimson's aide, "Am I making the right kind of speeches for Harry?" Frankfurter delicately pointed out the *World*'s scoreboard and suggested that he had "a slight tendency to subordinate the candidate." "Oh, I'm so sorry," TR said. "Oh, I mustn't do that. This is too bad. I must stop doing that. I must bear that in mind." Formidable though the task may have been, the next day in Buffalo, TR bore down heavily on Stimson—praising his integrity and his record as U.S. Attorney. Stimson, he emphasized, was the issue. "Of course," he exclaimed, "I know they want to make you believe that I am the issue. It's got to such a point that I can't even say *My Country 'tis of Thee* without being accused of egotism."

But, alas for the Republicans, election day in November brought, in Taft's words, "not only a landslide, but a tidal wave and holocaust all rolled into one general cataclysm." Translated, this florid outpouring meant that the Democrats after sixteen years had gained control of the

House and Senate and that the strength of the Republican party lay in progressivism rather than in conservatism.

This defeat was shared by both TR and Will Taft. Stimson lost in New York, and Taft's Ohio went to the Democrats. Even the undiscerning were able to read significance in an election in which Old Guardsmen lost in the East and only progressive Republicans won in the West.

Following this debacle, President Taft, accompanied by his brother Charlie, sailed off to Panama, where blue skies and tropical warmth evoked the happier days in the Philippines. During Taft's absence from Washington, TR came there for an American Geographical Society meeting and visited the White House, where he had an affectionate reunion with the staff. No Tafts were present; Mrs. Taft was in New York. "I was amused," wrote Horace to Will, "at her finding it necessary for her to come to New York on the day that Teddy arrived in Washington."

Yet, there was a possibility in the air of a break in the hostilities between the two men. Taft, at Archie Butt's suggestion, invited TR to stay at the White House if he came to Washington for the Gridiron Dinner (though Taft said he would say nothing about it to Mrs. Taft until he found out whether TR would come). TR thanked him for the invitation but said he wasn't going to the dinner. Taft immediately wrote again, addressing his letters "My dear Theodore," to express the hope that "occasion will arise when we can have you and Mrs. Roosevelt under the White House roof and resume in some way our relations of yore."

There was a little more to the possibility of reconciliation than wishful thinking and polite gestures. After all, Charles Norton, a leading source of provocation, had lost much of his influence on Taft, and was now casting about for a bank position. Taft was now relying for political advice on Charles Hilles, Assistant Secretary of the Treasury, who had been planning on resigning and going into private business. Taft asked him to remain. "I have got to have an understanding with the President," Hilles told Archie Butt, "for if I remain he will have to give me authority to patch up some sort of truce with Colonel Roosevelt." TR, Hilles said, "knows of Norton's vilification of him and of course attributes it to the President."

Before long, White House conversation—particularly that of the President—took on a note of kindlier sentiment toward TR. Indeed, Taft, in a glow of good feeling, was even heard to say, "I do not think that anyone can ever say he has heard me say anything against the Colonel."

Taft also wrote TR a long friendly letter, giving him an account of the progress of the Panama Canal and reporting that it would be finished in about 1913—"a date," he wrote, on "which both you and I will be private citizens and we can then visit the Canal together." He also sent TR the manuscript of his annual message to Congress for his opinion, and TR replied with commendation, opinions, and advice. "If you care to have me," he offered, "I'll write you my general views on the Japanese question"; however, he wrote Taft, "I don't wish to but[t] in."

It was almost like the old days. All in all, on the last day of 1910 Archie Butt hopefully looked ahead to a brighter horizon in 1911.

Fourteen   Silver and Steel

For Theodore Roosevelt, who had aroused such excessive adulation among his fellow citizens, the tortuous events of 1911 came as cold confirmation of his own omniscience. The insurgent Western states, where he had campaigned, had defected to the Democrats; in the conservative East, New York—his own state, where he had so vigorously supported Harry Stimson—had also defected. Popular opinion held him responsible. It was, therefore, clear that his hold—to the Old Guard, his inexplicable hold—on the American people was over. He was, at last, "THRU!" He who had risen like a rocket now suffered a swift descent. The battle cry, "Back from Elba," had become "Back to St. Helena." But had he not often predicted, in those recurring periods of melancholy during his years of power, that this would be his fate? "I am going down like Dewey," he had told Lawrence Abbott in June of 1910, and he had then maintained that the hysterical reception given him on his return from Africa could only terminate in popular revulsion. "I was like Peary at the North Pole," he wrote a friend in January of 1911, "and any way I walked I could not help walking South."

But despite this determinedly philosophical acceptance of human nature's vagaries, TR's mood was one of dejection. The number of prominent men—progressive and orthodox Republicans—who either made the pilgrimage to Oyster Bay or stopped for lunch at *The Outlook* offices on Fourth Avenue had diminished.

Word of TR's despondency soon reached Will Taft in Washington. Archie Butt, hoping to arouse Taft's sympathy for TR, reported that Lloyd Griscom, in a visit to Sagamore Hill, "had found the Colonel in a most depressed state of mind; all his old buoyancy was gone, and he really seemed to him to be a changed man." Mrs. Roosevelt, Griscom thought, seemed even more depressed than her husband.

"Tell me again," Taft asked Butt, "what Griscom said." Butt's account of Theodore and Edith Roosevelt's bleak depression elicited the kind of sympathy he had hoped for, in the form of an analytic exposition.

"Archie," Taft said, "I don't see what I could have done to make things different. Somehow people have convinced the Colonel that I have gone back on him and he does not seem to be able to get that out of his mind. But it distresses me very deeply, more deeply than anyone can know, to think of him sitting there at Oyster Bay alone and feeling himself deserted. I know just what he feels. It is a dreary spot in winter and the surroundings must have a bad effect on both of them."

Taft paused and gazed straight ahead. Then Butt observed that "he reached up and wiped his eye." "I don't know," Butt wrote to his sister-in-law, "whether a tear had formed there or not, but I could see that something of a big nature was going on in his mind. He may have been reviewing all those years of intimacy and come face to face with some thought of disloyalty on his own part."

Butt started to leave, but the President waved him back. After another silence, Taft spoke again, saying, "It may be that a break had to come. The situation was a most difficult one for both of us, but no harder for him than for me, and I don't think he ever saw my side of it. What he is undergoing now may be the thing most needed to get him back to a normal frame of mind. The American people are strange in their attitudes toward their idols. This is not the first time this sort of thing has happened. They have even led their idols on and on to cut their legs from under them later and apparently to make their fall all the greater. Where I do blame Roosevelt," he went on, "is for allowing them to get him in this position. He should have kept aloof and not given the people an opportunity to do what they have done. But I don't know when I have had anything to affect me as deeply as the picture which this conversation brings to my mind. To feel everything slipping away from him, all the popularity, the power which he loved, and above all the ability to do what he thought was of real benefit to his country, to feel it all going and then to be alone! I hope the old boy has enough philosophy left to take him through this period; that is all. If he could only fight! That is what he delights in, and that is what is denied him now. The papers in the East have adopted a policy of ignoring him, of never mentioning him. I had heard this was done with a view of driving home the iron. This robs him of the right to hit back, to fight, and leaves him in a way without an audience. I hear Pinchot has deserted him and that his old allies are weakening. It is all sad!"

The rumor Taft had heard of a deteriorating relationship between

Pinchot and TR contained an element of truth. Their main source of friction was, of course, Will Taft. Pinchot could not tolerate any references to Taft except the most condemnatory ones. Therefore, for several months after the election of 1910, his sense of outrage impelled him to engage in a running argument with TR over the latter's use of "upright" in describing Taft. Now he and his brother Amos and other progressive politicians were backing La Follette for 1912. "Gifford is going in with some of the extremists in Congress with the expectation of trying to form a third party if Taft is nominated," TR wrote to his friend Robert Bacon. "He has become identified with the ultra-extremists, and I can only work with him now to a very limited extent."

Will Taft's analysis of TR's situation was not too different from TR's own views. He had been rebuked, he felt, by the electorate, who did not wish to be so relentlessly advised. "People," he wrote William Allen White, "very much resent the effort to make them more virtuous than they feel inclined to be! So my present feeling is that I had better keep out of active participation in politics."

It was easier to place this restriction on himself than to carry it out. His method consisted not of absolute withdrawal from the political scene—which would, in any case, have been impossible—but of treading carefully on a precarious course between the progressive and the administration Republicans. It was an exercise not unlike the one in the old days when he and Gifford Pinchot had walked "the Crack" in Rock Creek Park. Unfortunately, trying to keep his balance between opposing poles of Republicans proved neither as simple nor as enjoyable. When the progressives demanded that TR become a member of the newly formed National Progressive Republican League—the Paterson *Call* said it should have been called the National Party-Buster League—TR gave his refusal in somewhat the manner of a patient, understanding adult reasoning with a sullen child. "Now, my dear Senator," he wrote La Follette, "don't you think that the way I can best help the league is by cordial endorsement of it over my signature in *The Outlook?* At the moment I am very anxious not to seem to take part prominently in any political movement, in the sense of managing the details."

In balancing this conciliation of the progressives, he once more engaged in a friendly correspondence with Will Taft. They exchanged views— TR's frequently crossing the line into advice—on Japanese exclusion, Canadian reciprocity, and the Mexican revolution. The latter situation led TR to write: "If by any remote chance—and I know how remote it is—there should be any war, a war in which Mexico was backed by Japan or some other big power, than I would wish immediately to apply for permission to raise a division of cavalry, such as the regiment I commanded in Cuba."

Such a swashbuckling recouping of glory was a recurrent daydream. Now, prosaically, in early March, TR and Mrs. Roosevelt set off on a trip to California, where they would visit with Ted, Jr., and his wife, and where TR would deliver a series of lectures at the University of California at Berkeley. They went by regularly scheduled trains, for TR's semi-pariah status obviated the necessity for special cars. Nor was there any need for a separate railroad car for reporters, as there had been in 1910, for no reporters accompanied them. Gloatingly underscoring his fall, the San Francisco *Argonaut* declared, "Mr. Roosevelt has ceased to be an epidemic and has become merely a local irritation."

TR's one real pleasure was the expectation of the birth of his first grandchild, in August. Characteristically, he imputed to childbirth high national purpose. "I love to think how my eldest son and his darling wife are doing their duty," he wrote his daughter-in-law, "in every way, just as I would most wish to have it done."

From San Francisco TR wrote Taft a letter in which, without making a definite promise, he clearly tried to give Taft assurance as to his intentions for 1912. "Well, thank Heaven!" he wrote, "I am coming to the end of the last speaking tour I shall ever make. When I end this I will have practically covered the United States, according to the plan I announced before I left for Africa; and while I shall of course have to speak now and then on different occasions, it will be a case of making one speech and coming back, and never again will I have to make a tour; or have to make more than an occasional speech." (One can only conjecture whether Will Taft found the implication of this statement comforting or if his uneasiness might have been increased by the date of the letter, April 1.)

"If he could only fight!" Will Taft had said. Insights engendered by a long friendship enabled Taft to prescribe for TR's depressed state. The opportunity for that therapeutic combat—which would eventually engulf Will Taft—was in the process of development in the spring of 1911.

At the beginning of that year, the first Democratic majority in the House since 1895 met and, following one political tradition as ritualistically as if it were set down in *Robert's Rules of Order*, formed various committees to investigate the past activities of the Republican administration. One committee, the Stanley Committee, chaired by Democratic Representative Augustus O. Stanley of Kentucky, set forth to detect wrongdoing in the acquisition of the Tennessee Coal and Iron Company by the United States Steel Corporation during TR's administration. (The *Wall Street Journal* pointed out that at the beginning of a bitter attack against U.S. Steel by Congressman Stanley, U.S. Steel common stock was selling at 80 3/4 points, and that forty-five minutes later, when he finished, it had risen to 81 3/4.)

How the merger came to be had its roots in the Panic of 1907, when the price of shares for Tennessee Coal and Iron, held as collateral for loans by an eminent New York brokerage house, fell below the sum of the loans. Inevitably, these shares would have had to be thrown on the open market, which would have further decreased their value, thus causing the brokerage house to fail and the network of Wall Street banks to tumble after it. As a result, the country would have suffered an even more formidable financial disaster.

To the rescue came the United States Steel Corporation, represented by J. P. Morgan, Judge Elbert Gary, and Henry Clay Frick. They offered to buy the Tennessee Coal and Iron stock for twice its value at the time, emphasizing that it was in order to avert a national crisis. Fearful, however, that such an action might be subject to prosecution by the government as a violation of the Sherman Anti-Trust Act, the steel magnates arranged a hurried meeting with President Roosevelt. Traveling by night in special cars, Gary and Frick arrived at the White House before TR sat down to breakfast. They explained their plan and reiterated that "little benefit will come to the Steel Corporation from the purchase" of the Tennessee company, but that they felt it was "immensely to their interest as to the interest of every responsible business man, to try to prevent a panic and general industrial smash-up." After consultation with Elihu Root, TR told them he felt it was "no public duty of mine to interpose any objections."

The merger became a reality; the banks did not fail. But in the three and a half years that had transpired, criticism of U.S. Steel's purchase of the Tennessee Coal and Iron Company mounted. It attributed to U.S. Steel a less altruistic motive than patriotism: to secure a valuable property at a very low price, a plan carried out either with the connivance or through the credulity of Theodore Roosevelt. Though TR had always been able airily to dismiss charges that he aspired to be dictator, to be king, or that he was a political opportunist, a radical—even a madman— this charge that he had corruptly plotted with "malefactors of great wealth" or been used as a tool by them made him boil with rage.

At the beginning of June, the Stanley Committee indicated that former President Roosevelt might be subpoenaed as a witness, and TR wrote his former secretary, William Loeb, asking him to find a letter he had written to his Attorney General "giving a statement of just what was done."

Less than a week later, at a celebration of Cardinal James Gibbons' jubilee in Baltimore, TR and Will Taft met in the reception room of the Fifth Regiment Armory. Surrounded by reporters, they shook hands, "chatted, laughed and behaved," said the New York *Times*, "just as they used to when Mr. Roosevelt was in the White House and Mr. Taft was Secretary of War." After a few moments, TR looked around for Archie Butt, who came forward to have his hands warmly clasped. "Mrs. Roosevelt sent her love," TR said to him, "and told me not to come back unless I saw you and gave her message to you."

As Butt—now promoted to Major—observed, his two big friends "played the game beautifully through the program." The eyes of everyone in the hall "were riveted on the faces of Taft and Roosevelt, eager to catch any signs which might be construed into friendship or hostility. Once when they whispered together and got to laughing, it so pleased the people that they all broke into cheering and applause."

Earlier, they had had a ten-minute conversation, out of public earshot, if not of vision. This conversation, they later maintained to reporters, had been devoted to talk "about Mrs. Taft's health." However, another subject they discussed went unmentioned: the Stanley Committee's investigation. Taft had asked TR to refuse to appear before the committee if he was summoned, for this was within his rights as an ex-President. "I told him," TR wrote Nick Longworth, "that this was a position that I was not willing to take, that if I were asked to appear before the committee I certainly should do so."

On parting, Taft invited TR and Mrs. Roosevelt to be guests at the White House for the silver wedding anniversary he and Mrs. Taft were to celebrate in two weeks. TR said they'd try to come.

The Washington correspondent of *Harper's Weekly* asserted that no one having any dealings with Charles Dyer Norton ever suspected him of being naïve. "He very readily knew the difference between a hawk and a handsaw, or, for that matter, between an insurance agency in Chicago and a steppingstone." But whatever ambitions Norton may have had in regard to his position as presidential secretary in 1910, it was evident to him by early 1911 that a vice-presidential post in the First National Bank in New York was preferable to the frustration encountered in trying to be the power behind William Howard Taft. In actuality, the choice had not been left wholly up to him. Pressure for his removal had come from scattered sources. Even Senator Murray Crane, Norton's old ally of the previous summer, had turned on him. Did Taft know that Norton "has separated him from almost every friend he's ever had in public life," Crane exclaimed to Archie Butt, "and has almost made him hateful in the eyes of the House and Senate and with every public man who was his friend?"

Many of the congressmen's egos had been bruised when, upon being summoned to the White House, they learned it was not the President but Norton who wished to see them. They retaliated by refusing to increase the salary of a presidential secretary from six thousand to ten thousand dollars a year; finally, grudgingly, they had acceded to seventy-five hundred dollars a year. Cabinet members felt Norton's "practice of setting one person against another was seriously damaging Taft's prestige," and urged Taft's close friend, John Hays Hammond, to speak to the President. "You are closer to Taft than we are," they told Hammond, "and your position is a disinterested one. The President won't let us say a word against Norton." Shortly after Hammond went to Taft and began by saying, "I've come to tell you about Norton," Norton resigned.

Into the vacancy came forty-four-year-old Charles Dewey Hilles, a quiet, assured, unhurried man, "with an easy manner and a low and notably pleasant voice." Like Norton, Hilles had also been Assistant Secretary of the Treasury, but in Hilles' background was experience as Superintendent of the New York Juvenile Asylum in Dobbs Ferry. This career in the management of juvenile delinquents, the *Independent* declared, "in a way, not overly far-fetched, may prove of great value to him in many of the predicaments which will encumber his new position."

At about the same time that Norton left his position, Richard Ballinger, whom Norton had striven so mightily to oust, resigned from the Cabinet. Ill, with his normally thin nerves in a raw state, Ballinger returned to Seattle and resumed his law practice, rehabilitating his health and ego by casting rancorous remarks at the Roosevelt conservation policies—particularly at "the frothings of Gifford Pinchot." Ballinger's obvious feelings of ill-usage were increased by Taft's appointment of Walter Fisher as Secretary of the Interior. Fisher was not only a conservationist of the Pinchot persuasion, but he was also a friend of the former Chief Forester, circumstances indicating that his appointment was a sincere gesture of placation —at least, in part. "The circumstance of the appointment of Mr. Fisher as my successor," Ballinger wrote with an injured air to President Taft several months after his departure, "in view of his attitude toward your enemies and my enemies, was, I frankly confess, hard to bear. . . ."

Sympathetic reporters and pragmatic Republican politicians hoped that with these two political encumbrances removed from his path, Will Taft could gain public popularity and restore his old friendship with Theodore Roosevelt or—if that were not possible—the appearance of it.

There was some ground for the latter hope, because Taft and TR continued through the spring to carry on their friendly correspondence. But Will Taft remained stubborn, honest, and politically naïve, though he had begun to assume—in an almost playful manner—the trappings of a political maneuverer. To his dinner for Speaker Cannon—the largest dinner of this kind he had ever given—he had invited eighty-five guests, and Mrs. Taft indignantly upbraided him "for being so profligate in his invitations," though only seventy-two persons accepted. Laughingly her husband told her she had no political acumen, that she would find everyone at the dinner whom he hoped to "cajole" into voting for his reciprocity treaty with Canada. However, on the afternoon of the dinner, when the President told his wife that Cannon was fighting the reciprocity bill and the Old Guard "was playing the most dastardly tricks," Nellie Taft reproached him. "So you see this entire dinner is wasted," she said. "Twenty-five would have done just as much good as seventy-two. Now I do wish you would consult me before you do these things. I could have told you that nothing will move that old Cannon when he gets his head set, and it is a waste of good material to lay a dinner before him." It almost seemed as if, having had disillusioning experiences as First Lady, Mrs. Taft now was determined to get through the remaining two years of her husband's term as inexpensively as possible.

Throughout the afternoon of the day of Taft's dinner party, Cannon and the Committee on Rules battled off efforts by the Taft forces to bring the reciprocity bill to a vote; finally, the Rules Committee gave in, and the bill was brought in to be voted on. The President was informed that owing to the impending vote, his dinner guests wouldn't be able to get to the White House by eight o'clock. Deciding to postpone dinner until nine, Taft called his wife to consult with her. Archie Butt found the ensuing one-sided phone conversation "a most characteristic one." It indicated, he noted, "the methods which the President pursues when he wants to accomplish something very much."

"Is that you, my darling?" Taft spoke into the receiver. "I say," he repeated, "is that you, my darling? . . . Come closer to the phone, dear. Is that you, Nellie? . . . It would be a little more grammatical to say, 'It's I' but I don't care what pronoun you use as long as you utter it sweetly. . . . Yes, 'me' does sound more natural, but we can't change the English grammar. I couldn't, at least; but I don't feel so sure about you. . . . Well, they can do without you for a few minutes. . . . Don't hurry me so. . . . I thought you might be interested in the good news. They have got the Reciprocity bill up in the House and are now voting on it. . . . Yes, I thought it would interest you. . . . I am afraid it will make some of the members who are coming to dinner late. . . . No, I don't see how we can help it. Would you mind having dinner a little later, say at a quarter to nine? . . . Too late, is it? Well, I don't want to upset your plans. What do you think we had better do? . . . All right, then, we will say half-past eight and I will notify all our guests at once. . . . No, I will do it from here. Archie is here, and he has the list. . . . That is sweet of you, my dear; then half-past eight. Better tell the cook. . . . Of course, I might have known that you would think of that. Good-bye, darling. You are a trump all right."

Hanging up, Taft turned to Archie with a "bland, childlike smile," and asked, "We can't come down until you notify us, can we, Archie?" Butt agreed that they couldn't, and the President said, "Send a telegram to each guest at once saying that the dinner is postponed until a quarter of nine, and you see to it that the cook knows of this corrected hour and see that she does not give our secret away and then have the operator call up the Senators at least by phone and notify them."

But while a Machiavellian Will Taft could manipulate a three-quarter-hour postponement of a dinner party over the wishes of his wife, the reciprocity bill proved more troublesome to him. In the end, by July, 1911, he had forced its passage through Congress, but at the price of alienating both progressive Western farmers and Old Guard Eastern manufacturers, thereby adding another obstacle to his re-election.

As his sister-in-law Annie Taft said, the reciprocity measure was like their old Walnut Hills house in Cincinnati—"of a peculiar architectural beauty that wudden't pleze manny [sic]." By the fall of 1911, the reciprocity bill didn't even please Canada, which, prompted by Taft's inept phrase that intimated annexation of Canada by the United States, refused to approve it. Thus, all of Taft's prodigious efforts to bring about a kind of free trade with Canada, which, he felt, would be of benefit to both countries even though it might "break the Republican party for a while," had come to nothing.

In contrast to the ugly political passions aroused between Capitol Hill and the White House over reciprocity, the scenic view along the Potomac was spectacularly lovely. The Japanese cherry trees that Mrs. Taft had planted the previous year had flowered, and Mrs. Taft "actually clapped her hands in delight when she saw the cherry blossoms." Even the President, observed Archie Butt, "waked up from his lethargy to show his pleasure in them."

By the beginning of May, Washington's spring entertainments had also begun to ease tensions, at least superficially. Mrs. Taft's White House garden parties, inspired by those given by the Emperor and Empress of Japan, were in full swing when she collapsed and suffered a relapse. Nothing, however, could stem the horse shows, theater and dinner parties, teas, and musicales. Even Mrs. Taft's garden parties continued unabated, with her husband, "half as buoyant as usual," and her daughter, Helen, "girlish but dignified," receiving in Mrs. Taft's place.

In truth, Will Taft's buoyancy had been subject to attack by his brother-in-law Dr. William Edwards, who with his wife, Taft's sister Fannie, had come from California for a visit. "The Doctor has that sort of candor that is proverbially uncomfortable among friends," Taft wrote his brother Horace, "and he feels called upon to make an unfavorable prognosis of everything in sight. He did not think I was sufficiently advised of the seriousness of Nellie's attacks, and he wished that I would call a consultation of doctors in order that I should be. My disposition is to be as cheerful as possible, and as optimistic as possible, and I did not feel like exaggerating bad symptoms and minimizing good ones. The Doctor, I think, is just the opposite. At any rate, we had one or two sharp passages, with Fannie acting as Moderator. However, I like him; he is a fine fellow."

Among official diversions was the White House dinner to receive the new senators elected in 1910, most of whom were progressive Republicans noticeably hostile to the President. Despite their evident animosity, Taft made a genuine effort to exude his customary geniality, even having an inferior violinist—a constituent of an insurgent senator—play in the East Room. So dreary was his performance, that Mrs. Taft, who was sensitive to and knowledgeable about music, declared that she would do "a good deal to propitiate the insurgents, but in the future she will draw the line on admitting their musical friends to the White House."

But it was not only in music that Mrs. Taft suffered disappointments. Her first two years as First Lady had fallen gravely short of her expectations. What was to have been the fruition of a lifetime ambition and the dawning of a splendid new era in White House social history under her aegis had soured and become disagreeable. Her husband's steady series of difficulties—with Congress, with the tariff, with Pinchot and Ballinger, with the insurgents—was painful, but tolerable. As for the ominous specter of Theodore Roosevelt and 1912 suspended over the White House, this was a danger that had always been clearer to her than to anyone else and did not cause her to flinch. But to be afflicted with an illness that frequently prevented her from taking her place as White

House hostess, an illness that had crippled her speech, and to know—as Ike Hoover, chief White House usher, cryptically recorded—that "the peculiarities rising from her condition caused many embarrassing moments, especially to the President," was almost unendurable for a proud, ambitious woman.

During that memorable week's visit to the White House in 1877, in which her presidential aspirations for a future husband had first taken shape, the Rutherford B. Hayeses had held a silver wedding anniversary celebration. Now, on June 19, 1911, came what Mrs. Taft was to recall as "the greatest event of our four years in the White House, our Silver Wedding."

It proved to be an occasion of monstrous proportions. More than six thousand invitations were sent out. They went to all of official America— the justices of forty-six states, governors, mayors, bishops of the Episcopal, Catholic, and Methodist churches, eminent rabbis. ("Our Rabbi Marks is invited," the San Antonio *Express* reported proudly.) "And presents, Clara!" Major Butt wrote in shocked emphasis to his sister-in-law. "Well I never knew there was as much silver in the world. It is hideous to see such profligacy."

As the night of the silver wedding anniversary approached, a constant parade of delivery wagons drove up to the White House, bearing more silver gifts. Vice-President Sherman and his wife sent a silver vase; the Supreme Court, a silver service; the Senate, a set of solid silver compote dishes; the House, three dozen solid silver service plates; the White House press room, a silver bowl; the Gridiron Club, a silver pitcher. Impressive as these gifts were, they were surpassed by the two-hundred-year-old silver soup tureen, rumored to be worth eight thousand dollars, sent by Elbert Gary of the United States Steel Corporation, which was even then under the scrutiny of the Stanley Committee, and by the cabinet of tea caddies from John D. Rockefeller, Jr., and his wife, the former Abby Aldrich. Taft, alarmed, directed his wife "to let no one see them, at least until certain ones have been secreted in cold storage."

Although willing to place lavish silver gifts from embarrassing sources in an inconspicuous spot, Mrs. Taft felt that though "silver was showered upon us until we were almost buried in silver [it] was incidental, we couldn't help it; it was our twenty-fifth anniversary and we had to celebrate it." (For many years afterwards, Mrs. Taft, to her husband's chagrin, made practical use of the prodigious number of silver objects they had received. She had the monograms changed and sent them off as wedding gifts.)

Remembering, in particular, the horrendous weather of her husband's

Inauguration Day, Mrs. Taft complained that "all my life the elements have been unfriendly to me." As if justifying her complaint, Willis Moore, the Weather Bureau Chief, who had forecast sunny weather for March 4, 1909, which had then misled the Tafts, appeared at the White House in late morning of June 19, 1911, to report to the President that the weather would be "most unfavorable." Rain, heavy rain, would drench Washington and the White House grounds where the reception—a night garden party—was to be held. But as it turned out—again to the embarrassment of Chief Moore—the night of the reception was remarkably clear. The lights playing on the Washington Monument made it stand out sharply against a deep-blue sky. The White House grounds were lighted by myriads of tiny colored lights on every tree and bush and by innumerable Japanese lanterns, and searchlights focused on the State, War, Navy, and Treasury buildings. Will and Nellie Taft marched across the festive lawn to stand under a canopy with electrically lighted figures: "1886–1911." There they stood for two hours and shook hands with five to six thousand people. For Mrs. Taft, the reception proved to be everything she had dreamed it would be, and, fortunately, she did not hear the "rather vulgar *sotto voce* inquiries" noted by Mrs. James Slayden, wife of a Texas Democratic congressman: "How much did you put up? Are you getting your money's worth?"

Among the thousands of guests invited had been relatives of former Presidents. Grants and Hayeses as well as relatives of Chester Arthur and of Andrew Jackson were there. James Garfield had been invited, but had not accepted. And, of course, as always, the daughter of one former President, in particular, received an excessive amount of attention. She was dressed in "electric-blue satin, flesh colored stockings and gold slippers." As described by the acute Mrs. Slayden, "she held the very scant skirt quite high, and when the band played, kicked about and moved her body sinuously like a shiny leopard cat. She has a way of throwing back her head and showing all her teeth just like her father, but hers are very white and handsome."

The invitation Taft had extended to Alice's father in Baltimore had not been accepted. While the Tafts and their five thousand guests were celebrating on the White House lawn, TR was working in Oyster Bay on a pamphlet for the American Museum of Natural History entitled "Revealing and Concealing Coloration in Birds and Mammals." He was, he maintained to Ted, Jr., "keeping as much aloof from politics as possible." Yet under the veneer of his semifriendship with Will Taft there rankled several offenses. He still held Taft responsible for the Republican debacle in New York the previous November and for the activities of a number of his associates who TR believed were engaged "in a perfectly dastardly campaign of slander and mendacity" directed at him.

Just a few weeks earlier had come another affront. TR opposed on several points Taft's arbitration treaty with Great Britain and France, which proposed "the adjudication of an international arbitral court in every issue which cannot be settled by negotiation." He wrote Cabot Lodge that Taft was "thinking sloppily" and "speaking sloppily" when in a Decoration Day speech, urging support of the treaty, he had maintained that "the horrors of either internecine or international strife far outweigh the benefits that may be traced to it." (James A. Drain, President of the National Rifle Association, wrote an editorial for the NRA magazine condemning Taft's antiwar remark and sent a copy of it to TR, who responded enthusiastically. "I liked too," TR wrote Drain, "the sentence in which you said that death was not a dreadful thing. To me there is something unspeakably humiliating and degrading in the way in which men have grown to speak in the name of humanity of death as the worst of all possible evils. No man is fit to live unless he is ready to quit life for adequate cause.")

So despite the appearance of cordiality at their meeting in Baltimore, Will Taft's short thank-you note for the anniversary gift of silver the Roosevelts had sent ended the correspondence that had so briefly buoyed up the hopes of the Republican party.

The Stanley Committee investigating the United States Steel Corporation was, in TR's view, a body of "dishonest jacks." In early August of 1911 TR appeared at New York City Hall to "put the case clear as a bell." He declared that when he told Gary and Frick they might acquire the Tennessee Coal and Iron Company he "did exactly right." Moreover, he asserted vigorously that he had not been deceived by Gary and Frick. He simply had to stop the panic. To form a judgment as to whether they were motivated by an avid desire for Tennessee Coal and Iron or "whether they were only anxious to save the situation caused by the panic" was not, in TR's opinion, his duty. "That both motives were in their minds I thought possible, and now think possible," he said. "What was the predominant motive was of no consequence." Expounding further several weeks later in *The Outlook*, he maintained he would have shown himself "a timid and unworthy public servant if in that extraordinary crisis I had not acted as I did . . . but I fully understood and expected when there was no longer danger, when the fear had been forgotten, attack would be made upon me." In concluding with a rather bitter comment on the nature of gratitude, he wrote, "If I were on a sailboat, I should not ordinarily meddle with any of the gear; but if a sudden squall struck us, and the main sheet jammed, so that the boat threatened to capsize, I would unhesitatingly cut the main sheet, even though I were sure that the owner, no matter how grateful to me at the moment for having saved his life, would a few weeks later, when he had forgotten his danger and his fear, decide to sue me for the value of the cut rope."

Despite all his dissatisfactions with his successor, TR still privately clung to the need to support him. When Ted, Jr.—as of August, the father of Grace, the Roosevelts' first grandchild—wrote his father that he was thinking of supporting Wilson "if he runs next year," TR asked him to delay a decision, for, he said, "to take any public stand against, especially by supporting his Democratic opponent would cause me great embarrassment. . . . I don't pretend to say that I like Taft, or approve of him, or enjoy supporting him . . . [but] I believe that Taft, plus the Republican Party would do better than the Democrats could do."

Most of October was taken up with anxiety over Mrs. Roosevelt, who at the beginning of the month had fallen off a horse onto a macadam road and had not regained consciousness for over twenty-four hours. During a slow recovery, she suffered agonizing headaches, but by the third week in October TR wrote a friend, "Edith is now really on the mend."

However, the following week she experienced "a temporary setback," which was perhaps not unrelated to an occurrence of almost seismic consequence in the relationship of her husband and Will Taft. On the morning of October 27—his fifty-third birthday—TR opened his New York *Times* and read the black headline in the left-hand column of the front page: "FILES SUIT TO DISSOLVE STEEL TRUST." The Taft administration, through the office of Attorney General Wickersham, TR read, had instituted a suit against U.S. Steel for violation of the Sherman Anti-Trust law. In a descending order of headlines, the sixth carried the most lethal offense: "Roosevelt Was Deceived."

The case the government presented was a long one, and one paragraph received special attention.

The President [Roosevelt] was not made fully acquainted with the state of affairs in New York relevant to the transactions as they existed. If he had been fully advised he would have known that a desire to stop the panic was not the sole moving cause, but that there was also the desire and purpose to acquire the control of a company that had recently assumed a position of great significance.

When reporters rushed out to Oyster Bay to learn TR's reaction to the statement that he was "deceived by the Tennessee Coal and Iron Company deal," he "smilingly" refused to say one word to interviewers beyond his suggestion that they read the testimony he had given before the Stanley Committee.

But his personal reactions, revealed in letters and conversation, to having been labeled, he said, "either a fool or a knave," was a fierce, overwhelming, unquenchable anger. "Taft was a member of my Cabinet when I took that action," he wrote James Garfield. "We went over it in full and in detail, not only at one but at two or three meetings. He was enthusiastic in his praise of what was done. It ill becomes him either by himself or through another afterwards to act as he is now acting. I am sorry to say that I think you are right and that both he and Wickersham are playing small, mean and foolish politics in this matter." To Everett Wheeler, President of the Reform Club in New York, TR wrote, "What I did was right." As he told the congressional committee, he would do it again under the same circumstances. He again pointed out that Taft had been a member of his Cabinet; "we went over the whole transaction afterwards in the cabinet," he continued, "and Mr. Taft was emphatic in his commendation. Of course it was one of those cases where the protest should have been made instantly, or else from every consideration of honorable obligation never under any circumstances afterwards." "I suppose," he went on, scornfully, "that Mr. Taft did not know of Mr. Wickersham's action. Of course my own conception of the office of President is that he is responsible for every action of importance that his subordinates take, that is for every action sufficiently important to make it part of the Administration's policy."

Emboldened by the government's suit and its critical reference to TR, Congressman Stanley did not trouble to restrain his pubic utterances, declaring to reporters that Roosevelt had given U.S. Steel "a plenary indulgence to do business according to its own sweet will" and that Gary and Frick had "forced the strenuous Theodore to eat out of their hands." "I am curious to know," he added, "how they [the government] can indict the United States Steel Corporation without at the same time condemning this action of Roosevelt."

Though this question had been prompted by Stanley's partisanship, it was, nevertheless, a provocative one. How, indeed, could Taft indict U.S. Steel without condemning TR? But TR didn't pause to answer. With the strongest weapon at his disposal—the columns of *The Outlook*—he struck back, writing an eight-page repudiation of the government's case, entitled "The Trusts, the People and the Square Deal." Not once did he mention Taft by name. Instead, he dealt with the committee's assertion that he had been deceived by Gary and Frick. "This statement is not correct," he declared. "I believed at the time that the facts in the case were as represented to me on behalf of the Steel Corporation, and my further knowledge has convinced me that this was true. . . . I was not misled . . . and any statement that I was misled or that the representatives of the Steel Corporation did not thus tell me the truth as to the facts of the case is itself not in accordance with the truth." Following a lengthy defense of his integrity and acumen, TR dilated at even greater length on the whole subject of trusts, presenting the history of his administration in antitrust suits and trenchant criticism of the basis of the Taft administration's suit. Summing up, he wrote:

It is practically impossible, and, if possible, it would be mischievous and undesirable, to try to break up all combinations merely because they are large and successful, and to put the business of the country back into the middle of the eighteenth-century conditions of intense and unregulated competition between small and weak business concerns. Such an effort represents not progressiveness but an unintelligent though doubtless entirely well-meaning toryism.

This issue of *The Outlook* sold out immediately, and tens of thousands of copies of the article itself were reprinted to supply the demand. Suddenly everyone all over the country was again talking about TR; "the very mention of his name stirred the people as nothing else would do. . . ." All those progressives who had lost patience with him took heart and once more flocked to Sagamore Hill. Even more astonishing, *The Outlook* article had created, as Henry White wrote TR, "a great impression in Wall Street Circles." For, by attacking U.S. Steel, Taft had called down upon himself the wrath of the business world. Upon reappraisal, corporation men began to question certain of their tenets. Was Taft really a friend of business? Was TR really an enemy? Consequently, before long, several substantial men of Wall Street motored out to Oyster Bay.

"I feel badly over the editorial of the sage of Oyster Bay," Mabel Boardman wrote sympathetically to Will Taft, "only because it would give you that pinch of pain such an act on the part of one you had loved and trusted would bring. I knew it meant to you a personal not a political hurt and that probably made me resent it all the more."

But Miss Boardman erred in feeling that Taft had not suffered political harm from *The Outlook* article. For a corollary of the great revival of favorable political interest in TR was a resurgence of TR's self-confidence—in abeyance during most of 1911. Earlier that year, Taft had prescribed "the right to hit back" for TR's despondency. Now Taft provided him with both opportunity and target. For, as TR wrote a friend in barely subdued jubilation, the article's appearance "caused what evidently had been a very strong undercurrent to come to the surface in the shape of talk about my nomination for the Presidency."

In October, several days before the government suit against U.S. Steel had been filed, TR had written William Allen White that he expected every friend of his to do their utmost "to prevent any movement looking toward my nomination, no matter what the circumstances may be." But on December 5, three weeks following the publication of his *Outlook* article, he wrote Judge Ben Lindsey, in a letter marked "Personal & Confidential," that he could consider it "a calamity" to be nominated in 1912, for, he said, "poor Taft with the assistance of Aldrich, Cannon and others, has put a burden upon the Republican Party under which any man who attempts to lead it will stagger." Although he reiterated to Judge Lindsey that he sincerely did not want the nomination, he admitted, "speaking confidentially, I should add:—that of course circumstances might conceivably arise when I should feel that there was a duty to the people which I should not shirk, and so would accept the nomination." In between these two letters had come the steel suit, *The Outlook* article, public response, and the amusing coincidence of representatives of both Taft and La Follette forces coming out to Oyster Bay to ask him to declare that he "would not under any circumstances accept the nomination."

"Of course," he wrote Cabot Lodge, "I refused point blank. I told them that I emphatically did not want the nomination . . . but that I should certainly not definitely state that if it did come in the form of a duty I would refuse to perform that duty; in other words, that as Abraham Lincoln used to say, no man can justly ask me to cross such a bridge until I come to it." (Horace Taft felt that TR's "quotation of Lincoln in support of any position of his own indicated a lack of a sense of humor.")

The political renascence of TR produced the inevitable rumors and rumors of rumors. Alice Longworth's sister-in-law, Clara de Chambrun, called Archie Butt on a Monday in late November to say she "must see the President for ten minutes only." It was, thought Archie, a funny request and, speculating on what revelation she would make, he noted, "as she is most hostile to Colonel Roosevelt, it may be that she has discovered some deep plot directed against the President. The Longworths are great at discovering plots." The feeling of covert activities might have been in the air, for on the same November Monday that the Countess de Chambrun called Archie Butt, the sharp-witted Mrs. James Slayden, having attended a tea given by Mrs. Pinchot, wrote in her diary that "Mrs.

Pinchot's hatred of the Administration is an obsession. She talked about 'Progressives,' 'Insurgents,' and such political shades and plans until I pictured her and Gifford as a pair of deep conspirators with Jimmy Garfield stepping softly in front carrying a dark lantern."

The conspiratorial manner also cloaked Alice Longworth, "simply jubilant" over the upturn in her father's political fortunes. At a dinner party on the following Sunday, she took Archie Butt aside to whisper, "Isn't it the most wonderful thing in the world, Butt? Of course he would not have the nomination this time, but it just shows what is in people's hearts." The following week, returning from a visit to Oyster Bay, she called Major Butt and with a great air of mystery asked him to come around and see her. "I brought a message from Father," she said, "which I think I had better deliver to you in person."

"Now, Butt," she said when he arrived at her house, "you know that we are all devoted to you. Father looks upon you as a son, almost. Certainly I have never known him to be fonder of anyone outside his own family than he is of you, so you must understand what he meant when he told me to give you this message." Then she hesitated, afraid, she said, that he would not understand. Finally, after some urging by Archie, she revealed that when she was having lunch with her father in New York, he had said ("and very seriously, Butt, too, he said it"), " 'Alice, when you get the opportunity, tell Archie from me to get out of his present job. And not to wait for the convention or election, but to do it soon.' " What had he meant? asked a bewildered Archie, and Alice replied enigmatically that "he meant just what he said," and refused to say more. But she did give him her advice: "to get from under the edifice before the crash came . . . the President can't be elected, and it looks doubtful if he can even be nominated." However, Major Butt was incapable of taking such advice, for he felt "it would be a cowardly thing to do."

As 1911 ended, a pair of antithetical cycles had been completed with a precision and symmetry that seemed in obedience to some natural law. TR's depression at the year's beginning had now been displaced by an elated aggressiveness. But Will Taft, so hopeful in January, was, on the last day of December, being importuned by Mabel Boardman to "stop showing his depression" and to "appear optimistic whether he felt so or not, for his half-disconsolate statements were having a depressing effect on the electorate. . . ."

Fifteen   "TR: RU or RU Not?"

"If you were to remove Roosevelt's skull," Will Taft had said, "you would find written in his brain '1912'"—a year that now had arrived, ushered in with a New Year's Day reception for eight thousand at the White House. But the President's impulsive utterance had expressed irritation rather than conviction. At times he maintained TR would not seek the nomination, but on receiving a confidential memo from Charles Hilles reporting a rumor that TR "said that he would not become a candidate, but would accept the nomination if the Convention forces it on him," the President wrote across the top of the memo, "I am not surprised." His brother Harry believed TR "would take it if he can get it," and the Philadelphia *Inquirer* stated: "Mr. Roosevelt's position seems to be that he positively will not say he is a candidate, but dares anyone else to say he isn't." Mrs. Taft's opinion held no equivocation; she knew. She told her husband, often and with great certainty, that Roosevelt would attempt to get the nomination.

What a German paper called "the Teddy *Leitmotiv*" occupied the thoughts of a great many people in those early weeks of 1912. No less a power than George Walbridge Perkins, Vice-President of the New York Life Insurance Company and a partner of J. Pierpont Morgan, made the trip from shadowy Wall Street to sunny Oyster Bay to persuade TR that the country needed him. Elegantly slim, Perkins spoke softly and was as "careful of punctilios as a preacher at the front door of the church." He favored gray, the color of his delicately curled mustache and the sprinkling in his brown hair, and wore a gray alpaca suit. The country had much to gain from TR's nomination, he believed, for TR had stated that size did not make a trust bad, that the government should not destroy trusts, but regulate them.

Perkins was only one of the swarm of visitors that descended on Sagamore Hill—newspaper editors, political bosses, full-time idealists, Rough Riders, cartoonists, former members of his Cabinet, governors, senators, members of the House, publishers, college professors. All urged him to change his mind about the nomination; many had been waiting impatiently for the day Taft would leave office and TR take his place.

One senator, Robert Marion La Follette of Wisconsin, did not appear; if he had, it would have been for exactly the opposite reason that had brought all the others. La Follette had already asked TR to make it clear by a formal statement that he would not be a candidate for the nomination, so that all progressives could rally around La Follette. TR had not obliged. This might have indicated to TR's devoted followers that he was seriously considering being a candidate, but that would have been overlooking the antipathy the two men had for each other. Back in 1908, TR had spoken of "the La Follette type of fool radicalism." When TR and La Follette met for the first time, they mumbled what might pass for the expected amenity and started moving from each other while still going through the motions of a handshake. It suggested the wary, tense meeting of dogs encroaching on each other's territory.

But La Follette was the exception; the devotion, the blatant idolatry exhibited at Sagamore Hill and in *The Outlook* offices duplicated what TR had experienced in Europe in 1910.

Still, some of TR's advisers felt that he should "not have the nomination this time," for the Democrats would win in 1912, just as they had won in 1910; therefore, they reasoned, let Taft have his nomination and defeat, and then TR could win in 1916. TR, by temperament, was not one for such long-range planning. The impulsive act—or what appeared impulsive—characterized him, but he also believed the mark of the statesman was to temporize.

The technique became obvious, and the New York *American* spoke for everyone when it asked, "TR: RU or RU Not?"

With more forthright impatience, in December, 1911, Lincoln Steffens had complained, "The Colonel is mussing up the whole Progressive movement with his 'To be or not to be.' "

Finally, TR publicly altered his flat, unequivocal no. He would consider being a candidate for the nomination, he disclosed, but only on one condition: that the public overwhelmingly demand it. (In November, 1911, Taft had expressed the opposite view in a note to Mabel Boardman: "If the people do not want me I am entirely willing to retire.") It must be clear that people wanted TR; not that he, for personal reasons, wanted the nomination.

The anti-Roosevelt press viewed TR's requirement with cynical suspicion. Why did Napoleon, back from Elba, require the assurance of his subjects? One cartoon represented TR beating a big bass drum, identified clearly with the legend "CALL OF THE PEOPLE"; it showed him beating the drum with one hand, with the other cupped at his ear.

In spite of all the charges of megalomania and insincerity, TR had a hard, pragmatic basis for demanding a popular summons. He hadn't forgotten the defeat of 1910, and he didn't want to enter a contest that was hopeless. He knew that the Republican-machine politicians who might make victory possible would, if he had popular backing, regard him favorably.

To make sure he had sufficient popular support, he watched and analyzed the political situation—state by state—far into the night at Sagamore Hill.

Then, in Philadelphia on February 2, 1912, La Follette delivered a speech at a dinner attended by eight hundred journalists; the repercussions of what he said and how he said it brought TR to his decision.

Woodrow Wilson, then Governor of New Jersey, but slated by conjecture and destiny for a much higher post, had preceded La Follette. Elegant of phrase, and yet with a lightness fitting the occasion, he held his audience. (He pointed out to publishers that as a writer he was afraid they wouldn't publish him and now as a public figure he was afraid when they did.) La Follette's speech would have to be superb; a comparison between it and Wilson's was inevitable.

The audience did not know that La Follette, still weak from a ptomaine poisoning attack, had been working very hard that day—and it was ten at night before he began to speak—that his daughter was to undergo serious surgery the following morning, and that he had downed a tumbler of whisky in order to be able to speak at all. He started out with a polemic on money in the United States, prefacing it with an attack on journalism and journalists. Merely astounded at first, then angered, individuals in the audience began to leave as La Follette grew more and more vehement.

Their departure caused La Follette to shake his fist at them. "There go some of the fellows I'm hitting," he exclaimed. "They don't want to hear about themselves."

Continuing in this vein until twelve thirty—in a hall that had become half empty—La Follette finally sank forward on the table at which he was seated.

The next day, the progressives, who had been halfheartedly supporting La Follette, diagnosed his Philadelphia speech as evidence of a nervous breakdown; now they could swing to TR, who they felt had a much better chance than La Follette of winning.

Though the press had been the object of La Follette's irrational attack, one newspaper pointed out, "he is being ruthlessly hustled inside the hearse although he still insists that he is strong enough to occupy a seat alongside the driver."

Callers continued to come to Sagamore Hill and to *The Outlook* offices, but now, with La Follette no longer in the running, they became more importunate than ever. Though this whirlpool was TR's natural habitat, his wife decided to escape from it by going on vacation to Panama with their daughter Ethel; the Providence *Journal* interpreted this as "an ominous sign . . . let the women and children be removed; the fight is about to begin."

TR's political dilemma continued: both silence and anything he might say about the nomination would be subject to misrepresentation. To illustrate this problem, he said to a reporter one day in his office, "There are only two elevators in this building and I must use one or the other of them. If I go down by the side elevator, that is evidence of furtiveness. If I go down in front, that is proof of ostentation."

Finally, TR concluded: "The evil of my speaking out publicly is less than the evil of my refraining from speaking." However, he felt it was of the utmost importance that this statement be made in "the right way." Governors had written him, urging him to be a candidate for the nomination; and the "right way" stemmed from their correspondence. To one of the governors, Chase Salmon Osborn, he wrote his plan: "If four or five Governors wrote me a joint letter . . . which I could respond to . . . such procedure would open the best way out of an uncomfortable situation." And, he said, there must not be the "slightest manipulation." With this clear-cut understanding, the letter to the seven "little governors" was ingeniously assembled: parts from the governors' letters, from advisers and from TR himself. To get the signatures of the governors for this round-robin letter, Frank Knox went to see some of them at a Progressive conference in Chicago; even snared one, Young Governor Bass of New Hampshire, while Bass was on his honeymoon. By February 10 all the signatures had been obtained for this "somewhat 'cooked' letter," asking TR to accept the nomination of the Republican party if he were nominated; it was then put in an envelope, sealed, and sent off to TR. Straight-faced, Alice Longworth said the letter "did not take Father by surprise."

Over a week went by and the document still had not been made public. But TR, on the twentieth of February, wrote to Truman Handy Newberry, in the course of asking him to "take charge of things" at the Republican convention in Chicago. "You understand, my dear fellow, that probably Taft will be nominated. This is not a thing we can say in public, because of course such a statement discourages men; but I am in this fight purely for a principle, win or lose."

In the middle of February, Alice Longworth attended a dinner at the White House; with her knowledge of her father's political plans, she strongly suspected that it was the last time she "would see the inside of the White House while the Tafts were there, as indeed it was."

Although William Allen White had suggested the need for someone to put "cayenne pepper where it will do the most good," he felt that TR had gone too far in a speech on February 21 to the Ohio Constitutional Convention. For even White, loyal progressive though he was, believed the speech probably "crippled him [TR] more than any one thing that he did in his life." In presenting a series of proposals, essentially his personal platform, TR, to the shocked dismay of Republican regulars, advocated the recall of judicial decisions. If enough people, he said, "feel that the decision is in defiance of justice," then it should be voted on. If the voters reversed the court's decision, their reversal would stand "subject only to action by the Supreme Court of the United States." ("Why did your Father except the Supreme Court?" Nick Longworth asked his wife "saturninely.")

The import of the speech "sent the Country into convulsions," and appeared to some to be aimed at Taft personally, for he and the judiciary were as one. Conservative newspapers lashed out in fierce editorials, and the Wall Street men, who had turned their eyes speculatively on TR, now reeled back in aversion, as did regular Republicans who had been thinking TR might have a better chance of being elected than Taft. Even some progressives—White and Senators William E. Borah and Albert B. Cummins—found the recall of judicial decisions too radical. As for Cabot Lodge, he proclaimed in a statement to the press: "I am opposed to the Constitutional changes advocated by Colonel Roosevelt in his recent speech at Columbus."

Many critics of the speech misunderstood what TR had meant. A Boston friend of Roosevelt's and a judge, Robert Grant, tried to point out to some of these critics "that what he had in mind were not civil and criminal cases, but cases where the several States had declared humanitarian Acts passed by the Legislatures to be unconstitutional."

One noteworthy remark made by TR just before his Columbus speech was seemingly lost in the outrage generated by his speech. "My hat," he had told a reporter, "is in the ring." In spite of this remark, TR felt that because of the nature of the Columbus speech he should give any of the seven governors who found the speech "too radical" a chance to withdraw; therefore he did not reveal their letter and his reply announcing his willingness to accept the nomination until February 24.

To Archie Butt's virtues of loyalty, romanticism, gentlemanliness, decency, and etiquette was added the chivalry of the Old South. For Taft, to whom he owed allegiance, he bore a deep and compassionate concern. It had pained him—literally to the point of tears—to see his chief, with whom he traveled for fifty-eight days in the fall of 1911, visiting twenty-eight states, attempt to salvage something from the disastrous election of the preceding year with speeches that were "dry and full of statistics." The bad manners of "fellow citizens screeching and screaming 'Hello, Bill,' from one town to the other" appalled him. Even in the South, his South, he had to admit that he heard "saucy little brats sometimes yell, 'Hello, Fatty.'"

Taft had indeed put on weight, as he always did during stress. He spoke of going on a diet, for he weighed three hundred and thirty-two pounds, and said to the White House housekeeper with a laugh, "Things are in a bad state of affairs when a man can't call his gizzard his own." They were also bad because during those days of January and February, 1912, "the Teddy *Leitmotiv*" sounded loud and discordant to Taft. Four days into 1912, Henry Adams, that aristocratic—and malicious—voice of doom from across Pennsylvania Avenue, wrote a friend: "I went out and crossing the square was stopped by a big man who hailed me loudly. It was a hippopotamus! . . . It was the President himself wandering about with Archie Butt, and I joined them as far as the White House porch. He, too, gave me a shock. He [Taft] looks bigger and more tumble-to-pieces than ever, and his manner has become more slovenly than his figure; but what struck me most was the deterioration of his mind and expression. He too is ripe for a stroke. He shows mental enfeeblement all over, and I wanted to offer him a bet that he wouldn't get through his term."

Though Adams, as usual, reflected his own obsessively dismal outlook rather than reality, Will Taft was, unquestionably, fatter and more harried. To cheer him, Archie Butt belittled the idea of TR accepting the nomination, and added, "He would be sure of defeat if he took the nomination this time."

Taft nodded. "But the trouble is, Archie, that the Colonel, I fear, is encouraging this talk. . . . The Progressives see that it is impossible to nominate La Follette, and so they turn to Roosevelt. It is bringing about an awful split in the party." Turning to Mrs. Taft, he said, "But I remember that it looked just as blue for me four years ago. Don't you remember it, dear, when we got back how black everything looked?"

"Yes," she said, "but I was always hopeful then. I am not hopeful now. Things are different."

"Well, you are not hopeless about the nomination?" Taft asked worriedly.

Still finding it difficult to enunciate clearly, Nellie Taft said slowly, "I think you will be renominated, but I don't see any chance for the election."

"Well, I am chiefly interested in the renomination, so don't get disconsolate over that. If we lose the election I shall feel that the party is rejected, whereas if I fail to secure the renomination it will be a personal defeat."

The strain bore down with increasing heaviness on President Taft and on Archie Butt, who was torn between his devotion to both TR and Taft. Butt worriedly noticed that Taft's skin had taken on a waxy look, and that he had developed "unhealthy bags" under his eyes. And his tendency to drowsiness had become stronger. In church on Sundays the ritual of arising and sitting down kept him awake, but the sermon had a soporific effect on Taft. Relating one such incident to his sister-in-law, Archie Butt wrote: "I had not suspected that he was asleep until I heard an audible snore, and then I punched him, and he woke with such a start as to attract the attention of everybody around him. Then as I could see he was dozing . . . I resorted to my old trick of having a spell of coughing. He knows what that means, and it straightens him out for a time. The people around me yesterday must have thought me consumptive, for I had to keep it going throughout the long tiresome sermon."

On weekdays Major Butt was also close to the President. In the mornings, Taft had a masseur, and every afternoon he walked with Butt, panting for breath with each step he took. Butt hoped the walks would "bring him around," but he saw that the condition of neither the President nor himself was improving. His compassion grew as Taft became more and more in need of understanding and sympathy. Then the daily walks had to be halted, for Taft's gout flared up, producing pain in both feet. Butt was also aware that "the trouble with the Colonel hangs over him like a big, black cloud and seems to be his nemesis. He frets under it."

"I don't understand Roosevelt," he would say to Archie. "I don't know what he is driving at except to make my way more difficult. I could not ask his advice on all questions. I could not subordinate my administration to him and retain my self-respect, but it is hard, very hard, Archie, to see a devoted friendship going to pieces like a rope of sand."

To see Taft in this despairing state pained Butt. Moreover, he felt obliged to speak, but could not, for the situation required that he comfort Taft by speaking against TR. And this he could not possibly do. He simply could not "talk against the Colonel."

Still, with sadness, he realized that both TR and Taft were to blame. His devotion forced him to an impartial criticism, which stemmed completely from affection. "The President has done what he should do publicly," he wrote, "but I think he has been greatly at fault in the past. He has talked against the Colonel, speaking slightingly of him in private, and all these remarks have been repeated. There was a lot he could have done at the beginning."

Emerging from Taft's office one day in mid-January, Charles Hilles whispered to Archie Butt to come downstairs with him. There, in the confidential confines of the White House basement, Hilles told Archie that Robert Bacon, one of TR's old Tennis Cabinet members, had resigned as Ambassador to France and that President Taft believed he did so "at the suggestion of Colonel Roosevelt."

In an exchange of confidences, Archie revealed the message he had gotten from TR through Alice Longworth—"to get out and to do so before the nomination." Others who had been close to TR had received the same warning, Hilles said. "There is going to be great bitterness between the two before and during the Convention and I think the Colonel wants to notify his old friends that they had better be prepared for the fight to the finish, for no one can remain neutral during the next few months." On two occasions, Hilles said, he had sent the Secretary of War, Harry Stimson—like Butt, Stimson, too, was torn in his loyalties to Taft and TR—out to Oyster Bay to "sound the Colonel out" on his position. Both times Stimson could merely report that "the Colonel was as hard as nails and utterly implacable," and that this animosity dated from the U.S. Steel suit.

Two days later, during lunch at Alice Longworth's, Stimson's findings were confirmed when Archie talked to Corinne Robinson, TR's sister, who gave him the impression that the "breach was irrevocable."

"When I think," she said sadly, "of the old days at the White House and how these two men seemed to love one another it makes me very unhappy to think of the great chasm which lies between them now. How they would get together and talk and discuss matters! And I remember the way their laughs would mingle and reverberate through the corridors and rooms, and Edith would say: 'It is always that way when they are together.'"

If only TR could see Taft as he had seen him, Archie told her, he was sure the Colonel would be moved by his old friend.

"Oh Major Butt," she said "it is too late now. If it had not been for that Steel suit! I was talking with Theodore only last week, and he said that he could never forgive."

"Of course you know," Archie told her, "that the President never saw that suit until it was filed."

"Yes," Mrs. Robinson replied, "and Theodore knows that, and that in his eyes is the worst feature of the case—that such a thing could have been done without his knowledge."

On a Sunday at the end of the month, when he motored out to Oyster Bay to spend the day with the Roosevelts, Major Butt was able to judge for himself the chances of a *rapprochement*. Though he had received Taft's blessings for the visit ("Go by all means. It will cheer them and I know will make you happy"), Archie had heard that reporters were "on all the surrounding hills," and feared his appearance at Sagamore Hill would start the rumor that he had deserted to the "Roosevelt Camp."

The Roosevelts' other guest, the elderly French Ambassador, Jean Jules Jusserand, had the same fear, for when TR greeted Archie, he told him he had "old Jusserand hidden away in the back room." Then, leaning over, TR whispered in Archie's ear, hissing between his teeth, "He seems to be afraid of being seen, the sly old fox." When Archie suggested to Mrs. Roosevelt that Jusserand might like to return to New York with him by car, she said the Ambassador had said that "he wanted to keep his visit unknown for fear of giving offense to the President."

Despite this semiclandestine atmosphere, Major Butt found his visit was "like a leaf out of an old book. . . . They were just the same dear people. . . . The fireplaces were filled with huge logs which the Colonel cuts down for exercise . . . [and] the dogs were following one all over the house."

To Archie's amusement, an incident occurred that was another bit of nostalgia, characteristically Rooseveltian. TR's tree-cutting exercise that day led to his inadvertently cutting down all the trees holding the telephone wires, thus throwing the phone out of order. Informed of this at lunch, TR was also told he hadn't even "pulled the wires out after the trees fell."

TR looked guilty, and Mrs. Roosevelt began to laugh. "Now, Edie," he said, stopping her quickly, "don't you say a word. It was your own fault. You always mark the trees I am to cut down, and you did not do it. No, Edie, you did not do your duty as forester of this establishment, and you ought to be punished, but I will say nothing more about it and not hold you up to scorn before your children if you will let the subject drop once for all."

"It seems to me," said Jusserand, "that no one has said a word but yourself."

"Ah!" TR exclaimed. "But you don't know my wife. She has a language all her own. That telephone will never ring now that my wife will not begin to chuckle to herself, and if the cursed thing ever gets out of order, which it most frequently does, she will tell the servant to see if the wires are still up or if the trees are down. No, my dear Mr. Ambassador, people think I have a good-natured wife, but she has a humor which is more tyrannical than half the tempestuous women of Shakespeare."

In his desperate desire to mend relations between the Roosevelts and Tafts, Major Butt resorted to a slender thread. He told Mrs. Roosevelt that Mrs. Taft had determined "to make the Roosevelt china the White House china and to have no Taft china." Mrs. Roosevelt observed that "this showed a good unprejudiced mind." Whether this comment further displayed Edith Roosevelt's singular humor was not revealed.

As for the Colonel, not once did he mention Will Taft. As Archie and Jusserand prepared to leave (upon reflection, the Ambassador decided it was safer to return by car "than risk the station where most of the newspaper men stand on guard"), Mrs. Roosevelt sent her love to Taft, but TR, suddenly laconic, said only, "Give my best regards to Stimson."

Butt met the Tafts, according to prearrangement, at Harry Taft's house in New York. He found them "itching to know what had happened at Oyster Bay." Despite strong hints from Mrs. Taft "to tell them something," Archie took malicious delight in keeping silent. Later, however, when he and the President were alone, Archie gave him Mrs. Roosevelt's message.

"And the Colonel, Archie?" asked Taft.

"He said nothing, sir. I don't believe he is a candidate, but I simply caught this from the atmosphere; but he will never forget the Steel Trust suit, in my opinion."

"If he is not a candidate," Taft persisted, "why is he sending for governors and delegations all the time?"

"It is all a mystery to me," Archie admitted, "but the fact that he would not send a message to you by me was significant."

Dinner at the White House on February 25, 1912, was served at seven thirty. Mrs. Taft had specified this early hour, for she and her husband were going to the Belasco "to hear Buffalo Jones describe in a ludicrous way his catching of live animals," which Taft had said made "animal hunting in Africa ridiculous."

As President Taft and his wife and guests moved into the dining room, a note from the Associated Press was handed to the President. He read the note and then passed it to the others. Each one read what was on the piece of paper, and the silence that ensued was palpable. TR, the press dispatch said, had announced that he would accept the nomination if it were offered to him.

Mrs. Taft broke the silence, but not until everyone had been seated. "I told you so four years ago," she said to her husband, "and you would not believe me."

The President laughed—surely not without some bitterness—and said, "I know you did, my dear, and I think you are perfectly happy now. You would have preferred the Colonel to come out against me than to have been wrong yourself."

While strained conversation continued, TR's entire letter announcing that he would be a candidate for the nomination arrived from the office. It was the reply TR made to the letter that he had helped the "seven little governors" write:

Gentlemen: I deeply appreciate your letter, and I realize to the full the heavy responsibility it puts upon me, expressing as it does the carefully considered convictions of the men elected by popular vote to stand as the heads of government in their several States.

I absolutely agree with you that this matter is not one to be decided with any reference to the personal preferences or interests of any man, but purely from the standpoint of the interests of the people as a whole. I will accept the nomination for President if it is tendered to me, and I will adhere to this decision until the convention has expressed its preference.

One of the chief principles for which I have stood, and for which I now stand, and which I have always endeavored and always shall endeavor to reduce to action, is the genuine rule of the people, and therefore I hope that so far as possible the people may be given the chance, through direct primaries, to express their preference as to who shall be the nominee of the Republican Presidential Convention. Very truly yours, Theodore Roosevelt.

After Taft read the letter aloud, "everyone took a whack at it." "It is characteristic of him," the President said, "and it will be a rallying cry to the Progressives of the Country and to the discontented." However, he felt that in a short time "there will be a great sag in the sentiment which will at first be aroused by it."

One of the sentiments aroused by TR's announcement was expressed earlier in the day. In the West Wing, in Secretary of War Harry Stimson's office, Stimson and his law officer, Felix Frankfurter, were working when Congressman William Kent of California—a progressive and a friend of TR's—came in.

"Well, Harry," Kent said. "Terrible Ted has gone and done it."

"What's happened now, Will?" Stimson asked.

"Well, Teddy went with the girl so long he finally had to marry her."

Charles P. Taft expressed a less whimsical sentiment. He wrote his brother Will the next day, "While I was mad at Roosevelt this morning it did me good to go through the banks, brokers' offices and other places to hear the universal condemnation of Roosevelt. The universal theory seems to be that he is crazy. . . ." The following day, Charles P. sent off another letter to Will, assuring him that "everybody here is against the Colonel. If this kind of sentiment grows I do not see where the Colonel is coming in at all."

The night he learned of TR's intention to accept the nomination, Archie Butt lay awake for a long time, unable to sleep, trying to decide whether he should take his planned trip to Italy. Exhausted by the emotional crisis produced by dual loyalties, he had been advised by his doctor to take a rest. Duty. It was a matter of duty. What did duty require of him? Just a few days before, he had written, "No matter how much we may love the Colonel, we must remain true to the President." It was obvious Taft hated to see him go—and to go would make him feel like a quitter.

The next morning he canceled his sailing orders and told the President he wasn't going. Taft, however, insisted that he go. "I think," Butt observed, "he feels that I will break down just when he needs me the most if I don't go now."

And so Major Butt sailed to Naples on the S.S. *Berlin,* a North German Lloyd steamer.

"Don't forget that all my papers are in the storage warehouse," he wrote his sister-in-law, "and if the old ship goes down you will find my affairs in shipshape condition. As I always write you in this way whenever I go anywhere, you will not be bothered by presentiments now."

In April, he was to sail for home on the *Titanic.*

Elihu Root said of his old friend Theodore, "When he gets into a fight, he is completely dominated by the desire to destroy his adversary completely."

In this battle Roosevelt's plan of attack dovetailed nicely with his insistence all along that he would only serve on the condition that the rank and file Republicans needed and wanted him. The people must have the right to determine who the nominee would be; if they did not do this, by means of direct primaries, the machine, the bosses would pick the nominee. Because TR by now had linked Taft with these bosses and their corruption, he felt completely justified in attacking his former friend.

Though the Colonel might be "as hard as nails," a gentler strain in Taft kept him from relinquishing his friendship with TR's stern un-equivocalness and speed. In early March, Henry White attempted to make peace by writing TR that Taft had said he would never say any-thing against TR personally; "he never can forget the old and happy relation of intimacy . . . he could not help hoping that when all this turmoil of politics had passed, you and he would get together again and be as of old," White wrote.

It was a futile message. The litany of tribulation among Roosevelt and Taft intimates was itemized by Henry Adams with his customary re-morseless mockery. "All our friends are in real distress," he wrote on March 3, 1912. "Theodore has put them in a deadly box and is jumping on them with both feet. . . . Edith ran away in advance, with Ethel. . . . Mrs. Cowles is in Michigan bent like a cork-screw with rheumatism; Root and Cabot and all his old friends are thrown away and discarded. . . . Of course the whole strain centers on Sister Anne [Mrs. Lodge], as usual, but you can imagine how it squeezes her all round, for Gussy's [Augustus Gardner, Lodge's son-in-law] seat is in danger, and the danger affects Gussy's heart and temper. Constance [Gardner, Lodge's daugh-ter] and Alice Longworth are in the mess. From Boston I get only ominous silence. They are scared blue. . . ."

The pressure of primaries exacerbated the already rancorous feelings. When TR lost the primaries in New York and Indiana and Michigan and Kentucky, the Colonel began the chore of "not leaving an adjective un-turned." He not only shouted "fraud" when New York fell to Taft, but he linked Taft with William Barnes, Jr., New York's corrupt boss.

Noting TR's rage and that people were saying that TR had both lost his reason and was drinking, Taft remarked that he didn't believe TR was drinking. In a speech at the Lincoln Day Dinner of the New York Republican Club, Taft had declared that some of the progressive move-ment's leaders were extremists, "political emotionalists or neurotics." TR immediately maintained that "neurotic" had been meant to apply to him. (To the lay public—not yet aware of the universality of neuroses, or of the new science of psychoanalysis—the word "neurotic" meant "crazy.")

Then the picture concerning the primaries began to change; TR gained a victory in Illinois and exulted, "we slugged them over the ropes." This loss was difficult for Taft to take, for, like Roosevelt, he believed the fight was being fought for eternal principles. Constitutional law and Taft stood against TR's wild radicalism. From TR's point of view, he and social justice were fighting Taft and special privilege.

Nonetheless, Taft disliked "to speak with directness about Theodore Roosevelt." However, on April 14 he wrote to his brother Horace, who felt that "a snake in the grass is a pretty respectable sort of gentleman compared with T.R.," that he could not "expect those in charge of the campaign to refrain from pointing out his mendacity," and mendacity was carefully chosen over a shorter, stronger, more commonly employed synonym.

Still, TR not only viewed the work of the Taft managers of the campaign as "infamous," but he was also certain Taft was "conniving at it and profiting by it." The tenor of the conflict was such that Representative William B. McKinley—a cousin of the late President and Taft's campaign manager, a little man, blue-eyed, with a boyishness that baldness contradicted—was accused of using his congressional frank to send out literature in favor of Taft.

The battle between the President and TR continued to be such news that the Democratic party and its forthcoming convention in Baltimore received the briefest of mentions, paragraphs lost in the depth of the paper. This extreme neglect attracted some notice. The Indianapolis *News*, for one, pointed out that since the "Democratic nominee is likely to be elected," it was certainly time "the people were giving some attention to Democratic politics." (Even less mention was made of the Socialist party and its candidate, Eugene Victor Debs, making his fourth run for the presidency. The Socialist party predicted Debs would receive two million votes.)

But on Monday, April 15, startling, stunning nonpolitical news broke on the front pages, taking some space from the Roosevelt-Taft dispute. Around midnight of the previous day the *Titanic*, "the unsinkable ship," speeding through smooth-as-glass sea, brushed against an iceberg which tore a hole in its hull. For the 2,207 passengers there were only twenty lifeboats—sixteen wooden ones and four that were canvas and collapsible. The passenger list included such names as Astor, Guggenheim, Straus, Harper. Archie Butt was also aboard.

After a month of relaxation Butt was returning on the *Titanic* "to be with the President when he passes the flag or else be some support to him should he come in second."

Late on the night of April 14 Archie played bridge in the smoke room on A Deck. When the collision with the iceberg occurred, the shock was so little felt that he and the others didn't even stop the game momentarily. They also ignored the sounds made by the turmoil on the boat deck.

On April 15 the first news about the *Titanic* appeared, and it contained no information as to whether or not Archie Butt had been rescued. The fate of the friendship of the two men to whom he had been equally devoted was clearer. Beside the newspaper columns devoted to the *Titanic* there was an item concerning TR's primary victory in Pennsylvania —that it was growing. Incomplete returns gave Roosevelt sixty-five of the seventy-six delegates. "We hit them middling hard," TR said with an understatement that was part of the jubilation he felt, for this victory indicated popular opposition to the "bosses"—and Taft.

The Pennsylvania victory also marked a definite turn in favor of the progressive forces. Senator William E. Borah flatly declared, "There can be but one result, and that is the nomination of Mr. Roosevelt." As certain of the victory's significance, George Norris of Nebraska said, "Taft is out of the race." More analytically, Senator Miles Poindexter of Washington pointed out, "If President Taft cannot carry standpat Pennsylvania with the organization he had behind him there, the chances are against him everywhere."

The truth of all this caused William B. McKinley to strike back angrily, in the editions that carried the first news of the *Titanic*. That TR said he was wearing the mantle of Lincoln was, he declared, "evidence that the acme of demagogism has been reached." Moreover, TR, committing the Republican party to "rank socialism," was waging a campaign of "vilification and assault." Taft's campaign manager had still more to say. Taft, he said, in keeping with the dignity of his office, had "patiently submitted to misrepresentation, vilification and insult without reply." He had done this even though they had gone so far as to charge him, the President of the United States, with being "a receiver of stolen goods."

In those same editions—which went out into "a day of strange quietness, a spiritual numbness, a sense of mysterious horror at the loss of the *Titanic*"—Representative A. P. Gardner, who, like his father-in-law, Cabot Lodge, had been a long-time friend of TR's, challenged TR in a public letter to a debate on the issues of the campaign. It was his fear of losing his House seat that drove Gussy Gardner to throw down the gauntlet. Although the letter's salutation was "My dear Colonel," it closed with words that had the ring of a challenge to a duel: "The time and place for the debate I leave entirely for your decision." In a stinging telegram from Silver Creek, Nebraska, TR flatly refused to debate Gardner.

In his tirade McKinley had made a sober formal statement: "The President is in this fight to stay. He will be the nominee of the Republican convention at Chicago. He was nominated four years ago without the votes of Illinois, Pennsylvania, Indiana, New York or Wisconsin."

But Henry Adams in his bleak view of society linked Taft with the

Titanic, describing them as a pair of sinking leviathans. "I do not know whether Taft or the *Titanic* is likely to be the furtherest-reaching disaster. The foundering of the *Titanic* is serious, and strikes at confidence in our mechanical success, but the foundering of the Republican Party destroys confidence in our political system."

On the morning of the sixteenth, Taft faced the grim reality of the depressing bulletins concerning the *Titanic,* which were brought to him personally. In addition, the solemnity of almost everyone—moving slowly, speaking softly, as at a funeral—inevitably added to his gloom. Worst of all, though the bulletins came, and the newspapers released extra after extra, Taft did not receive the news he desperately wanted—news about Archie Butt.

Finally, Taft wired Vice-President Philip Franklin of the International Mercantile Marine Company: "Have you any information concerning Maj. Butt? If you will communicate with me at once, would greatly appreciate."

The next day, having received no reply, Taft could no longer bear the strain. He therefore ordered the cruisers *Salem* and *Chester*—on their way to meet the *Carpathia,* carrying the rescued to port—to flash word as soon as they had news of Butt.

Oblivious of Taft's emotional burden, his friends started at this time to pressure him to fight Roosevelt with Roosevelt's weapons. The time for sentiment and the niceties of gentlemanly behavior—which had meant so much to Archie Butt—was past. After all, they argued defensively, "Col. Roosevelt is deliberately trying to wreck the Republican Party."

During the day, Taft received a number of telegrams from the White Star Line Company containing lists of survivors, but Butt was not among them. The company pointed out that his name might be reported later. Taft sent copies of these wires to Butt's family in Augusta, Georgia, "and added hopeful words of his own."

TR, on this same day, delivered a speech in Omaha, Nebraska, in which he declared emphatically that the bosses were behind Taft. These bosses had been opposed to Roosevelt, TR made clear, in 1908, in 1904, and when he was nominated for Vice-President. He presented Taft's strength in this way: Taft's delegates in the Southern states represented "nothing whatever but the Federal officeholders"; and in states like Michigan, Colorado, Indiana, and Kentucky, as well as in the City of New York, his totals were a result of swindling.

Butt would not know of this speech—and of the more bitter verbal conflict ahead. Finally, word had reached Washington that Major Archie Butt had gone down with the *Titanic.*

Coincidentally, the last person who had seen him and survived had been associated with the White House and TR. When Roosevelt was President, Miss Marie Young gave the Roosevelt children special music instruction. Her face, framed by the huge coiffure of the period, was long but delicate, and had a sad, somewhat apprehensive quality.

In an interview in New York, she told of her departure from the *Titanic*. Butt, an old friend of hers, had been the last person on the *Titanic* to whom she spoke. "Archie himself put me into the boat," she said, "wrapped blankets around me, and tucked me in as carefully as if we were starting on a motor ride." He did all this calmly, "as if death was far away instead of being but a few moments removed from him." Then, she continued, "he stepped upon the gunwale of the boat and, lifting his hat, smiled down at me. 'Goodby, Miss Young,' he said, bravely, with a smile, 'Luck is with you. Will you kindly remember me to all the folks back home?'"

Butt stepped back onto the *Titanic*'s deck; he remained at the rail, watching the long, eighty-foot descent of the lifeboat through the darkness to the black water that was "as still as water in a tumbler."

When the boat left the steamer's side, Miss Young, looking up, saw Archie at the rail. "The picture he made," she said, "as he stood there, hat in hand, brave and smiling, is one that will always linger in my memory."

Taft also had fond memories of Archie Butt—of his heroic stance in the ornate uniforms for which he had a penchant, or as he sat gallantly erect on horseback, and of his gaiety and gentleness. And he recalled with affection the statement he had made one night, while on a Southern trip. Major Butt had interrupted his conversation with several newspaper correspondents to say that it was his bedtime. "I have four bosses," Taft had said, "and Archie is the hardest." Now, he wrote Archie's niece in England, "our dear Archie is gone."

All Washington stopped its social life and made tribute to "One of God Almighty's gentlemen." In Lindsborg, Kansas, where he was on the trail of convention delegates, TR said, "I and my family loved him sincerely." Taft's eulogy bore a striking resemblance to TR's. "He was like a member of my family, and I feel his loss as if he had been a younger brother." And Alice Longworth wrote: "High-spirited, warm-hearted Archie Butt; so torn between his loyalty to Taft and his loyalty to Father. . . . It was difficult to realize that Archie was lost."

And with his loss, lost, too, was the link that, at least in a tenuous figurative sense, joined TR and Will Taft by friendship.

Part V   TR vs. Will

Sixteen   Armageddon

It does not follow, in the form, rhythm, and truth of a mathematical formula, that two men who feel affection for the same individual will have affection for each other. Nor does tragedy—even though it be as dramatic and spectacular as the sudden mass drowning of fifteen hundred individuals—humble mortals for very long. And Will Taft had said with sadness of one of those hundreds, "I cannot refrain from saying that I miss him every minute, and that every house and every tree, and every person suggests him. Every walk I take somehow is lacking in his presence and every door that opens seems to be his coming." Still, bickering, pettiness, vanity quickly assert themselves, blot out the momentary insight, as a result of tragedy, into one's mortality and the kinship by death of Democrats and Republicans, progressives and standpatters.

Taft, it must be said, had held out against McKinley and all the others who urged that he be more combative. In February he had felt a candidate ought to be able to present his views to the voters "without the use of denunciation and personal attack." But by the last week in April, he had reluctantly capitulated and had written Mabel Boardman, "I agree with you that the time has come when it is necessary for me to speak out in my own defense. I shall do it sorrowfully. I dislike to speak with directness about Theodore Roosevelt but I can no longer refrain from refuting his false accusations."

Consequently, on April 25, President Taft rode on a special train cutting catty-cornered across Massachusetts, heading northeasterly from Springfield to Boston. The train stopped at a string of small towns and cities that dotted the rail route to Boston, and he stood on the rear platform—or at times went into town—and spoke. At all the towns— among them Springfield, Palmer, Worcester—he exclaimed in an anguished outcry, "This wrenches my soul!"

"I am here," he would say over and over again, "to reply to an old and true friend of mine, Theodore Roosevelt, who has made many charges against me. I deny those charges. I deny all of them. I do not want to fight Theodore Roosevelt, but sometimes a man in a corner fights. I am going to fight. Neither in thought nor word nor action have I been disloyal to the friendship I owe Theodore Roosevelt. . . ."

That night in Boston's Arena, Taft spoke to an audience of ten thousand. The crowd sang, "We'll hang Teddy's hat to a sour apple tree." With sweat streaming down his face, Taft repeated TR's charges against him.

He charges that the patronage of the government is being shamelessly used to secure my renomination, and that in the conventions and primaries which have been held, fraud and violence have been systematically used to defeat the will of the people and to secure delegates for me. He says that I am not a progressive, and after election joined the ranks of those who opposed me for the nomination; and he intimates that I have not the spirit of the progressive, or the imagination or the clearheaded purpose essential to the make-up of such a person. In short, he intimates pretty broadly that I am puzzle-witted. . . .

The speech went on and on, in the manner of Taft's speeches, each of eleven points were considered meticulously as in a matter of law, and he substantiated his denials by statements of his position and by quoting lengthy excerpts from his letters to TR and TR's letters to him. TR had, he said, misrepresented his views and actions. He suffered and the audience suffered. How long, after all, could "We'll hang Teddy's hat to a sour apple tree" sustain one? In conclusion, he referred to the recall of judicial decisions.

One who so lightly regards constitutional principles and especially the independence of the judiciary, and who is so naturally impatient of legal restraints, and of due legal procedure, and who has so misunderstood what liberty regulated by law is, could not safely be entrusted with successive presidential terms. I say this sorrowfully, but I say it with the full conviction of truth.

Taft then presented a condensed version of the speech to an overflow crowd at Symphony Hall. It had to be brief; the speeches of that long day had reduced his voice to a weary whisper and had depressed his spirits. Finally, he was driven to the Boston railroad yard, where his special train waited which would take him back to Washington.

Louis Seibold, a New York *World* reporter who was traveling with the presidential party, entered the car to ask the President a question. He saw Taft slumped forward on a lounge with his head in his hands.

Taft looked up. Seeing Seibold, he said, despairingly, "Roosevelt was my closest friend." Then he broke down and wept.

The occasion for Taft's Massachusetts speeches was the upcoming Massachusetts primary, for which TR had also planned an assault on the Bay State. On the twenty-sixth the Colonel left Oyster Bay for Worcester with a prepared speech. But after reading the complete text of Taft's attack against him in the morning papers, he discarded his prepared speech. His anger—his complete outrage—could supply him with what had to be said.

Instead of singing, "We'll hang Teddy's hat to a sour apple tree," the crowd that had come to hear TR talk shouted, "Hit him again, Teddy. . . . Put him on the ropes."

And TR did that. His normally high-pitched voice became shrill as he gesticulated with tightly clenched fists and charged that Taft had "not only been disloyal to our past friendship, but had been disloyal to every canon of decency and fair play." That Taft's soul had been wrenched by what he had to do, he damned as hypocritical. "He only discovered I was dangerous when I discovered he was useless to the American people. . . . I believe that he has yielded to the bosses and to the great privileged interests." As for reading his letters before the Boston audience, that TR branded "an unpardonable sin." Thereupon he did the pardonable in his eyes, by reading one of Taft's letters, in which Taft had expressed his obligation to TR—"in selecting me as your successor"—commenting bitterly, "It is a bad trait to bite the hand that feeds you."

The spectacle of an ex-President and a President engaging in such a corrosive exchange shocked everyone, including humorists. Mr. Dooley, with wide-eyed awe, said, "I wonher who ar-re th' professors iv personal abuse at Yale an' Harvard. They're good men whoiver they ar-re." And FPA declaimed in verse in the New York *World:*

T.R. to W.H.T.

For many a sun has set and shone
On the path we used to trudge
When I was a king in Washington
And you were a circuit judge.

I passed the lie and you passed it back;
You said I was all untruth;
I said that honesty was your lack;
You said I'd nor reck nor ruth;
You called me a megalomaniac—
I called you a Serpent's Tooth. . . .

The battle lines had now been drawn. What had been only thought—at worst, spoken in private—had now been declared on an open platform and disseminated by the press. The Democratic party, which had known fifteen lean years, could once again, because of this Kilkenny brawl, feel more than vain hope.

Will Taft had become a fighting Will Taft. His new-found aggressiveness in no way tempered his unfortunate gift for saying the wrong thing. On the night before the Massachusetts primary, he declared, "I was a man of straw but I have been a man of straw long enough. Every man who has blood in his body and who has been misrepresented as I have is forced to fight." After all, TR was hitting him in both eyes and above and below the belt, and he was backed to the wall; and so, he declared, "by George, if you have any manhood in you, you have got to fight."

A man of straw is usually not considered as bad as a rat. In a few days' time, Taft deteriorated figuratively, for in Hyattsville, Maryland, he said, "I am a man of peace, and I don't want to fight. But when I do fight I want to hit hard. Even a rat in a corner will fight."

"I Believe in Giving Every Man a Square Deal"—Theodore Roosevelt. By E. W. Kemble, *Harper's Weekly*, March 9, 1912.

As April ended and the campaign for a primary victory in Ohio began, Taft again said the wrong thing, this time in the form of a prediction. He stated with all the definiteness of a declarative sentence that the one who was victorious in Ohio would be certain to receive the nomination in Chicago in June.

Both TR and Taft, therefore, put everything they had into the Ohio campaign: TR spoke about ninety times; Taft even oftener. In one day TR spoke in Bellaire, Bridgeport, Martins Ferry, Steubenville, Wellsville, East Liverpool, Youngstown, Girard, Niles, Warren, Alliance, and Canton. Although the private trains of both men were in Steubenville at the same time one evening, there was no communication between them. Disappointment, therefore, struck those who had gathered expecting a street fight.

The virulence of the exchange in Massachusetts—where Taft won a narrow victory—had festered. TR's statement to his son-in-law that he would "avoid attacking the President unless he makes it impossible for me to refrain" meant nothing, for Taft used the terms "egotist" and "demagogue" and in return TR hurled "puzzlewit" and "fathead."

In Marion, Taft accused TR of saying "I—I—I" and not much else, and derided him with "honeyfugler." In Cambridge, he damned TR as a flatterer, as one not saying what he meant.

Andrew Carnegie did not approve. President Taft, he declared, deserved the nomination, but he should have maintained a dignified silence.

Taft's schoolmaster brother, Horace, felt not at all like the wealthy Scot, for he advised Will, "Don't be too personal in your attacks on Teddy. Generally you call him a liar in a perfectly dignified way."

"Apostate," "Jacobin," "guinea-pig brain" were brought forth from the verbal arsenal. No wonder the Atlanta *Constitution* said TR may have won the Nobel Peace Prize in 1911, but he would not win it in 1912. And Mr. Dooley observed that something new characterized the leaders of this republic. "Ye niver heard," he said, "iv George Wash'nton goin' around th' counthry disthributin' five-cent see-gars an' tellin' people that Thomas Jefferson run an illicit still."

The accusation of drunkenness was leveled at TR—which in some states was considered worse than running an illicit still. The country wanted to know how much TR drank, and when it heard that his capacity matched that of Lyman Abbott, the white-bearded editor of *The Outlook*, who looked like an Old Testament prophet, the question became, "How much does Lyman Abbott drink?" Abbott answered the question, but since he was a friend of Roosevelt's, how much reliance could one place on his answer? He spoke of light wines with meals and brandy used solely for medicinal purposes.

But the accusations of alcoholism continued. The "scoundrels" responsible for this unfounded calumny angered TR; he considered suing the Salina *Union* for reporting that he had been drunk while touring Kansas. While the charge of drunkenness was a nuisance, it was a relatively simple one to deny. To squelch the third-term controversy, which had arisen because of TR's statement in 1904 never to "be a candidate for or accept another nomination" proved more difficult. Now TR maintained that he had meant a third *consecutive* term, for if the terms were not consecutive a President could not use the power of his office to keep renominating himself. His friends at *The Outlook* stated TR's position with a vivid analogy: "When a man says at breakfast in the morning, 'No, thank you, I will not take any more coffee,' it does not mean that he will not take any more coffee to-morrow morning, or next week, or next month or next year." This explanation led the opposition to say that the real issue was not highballs or cocktails, but that third cup of coffee.

Soon another source of conflict emerged. Onto the emotionally charged Ohio landscape rode "Fighting Bob" La Follette, trying to recover from the political effects of his speech in Philadelphia. Stopping in Bowling Green, he lashed out against both TR and Taft; his style was the style of his adversaries. TR, he said, was an "inconsequential playboy."

Taking his usual omniscient view, Mr. Dooley declared all this billingsgate, slander, and personal animosity "pleasant and homelike." He went on to explain the paradox. "Ivrybody callin' each other liars and crooks not like pollyytical inimies, d'ye mind, but like old frinds that has been up late dhrinkin' together."

This alcoholic congeniality did not exist in the real world; rather, its atmosphere had the prosaic, stark, painful quality of the morning after. It was a morning, moreover, in which the sun had risen in the west; Republicans hated Republicans instead of Democrats, and conservatives had become revolutionaries.

Taft, speeding from one peaceful Ohio town to another, knew no peace. For one thing, Root, he told Horace, "has failed me." Elihu Root explained to Taft that though he wanted him to win the nomination, he could not come to Ohio and engage in the primary campaign. Root loved TR. He had served him in a confidential capacity. Therefore, he could not possibly enter into discussions concerning the right and wrong of the two administrations without deserving the charge of "betraying the confidence and disloyalty." Though Taft may have been justified in attacking TR, for he acted in self-defense, TR had not attacked Root. "He has never said a word . . . regarding me which was not kindly and laudatory," Root explained, and added, "My fighting days are over. . . ."

Root had hoped four months earlier to avoid the whole fight between TR and Taft, to retire to his farm in Clinton, New York—"under the protection of a force of accomplished liars who will say that I am not at home," he quipped.

Harry Stimson, too, as he had told Archie Butt at the end of February, was "in a hell of a fix," and had had to make a painful decision. In a speech for Taft that he delivered in Chicago, he said that though he had been inspired to public life by Theodore Roosevelt and believed firmly in his national policies, he "believed that those who are forcing him, contrary to his original intention, into the arena against Mr. Taft, are jeopardizing . . . the real cause of the progress of the nation."

"Heaven's sakes!" TR wrote Stimson genially, "you have so often been right that it is perfectly possible that I am wrong. . . ." He would not, he said, take seriously anything that reporters wrote about their relationship. Stimson made no such promise. Even if he had, the news item that TR had accused Stimson of being ungrateful, considering the campaigning Stimson had done for him in 1910, could not have been casually dismissed.

The tangle of ill feeling also trapped those related to the principles in the drama. When in Washington, Alice—a Roosevelt by birth, a Longworth by marriage, and irreverent by nature—realized she was in enemy territory. Washington, after all, liked Taft even though the rest of the country didn't. As for TR, the entire country—except for Washington— liked him.

Alice Roosevelt Longworth knew wisdom dictated that she refrain from talking politics. This called for painful self-control when individuals stepped forward and told her what they thought of her father's efforts to gain the nomination. In order to keep their relationship from being severed completely, Nick's sister Clara and her husband, Bertie de Chambrun of the French Embassy, made a pact with Alice not to talk politics.

All this silence, this "bottled-up savagery" affected Alice. She enumerated the results with objectivity and candor: "I had a chronic cold and cough, indigestion, colitis, anemia and low blood pressure—and quite marked schizophrenia."

Two weeks before the Ohio primary, Nick went to Ohio for speechmaking. According to their plan, Alice was to meet her husband in Cincinnati, but Nick phoned her not to come, "as the feeling was unbelievably bitter, particularly in his immediate family." He also advised her against another plan she had: attending a meeting of her father's in Cleveland. Gossip would seize upon this, would speculate as to why she had gone to Cleveland but not to her husband's district. From Cincinnati, Nick's other sister, Nannie Longworth Wallingford, had written Will Taft in late April, "It is almost intolerable to me not to put the deep loyalty I feel to the slightest use to you. You stand for everything I'd like to fight and work for." Alice had often remarked that she had "married into a family of lunatics," and so the day after TR's Columbus speech, Nannie wrote Taft, "I could hardly resist wiring her . . . 'Who's loony now?' "

When Alice did encounter her in-laws, she found them working devotedly to get votes for Taft. All Alice could do was phone her mother at Sagamore Hill and blow off steam, "and get large soothing doses of sympathy," but poor Nick had no such comfort; he continued to be "surrounded by furious females pulling him in opposite directions."

Unlike his daughter, TR bore antagonism and the desertion of friends with, to all appearances, a cheerful magnanimity. He understood his son-in-law's position perfectly. "Of course you must be for Taft." Cabot Lodge, who had been TR's dear friend for thirty years, had had to tell him he could not come out in his behalf. But he added, "As for going against you in any way or supporting anyone else against you, that I could not do." To this TR replied with an ebullience that did not seem quite apt. "My dear fellow," TR wrote Lodge from his office in *The Outlook*, "you could not do anything that would make me lose my warm personal affection for you. For a couple of years I have felt that you and I were heading opposite ways as regards internal politics. . . . Of course you will stand by your convictions. Now don't you ever think of this matter again."

Where genuine enmity existed, TR's victory in Ohio intensified it. It was a complete, unqualified victory: TR, 165,809; Taft, 118,362; La Follette, 15,570. Moreover, part of the story these figures told was of the repudiation of Taft's administration by his own state. La Follette, Wisconsin's "Little Giant," couldn't resist saying, "If it wasn't for being personal, I'd say I was the only candidate who could carry his own State." Ohio, the mother of Presidents, had indeed behaved like a stepmother.

Smooth-shaven, dark, with a manner both Southern and impressive, Senator Joseph Dixon had the agility of a good campaign manager. He released this statement to the press: "There is no further room for argument. On last Thursday at Columbus Mr. Taft in his speech said: 'The vote in Ohio, my home state, will be the decisive one, and will settle the question of the nomination.' Ohio has spoken. . . . Roosevelt will have 42 of the 48 delegates in Mr. Taft's own state."

After the Ohio victory, TR expressed his feelings in regard to the talk of a compromise candidate to unite the Republican vote. He was the compromise candidate, and the platform would be his platform.

TR had a strong basis for this forthright, cocksure assertion. After Ohio, he won the New Jersey primary. From the thirteen states that chose delegates through primaries, TR had gathered 278 delegates, losing only 82. Not only did the rank and file of the Republican party want TR; his victories also showed that the party had been strongly colored by progressivism.

But TR had not defeated Taft yet; the convention—and the outcome as to who would control it—lay ahead.

As May and the primaries drew to an end, Roosevelt and the President left their special trains, their speechmaking once again finished. But schedules cannot control enmity; their rancor continued. It made little difference that Taft's men had replaced Taft as a combatant, that the participants' camps were now the convention offices of the Coliseum annex and Sagamore Hill.

After going to the polls in Cincinnati with his brother Charles P. and casting his vote, Taft had been happy to return to the comparative quiet of Washington. There, with the calm of a church announcement, he said he would be nominated on the first ballot and that fellow Ohioan Warren G. Harding, who had a fine voice, would place his name in nomination at the convention.

But as so often in the past, the spotlight focused on TR rather than on Taft. Reporters twice a day climbed the mile-long hill from Oyster Bay to TR's front porch. Would he go to the convention? That was an oft-repeated question, a spectacular, newsworthy one, for a docile nominee, obeying tradition, never appeared at a convention.

On June 1, one of June's perfect days, TR gave the perfect answer from a newspaperman's point of view. Shaking his head vigorously, TR said, "I have no intention of going unless circumstances make it necessary. At present I don't think it is necessary."

That "at present" had an ominous, intriguing quality. The strong implication was there that circumstances might very well arise that would make TR's presence at the convention necessary, and "TR's presence" was a euphemism for TR's singularly colorful, unpredictable belligerence.

A few days later, TR clarified his statement, not to reporters, but to Roosevelt-pledged delegates from Illinois who had come to Sagamore Hill to persuade TR to come to the convention. He'd come to the convention, he told them, if "a grave emergency in the shape of unfair play" arose.

Roosevelt knew there was a strong possibility such an emergency would arise. Some states—whether they used the primary or state conventions

to pick delegates—had failed to arrive at a conclusive selection of delegates and had therefore sent two sets of delegates, "contesting delegations."
Out of the 1,078 delegates 252 involved contests, and it was the Taft-
dominated National Committee that would decide these contests and
thus determine whether Taft or TR received the nomination.

In addition to considering them "thieves," TR regarded the Taft men
as devilishly shrewd. Every minute of the day and night, he had to be on
top of their machinations, and so workmen joined the flow of visitors to
Sagamore Hill to connect it and Chicago telegraphically. A direct phone
line would be tapped. Besides, TR detested phones; in communicating
with the village, he favored sending a boy on a pony to using a phone.
Two telegraphers at each terminus—the third-floor gun room at Sagamore Hill and Senator Dixon's Congress Hotel bedroom in Chicago—
made possible round-the-clock communication.

An early strategic move—to embarrass, to trick TR—was the scheme
to select Elihu Root as the temporary and then permanent chairman of
the convention. A superb parliamentarian, Root would scotch any out-of-
line maneuvers on the part of progressives. The real beauty of the plot
was that TR, politically astute though he might be, could not object to
Root, for he had described him as a brilliant, dedicated public servant.

Speculation continued, stronger than ever, as to whether or not TR
would go to the scene of the battle. Meanwhile, TR continued to direct
his men at his headquarters in Oyster Bay. Frank A. Munsey, George
Perkins, and Walter Brown arrived to talk about the platform. To keep
out from underfoot, Alice Longworth, who was home for a visit, went
with her mother to the summer house. Theodore, Jr.'s wife, who with
their infant daughter was also at Sagamore Hill on a visit, said, "The house
was always full of people. Conferences went on all day." In spite of the
hectic activity, the Roosevelt family, she recounted, "stayed downstairs
until nearly midnight; then talking at the top of their voices, they
trooped up the wide uncarpeted stairs and went to their rooms. For a
brief moment all was still, but just as I was going off to sleep for the
second time they remembered things they had forgotten to tell one another and ran shouting through the halls."

Just as the country had wondered with impatient curiosity if TR
would cast his hat into the ring, they now continued to speculate if he
would leave Sagamore Hill's special turmoil for Chicago.

On June 5 a coach of the Twentieth Century, bearing both TR and
Taft partisans and therefore called the "Harmony Special," left for Chicago.

Two days later TR sent Bill Flinn to Chicago to assist Senator Dixon.
"I may go," TR said on this occasion. "I haven't decided yet."

In the thousands of handbills that had been passed out and were littering Chicago's streets it was assumed TR would come. The leaflets announced that "at three o'clock Thursday afternoon Theodore Roosevelt will walk on the waters of Lake Michigan."

The decision on delegates by the committee made up TR's mind. Twenty-four delegates from Alabama and Arkansas went to Taft, and TR didn't object. But when the committee gave Taft Kentucky's delegates, TR yelled "robbery" and started packing his bags. (He included volumes by Ferrers and Herodotus—"to amuse myself and get my mind off the business.")

TR arrived at *The Outlook* office, 278 Fourth Avenue, late that Friday morning, June 7. Reporters were already there, eager for details. At last they received the answer for which, day after day, they had been patiently waiting. He was going to Chicago! What's more, TR had a new, broad-brimmed, black felt hat, of the type that had become associated with him as a colonel, a warrior. When cartoonists showed the ring and the hat that had been tossed into it, this was precisely the hat they drew.

As the train sped westward, on June 14, and bore northward, a crowd began to gather at Chicago's La Salle Street station. It was not the special train on which he had done his campaigning, for there was not to be any speechmaking along the way; TR's strength must be saved for the battle to be waged in Chicago.

Since the Republican National Committee began its "wholesale theft" of delegates, Chicago had become an emotionally keyed-up city. Of all mortal sins, theft suddenly ranked as the worst. The eighth commandment had become first in importance. A Roosevelt delegate, spotting a Taft delegate—his badge giving his allegiance away—shouted "thief" reflexively, and in sudden, automatic response a street fight started. Fist fights also occurred in bars and hotels—wherever Republican thieves met Republicans who had been robbed. (The manager of the Congress Hotel bar developed a novelty drink for identification purposes. He shaped a lemon peel like TR's Rough Rider hat. The rim of the glass represented the ring. If the customer drank with the "hat" in the "ring," he was a TR man; if he flipped it out, he was for Taft. The recipe for the Campaign Drink: Fill mixing glass with chopped ice, and add a dash of bitters, ½ pony raspberry syrup, 1 pony gin, ½ pony French vermouth, ½ pony Dubonnet. Shake well. Strain into glass. Drop in lemon-peel "hat" as you serve.)

From noon of June 15—which was hot and sticky, with a threat of rain—people began to gather on Michigan Avenue to await the arrival of Colonel Roosevelt. At the La Salle Street station, where TR was scheduled to arrive at 4:00 P.M., the noisy holiday-merry crowd had grown by midafternoon so that it covered the railroad yards, and police labored to keep it from overflowing and engulfing the train shed. A voice cried, "Hurrah for Teddy!" That was all the crowd needed to break through the restraint of the police.

As though influenced by TR's eagerness, the train arrived at 3:59 P.M., a minute ahead of time. The instant the porter opened the door of the coach, TR bounced out and was greeted by a great roar of cheers. He was met by A. H. Revell, head of the Roosevelt National League.

TR removed his big new black hat and waved it. He then walked briskly to the waiting room. The police made way for him, and he followed behind them through the station and down to Van Buren Street, to his automobile. Three brass bands were playing, but the cheers drowned them out. Those close to the cornets knew the bands were playing "There'll Be a Hot Time in the Old Town Tonight" and "Everybody's Doing It Now." At a distance of merely ten yards, however, one couldn't even hear a bass drum above the cheers. (Mrs. Roosevelt, who had accompanied her husband, remained in the station and later went to the hotel by a different, private route.)

"Thank you! Thank you!" the Colonel shouted, then smiled, shook his head, and gave up trying to speak.

Mounted police cleared the struggling, raucous mass from in front of the topless automobile, its stiff perpendicular barrier of windshield decorated by two large American flags, one on each side. The police made enough room for one of the bands; it was to lead the way to the Congress Hotel. Finally, the procession started. Its route was to be down La Salle Street, past the Board of Trade building, into Jackson Boulevard, east to Michigan Avenue, and south to the hotel.

TR stood up all the way, waving his hat without favoritism to those lining both sides of the street. During all those months before he had cast his hat into the ring, he had wanted to be sure the people wanted him. They had answered through the primaries. Now, vividly, spectacularly, TR was being given a representative sample of the people's affection for him. They filled the windows of hotels and office buildings, stood on window sills and on the tops of automobiles, clung to lampposts, overflowed the curbs, ran beside the automobile in which he rode.

When TR finally reached the Congress Hotel, Captain Schuettler of the police preceded him. Tossed about by the crowd, Schuettler, a normally quiet, efficacious man, became visibly angry, for, after all, he was a police officer protecting an ex-President. It appeared, finally, that TR helped the Captain to the door of the Congress Hotel, rather than the other way around.

A lane had been formed through the hotel lobby, but a crush developed at the elevator and in it TR's glasses flew off into the crowd and were not recovered. A suffragette tried vainly to get in a word for her cause. The elevator took TR to the Roosevelt headquarters on the second floor, just off the Florentine Room, a banquet room at the head of the main stairs.

Meanwhile, the crowd that had gathered in front of the hotel, filling the street from Harrison to Congress streets, waited, demanding a speech from TR. One man shouted, "Here's the regiment! We want the Colonel!"

TR didn't make his appearance for a long time, but the crowd waited and waited. It spread across the boulevard and out into Grant Park; it stretched almost the full length of Harrison Street.

TR, who had felt obliged, when campaigning, to appear and speak even at a whistle stop, to a mere handful, in order not to disappoint them, certainly was not to let down "the regiment" in front of the Congress Hotel. He went to an adjoining room, raised the window, and climbed through it onto a gray stone parapet not far above the heads of the people.

When he appeared, clutching his hat in his right hand, and with the grin that showed all his teeth, the crowd's cheers doubled and redoubled. Finally, they quieted enough for him to say "My friends," which set off wild applause. Slowly, with extremely careful enunciation, he then said, "Chicago is a bad place for men to try to steal in." This caused even wilder cheering, to which were added the screaming of automobile sirens and the roar of open mufflers. Each sentence after that continued to be punctuated with cheers. When he saw a banner that bore the legend, "California's solid vote for Roosevelt," TR said, "California's twenty-six votes are mine and shall be counted as such. And, mind you"—TR thrust his head forward with the passion of his words—"the receiver of stolen goods is no better than the thief." He assured them that the people would win in their battle with "the professional politicians representing all that is worst in the corruption of business." Finally, into the din below him, he stirred up a fresh surge of cheers by concluding, "It is a naked fight against theft and thieves, and thieves shall not win."

The crowd could leave now; TR had satisfied them with a call to battle.

Of the many newspapermen who saw him before dinner, which he had with his wife and son Kermit, one, curious as to whether or not TR could stand up to the rigors of what lay ahead, asked TR how he felt. TR exclaimed, "I'm feeling like a bull moose!"

Until then, a bull moose had simply been the huge-antlered male member of the largest deer family, of the genus *Alces Americana,* but TR's simile made it the symbol of a fighting cause.

On Monday, June 17, the day before the start of the convention, TR was to coin yet another rallying cry. In the afternoon his wife and his daughter Alice read the speech he was to deliver that night in the massive Auditorium, a building that was half hotel, half theater. At their suggestion he deleted certain passages. Wisely, they did not tamper with the one that captured the country's fancy.

Doors to the Auditorium opened at seven, and ticket holders began to come through. Seats had been reserved in the first two rows for one hundred and twenty-five Grand Army veterans, guests of honor, who marched to the Auditorium from the Congress Hotel in a body.

Before the meeting started, a quartet stood near the organ and sang "Four Years More of Theodore." At a little after eight, Senator Borah was introduced; he was to speak briefly on "The Clean Road."

"We are in favor of Colonel Roosevelt's nomination because he can be elected," Borah said. "That ought to be one qualification of a candidate. If we name a man who can not be elected, what avails it? Now, in California—"

A great roar interrupted Borah; he turned and saw that TR had entered. The organ began playing "America," and the people obligingly sang. As soon as they finished, they once again roared for "Teddy— Teddy—Teddy!"

TR, with outstretched arms and a beaming smile, finally stopped them. Twenty thousand had come to hear TR, but fewer than five thousand were able to get into the hall. For forty-five minutes the fortunate ones heard TR at his best, even though their enthusiasm did not require this, for they "would cheer at anything he said." At the start he declared heroically, "As far as Mr. Taft and I are personally concerned, it little matters what the fate of either may be." He spoke for the underdog and, consequently, against privilege and all the injustices, economic and political, of society. He spoke against Taft and the bosses, who were attempting to steal the nomination. He pointed out, "What happens to me is not of the slightest consequence: I am to be used, as in a doubtful battle any man is used, to his hurt or not, so long as he is useful, and is then cast aside or left to die. I wish you to feel this. I mean it; and I shall need no sympathy when you are through with me, for this fight is far too great to permit us to concern ourselves about any one man's welfare. . . . We fight in honorable fashion for the good of mankind; fearless of the future; unheeding of our individual fates; with unflinching hearts and undimmed eyes; we stand at Armageddon, and we battle for the Lord."

It did not matter that bitter Republicans were to equate "the Lord" with the Democrats and that the press collected their readers' earnest attempts at identifying Armageddon: a township in Oklahoma, a skirmish in the Revolution, an Alaska post office, a Pullman car. To TR, Armageddon "wasn't just flapdoodle," Felix Frankfurter recalled. "That's the way he felt." This was just as true of his followers.

The battle at the convention, which was to start on the following afternoon, was definitely going to have the fire and dedication of men who were battling for the Lord.

Seventeen

"Old Friends Are Foes in the Coliseum Today"

As the June solstice drew near, advertisements proclaimed that for as little as fifteen dollars one could be the possessor of a Victrola Talking Machine—the "Best Summer Entertainment." The exaggeration of advertising blithely ignored one stellar entertainment: the Republican convention scheduled for June 18 in Chicago's Coliseum.

The Washington *Post* on that day announced what the convention had to offer; a full-length, four-column picture of Theodore Roosevelt and William Howard Taft was captioned "Old friends are foes in the Coliseum today." Between the lines, if not in the lines themselves, was revealed the intransigent determination of each man to prevent the other from gaining the nomination.

In keeping with this spirit, when William Jennings Bryan applied for a ticket to the convention—he was covering it for a newspaper syndicate—he wrote, "If you will send me a ticket, I will agree not to say anything worse about Taft and Roosevelt than they say about each other—a promise I feel sure I can live up to."

Even the weather forecast hammered away at this theme. Though the standard forecast for the convention was for fair and comparatively cool weather, another one—political in nature—was issued the day before the convention. "Area of extreme excitement forming in Michigan Avenue, centering tonight in the Auditorium and extending tomorrow to the Coliseum, with low barometric pressure and indications of violent storm. Air waves generally through the week over a heated sub-strata. Look out for tornadoes."

The promise of drama—and of good weather—drew the largest crowd ever to attend a national convention. It even separated Alexander P. Moore, editor of the Pittsburgh *Leader*, from his bride. The day before, in the Hotel Schenley in Pittsburgh, he had married the beautiful Lillian Russell, star of light opera. But Moore was "a red-hot Roosevelt man," and though he loved his bride, he didn't want to miss any of the excitement of the convention. "I abandon a honeymoon to come to these proceedings," Moore said, concluding somewhat ungallantly, "and they are worth it."

Ill with a cold and somber with thoughts of what lay ahead, Elihu Root, upon his arrival in Chicago, said the situation in the Republican party was very grave. Yes, he regarded both Theodore and Will "with the warmest personal feelings," and he felt, he said, that "the scrap between these two men is comparatively insignificant." It was the survival of the party that was all-important; he would hate to see it broken up.

Henry Taft came from New York, stepped from the train, cane in hand, and said with the sardonic humor of his brother Horace, "I think somebody is liable to be nominated on the first ballot if somebody does not steal something from somebody."

Alice Longworth, wearing a simple, dark-colored tailored dress of swagger cut, was interviewed shortly after her arrival at the Blackstone, where more Tafts than Roosevelts were registered. She was asked, "How does the campaign compare with the last one your father was in?" "Well, it's a bit more exciting," she answered, "but the result is going to be the same."

Dooley also thought it would be exciting—"a combynation iv th' Chicago fire, Saint Bartholomew's massacree, the battle iv the Boyne, th' life iv Jesse James, and th' night iv th' big wind." He therefore decided that he would "get a seat somewhere [so] that I can see th' sthruggle f'r human rights goin' on but fur enough away so I won't be splashed."

Hoosier George Ade, Dooley bereft of dialect, maintained the factions at the convention were irreconcilable. They were so far apart, he declared, that they couldn't "agree on the number of ounces in a pound."

Essentially, ex-Senator Chauncey M. Depew, former New York Central president, famed orator and champion of special interests, expressed the same view: "Delegates are not in mind to take things frivolously; they feel there's going to be a funeral no matter which faction wins."

Out of such statements—and innumerable anonymous ones—dark rumors sprang and proliferated. One stoutly insisted the convention hall would literally be seized by armed men; according to a more elaborate version, TR would, in San Juan Hill style, lead a charge on the Coliseum at 3:00 A.M. Another report claimed a horde of TR followers would swamp the platform and snatch the gavel away from the chairman.

Because where there were so many rumors there might be some truth, Governor Charles S. Deneen of Illinois stood poised, ready to send the National Guard to the rescue, and "nearly a thousand policemen" strode the convention aisles. Moreover, concealed under the gay, colorful bunting that decorated the railings and posts of the platform was barbed wire. As an extra precaution farsighted officials had the steps leading to the platform removed.

Even music contributed to the explosive situation, for bands paraded down the streets and through the hotels deliberately pounding out blood-stirring martial music.

More directly, Boss Bill Flinn of Pittsburgh—who had defeated the pro-Taft Philadelphia machine of Senator Boies Penrose for control of their state's delegation—instructed his delegates from Pennsylvania, "Pick an argument with a candidate wherever possible and convince these fellows that Taft hasn't a chance. They are beginning to weaken already, and we will soon have them all over on our side."

One who had weakened waited outside TR's office on the second floor of the Congress Hotel, waiting to shake TR's hand. When TR emerged— he only left his work long enough to eat—"he had on a rumpled business suit and his hair was tousled," the delegate reported, "but his teeth were exactly what you have seen in the lithographs." (During the convention, an exhibition at the Field Museum featured pre-Columbian artifacts from islands off British Columbia. These artifacts, engraved with large fierce teeth and spectacle-type eyes, were discovered to be virtually replicas of the standard TR features of the newspaper cartoons, leading some lay authorities to claim that TR had been foretold by prehistoric man. "The whole Pacific Northwest," said the museum director, "is one panorama of allegorical pince-nez and symbolical teeth.") TR shook hands left and right, and when he shook the hand of his new delegate, he pumped it hard and said, "Very glad to see you!"

Although he remained in Washington, Taft was as close as possible to the tense Chicago scene; in addition to having access to a long-distance telephone, he received newspaper reports by telegraph. An arranged diversion had him scheduled to see a game on the eighteenth between Washington's own Nationals—on a winning streak, a record-breaking fifteen games in a row—and the Philadelphia Athletics. (In 1910 a magazine had linked Taft and the Nationals as perennial losers. Now that the ball club was winning, might this have a favorable significance for Taft?) But that the President would occupy the special flag-trimmed box reserved for him suddenly became doubtful, for he had heard that the Roosevelt managers planned to force the fight from the opening hour of the convention. Duty and apprehension were dictating that he stay near his long-distance telephone.

Though the convention was not scheduled to start until noon, it was open to the public at ten; by ten thirty a solid line of policemen stood up against the waist-high speaker's platform and faced the "arena."

Victor Rosewater, editor of the Omaha *Bee*, had been chosen by the Taft forces to open the convention. He didn't appear on the platform until quarter past eleven. He was slight and pale, with a thin voice; in his delicate white hand the gavel appeared ludicrously big, heavy. To convey Rosewater's wraithlike quality, George Ade said of him: "We never did hear Victor Rosewater. We didn't even see him."

But Rosewater was heard when he announced, before the convention was called to order, that a flashlight photograph would be taken. From the Indiana delegation, a voice called out, "It's the last time the convention will look pleasant." This prediction proved inaccurate, for the panoramic expanse of faces in the picture conveyed an irrevocable, enduring air of solemnity and grim purpose.

Then dutifully all arose for the playing of "The Star-Spangled Banner" by the band, and "hundreds of women joined in with their timid little sopranos." All this had the calm of an afternoon tea and was most irksome to the thousands present who were taken up with principle and intent on belligerence.

The prayer-meeting atmosphere that forthwith displaced the bland one was certainly not an improvement. Father James F. Callahan, of St. Malachy's Roman Catholic Church—tall, young, good-looking—came forward and attempted to lead the assemblage in the Lord's Prayer. It was soon apparent to the priest that the convention was not familiar with the prayer; real trouble started at "Thy will be done," and the supplicants came hopelessly to grief when they arrived at "Lead us not into temptation." The delegates continued their mumbling, with their heads at least reverentially bowed, but it was Father Callahan alone who really finished the prayer.

The moment the convention was called to order, Governor Herbert Hadley of Missouri climbed to the platform. (TR at this time was making his way to a room in the Congress Hotel, where a private line to the Coliseum had been installed, in order to take personal command of his forces in the fight against Taft.) Though Hadley, too, was young—and "a clean ministerial type"—he "demanded the expulsion of the black sheep," and from that moment on the convention took on the noisy, delirious, explosive characteristics that its very nature required.

Hadley's gestures were "easy, free and natural," and his clear, penetrating voice could be heard in the remotest part of the huge hall. The seventy-two Taft delegates adjudged winners by the National Committee, he said, had not been elected honestly, and he moved that the seventy-two Roosevelt delegates "elected by the honest votes of the Republican voters" be substituted for them.

In the debate that followed, former Governor John Franklin Fort of New Jersey tried futilely to second Hadley. General raucous laughter unnerved him, and he, therefore, tried to explain, when no explanation was really required. But he did manage to say, "Shall this convention sustain the National Committee?"

"No!" voices cried, loudly and continually.

"Let's determine this question now—if not, it might be too late."

This led to shouts that he get off the platform, that he shut up, that he sit down; finally, he had no choice but to comply.

Then the Roosevelt forces had their chance to get even, for the next person to speak was Congressman Sereno E. Payne of New York, author of the Payne-Aldrich Tariff Act. He orated grandly that the question was one between orderly procedure and chaos, when somebody yelled irrelevantly, "How about that tariff bill of yours!"

This set off an explosive hurricane; in its eye, Payne stood smiling genially.

Finally, he tried to speak again and was actually able to say, "The question is shall we organize in the usual way, through the National Committee, or shall—"

"No!" yelled a Roosevelt supporter. This small word, made big with emotion, triggered another din that went on and on, driving Payne from the platform.

At last Rosewater, fragile though he appeared, made a decision on Hadley's motion, a motion he had anticipated and with which he had gone, he said, to "many distinguished gentlemen more learned in parliamentary law than myself." He had been warned by Senator Penrose, "Victor, as soon as you've made that decision, jump off the platform, for someone is going to take a shot at you sure." It was not evident that he made the decision; "the impression of those who sat in front of the chairman and watched the play of his throat muscles was that he swallowed it." But he did not jump. After an explanatory prologue, he had a clerk read the arguments of his advisers, on which he based his decision that the Hadley motion was out of order and that the seventy-two contested Taft delegates should remain on the temporary roll.

Rosewater then went on to perform his last duty: the election of the convention's chairman.

Everyone present knew that the nomination depended on the outcome of this election. After all, the delegates who would elect the chairman would also, undoubtedly, vote for the man the chairman represented. This was a crucial test; during it both Taft and Roosevelt stayed close to their phones.

The Roosevelt delegates had decided on Governor Francis E. McGovern of Wisconsin, for they reasoned that the twenty-six La Follette delegates would contribute their votes to elect someone from Wisconsin. When Henry F. Cochems of Wisconsin put McGovern's name in nomination, all those in the Roosevelt camp assumed, with suppressed jubilation, that Cochems was speaking for La Follette's supporters.

Job Hedges, a delegate from New York and a Taft supporter, then arose to nominate Elihu Root for the chairmanship. The audience blew up a storm of sound, but Hedges remained unruffled; while he waited for some calm in which to speak he smiled and enjoyed the little trick he was about to play.

TR had once said of his old friend, "Elihu Root is the ablest man that has appeared in the public life of any country in any position in my time." Now Hedges repeated this high praise and added, "If he's good enough for Roosevelt, he's good enough for me."

The last word, however, was had by someone somewhere in the Illinois delegation, who shouted, "Roosevelt hadn't found him out then!"

The seconding speeches went on.

Smooth-faced Governor Hiram Johnson of California, with a "paunch and a punch," shook his fists and his thick forefinger at the delegates in the course of telling them that California cast twenty-six votes for McGovern. This stirred up hisses and derogatory shouts.

"We deny the right of any moribund national committee," he shouted back, still shaking his fist, "to choose our chairman for us."

More and more seconding speeches made the convention begin to grow a little impatient.

Then Francis J. Heney, a lawyer from California, arose, attired in a bobtail coat and linen vest with three badges. He was "a shrewd-looking . . . long-nosed, large-mouth, bespectacled individual." He started his seconding speech for McGovern by predicting that if Taft were nominated, he would be defeated at the polls. This set off a "typhoon of noise." With a smirk that was as much a noticeable part of his face as his nose, he compared a Taft leader who had helped make up the temporary roll with Abe Ruef, the notorious Mayor of San Francisco, whom he had prosecuted and put behind bars. This caused what the official stenographer set down in beautiful understatement as "disorder and confusion in the hall." After Rosewater had pounded as best he could with the gavel and there was enough quiet in which to continue, Heney pointed out that the seventy-two disputed Taft delegates had "no legal, moral or ethical right to be in this convention," and that their voting for the chairman of the convention was like having a corrupt judge sitting in on his own case.

That finished Heney's offering—for the moment. Senator W. O. Bradley of Kentucky—big, stout, gray-haired, and afraid of nothing—had no sooner arisen when Heney jumped up and shouted, "You voted for Lorimer." William Lorimer had been expelled from the Senate for having paid for the votes of several members of the Illinois legislature.

Bradley's eyes widened and blazed; he walked the length of the platform, pointed at Heney, and shouted, "Yes, I voted for Lorimer and when I did, I voted for a man ten thousand times better than you."

The uproar made all the other noises that afternoon seem like virtual silence. When Bradley could be heard again, he waved his fist at Heney and shouted, "And the time shall never come when the great State of Kentucky will fall so low as to take moral advice from Francis J. Heney." As he brought the name out, he bent almost double, showed all his teeth, and fairly snarled it with a withering and contemptuous emphasis.

Finally, Rosewater announced that the next speaker, Walter L. Houser, La Follette's manager, would be the last one. Houser arose and repudiated Cochems' nomination of McGovern. Then with a curt nod he left the platform.

The Taft people were stunned, incredulous. What they had just heard meant the loss of twenty-six votes—crucial votes—by the Roosevelt forces. Their next reactions included jumping on chairs, waving flags and handkerchiefs, and yelling themselves hoarse.

Cochems, white in the face with rage, rushed up on the platform and demanded the floor on a question of personal privilege.

When Rosewater gave him the floor, Cochems, in a voice that shook with anger, announced that the vote in the Wisconsin caucus had been fifteen against supporting McGovern to eleven for him, and that he had a right to speak for the eleven who had voted for the Governor. "And," he shouted, waving his finger at the silent Houser, "I challenge any Progressive from Wisconsin to stand up in this convention and vote for Elihu Root and claim to represent the state."

Following the precedent of 1884, Rosewater ruled the vote should be taken on an individual roll call. And so, at 3:21 P.M. the call of the 1,078 names began.

Everybody watched the Southern delegates with intense expectation, because of the claim by the Roosevelt forces that they would switch.

The first break for Roosevelt came with Alabama. Two delegates were for McGovern. One of the delegates yelled out his vote at the top of his voice; this caused Roosevelt followers to jump on chairs and scream like Comanches.

During the Arizona roll call, Heney, up on a chair with a megaphone, tried to stop it. Men whose names had been placed on the roll, he maintained, had not been elected. The roll call went on, however, right through his shrill protestations.

A noisy but genteel demonstration occurred when Mrs. Florence Porter, a pleasant-faced matronly woman from California, arose and said, "McGovern." Mrs. Isabella Blaney, also of California, did the same, and the Roosevelt people demonstrated wildly for each. (Mrs. Porter was asked afterward how it felt to be the first woman to cast a national convention vote, and she said she felt a good deal like a Joan of Arc, and enjoyed the experience.)

The Taft men were reached in the California roll; Heney, with megaphone, tried futilely to stop it.

The New York vote was 76 to 13 in favor of Root.

Next came the Pennsylvania roll call, and Flinn of that state was spoiling for a fight. Though George Ade expected Flinn to be "large and overbearing" (very much, in fact, like the other Pennsylvania Republican boss, Boies Penrose), he turned out to be "a neat silvery gray person with spectacles." Still, the Chief of Police had been asked personally to watch him during the whole convention. Flinn started his offensive during the Pennsylvania roll call by protesting the vote of a Taft delegate; when it was to no avail, he shouted, "You are a pack of thieves."

He also made disturbances during the Texas roll call and when that roll was finished, even threatened to come up on the platform so that, as he euphemistically put it, "I can talk to you." The last disturbance he made was so great that it threatened to prevent the election of a chairman. It took more than a half-dozen policemen to prevail upon Flinn to sit down.

Then came the Washington vote, the final vote.

At 6:18 P.M. it was announced that Root had won—588 to 502.

Grim, gray, his weary eyes expressionless, Root moved forward to perform a difficult and embarrassing duty, one that would involve him in the fight between his two friends. At this point Flinn jumped up and shouted at him, "Receiver of stolen goods!"

Root stood calm, superior to the accusation and the passions of the delegates and of the spectators who packed the horseshoe gallery. This explained how he could begin by expressing his gratitude for the confidence the convention had reposed in him. Derisive laughter and catcalls broke in upon this amenity, and it was almost fifteen minutes before Root could continue. When he finally made a try, several hundred rose to leave. The noise of their departure was so great that Root sat down, and it was announced that he would not continue until all who wanted to leave the building had left.

The disturbance went on and on and, during it, Root sat silently, contemplatively. When Taft was TR's Secretary of War, he, TR, and Root had considered themselves jokingly as the "Three Musketeers," but they did not take lightly the closeness implied by this literary appellation. Circumstances had broken up the triumvirate. Root, with decided pleasure, had been chairman of the 1904 convention that had nominated TR. But in 1912 he had accepted the offer of presiding at the convention merely as a duty, before TR had announced he would be a candidate. TR fought his serving as chairman on the grounds that he now "opposed the men who stand for progressive principles" and had been "put forward by the bosses and the representatives of special privilege." Better to be in Washington, like Cabot Lodge, than to be in Chicago. . . .

Finally, Root arose—his face impassive, wintry—to deliver his keynote speech. Instead of speaking against whoever the Democrats would nominate at their convention in Baltimore during the following week, he praised the Taft administration and, by defending the Constitution and the courts, he obliquely struck out at Roosevelt.

In every respect, the speech was a difficult one to make; as much as Root liked Taft and felt an abiding loyalty to the American constitutional system, his affection for TR had deepened through the years. Just as Taft's soul had been wrenched in the spring of the year, now Root's, too, was torn by anguish.

After the convention, Root could no longer contain himself, and he cried out to a close friend, "I care more for one button on Theodore Roosevelt's waistcoat than for Taft's whole body."

Taft's feelings were also strong, but decidedly different. When word of the initial victory at the convention reached him, he wrote his brother Horace, "My office is empty. My usual callers are in Chicago, and all is quiet on the Potomac." It was a surface quiet, of course, and ominous rather than reassuring. But Root's election as chairman meant Roosevelt's eventual defeat, and there was bitter, vengeful satisfaction in that.

There had been no actual bloodshed on the first day of the convention, except when a Texan allegedly bit the head off a beer bottle. On the second day the convention had every opportunity to redeem itself, for the fight was to begin all over again from precisely where it had started.

Governor Herbert S. Hadley of Missouri would move that TR's honest delegates be substituted for Taft's crooked ones.

During the noon hour, groups of individuals in finery—with servants in tow, carrying lunch baskets—proceeded from the big hotels to witness the renewal of warfare in the Coliseum. Theodore Roosevelt, Jr., and his wife, staying at the Blackstone, were among those who carried basket lunches. (According to legend, observers picnicked at the battles of Bull Run and Balaclava, too.)

The fight on this day was primarily between Root—correct, opulent, in morning coat and dark-striped trousers—and Hadley, who wore a long, gun-barrel, double-breasted knee-length coat. For almost ten years Hadley, as a prosecuting attorney in Kansas City and Attorney General of Missouri, had fought for reform, had even cross-examined John D. Rockefeller, titan of privilege; so it seemed natural for him to face a man who for forty years "had been on the money side of lawsuits." Little wonder then that TR, in a letter dated May 28, 1912, stated that he thought Hadley would be an admirable running mate. (As for Root, the Baltimore *Evening Sun* punned, "Roosevelt is beginning to look upon Elihu as the Root of all evil.") There had also been considerable talk about Hadley as a compromise candidate, one who would keep the party from being split into two pitiful, helpless parts. Hadley's progressive record and his matinee idol appearance made him very popular at the convention. Unlike Root, who, though usually a man of trenchant wit, was now grim, Hadley had a relaxed, jocular, almost boyish manner.

He delivered what TR was later to describe as "a first-class speech about the packing of the delegates." When it was clear that his original motion could not possibly succeed, the Roosevelt forces modified it: the seventy-two contested Taft delegates should not be allowed to vote on the question of their own cases. Hadley pointed out, "It is written in the law of England that no man shall be a judge of his own case." He also made a seemingly irrelevant but all-important point. Even if Taft were nominated, he could not win the election.

Wearied by hours of speeches, the convention released its tensions and frustrations in a wild ovation for Hadley.

Alice Longworth viewed the demonstration with suspicion; she saw "the hand of the opposition in it." Taft and his followers would do anything to prevent her father's nomination.

Finally, a counterchant started: "Teddy! Teddy! We want Teddy!"

Every few minutes messengers ran into TR's main reception room at the Congress Hotel with telegrams from his leaders who were conducting the fight.

TR laughed when he read of the Hadley demonstration. "The cheering for Hadley," he told newspapermen, "has now lasted twenty minutes. That's right. There is nothing too good for him. He is splendid. He deserves it."

From his standpoint, any compromise candidate, honestly chosen, would be a victory for him; only Taft's nomination would mean defeat.

The ovation for Hadley died, unable to survive in an atmosphere heavy with Roosevelt feeling. Issues—even the dream of economic and social justice—could not completely explain the convention's emotion. Only bitter opposition to TR could, and the utter, joyous devotion of TR's followers.

This devotion was exhibited vividly. In the gallery, to the left of the platform, a pretty, rosy-cheeked brunette—wearing a suit of cream-colored linen, a blue straw turban hat, and with a bunch of pinks at her waist—leaned over the gallery and waved a picture of TR in time to the music of the band. Later it was learned that she was Mrs. W. A. Davis, the wife of a wealthy Chicago lumber dealer, and a wild TR enthusiast. Two nights before—as though in rehearsal for her performance in the Coliseum—she had climbed on a table in the Congress Hotel, waved a picture of TR, and incited a crowd to cheers.

Though the National Committee had "fixed things so that they couldn't be unfixed by anything short of an earthquake," the delegates jumped on chairs and cheered the woman whose gloved arm continued to wave a picture of TR. Fights broke out, motivated as much by sheer excitement as by concrete cause. Mrs. Davis' voice, audible because it was feminine and among male voices, urged, "Boys, give three cheers for Teddy."

But even cheers were not enough; Mrs. Davis was brought from the gallery to lead the state standards around the floor. Marching down the main aisle, with face flushed and eyes blazing with excitement, she led a parade of California, Oklahoma, and Missouri delegates and all the rest of her followers. Having reached the platform, she was lifted onto it, becoming the first woman in history to preside over a national convention. She stood at the table where Root—lost in the crowd now—had called for order, and, with a raised arm, called for cheers and songs. The audience responded.

No sooner did she return to the gallery than the whole performance started all over again.

"Go up into that gallery," Police Captain Schuettler ordered, "and make that woman sit down."

But the enthusiasm for TR couldn't be stopped by edict. Hadn't William Allen White said that TR had bit him and he'd gone mad? Earlier that day a rotund man had stopped in front of a group of TR supporters in the Blackstone Hotel and complained, "What did this man Abe Lincoln amount to anyway? Why, everything he did that was any good he copied from Teddy Roosevelt. He just followed Teddy and stole his ideas and that's what made him great with the people. Ain't that so?" A TR man answered, "Well, we don't want to go as far as that, but there is something in what you say, pardner; there's sure something in it."

At 5:32 P.M. Root issued his ruling. "No man," he stated, "can be permitted to vote upon the question of his own right to a seat in the Convention, but the rule does not disqualify any delegate whose name is upon the roll from voting upon the contest of any other man's right, or from participating in the ordinary business of the Convention so long as he holds his seat."

Root's ruling gave Taft control of the convention, virtually handed Taft the nomination. An infuriated TR vowed to fight "this outrageous and naked theft" to the end.

Eighteen

"Steam Roller!
Toot, Toot!"

William Jennings Bryan, viewing the fighting that was going on in the Republican convention, said, "If you didn't know where you were, you might think you were at a Democratic Convention." Partisan pride as well as amusement inspired the statement's claim, because not since the eighth Democratic National Convention of 1860 in Charleston, South Carolina—which was dominated by the explosive issue of slavery—had there been a convention as rough as this one.

"Th' language passed round has been magnificint," Dooley said. "This is partly joo to th' supeiryer iddycation iv th' Republicans. Th' curse iv the Dimmycrat party has always been its lack of cultur. Often whin confronted with gr-reat issues we've been unable to think iv innything bad enough to say about each other. But the Republican leaders ar-re niver at a loss f'r a wurrud. . . ."

All the conflict and wild, harrowing excitement at the Coliseum had its counterpart in Roosevelt's headquarters. The thunder and lightning of the storms in the conference rooms broke from clouds that a cartoonist would label "compromise" and "bolt."

As early as the beginning of June, Alice Longworth on a visit to Sagamore Hill had recorded: "If Father did not get the regular nomination there would be another ticket in the field." Even in May, TR had written friends about the chances of an "independent candidacy."

But TR knew the inevitable consequence of a bolt: he and the party would be defeated. And so, with the slowness of reflection, he put off making the irrevocable, hazardous step. In 1885, when Blaine ("Blaine! Blaine! James G. Blaine! The con-ti-nen-tal liar from the state of Maine") was nominated, TR had supported him rather than leave the party. But all around him now individuals were aflame with emotion, out of patience with hesitancy and caution and compromise. The wife of delegate Timothy Woodruff, who had been Lieutenant Governor when TR was

252

Governor of New York, said to her husband, "Timmy, if you don't bolt, I'm going to Reno." Stocky, aggressive Hiram Johnson—and other "hot heads"—also threatened to depart from the party and make a beeline to progressivism. Paradoxically, extremely conservative Republicans anticipated a split with delight, for they felt a bolt by the radicals would cleanse the party of extremism, Rooseveltism. On the other hand, many conservatives who would be running for office—and had something very definite to lose in the months ahead—vehemently opposed a bolt.

There was even talk of a Taft bolt. The rumor that emerged— probably from the Roosevelt camp—maintained that if TR were nominated, Taft would bolt to save the party from Roosevelt.

Thomas Woodrow Wilson also stood poised to save his party—by a bolt—if the Democrats nominated someone as conservative as Taft.

While some men talked of bolting the party—tantamount to defeat— others pleaded for compromise, saving the party, winning in November.

As a compromise candidate, Governor Hadley appeared the wisest choice, for though he was a reform governor, he was also conservative as compared with progressives like La Follette and Cummins. A compromise candidate, obviously, had to be one who was both conservative and progressive—but not too much of either. That Hadley met these specifications was indicated by the ovation he had received, for the followers of both Taft and Roosevelt had applauded him.

The day after he received that ovation, Hadley called on TR. (Alice Longworth saw him in her father's suite. She noted that "a large and obvious bee was buzzing in his bonnet," a fact she somewhat resented.) Earlier, TR had taken William Allen White aside and said, "What do you know about Hadley really?" It was then that TR learned, with shock and admiration, of Hadley's courage. Hadley had tuberculosis, and while he was acting as Roosevelt's floor manager at the convention, his temperature had climbed as high as 103. (Still, Hadley—a handsome shell—would outlive TR by eight years.)

"They have offered to nominate me," Governor Hadley told TR.

"Are you certain that it is a genuine offer?" TR asked.

Hadley wasn't sure the offer was genuine. He felt it might be an attempt on the part of the Taft forces to let Roosevelt know they would accept a compromise candidate—and that Hadley might possibly be their choice.

No honest man, TR told Hadley, would accept the nomination from a crooked convention. He would support Hadley should he be nominated —or anyone else except Taft—if, and only if, the fraudulent roll were purged. He made an exception of Taft because, he declared, Taft had "insisted on his representatives stealing the nomination for him, and under such circumstances I could not support him."

TR must have known the Taft people would never accept his stipulation that the seventy-two Roosevelt delegates be seated, for this would certainly lead to the nomination of TR rather than a compromise candidate. The stipulation, therefore, corresponded to what he had declared on other occasions. Before the convention began, he had stated flatly, emphatically, that he would "never under any circumstances compromise or agree to any compromise candidate."

The fight between him and Taft, after all, was a personal fight. And they were both ready for it.

On June 20 Taft said, "Roosevelt is struggling to secure as many of his followers as possible to join him in a bolt. . . . If he does not do it at once it will look like so many of his bluffs. . . . If I win the nomination and Roosevelt bolts, it means a long, hard fight with probable defeat. But I can stand defeat if we retain the regular Republican party as a nucleus for future conservative action."

And in July, TR wrote to Ambassador Jusserand, "I wish to Heaven I was not in this fight, and I am in it only on the principle, in the long run a sound one, that I would rather take a thrashing than be quiet under such a kicking."

Thursday, June 20, started as a "hot, sticky, gray day." The meteorological gloom deepened a psychological shadow. The convention was dragging on, and delegates could be seen morosely weighing bank rolls against hotel bills.

Having called the convention to order at noon, Root immediately recessed it until four o'clock that afternoon. Nothing could be done until the Committee on Credentials reported on the contested seats.

In sunny Washington, during the recess interval, Taft motored out to Chevy Chase to play golf with his son Robert. His smile was reported to be as cheerful as it had been the third week in June, 1908, when he sat in the War Department office with his wife, his daughter, Helen, and his younger son, Charles, and observed how the vote for his nomination was progressing.

At the Congress Hotel, during the convention recess, TR continued his work to put a stop to the wholesale brigandage of the bosses. Charles P. Taft, in an editorial in his newspaper entitled "The Evening of Waterloo," said, "When the full story of what occurred Thursday in those elaborately fitted Roosevelt headquarters on Michigan Avenue comes to light it will be worth reading. Roosevelt says he will start a new party.

Just now it looks as if it would have to be almost exclusively a Roosevelt party. Heney and Johnson and Pinchot and Garfield and some others of the type will follow him in a bolt, but the strong men who have given Roosevelt valuable support in his campaign up to date have made it fairly plain that they will not leave the party."

At the conclusion of the recess, the Coliseum was packed, because a rumor promised that TR would appear; just that—it did not stipulate the manner of his arrival, or his precise dramatic intent. The skimpy details of the rumor enhanced it and made it all the more intriguing.

The Taft forces—being apprehensively tense and diligent—had an entire scenario worked out in which TR, should he appear, would play an unrehearsed role. There would, of course, be a thunderous demonstration when he arrived. After it died down, Jim Watson of Indiana, a Taft leader, would ask that the Colonel be allowed the privilege of the floor. Walter L. Houser, La Follette's manager, was to object to the motion on the ground that La Follette, also a candidate, was likewise entitled to the same privilege. The Taft people would thereupon suspend the rules and permit TR to talk and, by means of this charade, show the Roosevelt people, graphically, undeniably, that there was no disposition whatsoever to deny Roosevelt the right to speak his mind. (William Barnes, Jr., the huge, jowly boss from New York, put it graciously: "Let him talk his head off. We don't care.")

But TR didn't appear, and the Committee on Credentials was not yet ready to report. Root, therefore, once again adjourned the convention, this time until eleven o'clock Friday morning.

The crowd showed its disappointment by remaining seated. It started to rain. The hall became so dark that lights were switched on. This was enough to cause the restless crowd to cheer, an expression more of despair than good humor.

An official seized a megaphone and bawled, "The lights in the hall will be turned out in five minutes!"

A man in the gallery started to wave his coat and yell, "We want Teddy!" This set off a demonstration, and the man's cry became a chant of "We'll *get* Teddy!"

The police on the platform went into a huddle, trying to determine how to empty the hall. When Police Chief Schuettler walked over to the speaker's stand, perhaps to make a final appeal, the crowd yelled, "Speech! Speech!" The Chief laughed and shook his head. The crowd was impossible; he was helpless.

Root and Watson withdrew to the rear of the platform and sat down resignedly. There were those in the audience who wanted to know why the men on the platform didn't set an example by leaving. A rumor arose that the Taft people were staying because they feared the Roosevelt people would seize the hall.

Finally, at 4:40 P.M., several hundred policemen marched purposefully up into the gallery and started to usher the people out of the hall and into the rain.

On the night of June 20 TR had his first full night of sleep since leaving Oyster Bay, almost a week earlier. The next morning he looked noticeably rested. As he rushed along—smiling, waving his hand—the three hundred or so of his followers who had been waiting for him in the lobby started a demonstration.

"Stick to the end!" a loud-voiced delegate from California cried, and others immediately took up his fervent plea.

TR paused for a moment to shout back over his shoulder, "You bet we will! Sure, sure!"

When TR reached the conference room, he had to be literally pushed into it to be free of the crowd.

Reporters lingered at the door. Borah, one of a series of men closeted with TR, told them when he emerged that he had nothing to say, but then he tossed them a gratuity: he didn't like the third-party idea.

Senator Dixon merely smiled when asked about his third-party sentiments.

When Governor Stubbs of Kansas left the conference room and reporters asked him if he was ready to join the third-party movement, he said, "I haven't even given thought to the matter. I don't know anything about it."

Perkins, upon whom continued financing would depend, had a talk with TR late that morning. Conjecture of what transpired dwelt on two possibilities: Perkins would either give TR financial backing without reservations, or he wouldn't back him unless he could be shown that there was a chance of success.

The first possibility seemed the more likely, for when a crowd collected in front of the Congress Hotel and shouted insistently for a speech, TR once again came out on the balcony and, waving his hand, called down to his audience, "My hat is in the ring and it is going to stay there more than ever."

TR's frenetic morning activity was not matched by that of the convention, for though the convention had been scheduled to get under way at eleven, the Committee on Credentials was not ready at that hour to make its first report. To fill the vacuum, a band played—futilely, for the crowd required something more stirring. The New Jersey and Massachusetts delegations tried cheering to start a Roosevelt demonstration, but nothing led to much in the way of a response.

"One thing they can't give," said a sour-minded Taft man from Ohio, "is the Electoral College yell."

The lack of spirits stemmed from the inevitability of the direction in which the convention was headed. Though an option on the Coliseum had been taken until the following Wednesday, this had simply been a "just-in-case" precaution, for it was generally expected that Taft would be nominated on the first ballot. Talk of a compromise candidate had died down—and then died out completely. In its place, the belief was expressed that if the Democrats nominated a radical at their convention on the twenty-fifth in Baltimore, TR wouldn't start a third party. But this rumor was discounted by a report that an option had been taken on a convention hall by the Colonel's friends, for dates in the middle of August.

Before noon, William Jennings Bryan arrived, in his role as a reporter; an instantaneous thunderous ovation greeted him. His wrinkled trousers appeared to have been slept in, and he wore an alpaca coat and a white vest. Several delegates called for a speech, and the band played "Auld Lang Syne." A fellow journalist told Bryan that if he didn't watch out the Baltimore convention of the Democratic party would nominate him. Bryan had already lost three presidential elections; his first defeat, by McKinley, went all the way back to 1896. And so Bryan said, "Young man, do you think I'm going to run for President just to pull the Republican party out of a hole?"

At 12:25 P.M. Root called the convention to order; the Committee on Credentials was ready to make its first report.

Instead of presenting a comprehensive statement, the committee had decided to announce its decisions on the contested seats by state in alphabetical order, with the convention voting on each case as it was announced.

Back of this procedure lurked clever strategy. If the usual custom were followed and the committee reported on all the cases at once, Hadley would be certain to ask for a substitution of a comprehensive roll of the TR contestants. On that motion none of the Taft men whose seats were contested could have voted, and Taft would be deprived of seventy-two votes at one fell swoop. By piecemeal arrangement, however, the only Taft men disenfranchised on each vote were the men whose seats were involved in that particular case—in accordance with the Root ruling. All Taft men from Texas, for instance, could vote on the Alabama report, and so on by state all along the line until the roll call reached Texas, in which instance the contested delegates would not be permitted to vote on their own case.

The convention began to grind its way through the reports of the Committee on Credentials—monotonously, mechanically, relentlessly voting the Roosevelt men down at every step. Roll call followed roll call, and Taft delegates were seated by a viva voce vote.

The Taft organization continued to bear down on the opposition and smash it with steam-roller tactics. The onlookers in the gallery—with the humor born of despair—visualized this abstraction in concrete terms; they whistled and hissed and made other steam-roller sounds every time Root made a decision. One gifted man produced a perfect steam-roller whistle. Numerous others, less favorably endowed but nevertheless ingenious, achieved the sound of escaping steam by rubbing two pieces of sandpaper together. As a consequence, sandpaper became scarce in Chicago, the demand exceeding the supply.

Root's face remained impassive through all the noises; his weary eyes held the pain of the duty he felt obliged to perform against his old friend Theodore. A few days after the termination of the convention, he admitted that his activities as chairman had been "clouded by regret & sorrow but never for an instant by any doubt."

During the long waits between reports of the Committee on Credentials, people rose, stretched, visited. The band played "You'll Do the Same Thing Over," an ambiguous yet significant allusion.

At exactly four o'clock, Root announced that the California case was ready for presentation to the convention. Immediately everyone sat up straight; talking stopped. It was generally known that TR's cry of fraud had a more solid basis in this case than in any other.

Heney made a "firebrand speech" and had the "dander of the Taft delegates up in a twinkle."

Root used his gavel. Sometimes he would lift it as high as possible so that he might bring it down as hard as he could, but in the deafening roar only the motion of the gavel could be perceived, not its sound.

Finally, when Root was able to speak, he told the convention, with a veiled threat for Heney, "The gentleman has not *yet* stepped over the line where he is to be called to order."

Heney managed to have the last word, screaming, "If President Taft accepts the votes of these two men in this convention he will be guilty of high treason." A chorus of cheers and hisses arose as he took his seat.

Hiram Johnson also spoke up. Though not known for evenness of temper, he seemed a model of restraint after Heney's outbursts. He maintained that the question was larger than the matter of seating two delegates. He went on to say, "The whole proposition of 'Shall the people rule?' is involved. . . . The struggle is on, North, East, South and West, for direct primaries, and the people all over the country will soon be given the right to choose their own representatives rather than let the bosses choose them. . . . Direct primaries in every State are coming as sure as night follows day."

Much applause, with Bryan leading it, followed this pronouncement, for popular rule was undeniably the larger question in 1912. In addition to advocating direct primaries, already in operation in thirteen states, the progressives believed the people should have a greater say in government by the direct election of senators and through initiative, referendum, and recall—that is, empowering them to initiate legislation, to veto legislation, and to recall an elected officer from his office. By 1912, twelve states had adopted the initiative and referendum, seven states the recall.

Mrs. Roosevelt had watched the convention from the galleries for several hours, but left after the Taft forces won on California. Her departure appeared to be a comment.

At the Congress Hotel, TR continued to laugh and joke with newspapermen, even after hearing the news that the two Taft delegates from California had been seated by a vote of 542 to 529. Since he had won the California primary by a majority of more than seventy thousand, he felt that such banditlike tactics of the Taft supporters would rouse the people against them.

By the time the Louisiana case was reached, darkness had fallen, and the crowd, having lost interest, was leaving the gallery.

Cries arose from those who remained to "speed up the steam roller."

"So long as you're going to work it," a California delegate yelled to Root, "speed her up!"

This outbreak and all that had preceded it had worn Root's nerves thin. As he was about to take the convention vote on the Michigan case, a shout of "all aboard" prompted him to point with the handle of the gavel at a disorderly Pennsylvania delegate and say in a loud, forceful voice, "If the gentleman sitting upon the other side of that aisle . . . does not cease his disorderly conduct, delegate or no delegate, the Sergeant-at-Arms will have him removed from the hall." In the silence that followed this ultimatum, from the platform where he sat in a large comfortable chair fanning himself, the "characteristic" voice of Pennsylvania's Senator Boies Penrose was heard to say in feigned awe, "Here, how rough he talks to the Mayor of McKeesport."

Root announced that no other cases were ready and adjourned the convention until ten the next morning.

During one uproar Root had said, "Evidently there are delegates here who do not wish to go home for Sunday," but it now appeared the convention would last only one more day. Contests on Oklahoma, Tennessee, Texas, and Washington remained. They would be followed by the adoption of the platform and by the nomination, and then the fifteenth Republican National Convention would be over.

Taft would be the nominee; but that night TR told a large number of his delegates, "I am proud of the manner in which you are fighting in the face of the steam roller. I love a dead game sport." With bitterness he scoffed at the delegates the Taft forces had thrown his way—after first being sure they had all the delegates they needed. He asked, "But if a man steals a pair of horses from you, do you expect to be satisfied if he brings you back one and says he has no use for it?"

With equal bitterness, Frank Munsey—financial backer of the progressives—told the press: "Mr. Roosevelt will be nominated for President by a new party. He refuses to have anything more to do with the Republican Convention now in session in this city. He would not now take a nomination from that body if it were given to him. He regards it as a grossly illegal organization, formed by the force of men fraudulently seated. Taft will probably be nominated late tomorrow. It is now the earnest wish of Mr. Roosevelt and his friends that the nomination go to him. They regard him as the proper nominee of such a convention."

The physical violence anticipated prior to the opening of the convention was finally to become a reality on Saturday, June 22, its closing day. But at first, good humor—laced with cynicism and bitterness and helplessness—characterized the convention's spirit. Nothing could stop the gathered momentum of the steam roller—or save the Grand Old Party from being ruthlessly smashed.

And so when Root asked for affirmative votes, everyone shouted "Aye." Then on a negative call, everyone hilariously yelled "No," and Root, with a trace of a smile warming his chill countenance, declared that the ayes had it. That was the way it went all day, with the steam roller taking care of Mississippi, Tennessee, Washington . . . to the accompaniment of cries of "Steam roller!" "Toot, toot!" "Choo choo!" "It's missing; go out and get gasoline." This steam-roller joke, it appeared, was all the Roosevelt forces had left, and they clung to it pathetically; the challenge was to create variations of it.

Delegate Clark Grier of Georgia, for example, made a mock point of order. "I make the point," he shouted with a laugh, "that the steam roller is exceeding the speed limit!"

A noisy, good-natured uproar broke through the entire hall.

Root waited till he could be heard, advanced a step, and shouted with a broad grin, "The Chair sustains the point of order." This brought down the house again; so Root had to wait. When he could continue, he said, "But unless you let that steam roller run on for a while there isn't any chance of our getting home for Sunday."

Strained though it was, that was the convention's last bit of lightness.

The assembly let that "steam roller run on for a while," concluding the contests. Then Root was made permanent chairman, and a five-minute demonstration followed; Roosevelt's followers did not participate.

"I thank you, my friends, from the bottom of my heart," Root said, "and my first duty as Permanent Chairman is to ask your unanimous consent that our Republican brother Henry Allen of Kansas be permitted to make a statement."

The consent was not unanimous, but Henry J. Allen spoke up loudly and clearly, belligerence coloring every word of his "masterpiece of amiable sarcasm," though he began with the formal amenity, "Gentlemen of the Convention."

We cannot in justice to ourselves share responsibilities of a convention which has said to Ohio—the home of President Taft—that a majority of 47,000 voters obtained in a legal primary election must stand aside for the political dictum of a National Committeeman discarded by that same majority. We cannot become parties with you in a declaration to Pennsylvania that a defeated committeeman, seated in an obscure room of this building, can nullify the 130,000 majority by which Pennsylvania gave expression to her wishes. We will not put ourselves in a position to be bound by any act in which you say to the majority which rejected Mr. Taft in New Jersey, to the majority which rejected him in Wisconsin, to the majority which rejected him in Minnesota, to the majority which rejected him in Maine, to the majority that rejected him in Maryland, to the majority which rejected him in South Dakota, to the majority which rejected him in Nebraska, in Oregon, Kansas, Oklahoma, West Virginia and North Carolina, that all these majorities added together went down under the mere rulings of a political committee. . . . Finally we have pleaded with you ten days. We have fought with you five days for a "square deal." We fight no more. We plead no longer. We shall sit in protest and the people who sent us here shall judge us.

Henry J. Allen of Kansas had still not finished; he read an angry statement released by TR on that day.

A clear majority of the delegates honestly elected to this convention were chosen by the people to nominate me. Under the direction, and with the encouragement of Mr. Taft, the majority of the National Committee, by the so-called "steam roller" methods, and with scandalous disregard of every principle of elementary honesty and decency stole eighty or ninety delegates, putting on the temporary roll call a sufficient number of fraudulent delegates to defeat the legally expressed will of the people, and to substitute a dishonest for an honest majority. . . . I hope that the men elected as Roosevelt delegates will now decline to vote on any matter before the Convention. I do not release any delegate from his honorable obligation to vote for me if he votes at all; but under the actual conditions I hope that he will not vote at all. The Convention as now composed has no claim to represent the voters of the Republican Party. It represents nothing but successful fraud in overriding the will of the rank and file of the party. Any man nominated by the Convention as now constituted would be merely the beneficiary of this successful fraud; it would be deeply discreditable to any man to accept the Convention's nomination under these circumstances; and any man thus accepting it would have no claim to the support of any Republican on party grounds, and would have forfeited the right to ask the support of any honest man of any party on moral grounds.

The fuse that had been burning throughout the reading of Roosevelt's statement reached the explosive charge with the words "on moral grounds." Taft and Roosevelt men punched each other in the nose. To stop the spread of fist fights, policemen threw fighting delegates out of the hall, but fights continued to break out here and there, and it was impossible to keep track of them all.

Former Vice-President Charles Fairbanks, tall, goateed, whose baldness made a smooth dome of his forehead, did not help matters when he took the platform to announce the report of the Resolutions Committee. As soon as he began, it was plain he would make one of his usual "large-sounding speeches." But he put too much strain on the temper of the Roosevelt delegation when he ill-advisedly declared, "The great Republican Party stands as it has always stood, for government of the people, by the people, and for the people."

When the tumult of jeers, hissing, and catcalls finally died down, Fairbanks read the conservative Taft platform in a firm voice that carried well, but he received little applause.

Suspense gripped the convention, for a roll-call vote on the platform would soon begin, and everyone eagerly waited to see if delegates would remain silent in accordance with TR's request.

When California, the first Roosevelt state, was reached, a Mr. Myer stood up importantly, threw back his shoulders, and shouted, "California declines to vote."

For a full five minutes, a continuous wild roar of applause made it impossible for the clerk to continue with the roll.

Then a succession of cheers and hisses followed as each state either refused to vote or gave its approval of the platform. Depth of feeling led those who refused to vote to express themselves as individually as possible: "Present, but not voting." "Present and won't vote." "Present and you can't make me vote." Ex-Governor Fort of New Jersey answered by shouting, "There are twenty-eight present and the twenty-eight decline to vote." Zeb V. Walser, leader of the North Carolina delegation, got a big laugh for saying, "Present, but not voting at funerals." Bill Flinn managed to hold sixty-three of sixty-four delegates from Pennsylvania, and they sat like images.

The final vote was 666 in favor of adopting the platform, 343 refusing to vote, 16 absent, and 53 against.

The time had come for nominations. As TR had requested, his name was not presented. At 6:15 P.M., Warren G. Harding arose to make a nominating speech; it included obligatory praise of the Republican party and a reference to George Washington's opposition to a third term. At the mention of Taft's name a demonstration started that went on for fifteen minutes. Through it all the Roosevelt and La Follette delegates sat grimly silent. Nick and Alice Longworth waited for the hubbub to end, without a smile between them, looking plainly bored.

Pounding his gavel, Root brought the meeting to order, but only for a moment, because Harding started a eulogy of Taft, which set off the biggest commotion of the convention.

Above the din, Harding, no doubt carried away by the moment, shouted in a shrill, impassioned voice, "President Taft is the greatest progressive of his time."

A fist fight broke out in the South Dakota delegation, and a dozen policemen scrambled over seats to get to it. This was but one element in the general wild disorder. Eventually, partial quiet was restored. Harding continued, after a fashion, but every word he spoke brought forth hisses and cheers. A fighting mood, a desire to start a riot, gripped half the convention.

Shoving Harding to one side, Root advanced grimly to the edge of the platform and, pointing with his gavel, said, "You delegates who announced your intention of sitting mute to preserve your self-respect, try and preserve it by remaining mute now."

Harding began again, but a fight broke out in the Pennsylvania delegation, and in a moment the entire hall was in turmoil.

Finally, Harding was able to continue. He declared that William Howard Taft was "as wise and patient as Abraham Lincoln, as modest and dauntless as Ulysses S. Grant, as temperate and peace-loving as Rutherford B. Hayes, as patriotic and intellectual as James A. Garfield, as courtly and generous as Chester A. Arthur, as learned in the law as Benjamin Harrison, as sympathetic and brave as William McKinley, as progressive as—" suddenly Harding could not utter the next name and resorted to mild anonymity—"his predecessor, with a moral stamina, breadth of view and sturdy manhood all his own." At last, he exclaimed in the traditional fanfare crescendo of nominations, "For one hundred millions of advancing Americans, I name for renomination our great President William Howard Taft!"

John Wanamaker and Nicholas Murray Butler, President of Columbia University, made seconding speeches. Then a short thickset man with a heavy shock of black hair nominated La Follette, and during the demonstration that followed the seconding speech, Root impatiently started the balloting.

Alabama gave 22 of 24 votes for Taft. Two delegates, in accordance with TR's request, declined to vote. It went on and on in this fashion until Taft was renominated by a vote of 561. Roosevelt received 107 votes, La Follette, 41, and 344 delegates had refused to vote.

At 10:35 P.M. the convention adjourned.

Chauncey M. Depew, of the bushy white eyebrows, muttonchop whiskers, and macabre wit, threw out to the delegates this *envoi:* "The only question now is which corpse gets the most flowers."

Taft told callers that just as he owed his nomination in 1908 to Roosevelt, he owed this one in 1912 more to Roosevelt than to any other man, because TR had refused to accept a compromise candidate. This was a statement of fact rather than of gratitude. Roosevelt reacted with more obvious bitterness, saying that he had hoped Taft would be the "receiver of stolen goods," for a compromise candidate could have said he had merely accepted the nomination but hadn't premeditatedly taken an active part in the theft of delegates. Taft, TR maintained, wouldn't be able to make that excuse.

Nineteen
". . . and We Battle for the Lord"

On that same Saturday night when the fifteenth Republican National Convention nominated William Howard Taft in the Coliseum, less than a mile away, in Orchestra Hall, a huge painting of Theodore Roosevelt was hung conspicuously behind the stage. Under the painting its subject stood and said, "If you wish me to make the fight, I will make it even if only one State willl support me." He even declared that when the convention of the new Progressive party assembled in August, if they wished to nominate another progressive, he would support the nominee. ("I do enjoy those pretty politenesses," Alice Longworth observed.)

Governor Hiram Johnson dismissed the meeting—it was only a meeting, a rump convention at most—after calling upon the delegates to get together on the following day. "I know it is Sunday," he told them, "but our work is holy work."

Without this self-induced religious fervor, this staff of comfort and hope, they could not have faced the rigors of the next four and a half months. No third party had ever won. Such an awesome precedent intimidated, discouraged.

Late the next afternoon, Alice and Nick Longworth boarded a train for Washington, a train filled with the emotion of Chicago and, she felt, "with enemies, and deserters who had been with us during the primaries but had decided to remain regular." Still, she and the others who remained loyal bubbled with inexplicable good humor, inexplicable because they were the defeated. Aware of the Republicans' cheerless future, the opposition press could gloat with staccato glee: Both TR and Taft wanted the nomination. Both got it. Everybody ought to be happy. The Democrats are.

Passing Elihu Root's table in the dining car, Alice—still fond of Root—bent over him and made a good-natured "toot-toot" sound of a steam roller. The Democrats' cause for happiness cast a thick pall of gloom over the President. "Whatever happens in November," he said by way of consolation, "we have achieved the most important end and that is that Roosevelt can not be President, or the absorber of the Republican Party."

Having stood at Armageddon, TR, unlike Taft, had access to the balm of Gilead for what lay ahead. He had often said he was no more than an instrument to be used and cast aside, and now he—without thought of self or of ephemeral victory—would be fighting for the establishment of a progressive movement.

TR's view of himself, however, did not always coincide with the free, heavy-lined caricatures that reflected how others saw him. In New Haven, for example, a new national anthem was being sung; Horace Taft sent a copy of it to his brother.

> My country 'tis of me,
> Sweet land of mostly me,
> Of me I yell.
> Land to which I am sent
> Beyond all argument,
> Choose me for president
> Or go to hell.

And Woodrow Wilson saw TR as an individual who had obligingly split the Republican party. "Good old Teddy," he said appreciatively. "What a help he is."

But the Democratic party also had vehement progressives and entrenched conservatives; therefore, the Democrats of 1912, recalling the terrible division of their party in 1860, were worried and felt fear. TR knew that in their divisiveness lay his only chance; if the Democrats selected a conservative as their nominee, he could defeat him.

Kermit Roosevelt said, "Pop's praying for Clark." He meant Champ Clark, Democratic Speaker of the House, who wore a black slouch hat and a frock coat, and had the obscure though intriguing slogan, "You got to quit kickin' my dawg around." Tammany Hall backed his conservatism, and so did William Randolph Hearst of the powerful yellow journals.

TR prayed for Clark's nomination because he didn't have a chance against Wilson, a liberal. Erudite, born in the South—in Staunton, Virginia—Wilson (who had a handshake like "a ten-cent pickled mackerel in brown paper" and a face that was thin and ascetic) was backed by the New York *World*. As Governor of New Jersey, he had given his state the primary and the direct election of senators and had secured progressive legislation governing child labor and workmen's compensation.

In the last week of June, during a punishing heat wave, delegates gathered in the Baltimore Armory to determine—as it turned out—whether their nominee would be conservative Clark or progressive Wilson. The conservatives won the first victory by electing as temporary chairman Judge Alton B. Parker, who had been the Democratic nominee in 1904, but then the progressives elected their man—Ollie M. James of Kentucky, "a flabby giant"—as permanent chairman. James had been a formidable member of the Pinchot-Ballinger investigating committee.

This seesawing continued; it characterized the entire convention and kept everyone in nerve-racking suspense, for the convention was picking not only the nominee but also, from all indications, the next President. On the third day, Thursday, June 27, both TR and Taft had unofficial emissaries, for Mrs. Taft took the ten o'clock train from Washington to Baltimore, arriving at the Armory at about eleven thirty; Alice and Nick Longworth arrived there about a half hour later.

Mrs. Taft, seated in the first row of the gallery, wore a dark-violet linen suit and a straw hat to match. As she listened to Ollie James denounce the President, reporters watched her closely in order to be able to tell their readers that "varying emotion was depicted on her face." When they asked her how she liked a Democratic convention, she replied, "It's very interesting, isn't it? I don't suppose I could expect them to endorse the administration of a Republican President, could I?"

A photographer took a picture of TR's daughter, in the gallery at the west end of the Armory; it caught her bent forward, elbows on the rail, with her head in her hands and an amused expression on her face.

The balloting and overt conflict began. Clark held a majority for seven ballots. On the eleventh ballot, Wilson was prepared to give up; he had a telegram written and ready to send which would release his delegates.

In Oyster Bay, though busy conferring with his supporters, TR was eagerly aware of developments in Baltimore. Taft also kept in close contact with the convention. As the ballots continued to be taken, tense crowds all across the country viewed the reports as they appeared on newspaper billboards, because the nation had come to the realization that progressive leadership was the alternative to revolution, to the socialism of Debs, who obeyed capitalist laws with the greatest reluctance, to anarchism. The nation was also in revolt against the preceding generation, and was demanding moral, economic, and political change. Women wanted a voice, too; they wanted suffrage. (It was not enough that their pressure had led to the lowering of trolley-car steps in New York to accommodate hobble skirts.) In labor, the IWW arose, gained power. (The Lawrence, Massachusetts, textile strike revealed that men had been working a fifty-four-hour week for ten dollars.)

On the fifth sweltering day in Baltimore, heat hung thick under the vast arched ceiling of the Armory. The discomfort of heat slowed time, and this intensified suspense. On the eighteenth ballot, Clark was slipping. The next day, on the thirtieth ballot, Wilson moved ahead of Clark for the first time.

Sixteen ballots later, as July 2 came to an end, Wilson was nominated, and the convention selected Governor Thomas R. Marshall of Indiana as his running mate. The progressives had lost in Chicago but won in Baltimore. However, unlike those in Chicago, the losers in Baltimore remained loyal to their party. TR and Taft would, therefore, be facing a shaken party, but not a split one. An old standpat Republican editor in Vermont summed it all up neatly, concisely: "Vote for Taft, pray for Roosevelt, and bet on Wilson."

Now the new Progressive party that was to be formed in August could not offer something clearly, sharply distinct from the old parties; Wilson's New Freedom and TR's New Nationalism were as close as fraternal twins. But TR had no trouble telling them apart. He viewed the Baltimore platform as the "exact reverse" of his own, as "not progressive at all."

That night at Sagamore Hill a family meeting was held. The spaciousness of the house and its warmth were in keeping with the spiritual closeness of the Roosevelts as a family unit. TR valued Edie's judgment, thought it better than his own. Since continuing the fight would affect the lives of his children, Ethel, Kermit, Archie, and Quentin were given the opportunity to express themselves.

TR presented the alternatives. He could stay in and make the fight. Or he could let Wilson trounce Taft and let himself be nominated in 1916.

Without argument, without hesitation or doubt, Mrs. Roosevelt and the children agreed that he should, as a matter of principle, lead the progressives in the Republican party in their fight.

The next day, though TR felt that the election in November would bring defeat and the end of his public career, he said, "Actually, I have no choice. If I don't run, everything I've stood for, and tried to advance politically, will be lost."

The height of the dog days had come to Washington: heat, a restless Congress in session, the President enduring a bachelor's solitude. . . . Once again, on Independence Day, Taft had escorted his wife to Beverly.

She still needed the tranquillity of its sea, wide verandas, and towering elms. He then had returned to the White House, which was not too comfortable in the summer, even though it was open on all sides, with a sweep of lawn rolling off to the south, much-used terraces flung out to the east and west, a cozy south portico opening from the Blue Room, and apartments that were lofty.

Taft knew discomforts that benign architecture and green vistas could not alleviate. His days bore a resemblance to that arduous first summer in office, the tariff summer. Similar elements made them seem—eerily—to have occurred before, to be preternatural repetitions. The late Archie Butt had shared his bachelorhood then, and now it was Charles D. Hilles. That summer it had been the feud with vulgar, tobacco-spitting Joe Cannon, and now it was vituperation directed against Theodore Rex—TR the King—"persistently lying . . . utterly unscrupulous." And then, as now, there had been golf and taking off "excess flesh" and daily letters to Nellie.

"The Colonel is going into the third party with seriousness," he wrote her in mid-July. "I suppose he will do us a good deal of damage. . . ."

Along with his letter, Taft sent some verses he had received from Nannie Longworth Wallingford, who wished, he said, "to do a lot of things in the matter of stirring up workmen to vote for me." Mrs. Wallingford's intense dislike of Theodore Roosevelt and her intense desire to help Will Taft were revealed in her political verses.

The Roosevelt Battle Song, A-R-M-A-G-E-D-D-O-N

> The Pinchot brothers (pinch with care)
>   Amos and dear Gif-ford
> Who says—I never change my mind
>   And never break my word—
> And Jimmy Garfield (Shady Jim)
>   All say with one accord
> That I must have at least three terms
>   To battle for the Lord.
>
> "Thou" means the other fellow
>   When I say "Thou shalt not steal."
> We have our little "Steal Trust"
>   And the Limited Square Deal.
> Their naked thefts of delegates
>   I greatly have deplored;
> But, *I'm* justified in stealing,
>   For I battle for the Lord.

In thanking Mrs. Wallingford for her verse, Taft said he would "give them to Mr. Hilles, and he will feed them to the public."

Will Taft had another fierce and feminine defender—Mabel Boardman, who, in a letter to a TR supporter, expressed her loyalty to her old friend. "I have known him [Taft], as I have known Mr. Roosevelt for some twenty years. When time gives a clearer vision, the two men will find their right place in history; one an unselfish and great statesman, working for justice, for world peace and for the welfare of all of our people. The other, an egotist, a demagogue, and a fooler of some, though not of all the people, working for himself."

Despite these evocations of faith, Taft was not hopeful. When Hilles asked him if Mrs. Taft would be "greatly disappointed in defeat," he replied, he reported to his wife, that "the contrary was the case, that you had for a long time not expected [me] to be reelected, and you were most gratified, as we all were in the accomplishment of the more important purpose of defeating Roosevelt at Chicago."

During the years of their friendship, Taft had always spoken admiringly of TR's ability to gain a public ear. Now he viewed it with alarm. "With the persistent lying of Roosevelt, with his constant harping on the same matter, day in and day out, he secures a public opinion that it is impossible for us to offset. The more I think of him in this light, the more dangerous he appears to be." Taft's staff was even more chagrined at his lack of news potential. "Hilles is sensitive because Wilson gets a column every day and so does Roosevelt on political subjects," he told Nellie, "and there is no news from me except that I play golf. I seem to have heard that before. . . ."

On July 31 he was to be formally notified that he was the nominee of the Republican party, and he began trying to write a speech for that occasion. "I am not quite certain what I ought to put into it and what I ought to leave out, and I am not quite sure that my heart is in the campaign at any rate," he wrote Nellie. "I seem to think that we have won what there was to fight about, and that which follows is less important, though it concerns both you and me more personally."

A relationship existed between Mrs. Taft's dim view of the coming election and her desire to keep the White House entertainment bills down. In regard to the notification luncheon, she wired her husband, "I will come home. Not over seventy-five to luncheon." Several hours later, aware of her husband's proclivity for extravagance, she dispatched another wire: "The committee is sixty-five. Invite a few women to go with them. That is all you need."

In reply, the President gave his arrangements for the luncheon: "We will have lobster Newburg, capon and ham, have enough for 400 guests en buffet. I know you want to keep them down to 75 but we can not do it, my dear. I have got to be more generous."

This was duty, not enthusiasm. Nor had he any more eagerness for the campaign ahead, especially since he was aware of the split loyalties of his associates. Elihu Root, he wrote Nellie, "is very timid in certain ways and sometimes makes you feel that he is afraid to get out in the open in his controversy with Roosevelt." Though Root lacked this combativeness, he did serve as a source of amused gossip in Washington. For Root, who had told Taft only a few months earlier that he was too old to get deeply involved in the campaign, was engaged in "a flirtation." "Root and Mrs. Corbin go out driving every afternoon in the park," Taft reported to his wife, "and wherever she goes he goes. The ladies say that he has spruced up, has bought new clothes, has new ties, and that his bang is more correctly cut, and he is really giving a great deal of attention to his personal appearance. What Clara [Mrs. Root] would say if she knew it, they can only conjecture. . . . Why should not the dear old boy and Mrs. Corbin flirt if they will? They are both so old it won't hurt anybody."

On August 1, the newly refurbished Senator Root of New York said in formally notifying President Taft of his nomination: "Your title to the nomination is as clear and unimpeachable as the title of any candidate of any party since political conventions began. . . ."

Root spoke from a platform raised a few feet above the floor of the East Room, which overlooked a terrace and garden with blooming scarlet geraniums and tall, waving green palms, with the Treasury Building in the background. Mrs. Taft sat just below the platform, among the four hundred guests.

Root spoke briefly, forcefully. But Taft, who followed him, read a ponderous ten-thousand-word speech, obviously having solved the problem of what to put in it and what to leave out by putting everything in. Like Warren G. Harding, who hadn't been able to speak Roosevelt's name in the nominating speech in Chicago, Taft avoided the names of both Wilson and Roosevelt. Together, they were "gentlemen." Individually, Wilson was referred to as the one who led the Democratic party; TR, the leader of former Republicans who had left their party.

Finally the speech ended, with a question and with syntax as difficult to deliver as it was to follow: "So may we not expect in the issues which are now before us that the ballots cast in November shall show a prevailing majority in favor of sound progress, great prosperity upon a protection basis, and under true constitutional representative rule by the people?"

Having asked this question, the President disappeared—as though in fear of receiving an answer—and when he returned to the buffet lunch that was being served, he wore a silk house coat instead of formal dress.

He carried refreshment to Mrs. Taft and other women, and then mingled among the guests, who appeared happier with the lobster Newburg, capon, and ham than with thought of the future.

Six days later, in Sea Girt, New Jersey, a more vigorous spirit characterized the ceremony notifying Woodrow Wilson that he had been nominated by the Democratic party. Ten thousand people stood on the green that stretched from the Governor's sedate pillared cottage to the ocean. They heard huge Senator-elect Ollie James—whose hand was so big that when raised it could obscure the view—score both TR and the President.

"A former President charges the present President," James said, "with being friendly with certain trusts, and failure to prosecute them. The present President charges the former President with being friendly with certain other trusts, and failure to prosecute them. We believe them both."

Then, in his direct notification, he reminded Governor Wilson that he had been unanimously nominated by the Democratic party on the forty-sixth ballot. "No cry of a fraud-controlled convention was heard, no charge of theft-made delegations was uttered, no bribery of delegates debauched that convention, no combination or trade, no bosses' mandate was responsible for nomination. But it came to you as untainted as the nation's honor."

With his running mate, Governor Marshall of Indiana, at his side, Wilson accepted the nomination and presented his political beliefs— which were progressive, those which the people and the time required. For far more personal reasons, Taft and Roosevelt were ready to accept the man who enunciated them. "If I can not win I hope Wilson will," Taft said, "and Roosevelt feels that if he can not win, he hopes Wilson will."

Sagamore Hill teemed with politicians in July, all busily conferring with TR: Woodruff, A. P. Moore (without his wife, Lillian Russell), Cochems, Perkins, Dixon, O. K. Davis, George Kirchwey, Flinn. They also came in groups and, therefore, with a degree of anonymity: Oyster Bay Progressives, Freeport, Long Island, Progressives, Minnesota Progressives, Vermont Progressives. . . . They came and kept coming, wending their way up the long hill from Oyster Bay, as to a shrine.

Fittingly, one weekend a kind of morality play took place, when TR and Nick Longworth decided whether or not Alice should attend the Progressive convention. "We sat on the piazza," she recalled, "Father and I in rocking chairs, both rocking violently, while they held a sort of court of justice on me." Finally, to her terrible disappointment, they decided it would be unfair to Nick if she went, and Alice spent the following weeks in Washington, "trying not to be too unpleasant," she said, "with, I think, only intermittent success."

The religious theme went from Sagamore Hill to Chicago's Coliseum, where bunting from the last convention still concealed barbed wire, and where at noon on August 5 the Progressive party, freshly named, opened its convention. The delegates and alternates made the trip from every state in the Union but South Carolina; like pilgrims or crusaders, they had paid their own way. Upon their arrival at the Coliseum, they beheld a fine specimen of a bull moose hanging over the entrance. The music into which they walked was not convention-shrill and secular like "There'll Be a Hot Time in the Old Town Tonight," but, rather, spiritually uplifting, inspiring, the roll of hymns.

Impatient with the tumult—indigenous to conventions, even progressive ones—Senator Beveridge called out, "Where is that blankety-blank preacher, we want him to start his prayer."

So perhaps it was "a Methodist camp meeting done over in political terms." But TR was not, as Taft believed, attempting to make "Holy Rollers" out of his followers. This even TR could not do, for those in attendance at the convention were middle-class, intelligent, educated people, no one among them making "less than two thousand a year" or "topping ten thousand." George Perkins, of course, was an exception, but he was contributing his wealth, as the others were giving their energies and spirit, for a cause.

Beveridge made the keynote speech; he spoke of "invisible government," a sinister, economic aspect of the two old parties that must be destroyed. With oratorical ornateness, he declared, "Hunger should never walk in these thinly peopled gardens of plenty." And he concluded solemnly, reverently, "My eyes have seen the coming of the glory of the Lord."

The next day, TR made his first appearance at the convention and was welcomed by a frantic, hour-long ovation that included the singing of hymns and waving of red bandannas, anticipating the revolutionary character of what TR was about to say. Though TR's "Confessions of Faith" speech was long enough to have been written by Taft, its contents were too radical for Taft to have even considered. It contained deeply felt beliefs, ones which TR had doubted he would ever be able to express publicly. Moreover, its content and the Progressive party's platform were essentially one; the platform, significantly, had been worked on by Pinchot, author of TR's Osawatomie speech. In essence, the platform stood for "using the government as an agency of human welfare." Government was to be an instrument of the people—not of the bosses and privilege—and women and children and the laboring man would be its concern. In concluding, TR said, "Surely there never was a fight better worth making than the one in which we are engaged. . . . I hope we shall win, and I believe that if we can wake the people to what the fight really means we shall win. But, win or lose, we shall not falter. . . . Six weeks ago, here in Chicago, I spoke to the honest representatives of a convention which was not dominated by honest men. . . . Now to you men . . . I say in closing what in that speech I said in closing. We stand at Armageddon, and we battle for the Lord."

The platform was then read—interrupted by cheers and hymns—and adopted; next, Beveridge presented TR and Hiram Johnson, the party's candidates; finally, the convention adjourned with the congregation singing, "Praise God, from whom all blessings flow." TR's "rough bass about a half tone off-key" joined in like a bull moose bellowing lustily.

A reporter objected to all the hymn singing of the new party, maintaining that the tariff and other such mundane matters—unlike the abolition of slavery—did not rate the "Battle Hymn of the Republic." He was overlooking the fact that the Progressive party's fight was against another kind of slavery, economic slavery, and that God's blessings were needed to attain this highly moral objective.

On a personal level both TR and Will Taft stood ready to do almost anything to defeat the other. In the campaign ahead they, at least, considered every possible means to that end.

Twenty   Elephant, Donkey, and Bull Moose

In the middle of August, TR—a campaigner once again—invaded the state in which Taft's summer home was located. He spoke in Revere Beach, Massachusetts, where red bandannas, the Roosevelt battle flag, "dotted the crowd with dabs of bright color." TR spotted a particular banner that amused him and gave a special wave of his hand to those who carried it, the Roosevelt Club of Beverly. "We love Beverly," the banner joyously proclaimed, "but oh you Oyster Bay!"

Though a middle-aged heaviness now thickened TR's waist, and gray had come to his temples, the fire of his personality blazed as high as ever. When a man in the crowd shouted, "Tell us about Taft!" TR shouted right back, "I never discuss dead issues."

Will Taft's enmity, however, was very much alive and equaled TR's. "As the campaign goes on and the unscrupulousness of Roosevelt develops," he wrote Nellie, "it is hard for me to realize that we are talking about the same man as that man whom we knew in the Presidency." (She, of course, did not find it at all hard to realize.) "It is true he gave evidences in his humorous and cynical way of indifference to moral restraint, but I always assumed that it was humorous. I knew of course that his memory was defective about the things he did not want to remember, that he was so intense in his pugnaciousness and in making his enemy aware of him that he could think almost as he wished to think, but it is impossible to conceive of him as the fakir, the juggler, the green-goods man, the gold brick man that he has come to be."

Despite all this, Taft insisted that he felt no hatred for TR, that he looked "upon him as a historical character of a most peculiar type in whom are embodied elements of real greatness, with certain traits that have now shown themselves in unfitting him for any trust or confidence by the people. I look upon him as I look upon a freak almost in the zoological garden, a kind of animal not often found."

Taft's irritation with Elihu Root also continued, because of Root's halfhearted commitment—a promise to deliver one address. Knowing that Root's real reason was his attachment to TR, Taft wanted him to "cut his bridges behind him and go as far as he can for the cause which he really believes in."

Nick Longworth's position was far more difficult than Root's. Because he was running for re-election on the regular Republican ticket, his wife, his father-in-law, his mother and sisters, and the conservatives of the Republican party—in whom reposed his political ambitions—required diplomatic handling. "I don't know what poor Nick Longworth is going to do," Taft observed.

In a report to his wife, Taft told her that her brother, Will Herron, "told me yesterday that he had a long talk with Nick Longworth and that Nick has told him that his whole sympathies were with me, but that the question which he had to meet was one of family feeling, and therefore he had to be quiet and was unhappy on account of it." Taft concluded with words that reflected his mood that summer: "I don't know how much of this is true, as old Nick is a good deal of a liar, but I guess some of it is. I think that Nick knows that I have always been very friendly to him. He has a good deal less difficulty with me than he has with his father-in-law."

Although Taft wanted the support of Root, Longworth, and every good Republican, he didn't want to campaign for it. That he had defeated Roosevelt for the nomination and thus proved that his administration had not been rejected may have satisfied him. As for that annoying demand that he go out and make headlines, he stated rhythmically—to make it all the more categorical—"I couldn't if I would and I wouldn't if I could."

TR, on the other hand, could and would and did. In visiting thirty-four states, he traveled ten thousand miles. Let the war be lost, he would still give his heroic all in winning the battles. Catching sight of Taft badges in Springfield, Missouri, he remarked, "They are the appropriate color of yellow." And he had to continue fighting the charge that he was a drunkard; it was renewed when, for security reasons, he was surrounded by guards on entering a hotel in Duluth and escorted up the hotel's stairs in that fashion. "Did you see that?" someone in the lobby exclaimed. "He was so drunk they had to carry him upstairs."

As persistent as the drunkenness fantasy was the assertion that TR, an ambitious egomaniac, wanted desperately to be king. The third term he was seeking was a steppingstone to a fourth, the fourth to a fifth, until, eventually, a throne would be ordered for the White House. This allegation amused rather than angered TR. "Good Lord," he exclaimed, laughing, remembering his 1910 encounter with royalty, "I know kings. Nothing would induce me to become one."

Editorially, the New York *Times* attacked TR for his skill at arrogantly justifying almost anything. For example, they said, if Roosevelt's grandmother's body, dismembered and boiled in oil, were found buried in the Sagamore Hill cellar, TR would have a letter from a friend explaining it all away. At dinner on the day the editorial appeared, TR was jokingly asked by O. K. Davis why he'd cut up his aged and respected grandmother and disposed of her in a highly unorthodox way. "Well, O. K.," he replied gravely, "she was a highly reprehensible old party, who ought to have been drawn and quartered and boiled in oil long ago."

Those were merely a campaign's annoyances—a cloud of gnats before one's face, the yipping of dogs at one's heels. TR knew that it was Wilson whom he was really fighting, and dispassionately assessed his vote-drawing power.

Though Wilson was TR's adversary, at the start of the campaign, Wilson concentrated on the Republicans, for he was able—with the objectivity of a professor—to view the admirable aspects of the new party. He had great respect for Roosevelt as a political animal. When he compared TR with himself, he humbly accepted second place. TR appealed to the public's imagination; he did not. TR was vivid; he was "a vague, conjectural personality, more made up of opinions and academic prepossessions than of human traits and red corpuscles."

Not long after the campaign started, Wilson had to shift his attack to the admirable new party and TR because TR ignored Taft, loftily, realistically, and was firing his heavy guns at the main target. TR said Wilson was "generally clearheaded," but he was "very wrong-headed on many issues." He pointed out, with the directness of dogma, "Wilson is a good man who has in no way shown that he possesses any special fitness for the Presidency." After all, said TR, Wilson had not the "slightest understanding . . . of our industrial and agricultural life." This vigorous attack pleased Mrs. Roosevelt, who remained at home, closely following the campaign. "Theodore is whacking at Wilson," she said, "who deserves all he gets."

Calmly Wilson said Roosevelt had "promised too often the millennium." He, on the other hand, did "not want to promise heaven," he declared, "unless I can bring it to you. I can only see a little way up the road."

Traveling about the country in an old wooden private railroad car, Wilson parried TR's hyperbole with understatement. TR wanted to have the government regulate trusts, but Wilson—aided by Louis Brandeis, who had shown him how to clarify the moribund Sherman Anti-Trust Act and make it effective—proposed to do away with monopoly and revive free competition. Wilson, however, aligned himself with social welfare and much of the Progressive party's specific progressivism: the prohibition of the injunction in labor disputes, direct presidential primaries, the election of senators by popular vote, federal income tax. As for Taft's Republican party, Wilson dismissed it as not having had an idea in thirty years—and then quickly corrected that figure to fifty.

It was inevitable that a campaign such as this should spawn scandal-mongers. Someone, it was reported, had an exchange of letters—that they were scandalous love letters was implied—between the highly respectable Mr. Wilson and a Mrs. Peck, recently divorced. After the letters were brought to the attention of Republicans and declined by them, the Progressive party was approached. That body, busily battling for the Lord, nevertheless found time to consider making use of the letters. Finally, the Progressives dismissed the whole idea, reasoning that since they had no concrete proof of the existence of the letters, an unsubstantiated charge might turn out to their disadvantage rather than to Wilson's.

Essentially, TR supported this view. He maintained that "those letters would be entirely unconvincing. Nothing, no evidence, would ever make the American people believe that a man like Woodrow Wilson, cast so perfectly as the apothecary's clerk, could ever play Romeo!"

Lacking the weapon of "salacious and incriminating" evidence, TR had to intensify his campaign. His voice began to give way under the strain; the final bit of punishment to which it was subjected was during a speech delivered in a packed tent, with the flaps open to accommodate the overflow crowd and through which a raw October lake breeze blew. The night of that speech, TR delivered another in Chicago's Coliseum, and his voice sank to a painful, ragged whisper that failed ludicrously to match his powerful gesticulations. Finally, he had to stop both gestures and speech, unable to complete his address.

The next day, October 14, TR was scheduled to speak at an evening meeting in Milwaukee. That morning TR's voice could not rise above a whisper, and Dr. Scurry Terrell of Dallas, Texas, a throat specialist who accompanied the campaign party, told TR that how long he would be able to campaign depended on how well he took care of his voice. Care meant not talking and, when possible, not whispering.

TR insisted—in vehement whispers—on going to Milwaukee; if he should not be able to speak, he would, at least, be present, and the audience would have visual if not auditory proof of his good intentions.

The train left at three in the afternoon. It made several stops along the way; at each of them TR appeared on the rear platform and shook hands, and—by prearrangement—Congressman Henry A. Cooper of Wisconsin did all the talking. At six, the train arrived in Milwaukee; the populace had eagerly been awaiting it.

One individual, a former New York saloonkeeper named John Schrank, had a singular reason for looking forward to TR's arrival. On September 21 Schrank had purchased a revolver in a gun store on Broadway and started following TR from city to city—traveling under the name of Walter Ross—waiting for a chance to kill him. In Chicago, he had wanted to do it at the railway station and again when TR had spoken at the Coliseum. Now he was waiting his chance in Milwaukee; he was not noticeable in the crowd, a bald, light-complexioned, stocky man, fairly well dressed. But anonymity did not alter his uniqueness; he believed "any man looking for a third term ought to be shot" and imagined that McKinley had appeared before him in a dream one night in the middle of September and said of Roosevelt, "This is my murderer; avenge my death."

Every detail that evening worked with a fine precision for the benefit of the would-be assassin. Incidents and decision aligned themselves so that TR received maximum police protection, and this, paradoxically, made possible the point-blank, deadly shot at TR at a distance of only a few feet.

After the stop in Racine, the last one before Milwaukee, the members of the TR party met and decided that TR shouldn't go to the hotel as originally planned. Instead, to conserve his energy—and his voice—he was to dine on the train and then go directly to the Auditorium, where he would say a few words and have someone read the rest of his speech.

At Milwaukee, a large civically dedicated committee boarded the train and was very upset to hear about the change in plans. All their arrangements meant much to them and to Milwaukee, and to the state of Wisconsin. After all, people lined the streets, waiting for the scheduled parade from the train to the Hotel Gilpatrick, where reservations had already been made.

No argument diminished their vehemence, and TR finally surrendered, saying he wanted to be a "good Indian." Dr. Terrell, as opposed as ever, hoped to salvage something. He would consent, but only on one condition: there must be extra police protection to save TR from the strain of pushing through crowds on entering and leaving the hotel, even in going to and from the hotel dining room. The committee agreed, and—unfortunately, as it turned out—kept its word.

TR—obeying Dr. Terrell only because of extreme weariness—did not stand up or greet the crowds that stretched for more than a mile, from the station to the hotel. He merely lifted his hat. At the hotel he napped briefly before dinner—unusual for him—in a rocking chair. After dinner he rested again before going down to the seven-passenger touring car waiting at the hotel door.

The committee, in keeping its promise, had done a thorough job; the hotel lobby and the sidewalks had been cleared by the police. Shortly before eight, TR and his party walked easily and directly to the waiting car. Ordinarily, TR would have been preceded into the car by two men, to shield him from the crowd, but now, because of the cleared sidewalk and street, the door of the car was courteously held open for TR, who was followed into the car by Elbert Martin, one of his secretaries. TR, wearing a big brown army overcoat, sat down, but a cheer from the crowd caused him to pop right up. As he faced the rear of the car and raised his right hand, holding his hat, he made a perfect target. Having just left the lighted hotel, he could not see the man in the dark who lifted his gun and fired at him. But a flash of metal caught Martin's eye; reflexively, he dove over the side of the car.

The bullet's impact, which he later described as being like the kick of a mule, staggered TR and caused him to sink to the seat of the car. However, he told Henry Cochems, a Wisconsin member of the Progressive National Committee, who had put his arm around TR's shoulders and asked if he had been badly hurt, "He pinked me." TR rose after saying that and coughed. Quickly he put his hand to his mouth to see if there was any blood. When he saw there was none, he deduced instantaneously that the bullet was in his chest and the "chances were twenty to one that it was not fatal."

TR also saw that Martin had the would-be assassin on the ground, locked in a half nelson, and was angrily doing his utmost to break the man's neck. Martin, a muscular former football player, had struck Schrank in leaping from the car and knocked him down. Then, as in a football scrimmage, another member of TR's party had jumped on top of Martin. Cecil Lyon, a Texas Republican leader and a very close friend of TR's, tried to shoot Schrank, but he couldn't find a clear passage to his target between the struggling bodies. Before Martin and Schrank had gone down together, Schrank had tried to take another shot at TR, but Martin had wrested the gun from him with his left hand while he held him around the neck with his right.

Angry cries arose in the crowd: "Lynch him! Kill him!"

Just as TR had calmly decided the bullet was not fatal, he continued to be master of the situation. In the emergency his voice returned. "Don't hurt him," he ordered Martin. "Bring him to me."

Martin arose, pulling the would-be assassin to his feet and twisting his face around so that TR could get a look at him. TR did not know the man. Standing in the car, he directed the police in the matter of taking his attacker into custody. Although TR had to save Schrank from Martin and the incensed crowd, he later candidly admitted, "I would not have objected to the man's being killed at the very instant, but I did not deem it wise or proper that he should be killed before my eyes if I was going to recover."

After the crowd had been pushed away from the car, Dr. Terrell told TR he wanted to see the wound. He also ordered the driver of the car to go to the hospital at once. Before the driver had a chance to obey, TR told the driver to take him to the Auditorium.

"No, Colonel," one of TR's secretaries said. "Let's go to the hospital."

"You get me to that speech," TR shot back angrily. "It may be the last one I shall ever deliver, but I am going to deliver this one."

All the way to the Auditorium Dr. Terrell pleaded with TR that he allow him to examine the wound, that they turn around, go back to the hotel.

"No," TR said adamantly, "this is my big chance, and I am going to make that speech if I die doing it."

Upon their arrival at the Auditorium, someone noticed the hole the bullet had made in TR's coat. TR put his hand under his coat, withdrew it, and discovered that the hand was bloody. Nevertheless he said, "I don't think it's anything serious."

Dr. Terrell began once again to insist that he have a look at the wound, and now TR consented. A few doctors in the audience were also contacted and asked to come to the dressing room. By the time they arrived, TR had opened his coat and vest and pulled up his shirt so that the wound could be examined. It was about a half inch below the right nipple and bleeding slightly; it had made a stain about the size of a man's fist on his white shirt.

Before the doctor could comment, TR put his hands on his chest, took a deep breath, expelled it, and took another breath. Then he told Dr. Terrell, "It's all right, Doctor. There's no perforation. I don't get any pain from this breathing."

Not willing to accept his lay diagnosis, the doctors informed TR they couldn't be sure of the seriousness of the wound and advised that he go to the hospital. But TR insisted he felt no pain, that he was all right. "I will make this speech or die," he said, "one or the other."

Overruled, the doctors made a temporary bandage out of a fresh handkerchief, and TR strode out onto the stage.

The packed auditorium responded with an enthusiastic ovation, unaware that an attempt had been made on TR's life. Henry F. Cochems, in introducing TR, had told the audience of the attempt, but apparently failed to make them understand. Perhaps they took the introduction figuratively, for Cochems said of the speaker that he "comes to you in the spirit of a good soldier. As we were leaving the hotel a few minutes ago, a dastardly hand raised a revolver and fired a shot at him, and the Colonel speaks as a soldier with a bullet in his breast—where we don't know."

TR raised his hands to silence the cheers. He then said that they didn't realize that he had been shot. "But," he concluded, "it takes more than that to kill a bull moose!"

A shudder ran through the audience, and because women predominated, there were many gasps that can best be described as "Oh, oh!"

As TR took the speech he was to deliver out of his pocket, he also removed his metal spectacle case, which the bullet had pierced. He turned and showed it to someone close to him on the stage. When he saw the bullet had also made a hole through the fifty folded pages of his speech, he held it up for everyone to see.

"And friends," he said, "the hole in it is where the bullet went through, and it probably saved the bullet from going into my heart. The bullet is in me now, so that I can not make a very long speech. But I will try my best."

The wound felt hot to TR, and he was also aware of his speeded-up heartbeat and that each breath he took was quick and short. But the audience only noticed that he spoke in a lower voice than usual, that his gestures were less emphatic.

"First of all," TR went on, "I want to say this about myself. I have altogether too many important things to think of to pay any heed or feel any concern over my own death. Now I would not speak to you insincerely within five minutes of being shot. I am telling you the literal truth when I say my concern is for many other things. It is not in the least for my own life. I want you to understand that I am ahead of the game anyway. No man has had a happier life than I have had, a happier life in every way. I can tell you with absolute truthfulness that I am very much uninterested in whether I am shot or not."

Then he pointed out that his all-consuming interest was the progressive movement, "a movement to try to take the burdens off the man and especially the woman in this country who is most oppressed."

As he continued, someone on the stage interrupted, asking that he stop, go to the hospital.

"I am not sick at all," TR declared, a bit impatient, annoyed. "I am all right."

But the audience could hardly believe this; they knew the man before them had been shot, that the bullet was still in him. They therefore could not keep from concentrating on his condition rather than on what he said. He gripped their attention when he opened his coat and vest to show them his blood-stained white shirt. It was the result, he told them, of the abuse heaped upon him by newspapers, "in the interests not only of Mr. Debs [the Socialist party candidate] but of Mr. Wilson and Mr. Taft, influencing a weak mind."

One white-haired old lady arose and asked him to stop, for he was making all those present suffer; they would rather have him go to a hospital to be taken care of than hear him speak.

TR thanked her, but he went on. "I give you my word, I do not care a rap about being shot, not a rap. I have had a good many experiences in my time and this is only one of them. What I do care for is my country."

His decided pallor and unsteadiness caused a number of individuals to form a ring at the edge of the stage so that they could catch him should he fall off.

Aware of what they had in mind, TR moved back from the lip of the stage. "My friends," he said, "are a little more nervous than I am. I have had an A-1 time in life, and I am having it now. I never in my life had any movement in which I was able to serve with such wholehearted devotion as in this."

Relief came to the audience when he said, "And now friends, I shall have to cut short much of the speech I meant to give you"; their relief was short-lived, for he added, "but I want to touch on just two or three of the points."

He spoke out against discrimination of all kinds. He spoke up for labor, of the laborers' right to organize for their own protection. He appealed to labor to denounce "crime or violence," "disorders and inciting riot," and to "proceed under the protection of our laws and with all respect to the laws."

When he finally finished his hour-and-a-half-long speech, appearing very weary and oblivious to the applause, he told Dr. Terrell, "Now I am ready to go with you and do what you want."

A half-dozen people climbed up on the stage to shake his hand. "Didn't they know," he said later in some annoyance, "that it is impossible for a man who has just been shot to shake hands with genuine cordiality?"

In spite of this delay, TR made it to a waiting automobile in just a few minutes; three doctors accompanied him to Emergency Hospital. There he sat on a table in the operating room and talked politics with the doctors, while waiting for the arrival of an X-ray machine to determine how deeply the bullet had penetrated. He told Dr. Joseph C. Bloodgood, "I do not want to fall into the hands of too many doctors and have the same experience that McKinley and Garfield had." He also busied himself dictating some messages. He requested that someone send a wire to his friend Seth Bullock at Deadwood, South Dakota, and to be sure and let Bullock know that he had been shot with a thirty-eight on a thirty-eight frame, for this would bring back memories of their ranching days. To his daughter-in-law, Ted's wife, he wired, "The bullet did not hit anything vital. I think they'll find it around somewhere."

A half hour later, at eleven o'clock, the news of the attempted assassination reached Washington. Since it was an early-to-bed town, a large portion of the population had already retired when the shrill voices of the newsboys, shouting "Extra!" violated the quiet streets.

The President could not be disturbed by their cries, for he was in New York to attend an official banquet at the Astor Hotel. It was there that a *Times* reporter broke the news to him. Taft said with feeling, but a bit formally, "I am delighted to learn that the dastardly attack was unsuccessful. The resort of physical violence is out of place in our twentieth-century civilization and under our form of government."

Mrs. Roosevelt was also in New York, at a musical comedy, "The Merry Countess," at the Casino Theatre. There she received the first report—that the bullet hadn't even hit her husband—and the second, that he had been merely scratched. Reporters noticed that she was crying when she left the theater. A wire from her husband, shortly after midnight, filled with comments to reassure her—the wound was "a trivial one"; he was feeling fine; his voice was in "good shape"; he was going to continue with his campaign speaking engagements—only caused her to remark, "That's just the sort of thing that was said when Mr. McKinley was shot."

Another Roosevelt—a fifth cousin of TR's and husband of his niece Eleanor—State Senator Franklin D. Roosevelt, who was recuperating from an attack of typhoid fever at his home at 49 East 65th Street, received an early report of the attempted assassination. Though he was one of Woodrow Wilson's chief backers in the state, the news made him very nervous, and he called the *Times* repeatedly for the latest bulletins from Milwaukee.

Woodrow Wilson sent words of sympathy.

Oscar Straus, in Amsterdam, couldn't understand how anyone would wish to harm "the greatest friend of the plain people the country has had since Abraham Lincoln."

A loyal Democrat expressed a painful dilemma: "I hope TR will not die, but this gives him the prestige of a martyr."

All across the country—and the world—the frightening word spread, and people reacted in individual ways.

At Emergency Hospital in Milwaukee, the X-ray machine finally came, and two pictures were taken of TR's chest. It had been decided, during all the waiting, that TR should make the short trip to Chicago, where he could be cared for by the famous surgeon John B. Murphy. TR left the hospital at 11:25 P.M. He walked to his private car unassisted—perhaps because no one dared make even a gesture suggesting help. They would surely have been further frightened off by his challenging "I am feeling fine."

On the train, the Mayflower, the two doctors who had accompanied TR tried to persuade him to go to bed immediately. He wouldn't hear of it; he was accustomed to shave before retiring, and he saw no reason for changing that practice. By this time, the doctors had come to realize the futility of trying to persuade TR by mere argument. Soon he was shaving, humming as he made the brisk razor strokes; his humming had all the contentment of a cat's purr.

Having finished shaving, he still did not lie down. He removed the studs and buttons from his bloody shirt and put them in a fresh shirt, for he thought doing this the following day might be difficult if he became stiff.

The anxious, impatient doctors were happy that he finally lay down in his bunk. His activity in the train had further tired him, and his rapid heartbeat and shortness of breath made him feel somewhat uncomfortable. After resting a short time, he carefully turned onto his unwounded side, and having made himself comfortable, he slept.

The engineer made the run to Chicago as quietly and gently as possible in order not to disturb TR's sleep—no bells, whistles, or sudden jerking stops and starts. Instead of terminating the journey in the city's new, bustling station, he considerately took the special train to the old, peaceful Northwestern Station, arriving at 4:00 A.M. on Tuesday, October 15. All these precautions achieved their objective, for TR continued to sleep, and since the doctors on the train believed sleep at this point was invaluable, they did not awaken him. The ambulance that had come to transport the patient to the hospital remained waiting beside the train.

TR left the Mayflower shortly after 6:00 A.M. The sight of the ambulance annoyed him; he wasn't a "weakling to be crippled by a flesh wound" and he didn't like the idea of going to the hospital "lying in that thing." However, when the flashes of the photographers popped all about him, his good spirits returned. "Oh, gosh!" he exclaimed. "Shot again!" To the crowd of about four hundred that had gathered he called out a cheery "Good morning!"

He was installed in a room on the third floor of Mercy Hospital. The hospital's staff had to adjust to his personality. He hadn't the least conception of the behavior expected of a patient. He ate breakfast—bacon, eggs, and tea—sitting up, kicking his legs vigorously over the edge of the bedstead. Flowers arrived in absurd quantity; he kept as many as was practical and aesthetically sufficient for his room, and routed the rest to other patients in the hospital. The surgeons and nurses tried to keep him from talking, wanted him to rest, but they didn't know where or how to take hold of the problem. What could they do when confronted by a series of rapid-fire political conferences? Of course, they could object to reporters—and they did—but TR said, "These men are my friends. You let me handle them." He kidded around with Martin, who had come in with the reporters; as they all left, he shook hands with the reporters, but not with Martin, saying, "I owe you a deeper debt of gratitude than a handshake can ever repay."

Almost as a concession, TR permitted the surgeons to administer an injection of tetanus antitoxin. To avoid infecting the wound, Dr. Murphy did not probe it. The X-ray pictures showed that the bullet had fractured and lodged in the fourth rib; he decided not to attempt to remove it unless infection occurred. The spectacle case had slowed the bullet; the fifty folded heavy glossy sheets on which his speech had been written had deflected the bullet upward and into the rib. If it had not been for those fifty folded sheets, the bullet would have gone between the ribs into TR's heart.

One doctor, a Dr. Butler, made an important nonmedical statement: "Mr. President, you were elected last night. It was the turn of the tide in your favor."

But Dr. Murphy and the other doctors were concerned for TR's life rather than his political welfare.

"Don't lose my place, Doctor, don't lose my place!" TR exclaimed when a doctor, who had turned back the covers to examine the wound, laid aside a book of essays by Macaulay.

TR, from a half-seated position, leaned his head forward and looked down at the wound. "That doesn't look bad, Doctor. What do you think?"

"That, as it is, doesn't bother us," Dr. Murphy said, nodding to the other doctors with him. "It is what you do to it."

TR raised his eyebrows questioningly. Once again he heard familiar admonition on the subject of rest. He smiled, reached for his book and said, "All right."

It had been, as he told Alice that day, "an amazingly interesting experience."

The attempt on TR's life led to an immediate doubling of the guard which was responsible for the security of Taft—a bigger and a more important target. Because of a threat—to "shoot Wilson the same as Roosevelt was shot"—Edward M. House, Wilson's adviser, sent a wire to a ranger named Bill McDonald in Quanah, Texas, telling him to come and bring artillery. McDonald arrived, wearing a white Stetson, a four-day growth of beard, and a gun that would kill a man without it being necessary to "give him a whole week to die in."

Taft and Wilson—like TR—realized that the possibility of being shot was a "trade risk"; adjustment included acceptance of this risk and being oblivious to it. Their more immediate concern was TR's behavior after being shot, a romantic gallantry certain to win the hearts of voters. ("What a melodrama we shall have when he is able to take the stump again," Horace Taft wrote his brother. "I have never been so disgusted about anything he has done as at the speech he made to his audience after the shooting.") All newspapers—even those opposed to TR and all he stood for—lauded his "pluck." Hapgood, in his lead editorial in *Collier's Weekly* the following week, pointed out that citizens should not cast their votes for TR simply because he had been shot. But he did admit that "no amount of argument, no amount of reflection concentrated in many months, could have influenced as many Americans as were stirred by the shot of a madman."

"I extend to you my heartfelt sympathy in your present distress," Taft wired TR, charging it to his personal account. "I earnestly hope and pray that you and your family and the country may be promptly relieved of suspense by news that all danger is past." TR replied, "I appreciate your sympathetic inquiry and wish to thank you for it." TR's wife, too, answered, "My family and I unite in thanks for your kind expression of sympathy." The amenities had been observed according to the rigid rules of etiquette.

But Taft also reacted in other ways. He angrily denounced Roosevelt's supporters, for they were, he said, "attempting to make all they can out of the shooting by charging it to the vituperation of my supporters. This is so palpably unjust that I rather hope they will continue it."

Wilson also had both public and private reactions to the shooting. For the electorate, he made the sportsmanlike gesture of calling off his campaigning; this was done on the advice of Colonel House, who often said, "The best politics is to do the right thing." Because this gesture was calculated to drain some sympathy away from TR, Wilson gloated, "Teddy will have apoplexy when he hears of this."

But TR also knew and practiced the best politics. He turned down Wilson's offer in a manner that would enhance his heroic image, for he urged that the campaign go on, saying, "so far as my opponents are concerned, whatever would with truth and propriety have been said against me and my cause before I was shot can with equal truth and equal propriety be said against me now, and it should be so said; and the things that cannot be said now are merely the things that ought not to have been said before. This is not a contest about any man; it is a contest concerning principles." Employing one of those stirring martial analogies for which he had a particular fondness, he said, "If one soldier who happens to carry the flag is stricken, another will take it from his hand and carry it on. One after another the standard bearers may be laid low, but the standard itself can never fall. . . . It is not important whether one leader lives or dies, it is important only that the cause shall live and win. Tell the people not to worry about me, for if I go down another will take my place."

Beveridge attempted to take over his speaking engagements, and Oscar Straus helped, too, speaking in the large cities—Chicago, Cincinnati, Cleveland—where he had been scheduled to make addresses. But TR would not let them carry the flag for very long. No sooner did he arrive home, only a week after the shooting, than he made it clear to his wife and especially to his doctors—and to the country in general—that he was definitely going to make his speech in Madison Square Garden in New York City on October 30, according to schedule. "I am in fine shape now," he declared. "The wound is still open but practically does not bother me at all."

A few days later, restive, tired of all the "mollycoddling," TR threw back the covers of his sickbed and left it.

The twenty-seventh, his birthday, Mrs. Roosevelt regarded as "a day of Thanksgiving for us all." She revealed her feelings in stating, "the horror of the deed still overshadows all who love him." Almost as a belated birthday present, the next day she permitted him to see the reporters who had been camping patiently on the Sagamore Hill doorstep.

When one of them asked how the wound felt, he said, "It feels like rheumatism. Only a lot worse." However, months later, in speaking of the bullet, he said, "I do not mind it any more than if it were in my waistcoat pocket."

As TR was rapidly recovering, Taft's running mate, Vice-President "Sunny Jim" Sherman, was nearing the end of his life. He died on October 30. Sherman's death was, Taft mourned, "very discouraging because it may induce many not to vote for the ticket." Mrs. Taft, too, regarded the Vice-President's death as a personal blow. "Sherman's death," she wrote her husband, "was very unfortunate coming just at this time. You have the worst luck."

The day after Sherman's death, a Thursday, Louis Seibold of the New York *World* called on Taft at the White House. He presented a plan, a last desperate attempt to keep TR from defeating Taft in the four-way election. First of all, he wanted—for nationwide publication on Saturday, November 2—Taft's forthright view of the issues. He also wanted—and this was, perhaps, even more important—Taft's whole account of his relationship with Roosevelt.

Taft agreed to the interview—in part, because Sherman's death might have confused the voters and lessened the Republican party's chances. Seibold interviewed Taft the next morning—and all went well. But that afternoon Seibold was informed that Taft wished to make some changes in the statements he'd given him. Since Taft was leaving Washington for Utica at five o'clock to attend Sherman's funeral, it was arranged for Seibold to go along as far as New York City to receive the revised interview en route.

Seibold accompanied the presidential party. He had dinner with Taft, during which he stressed the importance of having the story in time for publication on Saturday; space in Saturday's papers had been saved for it, and the election was imminent, on Tuesday, the fifth. Taft then went to his stateroom to make the changes. After an hour, a wait that seemed far longer to Seibold, Taft appeared and told him that he had second thoughts about some of the statements he had made and wanted to get advice from Root, Wickersham, and Barnes upon arriving in New York. This meant that the interview couldn't be in Seibold's hands until the next day.

"I'm afraid that's too late," Seibold said.

To which Taft replied, in seeming *non sequitur*, "But Roosevelt was my closest friend"—the very words he had spoken to Seibold after attacking TR in Boston, in the spring of the year. That time Taft had broken down and wept.

Another *World* reporter on the train and some of Taft's advisers made a strenuous effort to persuade Taft to release the interview, but they failed. And so this last chance to change the outcome of the election also failed.

(The election over, Seibold asked Taft for a copy of the interview—to be preserved as a historical document. Taft said there were no copies and that he had ordered the secretary present at the interview to burn his notes. Since the interview, according to Seibold, actually lacked sensational revelations concerning the Taft-Roosevelt relationship, it may be that Taft's thoughts and feelings at the time of the interview were of such a nature that Taft felt compelled to destroy all traces of what he had told Seibold.)

On November 5, 1912, a nation of ninety million people went to the polls to choose Wilson, Roosevelt, Taft, or Debs.

Wilson spent the evening with his family; after supper, they gathered around to listen to a reading from Browning. This simple tranquillity could not last, for word came that the head of the house had won the election—by a landslide. Wilson, like Jefferson and Lincoln, had profited by a split party. "I myself have no feeling of triumph tonight," he said. "I have a feeling of solemn responsibility."

Taft's immediate reaction to the returns was bitter, for he had won in only two states, Utah and Vermont, and had suffered the worst presidential defeat in the history of the country. As a form of comfort, he repeated privately and publicly that hundreds of thousands of Republicans had voted for Wilson in order to save the country from Roosevelt. ("It's too bad how it went," sixteen-year-old Charlie Taft remarked philosophically, "but it will be interesting to see what Wilson does.")

Reporters at Sagamore Hill found TR seated before a fireplace, reading; they found him—unlike Taft—"all buoyant and good-humored." He had lost, but he had also been victorious, for he had won a victory over Taft; he had received 4,126,020 popular votes to Taft's 3,483,922, and 88 electoral votes to Taft's 8.

Debs and Socialism had been victorious, too, in defeat. The votes cast for Debs, almost nine hundred thousand, nearly six per cent of the total vote, were over twice the number he had received in 1908.

Nick Longworth also lost—by only 97 votes. Alice attributed his loss to her attendance at a Bull Moose meeting for Hiram Johnson in Cincinnati in the latter part of the campaign; "that was quite enough to lose him just that number of votes," she said. Though she thought Nick would rebound in the next election, his mother and sisters felt his loss signified the end of his political career, and this intensified their acrimony toward TR. "You know the French proverb," Clara de Chambrun wrote to Will Taft following the election, "a country deserves the government that it has. Let us be thankful that we have not deserved the Moose!" During the campaign Nannie Wallingford had written Taft that on being lectured against hating anyone she had said that "if T.R. were cold and hungry I would take him in and feed and warm him and give him some old clothes of Buck's [Mr. Wallingford] and be glad of the chance. . . ." These charitable instincts, however, did not always dominate her feelings, and seven months after the election, Mrs. Wallingford suggested to one of her children who had chicken pox "to be sure to kiss Aunt Alice."

Paradoxically, TR's personal victory helped elect Wilson, whom he would come to hate with passionate intensity and who would, oddly enough, become the key piece in the strategy to reconcile Roosevelt and Taft.

Twenty-one   Reconciliations?

Presidents about to become ex-Presidents can fully appreciate Thomas Jefferson's declaration when he was shedding the presidency after enduring two terms: "Never did a prisoner released from his chains feel such relief as I shall on shaking off the shackles of power." Understandably, "such relief" might produce lightheartedness, which could inspire an irreverent suggestion for the handling and disposal of ex-Presidents. Taft, for one, recommended a somewhat drastic proposal. After being put to death by chloroform, the ex-President should be reduced "to ashes in a funeral pyre." This would not only be a fitting end, Taft argued, but "at the same time would secure the country from the troublesome fear" that the one who had occupied the highest office could ever come back.

In actuality, an ex-President moves in the direction dictated by his personality. In Taft's case, this would have meant returning to Cincinnati, to the practice of law. But Yale University invited him to become Kent Professor of Law, and this position Taft equated with tranquillity and dignity, a combination Taft's nature could not resist—even though the salary, the highest Yale paid, was only five thousand dollars a year. Still, being in a carefree, jubilant mood, Taft believed he could manage on such a salary, for he did "not expect to eat so much after leaving the White House."

As an ex-President in 1909, TR had sought not the quiet groves of academe but the unpredictable game trails of Africa. Now he found himself to be an "airedale pup in the company of tomcats," more of a pariah than he had been in 1911, for good Republicans blamed him for smashing their party. From this accusation, TR found sanctuary at Sagamore Hill, escaping into the past through the corridors of time as he began writing *Theodore Roosevelt, An Autobiography*. Dipping his pen in an inkwell made of a rhinoceros's foot, he began this journey with the words, "My grandfather on my father's side was of almost purely Dutch blood. . . ."

A single activity, especially such a sedentary one, could not sustain him. In the fall of 1913 he left for South America, accompanied by his wife and Kermit, to speak at half a dozen universities in Brazil, Argentina, and Chile that had invited him. This seemed rather pointless to TR; "as I speak in English . . . nobody will understand," he said. But part of the trip made sense to him. After the lectures, TR and Kermit, with a party, set out to map an unexplored thousand-mile-long river, the River of Doubt, which was later named Río Teodoro. The aim was also to bring back botanical and animal specimens for the American Museum of Natural History in New York. TR looked upon the adventure as his "last chance to be a boy," though by his own admission he now regarded himself as "a stout, rheumatic, elderly gentleman."

The adventure proved sufficient for any boy: this tributary of the Amazon was filled with an "endless succession of rapids and cataracts"; there was no human being in sight for forty-eight days; five of the party's seven canoes were lost in the treacherous waters; the rapids took one man's life; another member of the party "murdered the sergeant and fled into the wilderness"; and there were portages that had to be made through the steaming heavy jungle growth. To cap all these elements of adventure, TR caught his leg between a rock and a canoe and injured it so badly that he couldn't walk. For a time, the others carried him, but then he contracted a jungle fever, and this stopped the whole party. Spontaneously, TR showed the same romantic courage that he had that night in Milwaukee; not wanting to be a burden, he begged that they leave him behind. Finally, they all emerged, TR thirty-five pounds thinner, with the jungle fever germs—like Schrank's bullet—still in his body.

A little over a month after TR landed in New York, Archduke Franz Ferdinand—labeled by TR "a furious reactionary" when he met him in Europe in 1910—was assassinated. In addition to setting off a chain of events that led to World War I, it incidentally led to a constant shifting of TR's relationship with President Wilson and with his former friend, Will Taft.

Unlike Thomas Jefferson, who remained out of "the boisterous ocean of political passions," Roosevelt and Taft would be sucked back in by personal passions and cataclysmic events.

The start of the year, the turning of a corner in time, holds symbolic promise of change, of good fortune. But this is only hope, plaintive desire. After all, 1913 was separated from 1912 by only a tick of the clock—and was actually merely an uninterrupted extension of time.

Four days after 1913 began, Roosevelt and Taft attended the funeral services of Whitelaw Reid, American Ambassador to Great Britain, in the uncompleted Cathedral of St. John the Divine. Death had brought them together physically, and must also have inspired both of them with the sobering thought that we are all but grass to be cut down. Taft sat in the chancel, facing the chairs occupied by Mrs. Reid, her son, and other members of the Ambassador's family, and TR and his wife. But their nearness was simply a matter of physical proximity, nothing more.

The prayers having been said, Taft, his secretary, his military aide, and the Secret Service men arose. Customarily, after a ceremony, the President left first, but Taft, having started out, hesitated as though suddenly uncertain of protocol. This blocked the movement of the others and occasioned momentary confusion. Then, resolutely, all Taft's party headed for the doors at once, "making as much noise, on the stone floor," TR's daughter-in-law, Eleanor, reported, "as a troop of cavalry." TR, bending close to the person next to him, whispered, "This is the first time I ever saw a competition for precedence between corpses."

A few months later, when Ethel Roosevelt married Dr. Richard Derby, TR invited to the wedding George Meyer and Cabot Lodge, who had remained with the regular Republican party, but he did not invite Elihu Root and Will Taft. They would, he said, be "unwelcome guests." And to Will Taft, in 1913, TR was still "probably the most dangerous demagogue in history."

Two years later—in April, 1915—the awkward question of the Taft-Roosevelt relationship again arose in connection with a funeral. Thomas R. Lounsbury, Professor Emeritus of English at Yale, had died of a stroke in his seventy-eighth year. Taft wrote Charles Hilles, "His widow insists that T.R. and I shall both be pallbearers." After reflection, Taft accepted, but inquired whether Roosevelt knew that he was to be pallbearer. On learning TR didn't know, Taft suggested that he be informed, for otherwise he might "think he had been led into a trap." However, after TR was notified, he wired that the arrangement was satisfactory. ("It would have been simply silly for me to refuse," he wrote a friend.)

Taft was clearly uneasy about the meeting, even though, as he told Mabel Boardman, "I am not to walk with him. . . . I don't know how he will conduct himself, but I shall try to be pleasant. . . . I don't like to be on such bad terms with anybody that I may be embarrassed on meeting him."

Accounts of what happened when TR and Will Taft met are as numerous and varied as the witnesses who reported the incident. Some said Taft and Roosevelt extended their hands simultaneously for a handshake; but more maintained that Taft offered his hand first. One, standing behind the two men at the grave, merely observed that the "backs of their frock coats . . . seemed to show so plainly the difference in their characters. Mr. Taft's seemed very roomy and was hanging loosely . . . while Colonel Roosevelt's was very tightly drawn—so much so that there were horizontal creases across the back."

In any event, the meeting occurred in the vestibule of Battell Chapel at Yale, where Taft and the pallbearers who represented Yale waited for Roosevelt and two other pallbearers to arrive from New York City. When TR arrived, he went up to each member of the waiting party, approaching Taft last. TR said, "How do you do, Mr. Taft?" and Taft echoed just as formally, "How do you do, Mr. Roosevelt?" As he spoke, Taft noticed that Roosevelt did not "have as good color as he used to have," that his face seemed "fatter and flabbier," that he looked "a bit coarser." Then, after a moment's separation, TR stepped up to Taft again to inquire about Mrs. Taft and ask that his best wishes be given to her.

The following day, Taft reported in a letter to Gus Karger that the meeting with Theodore had been "pleasant enough" but "not cordial or intimate." Wilbur Cross, later Governor of Connecticut, revealed that Taft, after greeting TR, invited him to come to his New Haven home for a visit. Without hesitating, TR turned down the invitation, stating that he had to leave immediately after the funeral. Observing carefully, Cross noticed that "Taft was deeply hurt, as one could see, but his face quickly regained composure."

No more conversation took place between TR and Taft that afternoon. They sat in different pews during the funeral services, rode to the cemetery in different carriages, and stood at the open grave with another pallbearer between them.

Had Professor Lounsbury witnessed this hostile distance between his two friends and heard their verbal exchanges, he would undoubtedly have felt that their communication had been effective. As a philologist, interested in what had been done and could be done with words, he did not set up iron rules of usage or accept those formulated by fellow experts. And though he kept his infinitives undivided, he would defend those who preferred division in theirs. As for language in general, he believed its end was to convey thought and that there were many ways of achieving this end—one way being as "right" as another. The way employed by Taft and Roosevelt had worked. Now Taft knew definitely that their relationship was one of "armed neutrality." And Roosevelt was aware that he and Taft were no closer to being reconciled.

More than a year passed before they were to meet again, a year of war in Europe and of political maneuverings in the United States prior to a presidential election. During that year TR's hatred for President Woodrow Wilson had grown to nearly pathological intensity. (Epithet followed epithet—"infernal skunk in the White House," "yellow," "a Micawber," "abject coward"—as if he were compulsively striving to find the one that would be satisfyingly adequate.)

Roosevelt was irritated by the fact that Wilson, having defeated him in 1912, had gone ahead to make a reality of the Progressive party's program through legislature. Then, after TR had emerged from the South American jungle—emaciated, fever-weak, leaning heavily on a cane—he heard the incredible, insulting news that Wilson's Secretary of State, William Jennings Bryan, had negotiated a treaty with Colombia, agreeing not only to pay that country twenty-five million dollars for its loss of Panama, but also to apologize for the manner in which that loss had occurred. TR regarded the treaty as "an attack upon the honor of the United States," as "blackmail," and, of course, as a slur upon his integrity.

Aside from specific grounds for conflict, Roosevelt and Wilson had contradictory approaches to life: the reflective as opposed to the activist. They had one similarity, an absolute assurance that they were right, but this hardly endeared them to one another. And their views on war were irreconcilable. To TR, war was a bugle's stirring call, a sacrifice to honor, gallantry, love of country, the soul's desire; no phrase could be too purple or too embarrassingly lyrical. Understandably, Wilson's prosaic injunction to Americans to be "neutral in thought as well as in deed" set TR's teeth on edge.

On May 7, 1915, a submarine torpedoed the British liner *Lusitania* off the Irish coast. The "fastest and largest steamer" in the Atlantic service went down with 1,198 passengers, 128 of them Americans, among them Alfred Gwynne Vanderbilt, Charles Frohman, and Elbert Hubbard.

TR heard the details of the tragedy when he was awakened at midnight by a reporter who had phoned for a statement.

"That's murder!" TR exclaimed. (He was later to write an editorial entitled "Murder on the High Seas.") He then went on to give the reporter his statement, concluding it with: "It seems inconceivable that we can refrain from taking action in this matter, for we owe it not only to humanity but to our own self-respect."

Though as disturbed as TR, Wilson went into seclusion for three days of deliberation. At their conclusion, instead of holding Germany to "strict accountability"—taking action, according to TR's understanding of that phrase, "without an hour's unnecessary delay"—he drafted a note of protests. This he followed with a speech on May 10 in which he said,

"There is such a thing as a nation being so right that it does not need to convince others by force that it is right."

Though Wilson only reflected the moderation desired by Congress, the newspapers, and the people, TR placed the entire blame for inaction on him, for he merely continued to send notes of protest to Germany. When Alice Longworth mentioned to her father that another one had been sent, he said, "Did you notice what its serial number was? I fear I have lost track myself, but I am inclined to think it is No. 11,765, Series B."

Galled by the spectacle of some Progressives supporting Wilson and spurred by the pressure of the war, TR began, with the slow inevitability of glacial motion, his swing to the right. This was the time for battling not for the Lord, but on the side of the Allies against the Central Powers. TR became friends with his old enemies, the malefactors of great wealth, now substantial patriots. To defeat Wilson, TR called upon Progressives to return to the Republican party in 1916, refused their offer of the nomination, and killed the party that his personality had brought into being. ("If so soon it is to be done for," a couplet wailed piteously, "what the devil was it begun for?")

Woodrow Wilson had bitterly offended Will Taft, too, inflicting upon him, Taft declared, "one of the deepest wounds I have had as an American and a lover of the Constitution. . . ." For Wilson had appointed Louis Brandeis to Taft's beloved Supreme Court. Still embittered by the humiliations Brandeis had caused him in the Pinchot-Ballinger controversy, Taft felt the 1916 election was crucial. Although he and TR were in no way reconciled, he said, "Mr. Roosevelt and I are very anxious to secure the election of Mr. Hughes to the Presidency and to oust the present incompetent, meddling, muddling, opportunistic Administration."

Since the restoration of that friendship would provide a vision of a unified Republican party—the only way in which they could defeat Wilson—Elihu Root played conciliator. A reception for Charles Evans Hughes was to be held at the Union League Club in New York, Root wrote Taft, and TR would be present. He said it would help the ticket if Taft attended. There was also, Taft wrote Horace, "a very considerable part of the low-minded press that had given the impression that if Roosevelt and I met, he would curse me and I would curse him, and each would kick the other in the stomach." Therefore, it might be well to establish a peaceable basis on which to meet.

Taft had not the slightest objection, he wrote Root, "to meeting Theodore." Still, he told Clarence Edwards, it wouldn't be "a pleasant experience for either of us . . . he has already been quite ungracious in his language concerning it . . . [but] I have no reason to avoid meeting him."

"I only know that I am willing to meet anyone," he declared to his son Charlie, "if I have done nothing mean to him for I don't consider that I have done anything mean to Roosevelt. . . . I am very anxious to beat the politician and hypocrite now in the White House."

Finally, the "much discussed, long heralded get-together meeting which was to make the Republican Party great and united" occurred. For such an important performance there should have been a script, rehearsals. Undoubtedly because it was to be entirely extemporary, reporters were led into a side room, from which they could neither see nor hear the Roosevelt-Taft meeting. Velvet ropes also delimited the extent of their movement.

Taft arrived first and went directly to the library, where the reception was to be held.

When Hughes appeared, TR was already pushing his way through a crowded lobby to the elevator. The cheers that arose for TR mingled with those for Hughes. Murray Crane, an "unreformed porch climber," slipped into the elevator. He could be seen talking with TR, and though what was said couldn't be heard, that they were talking together indicated the party was being unified apace.

Leaving the elevator at the second floor, TR moved into the library's alcove; there he shook hands, left and right—eight, ten, a dozen hands, hands that wouldn't have touched him during the past four years. He even shook hands with Boies Penrose. Laughter followed jokes. Everyone rejoiced that TR, smiling, was back in the ranks, fighting for the success of the party. Then TR left the alcove for the library, where Taft stood. The two men confronted each other.

During all this, the reporters remained restive, though docile, behind the velvet ropes. A dozen versions of what had happened when TR and Taft met merely aggravated their captivity. Then Edward E. O'Brien, a member of the Reception Committee, showing an enthusiasm worthy of his calling, burst into the room and said, "They shook hands and there was the greatest cordiality. Yes, certainly! The greatest cordiality. I never saw such a smile on Colonel Roosevelt's face and also upon that of Mr. Taft. Don't forget that; it was most cordial."

But then a version—later known as the Taft version—was relayed to the newsmen by a friend of Taft's who reported Taft said, "We shook hands as any gentlemen might do and there was not a word said." (Taft, in describing the meeting to Nellie, contradicted this. "We shook hands with a Howdy do and that was all.")

After their meeting, TR and Taft stood together in a reception line, with Chauncey Depew between them like a buffer. Later Root, Hughes, and Roosevelt gave talks. Taft told Nellie, "He talked well and ill. But he talked long. He spoke six minutes longer than Hughes." In his speech—the last one—Taft said, "We are holding one of those exceptional meetings of the ex-Presidents' club. It is not a large membership and the members do not always entertain complete harmony of views. But there is one subject on which we are unanimous to a point which can not be exaggerated, and that is that we are going to elect in November another member."

Nevertheless, this effort failed to bring them closer. Even physically, at the supper that followed, they were separated; TR sat at table number two, Will Taft at table number three. Afterward, they went down in the same elevator together, but the atmosphere was cold rather than genial.

"I waited until he went out," Taft wrote his wife, "[and] followed him."

Two days later, a New York *Times* editorial summed it all up: "The inventor of morality laughed and jested with Mr. Penrose, but for Taft [he had] only the briefest, formal greeting. Was it worthwhile for the Republican managers to stage this 'reunited' party scene, which did but exhibit the leaders of the two factions as irreconcilable enemies?"

Less than a week after this appraisal appeared, Taft in a note to Horace substantiated it: "Roosevelt is going clear out to Arizona after speaking to working men in Pennsylvania and I am glad of it. The further he goes away the better."

The remembered relief and implied promise embodied in the slogan "He kept us out of war" helped Wilson defeat Hughes. But events hammered at the reflective, temporizing President, forcing him from his position of neutrality.

On March 7, 1917, TR was again at the Union League Club, at a war meeting this time, and again Root, Hughes, and TR delivered speeches. Now TR had nothing to say against Wilson—publicly—for not only had the United States broken off diplomatic relations with Germany, but also war was imminent; as soon as war was declared TR planned to approach Wilson and request that he be permitted to lead a division of volunteers into immediate action.

After the meeting, a group gathered in the club's grill, and TR asked for help in persuading Wilson to grant his request. He didn't expect to return, he said, and hoped to be buried in France. "Theodore," Root said in his old teasing manner, "if you can convince Wilson of that I am sure he will give you a commission."

Three days after war was declared, TR attempted to pacify the man he had so belligerently accused of being a pacifist, a leader of "the flub-

dubs and mollycoddles." "Mr. President," he said, as they sat most con-
genially in the Red Room, "all that has gone before is as dust on a windy
street." Nonetheless, Wilson eventually rejected not only TR's request,
but also Taft's plea to serve overseas.

Taft and TR now also had in common the bond of being fathers of
sons in time of war. All four of the Roosevelt boys were on their way
"over there." Bob Taft, unable to get into the service because of poor
eyesight, worked for Herbert Hoover's Food Administration. Little
freckled, mischievous Charlie, now over six feet tall and handsome—
married to Eleanor Chase, whom he had met at school—had enlisted as a
private.

To Taft the father, Charlie was still a little boy, in that he needed
guidance—and yet Charlie was a man. Before his son sailed for France on
January 10, 1918, Taft wrote to him, "Demoralization exists as never
before in France and you will almost be raped unless you brace yourself.
It is such a comfort to know that you have your sweet, loving wife,
Eleanor, to whom you have plighted your faith and whose appealing fond
glances will always rise before you when you are confronted by sinful
love. It is hard, my darling boy, to let you go. You are the apple of our
eye. But we would not have it different. If sacrifice is to be made who are
we that we should escape it? And now, Charlie my loving son, good-bye
till we meet again. You are knight *sans peur et sans reproche*. God bless
you and keep you."

In the spring, with word of a new German offensive, Charlie's mother
expressed her anguish by a simple flat statement, "I wish Charlie were not
over there." After all, he was her third child, her youngest.

Quentin, a close friend of Charlie's during the White House days, was
Mrs. Roosevelt's baby, too. This was a time for evoking memories. At the
age of nine, Quentin had said with unassuming candor that he was "of a
bubbling-over nature." At twelve, he saw his first airplane. "At one time
there were four in the air," he wrote, "it was the prettiest thing I
ever saw." In speaking of a model plane powered by a rubber band, he
exclaimed, "I have one which can fly a hundred yards, and goes higher
than my head!" At nineteen and a half, a sophomore at Harvard, engaged
to Flora Payne Whitney (whose grandfather had been very wealthy and
a member of Cleveland's Cabinet), he enlisted and went to the American
flying school at Mineola, Long Island. Now he would fly planes, real
planes—and neither they nor their objectives would be pretty.

But Ted and Archie and Kermit sailed before Quentin. Then Quentin's
turn came. The night before he left, his mother came to his bedroom and
tucked him in. She was later to admit that she found his going very, very

hard, but, at the same time, she realized that "you can't bring up boys to be eagles and expect them to turn out sparrows." (Quentin had said, "We boys thought it was up to us to practice what Father preached.") Still, she worried about Quentin's back, injured on a hunting trip in Arizona when his horse slipped. When she saw him off, she left a "paper bundle" in his cabin, the plaintive gesture of a mother concerned about the sustenance of her child. Long after he watched the "Statue of Liberty and the New York sky line dropping below the horizon," Quentin, feeling low, came upon his mother's package. "I opened it," he reported, "and found, neatly wrapped in a napkin—a loaf of bread, lots of chocolate, and a knife, with a note saying it was from Margaret, the cook!"

Quentin's half sister, Alice, had come with her father and mother to see the last of her brothers off. She had already heard her father say "how certain it was that several, perhaps all, would be wounded, possibly killed." She now remarked that "all the boys were gone," commenting, "it was bitterly hard for Father not to be with them. I used to say to myself, 'The old Lion perisheth for lack of prey and the stout Lion's whelps are scattered abroad.' "

TR's prey—and Taft's—was Wilson, for his "shilly-shallying." This common antagonist was to draw TR and Will Taft inevitably closer together. In speaking of the duty of all good citizens, TR maintained, "We must fearlessly insist upon the utmost efficiency in the handling of the war. We must fearlessly criticize whatever is wrong." Taft, who at first had backed the President's war efforts, would eventually be saying that Wilson was "one of the obstacles we shall have to overcome" in order to win the war.

TR found little comfort in his role of "slacker-in-spite-of-himself"; he feared he would be "regarded as merely a scold"; he felt left behind. He wrote Quentin, "My disappointment at not going myself was down at bottom chiefly reluctance to see you four, in whom my heart was wrapped, exposed to danger while I stayed at home in do-nothing ease and safety." But he envied them as any "man of gallant spirit" would. He could, therefore, tell Theodore, Jr., "You are having your crowded hours of glorious life; you have seized the great chance as it was seized by those who fought at Gettysburg and Waterloo and Agincourt and Arbela and Marathon."

Though he loathed speechmaking—earnestly wishing, he said, that "I was not to make another as long as I live"—he made speeches. He talked only because Wilson had not permitted him to act, because someone had to say the things that needed to be said. "Tell the truth and speed up the

War" summed up much of what he said. He wrote for the same reason that he spoke, but he revealed an additional incentive in a letter to Ted, Jr. "After October 1st, I shall write for the *Kansas City Star*, at a salary of $25,000; I shall still write a short monthly editorial for the *Metropolitan* at a salary of $5000. About all I can do now is to earn what money I can for Archie and perhaps Quentin, during the war, and have things ready for them to start after the war."

Taft's course ran parallel to TR's. After the trauma of Winona—and even before—speechmaking delighted Taft even less than it did TR, but he now traveled about the camps for the YMCA, explaining the war's meaning to the soldiers. He also made Liberty Loan speeches until his strained voice began to disappear and he complained to Nellie, "I hate money begging. They ought to arrange that without me but they say they can't. . . ."

Like TR, too, Taft was concerned about the financial future of his children; when Helen became Dean of Bryn Mawr, he told her he planned to leave an estate which would provide her with an income.

TR, frustrated at being removed from the danger and action of the "supreme crisis in the world's history," became wholeheartedly involved in the war effort. It was not enough to forgo eating wheat bread and bacon and to be able to say, "I have stopped having wine at the table." He bought sixty thousand dollars' worth of war bonds. When he heard Archie's men needed shoes, he sent two hundred pairs. He could do this because, he said, "thanks to my pen I am making money," and he wanted to spend it, he declared, on "your brothers and for your comrades if I can relieve their grinding needs." On September 11, 1917, he wrote General William C. Gorgas, a comrade "in the work of Panama" and now Surgeon-General of the U.S. Army, in behalf of his son-in-law, Richard Derby: "He wishes with all his heart to himself go over, to be as near the fight front as anyone. . . . This is the privilege, the privilege of being where at most risk to himself he can render most service to the army and the nation, which I ask for him." A little over a week later he wrote to Archie, referring to his wife's impending visit to Sagamore Hill, "I will most strongly express my approval of your staying by the line and refusing a staff position. We are fighting men; it is in the line that we can do our work to best advantage. I am sure I can make her understand." (When TR was told that Wilson's son-in-law was going into YMCA work in France, he pointed out maliciously to newspapermen, "How very nice. We are sending our *daughter-in-law* to France in the Y.M.C.A.!") As 1917 drew to a close, TR gave Quentin some fatherly advice concerning his failure to correspond regularly with Flora: "Now of course you may not keep Flora anyhow. But if you wish to lose her, continue to be an infrequent correspondent. If however you wish to keep her write her letters—interesting letters, and love letters—at least three times a week. . . . Write enough letters to allow for half being lost. Affectionately, A hardened and wary old father.'"

In January, TR went to Washington for four days to confer with senators and congressmen about a more vigorous prosecution of the war. In an address before the National Press Club, he advised, "Don't hit if it is honorably possible to avoid hitting, but never hit soft." He was, after all, "heartsick over the delay, the blundering, the fatuous and complacent inefficiency, and the effort to substitute glittering rhetoric for action. . . ."

Because his views accorded with the Republican party's course, the question of 1920 filled everyone's mind. TR appeared disdainfully above the matter, stating, "I am not in the least concerned with *your* supporting *me* either now or at any other future time. All I am concerned with is that you should so act that I can support *you*." The New York *Times* stated flatly, "Theodore Roosevelt has become the leader of the Republican Party." Just as the progressives and standpatters were joining forces for a common effort, TR and Taft could do the same.

In February, both of TR's ears became infected, as a result of a throat infection. Diagnosis upon his admission to Roosevelt Hospital was "bilateral acute otitis media, inflammatory rheumatism, and abscess of the thigh." Both eardrums were pierced, and surgery was performed on his thigh. A rumor started—on Wall Street—that he had died, but the thousands who called, snarling telephone lines, and the throngs who flocked to the hospital were told that he was "very much alive." TR dismissed his illness in a letter to Kermit as "entirely trivial," though he lost his hearing in the left ear.

"May I not express my warmest sympathy and the sincere hope that Mr. Roosevelt's condition is improving?" Woodrow Wilson wired Mrs. Roosevelt circumspectly.

In answer to Will Taft's message—"Hope for speedy and complete recovery"—TR sent a wire and a letter of thanks. That both men had their youngest sons in the war and had a mutual feeling that the administration was going about the war in a muddling, inefficient way was causing them to forget old hostilities.

Spring that year at Sagamore Hill brought forth "a green foam; the gay yellow of the forsythia"—all the beauty and promise of rebirth—but it also brought the implacable German offensive. TR, father and patriot in one, wrote Quentin not to "insist upon taking or staying in any position merely because it is more dangerous than another position in which your superiors think you can be more useful." And Taft told Charlie—though it might have been TR addressing his sons—"My dear boy, our prayers go with you. Whatever happens we know that you will do your duty and face death with a pure heart and a clear conscience. . . ." He pointed out, with all of TR's bitterness, that, as contrasted with the danger of Charlie's service, "some of us in the rear try to help with wind."

TR would not let old antagonisms mar his war efforts. He was to deliver an address—"Speed Up the War and Take Thought for After the War"—to be delivered to the Republican State Convention on March 28, in Portland, Maine. In his speech he urged one hundred per cent Americanism, longer working hours in war plants, universal military training, and an endless abundance of reforms for the postwar world. Copies went to Taft, to Root, and to Lodge, and TR asked for anything "in the way of criticism and suggestion." (In his note to Taft accompanying the speech, TR used the salutation "Dear Will" and closed with: "Pray give my warm regards to Mrs. Taft.")

Taft had no criticism—only two suggestions—and an overjoyed TR answered, "I have embodied both these suggestions. I think them capital. I am rather ashamed I never thought of them myself, and I am malevolently pleased that neither Root nor Lodge thought of them!"

TR was elated when he received news that Archie, wounded by German shrapnel, had received the Croix de Guerre. He wrote Clemenceau, "I am prouder of his having received it than of my having been President!"

TR never tired of revealing his pride in his four brave sons—to them and to others. He informed Quentin of Archie's great honor, concluding with more fatherly advice, "Why don't you write to Flora, and to her father and mother, asking if she won't come abroad and marry you? As for your getting killed, or ordinarily crippled, afterwards, why she would a thousand times rather have married you than not have married you under those conditions; and as for the extraordinary kinds of crippling, they are rare, and anyway we have to take certain chances in life. . . . I would most heartily approve of your getting married at the earliest possible moment. . . ."

Meanwhile, Taft felt obliged to explain the change in his relationship with TR to Charles P. "Roosevelt did me a great injury and great injustice, but he did himself more," he wrote his brother. "He would certainly have been President during the war had he held his hand against me. . . . I cherish no resentment against Roosevelt because such an attitude of mind is not congenial to me. It only worries the resenter and works little harm to the resentee. . . . I am glad to be on good terms with a man for many of whose traits and abilities I have great admiration, to whom I am indebted for many generous acts, and many great opportunities."

Since Taft felt as he did, his meeting with TR in May, 1918—no more than five blocks from the Coliseum, where the 1912 battles had taken place—followed naturally. Taft had arrived at the Blackstone from St. Louis; by coincidence, TR was dining there, prior to departing later that evening for Des Moines, for more and more speechmaking.

When Taft heard that TR was in the dining room—and dining alone— he walked rapidly up the steps from the lobby to the dining room. Since they had resumed correspondence, he reasoned, it was time that they met and their new relationship be established. During TR's convalescence, at a hotel, TR had invited him, but "a previous engagement" had prevented his accepting it. Now Taft felt it was his move. Life was too short to "preserve these personal attitudes of enmity."

Looking about, Taft finally located TR at a little table across the room and walked quickly toward him. Intent on his meal though TR was, the sudden stillness in the dining room caused him to look up. He immediately threw down his napkin and rose, his hand extended. They shook hands vigorously and slapped each other on the back. Those in the dining hall cheered, and it was not until then that TR and Will Taft realized that they had an audience and bowed and smiled to it. Then they sat down and chatted for a half hour.

Asked afterward by a reporter for the gist of their conversation, Taft said, "We just talked over things generally."

The press, after the Blackstone meeting, proclaimed that TR and Taft had buried the hatchet. Obviously, TR also felt that the ill feelings of 1912 had been dispersed like dust on a windy street, for he wrote Taft, "It was a very real pleasure to see you the other day. When you next pass through New York, do let me know. I will come in town to meet you, or I will get you to come out to Sagamore Hill for lunch, or for dinner and the night if that is convenient."

TR, at the end of June, advised "Dear Will" that he would be sending him a copy of another speech that, he said, "will be on the general outlines we have both been following." Those outlines encompassed unrelenting opposition to Wilson and a demand for increasing the army and speeding up the manufacture of munitions.

Taft, in a letter to his brother Charles—perhaps by way of pacifying him—minimized his new relationship with Roosevelt by pointing out that their common bond was a hatred of Wilson.

That summer TR was to have further reason for hating the President. For one thing, a ruling forbade the wives and fiancées of servicemen from going overseas. TR tried to maneuver around it. Flora wanted to go to France, to marry Quentin. "I hope she and Quentin can get married," TR wrote to his eldest son. "It is well to have had happiness, to have achieved the great ends of life, when one must walk boldly and warily close to death."

But regulations—Wilson—prevented Flora from going to France and to Quentin. TR felt it was "wicked" that they could not get married so that "even if he were killed, she and he would have known their white hour. . . ."

Deadly danger did indeed surround Quentin, now at the front where, TR wrote, "his part is one of peculiar honor and peril." As a consequence, TR, who had never had any trouble sleeping—not even during the hurricane of the presidency—now admitted, "I wake up in the middle of the night, wondering if the boys are all right, and thinking how I could tell their mother if anything happened."

All he could do to help them—and his country—was to speak. His frustration over not being in peril and participating in great deeds caused him to speak beyond his endurance, at a time when he was weak with fever, with the same unswerving determination he had shown that night when even a bullet could not stop him. He revealed how he really felt, beneath the ebullience and the great enthusiasm he displayed, when, in answer to someone who mentioned how well he looked, he said, "I feel as though I were a hundred years old and had *never* been young."

What the weeks ahead held would suddenly add years to his age. On July 10, north of Château-Thierry, Quentin downed his first plane. Premonition might be read into TR's proud reaction: "Whatever now befalls Quentin he has now had his crowded hour, and his day of honor and triumph." Within days this elation changed to dread and uncertainty, for Quentin was reported missing. He had been part of a patrol of thirteen planes which had encountered seven German planes, two of which turned on Quentin. His plane fell, but not in flames; a "chance exists," Mrs. Theodore Roosevelt, Jr., cabled from Paris, "that he is a prisoner."

Taft sent a wire and a letter to TR, offering comfort over "the distressing news."

After three days of anxiety and anguish, it was Wilson who confirmed Quentin's death. "He died serving his country and died with fine gallantry. I am deeply grieved that his service should come to this tragic end."

TR thanked Wilson for his courtesy, kindness, sympathy and "approval of my son's conduct."

Now, in addition to a jungle fever infection and a would-be assassin's bullet, an ineffable grief had become lodged within TR. Out of his pain, he said, "To feel that one has inspired a boy to conduct that has resulted in his death, has a pretty serious side to a father. . . ." And he commented, "It is very dreadful that the young should die and the old be left." Added to his suffering was the knowledge that Edie's heart would "ache for Quentin until she dies."

Under the circumstances, TR could not receive with enthusiasm Taft's well-intentioned urging that he run for Governor. "My heart is wrapped up in my boys at the front," TR wrote Will, "and I am not thinking in terms of New York State conditions."

Now Sagamore Hill—which he deeply loved—became a place filled with memories of Quentin. Ethel's son Richard, Quentin's favorite nephew, heard a plane while "on the piazza at Sagamore" and said to TR, "Perhaps that's Quentin."

To escape, TR and his wife went to Darkharbor, Maine, to Ethel's home. They did not find peace there—pleasure in their grandchildren, yes, but not peace. "Poor darling little Flora comes tomorrow," TR wrote to Ethel's husband. "Quentin's death has been even harder for her than for Mother!" And the letters that Quentin had written before his death were coming. TR dreaded the moment when Edie would receive "the letters from her dead boy."

When they returned to Oyster Bay, after two weeks, Quentin's last letters were there. He was, he had written, "at the fighting front, very proud and happy," and "would not for any consideration have been anywhere else." Fortunately, Alice was on hand—as always, when there was trouble—waiting for them at Sagamore Hill, and she was "a real comfort."

His opposition to Wilson kept TR going—in spite of his grief and illness. Germany must be completely defeated so that it would not rise again and fight again; only an unconditional surrender would, therefore, do, he felt. He wrote to Taft that he was for Taft's League to Enforce Peace, but with one qualification: he would back it, he said, "as an *addition to*, but not as *a substitute for*, our preparing our own strength for our own defense."

During a speaking tour of the West, Quentin remained in his thoughts.

While riding in the train, he was seen to put the book he had been reading in his lap and say as though in painful reverie, "Poor Quinikins!"

His sadness intensified physical pains, localized in muscles and joints; it was with difficulty that he managed to leave a sickbed to cast his vote in the congressional elections. A Republican victory gave him considerable comfort. But a few days later, he was "flat on his back." On Armistice Day, inflammatory rheumatism brought him back to Roosevelt Hospital.

When asked about 1920, he said sadly, "I would not lift a finger to get the nomination. Since Quentin's death the world seems to have shut down upon me. . . ."

He was able to leave the hospital to spend Christmas Eve at Sagamore Hill, and he told his Oyster Bay neighbors, "I'm all right now." But that Quentin would not "come home with the others" was hard, very hard, on both TR and Edith.

On January 5, a Sunday, TR spent a good day. Edith described the close of it in a letter to Ted.

> . . . as it got dusk he watched the dancing flames and spoke of the happiness of being home, and made little plans for me. I think he had made up his mind that he would have to suffer for some time to come and with his high courage had adjusted himself to bear it. He was very sweet all day. Since Quentin was killed he has been sad, only Ethel's little girl had the power to make him merry.

At eleven o'clock, she kissed him good night. Shortly after, he turned to his valet and said, "James, will you please put out the light?"

Those were the last words he spoke. During the night he died in his sleep, in his sixty-first year, of an embolism, a blood clot.

Snow fell from a solid-gray sky on the day of TR's funeral. During the afternoon of the day he had died, five airplanes had flown in V formation from Quentin Roosevelt Field to Sagamore Hill and dropped wreaths of laurel. For the next twenty-four hours, in tribute to Quentin and his father, two flights of army airplanes hovered continuously, night and day, over Sagamore Hill, but snow on the morning of the eighth of January caused them to give up their vigil.

The people of America and throughout the world found it hard to believe that such seemingly endless energy had come to an end. It would be "hard to get used to a world without Roosevelt in it" was sentiment generally expressed.

Even General Frederick Crayton Ainsworth, who had not been too fond of the Colonel, concurred. The news came to him by phone, and he responded with, "No-o? Heart disease, perhaps—or did someone pi'son him? It removes a storm center, doesn't it? It is hard to realize doing without him."

An editor of the San Jose *News* sat at his typewriter and wrote in somewhat shrill apostrophe, "Affectation, brutality, egotism—certainly you were full of all those things!" But then he went on to extol TR with unrestrained, verbose, early-twentieth-century lyricism:

. . . You smashed us with the word "red-blooded," you buffeted us with that old word "liar," which you gave a new vigor, you taught us what "big stick" meant, you insisted on trying to reform our spelling, our football, our army, our family. What, woman! Thirty years old and no children yet! Be bitterly ashamed. . . . What, you man! Can't you box? Can't you ride a broncho? Can't you shoot? Don't you love to wallow in blood? Shame on you! You're not a man, you're a mollycoddle! Thus it was you howled at us. And we howled back at you, and called you miserable old blatherskite and soapboxer and imperialist and everything else we could think of. But it was great sport and you loved it, and we loved it. . . .

Edgar Lee Masters described TR in an emotional free-verse narrative, recalling his last visit with him at Sagamore Hill.

> . . . He's drest in canvas khaki, flannel shirt.
> Laced boots for farming, chopping trees, perhaps;
> A stocky frame, curtains of skin on cheeks
> Drained slightly of their fat; gash in the neck
> Where pus was emptied lately; one eye dim
> And growing dimmer; almost blind in that.
> And when he walks he rolls a little like
> A man whose youth is fading, like a cart
> That rolls when springs are old. He is a moose,
> Scarred, battered from the hunters, thickets, stones;
> Some finest tips of antlers broken off.
> And eyes where images of ancient things
> Flit back and forth across them keeping still
> A certain slumberous indifference
> Or wisdom, it may be . . .

In Paris, when William Allen White came down to breakfast in the hotel in which he was staying, he saw the headlines of the Paris *Herald*. He read and reread them uncomprehendingly, disbelievingly. "Not since my father's death," he wrote, "has death stabbed me so poignantly. . . . I have never known another person so vital nor another man so dear." And in the heart of progressives, in addition to grief, was the knowledge that the Republican party, with TR's passing, would be attenuated and ineffectual for a long, long time. Only two months before his death TR had written to Cabot Lodge that the people "will not stand for the Republican Party unless," he declared, "we really go forward—as radically as may be necessary. . . ."

Understandably, Gifford Pinchot, who felt deep personal grief, expressed his additional concern in a letter to his brother; with his old chief gone, the reactionaries might gain such control, he said, "as to put the policies you and I are interested in back many years."

King George V remembered TR with affection, saying, "You should have seen him telling my children about lions and tigers and elephants in Africa. And finally he got down on the floor and played bear with them, crawling about and growling."

Grief overcame Cabot Lodge as he spoke in the Senate. His voice quavered, and he gripped the desk before him with both hands, but he could not still the shaking of his body. "At this moment, Mr. President," he said, "thought and memories so crowd upon me that I can say no more."

Harry Stimson, too, knew such grief that speech came with difficulty. "It comes too close to my heart to make a statement. It is the most irreparable loss that could have come to the country," he declared.

The Vice-President—Thomas Marshall—who had expressed the country's need in terms of good five-cent cigars, now stated as flatly, unequivocally, "Death had to take him sleeping. For if Roosevelt had been awake, there would have been a fight."

The President, traveling in northern Italy on his triumphal progress through all of Europe, received the news in a telegram, handed to him while he sat in a railroad car. Reporters watching him saw various emotions reflected in his face. The final expression—the one that lingered, that conveyed the summing up of his thoughts—suggested the satisfaction of victory. It was not until a few minutes later that the reporters knew the contents of the telegram Wilson had read. (In sending words of condolence to TR's widow, Wilson at first said he was "deeply grieved," but then, for the sake of accuracy, he changed "grieved" to "shocked.")

Also traveling, on a lecture tour, Will Taft was on his way to New York when he learned, in Newark, of TR's death. He immediately set to work "to prepare something"—an editorial eulogy for the Philadelphia Ledger, for which he wrote a syndicated column. He sent a wire to Edith Roosevelt, saying: "I am shocked to hear the sad news. My heart goes out to you and yours in your great sorrow. The country can ill afford in this critical period of history to lose one who has done and could in the next decade have done so much for it and humanity. . . ." But in a letter to his wife, Taft wrote in less lofty terms: "Roosevelt's death was a shock to me for in spite of all the past I had an affection for his good and great qualities that his defects did not neutralize." As though in answer to what Nellie might be thinking, he pointed out that Mrs. Roosevelt "has had her share of sorrow in this war and is entitled to our deep sympathy. We might have been in the same grief as hers as far as Quentin's death is concerned. . . ."

On reaching New York, Taft learned "the funeral was by card invitation"; he requested a card and received it. He also needed a silk hat, and so he and his brother Harry walked to Knox's to get one, though "the morning was moist with a wet snow." All about them there was evidence of mourning, from the flags at half-mast to the flags which drivers of wagons had affixed to their horses' harnesses and the streamers of crepe they had fastened to their manes.

When Taft arrived in Oyster Bay on the eleven o'clock train from New York, automobiles were waiting at the station. He saw Gifford Pinchot and his wife—the former Cornelia Bryce—and the Garfields getting in one car, but they did not see him. The snow—meager, fine—had stopped falling altogether, although the sky remained overcast. Taft walked to the church. Scarcely any snow clung to its steep-pitched roofs, and only a threadbare blanket of it covered the ground. Trees, sky, and the friends and neighbors who waited along the street at Christ Church for the arrival of TR's body were all in funereal shades of black and gray.

Inside, laurel, remaining from Christmas, decorated the church, and floral pieces covered the chancel. One piece, a wreath of pink and white carnations, had been sent in accordance with cabled instructions by President Wilson, who, in his proclamation ordering public mourning, stated that Roosevelt "had endeared himself to the people by his strenuous devotion to their interests and to the public interests of his country." An exhibit, of which TR had been especially proud, received a great deal of attention: two sheets of foolscap under glass bore the names of ninety-eight members of the parish who had entered the service. The first four names were Roosevelt, and a gold star distinguished only one name of the ninety-eight, Quentin's.

In spite of the solemnity of the occasion, people could not help but push and mill around while waiting to be seated by the ushers, for five hundred were attempting to enter a church with a capacity of three hundred and fifty. ("The plan for a private funeral," Taft wrote his wife, "was, I think, a mistake. Mrs. R., you know, is exclusive and it was her idea.") Alec Lambert, TR's physician, who had just returned from France, pushed Taft through the crowd toward the ushers. One of them, William Loeb, took Taft in hand and put him "in a pew behind the family in the same seat with the family servants." But Captain Archibald Roosevelt—thin and pale, not yet recovered from his wounds, with the Croix de Guerre of which his father had been so proud on his breast—saw Taft. He saluted, gripped Taft's hand, and said, "You're a dear personal friend and must come up further." He then seated Taft behind the Vice-President, who was there as President Wilson's representative, and in front of the Senate committee headed by Cabot Lodge and members of the House, among them Speaker Champ Clark and "Uncle Joe" Cannon. Elihu Root and other members of TR's Cabinet were "crowded into the back part of the crowd."

Shortly before the service began, the sun broke through the overcast; its rays illumined the stained-glass windows, "lessening the gloom in the church and touching it here and there with faint glows of purple, yellow and ruby."

At a few minutes before one, the rector, Dr. G. E. Talmadge, strode slowly down the aisle, intoning the words of the processional, "I am the resurrection and the life, saith the Lord. . . ." Behind him, borne by six men, was the flag-draped coffin, followed by the immediate members of TR's family.

The rector read the service—simple, brief, without an address or eulogy or music. "How Firm a Foundation, Ye Saints of the Lord," one of TR's favorite hymns, was read. At the close of the service, the rector moved to the head of the coffin and said, "Theodore, the Lord bless thee, and keep thee. The Lord make his face to shine upon thee, and be gracious unto thee. The Lord lift up his countenance upon thee, and give thee peace, both now and evermore. Amen."

As the coffin was borne out of the church, a bell tolled, and the bell of the Presbyterian church across the way tolled sadly in answer.

Taft accompanied the Senate committee to Young's Memorial Cemetery, a mile and a half from the church. The automobiles stopped at the cemetery gate; entering was out of the question because of the cemetery's narrow, steep, rough road and the absence of parking space. Senators, representatives in Congress, members of the Rough Riders, relatives, college friends, hunting and fishing friends, sparring partners, policemen, priests, and children from Oyster Bay Cove School, dressed in their best, climbed—bent forward as though walking against a wind—to the crest of the hill where, beneath bare locusts and green cedars, an open grave made a stark gash in the snow.

From the trees (one of them containing a spectator, a boy in a brown suit) melting snow fell on the banks of flowers that concealed the earth which had been removed from the grave.

"Do you remember the fun of him, Mrs. Robinson?" Captain Burke, the police officer in charge of the funeral, exclaimed tearfully to TR's sister. "It was not only that he was a great man, but oh there was such fun in being led by him."

Taft, too, had spoken to Corinne Robinson, and to Alice and Ethel, TR's daughters, and to Eleanor, Ted's wife. Mrs. Roosevelt had not come; her service had been the one held for the family that morning in the trophy room at Sagamore Hill. Of her sons only Archie could attend, for his brothers were still overseas. (He had cabled Kermit and Ted, "The old lion is dead.") Now Taft—whom TR had once told to smile, to reveal his genial nature, and to endear himself to the electorate—stood near the grave, his head bent, his face solemn.

Not long before his death, TR had said, "It is idle to complain or rail at the inevitable. Serene and high of heart we must face our fate, and go down into the darkness." Life and death, he felt, were all part of the same great adventure and "death wipes out all that is merely personal." Just the year before, at the time of TR's meeting with Taft in Chicago, Taft had attempted to pacify his brother Charles with a comparable bit of philosophy: "Life is too short to preserve these personal attitudes of enmity."

The simple burial service of the Episcopal Church came to an end. Taft walked away—somber, in great coat and new silk hat—his eyes cast down, watching his footing on the uncertain ground.

Punctually the next day, having resumed his lecture tour, he wrote Nellie from Punxswtawney, Pennsylvania, recounting the funeral in detail. With a mere trace of defiance, he stated, "I was glad I went." For completeness' sake he told her he had returned his hat "to Knoxes to be shipped to Washington," and that night he had gone to the theater to see "The Better 'Ole." He did not mention a mournful meeting with Oscar Straus after the funeral, during which he spoke of Roosevelt and said he "felt grateful that . . . he had some months earlier re-established their long-time friendship." As if in reply to a question Nellie might ask, Taft ended his letter to her by saying, "My going to Roosevelt's funeral did not lose me a night's engagement because I pushed the one for last night over to Tuesday night."

Roosevelt's death, which had obviously robbed him of the presidency in 1920, also dashed "the hopes of progressive Republicans for post-war control." The Republicans turned to Warren G. Harding and Calvin

Coolidge, thus remaining removed from progressivism. It was another Roosevelt, a Hyde Park Roosevelt—a Democrat—who brought fulfillment of TR's views. And fate, neatly tying up all loose ends, had Harding appoint Will Taft Chief Justice of the Supreme Court. But the appointment even at this time did not come without delays and uncertainties. During this trying period, Mrs. Taft expressed the wish that she had allowed her husband to go to the Supreme Court earlier. "She realized, afterwards," Taft's daughter recalled, "that he hadn't enjoyed the Presidency as much as she thought he would."

Fittingly, in 1921—the year Taft's long-cherished dream had finally come true and was making ample recompense for the anguish of the presidency and his defeat in 1912—Will Taft told TR's sister Bamie, "I want to say to you how glad I am that Theodore and I came together after that long painful interval. Had he died in a hostile state of mind toward me, I would have mourned the fact all my life. I loved him always and cherish his memory."

Bibliography and Index

Bibliography

Naturally, the Taft papers and the published Roosevelt letters provided indispensable material. By virtue of their obvious subjectivity, the Archie Butt letters provided a spontaneous, day-to-day history with qualities alien to remote objectivity. I've listed these sources below, and all the other works used in the writing of this book.

Abbott, Lawrence F., *Impressions of Theodore Roosevelt*. New York, Doubleday, Page, 1920.
———— *The Letters of Archie Butt*. New York, Doubleday, Page, 1924.
Adams, Henry, *The Education of Henry Adams*. Boston, Houghton Mifflin, 1918.
Amos, James E., *Theodore Roosevelt: Hero to His Valet*. New York, Day, 1927.
Bishop, Joseph B., *Theodore Roosevelt and His Time*, 2 vols. New York, Scribner, 1920.
Blum, John Morton, *The Republican Roosevelt*. New York, Harvard University, 1954.
Bowers, Claude G., *Beveridge and the Progressive Era*. Boston, Houghton Mifflin, 1932.
Busbey, L. White, *Uncle Joe Cannon*. New York, Holt, 1927.
Butler, Nicholas Murray, *Across the Busy Years*. New York, Scribner, 1939.
Butt, Archie, *Taft and Roosevelt: The Intimate Letters of Archie Butt, Military Aide*, 2 vols. New York, Doubleday, Doran, 1930.
Carter, Harold Dean, ed., *Henry Adams and His Friends*. Boston, Houghton Mifflin, 1947.
Chambrun, Clara Longworth de, *The Making of Nicholas Longworth*. New York, Long & Smith, 1933.
Chanler, Mrs. Winthrop, *Roman Spring*. Boston, Little, Brown, 1934.
Davis, Oscar King, *Released for Publication*. Boston, Houghton Mifflin, 1925.
Foraker, Julia B., *I Would Live It Again*. New York, Harper, 1932.
Ford, Worthington Chauncey, ed., *Letters of Henry Adams*, 2 vols. Boston, Houghton Mifflin, 1930, 1938.

317

Garraty, John, *Henry Cabot Lodge*. New York, Knopf, 1953.

Grey, Sir Edward, *Twenty-five Years, 1892–1916*. New York, Stokes, 1925.

Griscom, Lloyd C., *Diplomatically Speaking*. Boston, Little, Brown, 1940.

Gwynn, Stephen, ed., *The Letters and Friendships of Sir Cecil Spring Rice*, 2 vols. Boston, Houghton Mifflin, 1929.

Hagedorn, Hermann, *The Roosevelt Family of Sagamore Hill*, New York, Macmillan, 1954.

Hammond, John Hays, *The Autobiography of John Hays Hammond*, 2 vols. New York, Farrar & Rinehart, 1935.

Hapgood, Norman, *The Changing Years, Reminiscences of Norman Hapgood*. New York, Farrar & Rinehart, 1930.

Hoover, Irwin Hood, *Forty-two Years in the White House*. Boston, Houghton Mifflin, 1934.

Jaffray, Elizabeth, *Secrets of the White House*. New York, Cosmopolitan Book, 1927.

Jessup, Philip C., *Elihu Root*. New York, Dodd, Mead, 1938.

Johnson, Walter, ed., *Selected Letters of William Allen White, 1899–1943*. New York, Holt, 1947.

Kohlsaat, H. H., *From McKinley to Harding*. New York, Scribner, 1923.

La Follette, Robert, *Autobiography*. New York, Macmillan, 1911.

Leary, John J., Jr., *Talks with T.R. from the Diaries of John J. Leary, Jr*. Boston, Houghton Mifflin, 1920.

Lodge, Henry Cabot, *Selections from the Correspondence of Theodore Roosevelt and Henry Cabot Lodge*. New York, Scribner, 1916.

Longworth, Alice Roosevelt, *Crowded Hours*. New York, Scribner, 1933.

Lorant, Stefan, *The Life and Times of Theodore Roosevelt*. New York, Doubleday, 1959.

McGeary, Nelson M., *Gifford Pinchot, Forester-Politician*. Princeton, Princeton University, 1960.

Marx, Rudolph, *The Health of the Presidents*. New York, Putnam, 1960.

Mason, Alpheus T., *Brandeis: A Free Man's Life*. New York, Viking, 1946.

—— *Bureaucracy Convicts Itself*. New York, Viking, 1941.

—— *William Howard Taft: Chief Justice*. New York, Simon & Schuster, 1965.

Morison, Elting E., and Blum, John M., eds., *The Letters of Theodore Roosevelt*, 8 vols. Cambridge, Harvard University, 1951–1954.

Mowry, George E., *The Era of Theodore Roosevelt*. New York, Harper, 1958.

—— *Theodore Roosevelt and the Progressive Movement*. Madison, University of Wisconsin, 1946.

Muller, Julius, ed., *Presidential Messages and State Papers*. New York, Review of Reviews, 1917.

—— ed., *The Letters and Journal of Brand Whitlock*, 2 vols. New York, Appleton-Century, 1936.

Nevins, Allan, *Henry White: Thirty Years of American Diplomacy*. New York, Harper, 1930.

Norris, George W., *Fighting Liberal*. New York, Macmillan, 1945.

Pepper, George Wharton, *Philadelphia Lawyer*. Philadelphia, Lippincott, 1944.

Phillips, Dr. Harlan B., *Felix Frankfurter Reminisces*. New York, Reynal, 1960.

Pinchot, Gifford, *Breaking New Ground*. New York, Harcourt, Brace, 1946.

Pringle, Henry F., *The Life and Times of William Howard Taft*. New York, Farrar & Rinehart, 1939.

—— *Theodore Roosevelt, A Biography*, New York, Harcourt, Brace, 1931.

Rixey, Lilian, *Bamie: Theodore Roosevelt's Remarkable Sister*. New York, McKay, 1963.

Robinson, Corinne, *My Brother, Theodore Roosevelt*. New York, Scribner, 1921.

Roosevelt, Theodore, *An Autobiography*. New York, Scribner, 1926.

—— *Works*, 20 vols. New York, Scribner, 1926.

Roosevelt, Mrs. Theodore, Jr., *Day Before Yesterday*. New York, Doubleday, 1959.

Rosewater, Victor, *Backstage in 1912*. Philadelphia, Dorrance, 1932.

Ross, Ishbel, *An American Family*. Cleveland, World, 1964.

Slayden, Ellen Maury, *Washington Wife*. New York, Harper & Row, 1962.

Steffens, Lincoln, *The Autobiography of Lincoln Steffens*. New York, Harcourt, Brace, 1931.

Stimson, Henry, and Bundy, McGeorge, *On Active Service in Peace and War*, 2 vols. New York, Harper, 1948.

Stoddard, Henry L., *As I Knew Them*. New York, Harper, 1927.

Straus, Oscar S., *Under Four Administrations*. Boston, Houghton Mifflin, 1922.

Sullivan, Mark, *Our Times: The United States, 1900–1925*, 4 vols. New York, Scribner, 1926–1932.

Taft, Helen H., *Recollections of Full Years*. New York, Dodd, Mead, 1914.

Taft, Horace Dutton, *Memories and Opinions*. New York, Macmillan, 1942.

Taft, William Howard, *The Presidency*. New York, Scribner, 1914.

Tuchman, Barbara W., *The Proud Tower*. New York, Macmillan, 1966.

Tumulty, Joseph J., *Woodrow Wilson as I Knew Him*. New York, Doubleday, Page, 1921.

Walworth, Arthur, *Woodrow Wilson: American Prophet*, 2 vols. Toronto, Longmans, Green, 1958.

Wharton, Edith, *A Backward Glance*. New York, Appleton-Century, 1934.

White, William Allen, *The Autobiography of William Allen White*. New York, Macmillan, 1946.

Wister, Owen, *Roosevelt, The Story of a Friendship, 1880–1919*. New York, Macmillan, 1930.

Investigation of the Department of the Interior and of the Bureau of Forestry, United States Senate, 61 Congress, 3 Session, Document 719, 13 vols. Washington, 1911.

Official Proceedings of the Fifteenth Republican National Convention. 1912.
William Howard Taft Papers in the Library of Congress
Chicago *Tribune*
New York *Times*
Washington *Post*
Collier's Weekly
Harper's Weekly
Literary Digest
The Nation
The Outlook
Review of Reviews
Spectator
World's Work

Index